# Archaeological Theory Today

# Archaeological Theory Today

*Edited by Ian Hodder*

Polity

First published in 2001 by Polity Press in association with Blackwell Publishers Ltd

*Editorial office*:
Polity Press
65 Bridge Street
Cambridge CB2 1UR, UK

*Marketing and production*:
Blackwell Publishers Ltd
108 Cowley Road
Oxford OX4 1JF, UK

*Published in the USA by*
Blackwell Publishers Inc.
Commerce Place
350 Main Street
Malden, MA 02148, USA

ISBN 0-7456-2268-2
ISBN 0-7456-2269-0 (pbk)

A catalogue record for this book is available from the British Library and has been applied for from the Library of Congress.

Typeset in 10 on 12 pt Sabon
by Best-set Typesetter Ltd., Hong Kong
Printed in Great Britain by MPG Books Ltd, Bodmin, Cornwall

This book is printed on acid-free paper.

# Contents

# Figures and Tables

## TABLES

# Contributors

**John C. Barrett** is Reader in Archaeology at the University of Sheffield.

**Mary C. Beaudry** is Associate Professor of Archaeology and Anthropology at Boston University.

**Chris Gosden** is Lecturer and Curator in World Archaeology at Pitt Rivers Museum, University of Oxford.

**Ian Hodder** is Professor of Anthropology at Stanford University.

**Vincent M. LaMotta** is a doctoral candidate in the Department of Anthropology at the University of Arizona.

**Robert D. Leonard** is Associate Professor in the Department of Anthropology at the University of New Mexico.

**Lynn Meskell** is Assistant Professor in the Department of Anthropology at Columbia University.

**Steven Mithen** is Professor of Early Prehistory at the University of Reading.

**Stephanie Moser** is Lecturer in Archaeological Representation at the University of Southampton.

**Colin Renfrew** is Disney Professor of Archaeology and Director of the McDonald Institute of Archaeological Research, University of Cambridge.

**Michael B. Schiffer** is Professor of Anthropology at the University of Arizona.

**Michael Shanks** is Professor of Classics and of Cultural Anthropology at Stanford University.

**Julian Thomas** is Professor of Archaeology at the University of Manchester.

**Anne Yentsch** is Associate Professor of Historical Archaeology at Armstrong Atlantic State University, Savannah, Georgia.

# 1

# Introduction: A Review of Contemporary Theoretical Debates in Archaeology

## Ian Hodder

There has recently been a marked increase in the numbers of volumes dealing with archaeological theory, whether these be introductory texts (e.g. Johnson 1999), readers (Preucel and Hodder 1996; Whitley 1998), edited global surveys (Ucko 1995; Hodder 1991) or innovative volumes pushing in new directions (e.g. Shanks and Tilley 1987; Schiffer 1995; Skibo, Walker, and Nielsen 1995; Tilley 1994; Thomas 1996, etc.). It has become possible to exist in archaeology largely as a theory specialist, and many advertised lecturing jobs now refer to theory teaching and research. Annual conferences are devoted entirely to theory as in the British TAG (Theoretical Archaeology Group). This rise to prominence of self-conscious archaeological theory can probably be traced back to the New Archaeology of the 1960s and 1970s.

The reasons for the rise are numerous, and we can probably distinguish reasons internal and external to the discipline, although in practice the two sets of reasons are interconnected. As for the internal reasons, the development of archaeological theory is certainly very much linked to the emphasis in the New Archaeology on a critical approach to method and theory. This self-conscious awareness of the need for theoretical discussion is perhaps most clearly seen in David Clarke's (1973) description of a loss of archaeological innocence, and in Binford's (1977) call "for theory building." Postprocessual archaeology took this reflexivity and theorizing still further. Much of the critique of processual archaeology was about theory rather than method, and the main emphasis was on opening archaeology to a broader range of theoretical positions, particularly those in the historical and social sciences. In fact, anthropology in the United States had already taken its historical and linguistic "turns," but it was only a narrow view of anthropology as evolution and cultural ecology that the New Archaeologists had embraced. When the same "turns" were taken in archaeology to produce post-processual archaeology, the theorizing became very abstract and specialized, although such abstraction is also found in other developments such as the application of catastrophe theory (Renfrew and Cooke 1979). In fact all the competing theories have developed their own specialized jargons and have a tendency to be difficult to penetrate.

One of the internal moves was towards a search for external ideas, and external legitimation for theoretical moves within archaeology. There has been a catching up with other disciplines and an integration of debate. Similar moves towards an opening and integration of debate are seen across the humanities and social sciences. Meskell argues (chapter 8) that contemporary, third wave, feminist writers seek to open debate to a theoretical pluralism. There has also been a looking into archaeology from the outside, especially in philosophy but also in other fields. Shanks (chapter 12) shows how the metaphor of archaeology has wide resonance in cultural studies today. Indeed, he disperses archaeology into broad cultural and interdisciplinary fields. There are numerous examples of close external relations between archaeology and other disciplines in this book. Leonard (chapter 3) describes the productive results of interactions between biology and archaeology. An important emerging area of interaction is with various branches of psychology. Mithen (chapter 4) discusses the links to evolutionary psychology, and both he and Renfrew (chapter 5) describe debates with cognitive science and cognitive psychology. Barrett (chapter 6) shows how the agency debate in archaeology owes much to sociology, and indeed he argues that archaeology needs to be further informed by sociology. Thomas (chapter 7) shows how archaeological work on landscapes has been greatly influenced by geography, especially by the recent cultural geographers, and by art history. But it should be pointed out that these interactions with other disciplines are not seen as borrowing from a position of inferiority. Both Mithen and Meskell in their chapters (4 and 8) argue specifically that the particular nature of archaeological data, especially their materiality and long-termness, has something to offer other disciplines in return.

Gosden (chapter 10) and Shanks (chapter 12) point out the need for archaeologists to engage with postcolonial theory. The critique from other voices and from multiple non-western interests has often forced theoretical debate. For example, Norwegian archaeology saw a long theoretical debate about the abilities of archaeologists to identify past ethnic groups as a result of Sami-Norwegian conflicts over origins. Reburial issues have forced some to rethink the use of oral traditions in North American archaeology (Anyon et al. 1996). Indigenous groups in their claims for rights question the value of "objective science" (Langford 1983). A similar point can be made about the impact of feminism. This has questioned how we do research (Gero 1996) and has sought alternative ways of writing about the past (Spector 1994), opening up debate about fundamentals. The same can also be said of debates about representation in cultural heritage and museums (see Moser in chapter 11; Merriman 1991). These debates force a critique of interpretation. They challenge us to evaluate in whose interests interpretation lies, and to be sensitive to the relationship between audience and message.

## The community of discourses model

It can be argued that archaeology has a new maturity in that, as claimed above, it has caught up with disciplines in related fields in terms of the theories and issues being discussed. Many now, as we will see in this book, wish to contribute back from archaeology to other disciplines (e.g. LaMotta and Schiffer, chapter 2) – this emphasis on contributing rather than borrowing suggests a maturity and confidence which I will examine again below. This maturity also seems to involve accepting diversity and difference of perspective within the discipline.

There are always those who will claim that archaeology should speak with a unified voice, or who feel that disagreement within the ranks undermines the abilities of archaeologists to contribute to other disciplines or be taken seriously. A tendency towards identifying some overarching unity in the discipline can be seen in some of the chapters in this volume. Renfrew (1994) has talked of reaching an accommodation between processual and postprocessual archaeology in cognitive processual archaeology. LaMotta and Schiffer (chapter 2) argue that other theoretical approaches can be formulated in and be contributed to by behavioral approaches. Mithen (chapter 4) notes that a number of different paradigmatic positions have recently converged onto the problem of mind. Even the claim of postprocessual archaeology, or by Meskell (chapter 8), for theoretical pluralism can be seen as a strategic attempt to embrace and incorporate within one position (in this case the position of pluralism).

There is often an implicit assumption in discussions about the need for unity in the discipline that real maturity, as glimpsed in the natural sciences, means unity. But in fact, Galison (1997) has argued that physics, for example, is far from a unified whole. Rather he sees it as a trading zone between competing perspectives, instrumental methods, and experiments. In archaeology too, there is a massive fragmentation of the discipline, with those working on, say, Bronze Age studies in Europe often having little to do with laboratory specialists working on isotopes and little in common with Palaeolithic lithic specialists. New Archaeological theories were introduced at about the same time as, but separate from, computers and statistics, as the early work of David Clarke (1970) and Doran and Hodson (1975) shows. Single-context recording (Barker 1982) was introduced to deal with large-scale urban excavation, and was not immediately linked to any particular theoretical position. And so on. In these examples we see that theory, method and practice are not linked in unified wholes. While the links between domains certainly exist, the history of the discipline is one of interactions between separate domains, often with their own specialist languages, own conferences and journals, and own personnel. As Galison (1997) argues for physics, it is this diversity and the linkages within the dispersion (Shanks, chapter 12) which ensure the vitality of the discipline.

We should not then bemoan theoretical diversity in the discipline. Diversity at the current scale may be fairly new in theoretical domains, but it is not new in the discipline as a whole. These productive tensions are important for the discipline as a whole.


## From "theory" to "theory of"


The partial disjunction between theoretical and other domains identified above, as well as the specialization and diversification of theoretical positions, have all reinforced the view that there can be something abstract called "archaeological theory," however diverse that might be. For many, archaeological theory has become rarified and removed. In this abstract world, apparently divorced from any site of production of archaeological knowledge, theoretical debate becomes focused on terms, principles, basic ideas, universals. Theoretical debate becomes by nature confrontational because terms are defined and fought over in abstract terms. The boundaries around definitions are policed. Abstract theory for theory's sake becomes engaged in battles over opposing abstract assertions. Theoretical issues very quickly become a matter of who can "shout the loudest," of "who sets the agenda?" (Yoffee and Sherratt 1993).

But in practice we see that the abstract theories are not divorced from particular domains at all. Rather, particular theories seem to be favored by certain sets of interests and seem to be related to questions of different types and scales. Thus evolutionary perspectives have been most common in hunter-gatherer or Palaeolithic studies; gender studies have had less impact on the Palaeolithic than on later periods; subsistence-based materialist theories tend to be applied to hunter-gatherers; power and ideology theories come into their own mainly in complex societies; and phenomenology seems to be particularly applied to prehistoric monuments and landscapes.

When archaeologists talk of a behavioral or a cognitive archaeology they tend to have specific questions and problems in mind. For Merleau-Ponty (1962), thought is always "of something." In this book, Thomas (chapter 7) describes how for Heidegger place is always "of something." So too, archaeological theory is always "of something." Theory is, like digging, a "doing." It is a practice or praxis (Hodder 1992; Shanks in chapter 12). This recognition undermines claims for a universality and unity of archaeological theory.

Of course, it can be argued that archaeology as a whole is engaged in a unified praxis, a unified doing, so that we should expect unified theories. But even at the most general theoretical levels, archaeologists are involved in quite different projects. Some archaeologists wish to make contributions to scientific knowledge, or they might wish to provide knowledge so that people can better understand the world around them. But in a postcolonial world, such aims of a distanced objective archaeology can easily appear narrow, self-interested and even colonial. As Gosden (chapter 10) shows, in a postcolonial context of multivocality, a negotiated past seems more relevant. This may involve negotiation and accommodation of the idea that past monuments may have a living presence in the world today – that they are "alive" in some sense. In the latter context, abstract theory deals less with abstract scientific knowledge and more with specific social values and local frameworks of meaning.

It is in the interests of the academy and of elite universities to promulgate the idea of abstract theory. The specialization of archaeological intellectual debate is thus legitimized. But critique from outside the academy has shown that these abstract theories too are embedded in interests – they too are "theories of something." Within the academy, archaeologists vie with each other to come up with yet more theories, especially if they can be claimed to be meta-theories that purport to "explain everything." In fact, however, this diversity comes from asking different questions – from the diversity of the contexts of production of archaeological knowledge.

## Variation in perspective

As a result of such processes, there are radical divergences in the way different authors in this book construe theory. In summary, these differences stem partly from the process of vying for difference, with innovation often influenced by developments in neighboring disciplines. The variation in perspective also derives from the fact that radically different questions are being asked from within quite different sites of production of knowledge.

Many of the differences of perspective remain those that have dogged the discipline since the 1980s or earlier. For example, on the one hand Renfrew (chapter 5) repeats the science versus relativism opposition, and the emphasis on hypothesis testing is dominant in the approach of LaMotta and Schiffer (chapter 2). On the other hand, Thomas's (chapter 7) idea of the "reanimation" of ancient monuments and landscapes tries to move beyond this dichotomy (for a wider discussion of this issue see Wylie 1989 and Lampeter Archaeology Workshop 1997). Another dichotomy which still seems to occur concerns whether archaeology is seen as anthropology or history. For LaMotta and Schiffer in chapter 2 it is clearly a cross-cultural anthropology, even if they also put emphasis on historical issues at various scales. Generalization is a key theme throughout many chapters, but for some authors, especially Leonard, LaMotta and Schiffer, Renfrew, and Mithen (chapters 2–5) it plays a key role. Gosden (chapter 10) places the opposition between general information and local knowledge within wider contexts. It is indeed remarkable that many grant-giving bodies in English-speaking western countries evaluate proposals solely in terms of their contribution to general knowledge. There are often no questions asked about the impact of a project on local communities or about the relevance of the project to local knowledge. It is rather local museums and heritage projects, and those concerned with land rights and identity claims of minority groups that are likely to eschew universal science and to focus on local issues. Here the relationship between theory and the context of production of knowledge is evident.

Some authors, such as LaMotta and Schiffer, Leonard and Mithen (chapters 2–4), separate culture, history and contingency from behavioral or evolutionary processes. This oppositional stance is clearly seen in Schiffer's (1999) behavioral approach. "Readers may be nonplussed at the absence in the new theory of much vocabulary ... such as meaning, sign, symbol, intention, motivation, purpose, goal, attitude, value, belief, norm, function, mind, and culture. Despite herculean efforts in the social sciences to define these often ethnocentric or meta-physical notions, they remain behaviorally problematic and so are super-fluous in the present project." In the evolutionary approach as represented by Leonard (chapter 3), history and contingency are a part of the Darwinian evolutionary process, and culture is its product, but I would argue that at a certain scale of analysis the selective material process dominates. For Yentsch and Beaudry (chapter 9) material culture is universal; its use, form, substance and symbolic meaning are cultur-ally relative. At least at the analytical level, a separation is made between objective physical materiality and the meaning that is assigned to it. They see this analytical separation as one step toward an anthropological understanding of how meaning is assigned and how relations within society shift and thus cause changes in meanings of objects. The division of meaning from object allows archaeologists to sort artifacts into dif-ferent categories and begin to evaluate their significance within a society.

Thus the Cartesian oppositions of material/meaning and subject/object are held to. Thomas and Meskell (chapters 7 and 8) attempt to transcend these dichotomies. They argue against the idea that there is a material existence onto which meaning is added. Rather, for them, material existence is always already meaningful and meaning is always already lived in the material world by embodied beings. At the theoret-ical level, many authors dealing with historical specificities, including Yentsch and Beaudry, would take this view. A not dissimilar position is taken by Renfrew (chapter 5), for whom symbols are active and consti-tuting. For him too, the symbolic is part of daily life and it helps to con-struct the world.

It is possible to see then how these different perspectives are linked to different sites of the production of archaeological knowledge. There are clear underlying differences between the types of interests and questions of those using general evolutionary approaches and those concerned with history and agency. Within this array, individual authors take their own positions. Discourses specific to each approach emerge, and schools are defined. Distinct literatures emerge and separate conferences and circles of citation. Even if these different communities are working along very similar lines they do not communicate well. For example, LaMotta and Schiffer discuss an emulation model without referring to Miller's (1982) agency version. Barrett's (1987 and see also chapter 6) notion of a field of social practice has parallels with LaMotta and Schiffer's notion of activity, but again there is no cross-reference. Renfrew's (chapter 5) idea that "weight" can only be "weight of something" is identical to Merleau-Ponty's (1962) phenomenological discussion but is couched in cognitive processual terms.

With this separation into different communities, communication is difficult as people talk across each other. The differences become exacerbated and entrenched and convergence difficult. I do not wish to deny there are real differences – but they become difficult to transcend because of discourse.

## Convergences

In the chapters in this volume two areas of convergence stand out. Both concern something distinctive about archaeological evidence – a base from which to contribute to other disciplines. Because of the distinctive nature of the archaeological evidence in relation to these two areas, archaeologists feel a confidence in contributing to wider debates. The two areas concern the long term and material culture.

As regards the long-term perspective offered by archaeology, there is a general recognition by the authors in this volume of the importance of multi-scalar approaches in addressing a wide range of issues. As already noted, the scale at which questions are asked has wider implications in the contexts of production of archaeological knowledge. Gosden (chapter 10) suggests making a distinction between general information of wider relevance, and local knowledge of relevance to local communities. This point is illustrated in the case studies provided by Yentsch and Beaudry (chapter 9). All the authors in this volume recognize the need to distinguish short-term and long-term influences on human behavior. LaMotta and Schiffer (chapter 2) make a threefold distinction between interactions occurring at the micro level, activities involving the performance of tasks, and systemic interactions occurring within everything from households to nation states. They put most emphasis in their work on the proximate (especially activity) scale. Both Leonard and Mithen (chapters 3 and 4) deal with longer-term phenomena, but as Leonard points out, this involves dealing with the issue of whether selection operates at group or individual levels. Renfrew (chapter 5) castigates postprocessual archaeology for its emphasis on individual experience, but he stresses the need to work at the micro level of the individual and at the macro level of society without confusing the two, especially when it comes to the value of generalizing statements and sensitivity to context. Barrett (chapter 6) emphasizes how long-term processes need to be understood in terms of the working out of micro-processes, such as the tempo of gift-giving, or the direction of paths of movement in Iron Age round houses. Meskell (chapter 8) contrasts the individual, fluid processes of daily identity construction and the more slowly changing social mores about identity categories. Disagreement may occur about the relative importance of the different scales, about the nature of the interactions between scales, and about the degree to which the different scales can be accessed with archaeological data. But there seems to be a general recognition that a multiscalar approach is needed and that archaeology can contribute to a study of the interactions between scales.

Another frequently occurring general theme in this volume is that material culture has a central role to play in what it means to be human. Most authors here seem to be suggesting some version of a dialectical view in which humans and things are dependent on each other. This is a reformulation of the Childean Marxist view that "man makes himself" (Childe 1936) or the Geertzian view that it is human nature to be cultural (Geertz 1973), but with a new emphasis on the "material cultural." LaMotta and Schiffer (chapter 2) argue that behavior includes both people and objects. Leonard (chapter 3) suggests that the human phenotype includes behavioral and material culture traits, so that material culture can be described as the hard part of the human phenotype. Mithen (chapter 4) discusses the notion of "the extended mind," whereby even religious thought is seen as dependent on material objects. Renfrew (chapter 5) and Gosden (chapter 10) suggest that it is odd that archaeologists have not paid more attention to materiality and the significance of things. Renfrew refers to Donald's (1991) ideas on "external symbolic storage," and talks of the origins of sedentism in terms of a new embodiment and a new materialization. The theories of behavior used by Barrett (chapter 6) include Bourdieu's account of human agency in terms of daily practice, while Thomas (chapter 7) follows the experiential approach of Heidegger in describing bodily being in the world. Meskell (chapter 8) talks of identity being grounded in the materiality of the body. For Shanks (chapter 12), people are always linked to objects – cyborgs are the norm. Thus, for him, material artifacts are not "objects" in any simple sense. Rather, they disperse into networks of linkages between a great variety of factors.

In all these ways, then, it is being argued that an understanding of human behavior, agency, and culture needs to include a close study of the ways in which human beings depend on the material world. Disagreement may exist amongst the authors about how humans and material culture interact. Some may argue that humans depend on material culture generally just as they depend on tools specifically. Others assert that the relationship with material culture has to be understood in terms of the very construction of self and being. Thus the "I" or the "we" are always already partly material, as are the most abstract of concepts and theories. This emphasis on situatedness foregrounds an archaeological perspective – on the past and on the present.

While it might have been expected that wide divergencies occurred in the formulation of the relationship between humans and material culture, one key idea returns repeatedly in the chapters in this volume. This is the idea that material culture differs from language. Schiffer (1999) and LaMotta and Schiffer (chapter 2) develop a behavioral approach to communication theory. Most authors in this volume have moved away from the view that material culture is manipulated by humans in a language-like way (see Yentsch and Beaudry, chapter 9). At one scale, this issue can be seen in evolutionary terms. Mithen (chapter 4) argues that the evolution of material culture and language do not necessarily correlate, and Renfrew (chapter 5) decouples the early use of language from later more significant shifts in how humans made material culture. At another scale, a similar point can be made in terms of historical and ethnographic observation. Meskell (chapter 8) notes that medical science may have developed a more complicated discourse about livers than had the ancient Greeks, but "it does not follow that my liver is more sophisticated than was Plato's liver" (Craib 1998: 109).

In response to the need to develop a theory of behavior which goes beyond the models of language and discourse, Barrett (chapter 6) uses Bourdieu's and Giddens's theories of practice and structuration. Their account of behavior foregrounds the use of non-discursive knowledge in daily practice. Thomas (chapter 7) uses Heidegger's and Ingold's ideas of being in the world. Moser (chapter 11) adds that the non-verbal (in this case visual images) may express things we are not aware of. A similar point is made by Yentsch and Beaudry (chapter 9). Moser defines the non-linguistic conventions that are used to make visual images meaningful. These conventions deal with, for example, authenticity and singularity. Shanks too, in chapter 12, points to the importance of the visual in human, and specifically archaeological, behavior. Again, then, specific theories might vary, but there is a widely accepted view that archaeologists need to focus on the particular material character of their data and develop specific, non-language-based, models.

## Conclusion

So the conclusion, based on this small sample of essays, is positive. Despite the enormous gaps and disagreements about fundamentals, and despite the evidence that archaeological theorists are trapped in separate non-communicating discourses, there is at least some indication of moves forward. In particular, there is abundant evidence of increasing engagement with other disciplines, and the entry of archaeology into wider debates. This more extensive engagement has occurred at a time when archaeologists sense a greater confidence about the particular character of their evidence. In particular, there is a wide recognition that archaeologists have a particular expertise regarding both the long term and the materiality of human life. There is thus emerging evidence of archaeologists contributing to wider debates, not just borrowing. These contributions involve archaeologists speaking in their own right, not as anthropologists or historians. There is thus a new maturity and confidence.

Perhaps adding to this maturity and confidence, but also undermining it, is a new phase of reflexivity and critique as archaeological theorists try to respond to the challenges of working within a global and plural environment. The opening of debate to a wider range of voices from feminism to indigenous interests and minority groups has led to questioning about first principles and taken-for-granteds within the discipline. The chapters in this volume indicate some directions which respond to this situation and focus on issues of representation and power (e.g. Moser and Shanks in chapters 11 and 12). The processes of post-colonialism and the new information technologies create a new context in which archaeology will work. But it is a fluid and complex context in which theory and practice are in a continual state of challenge and re-negotiation. This volume may help that process forward, but it cannot hope to define it or structure it.

*Note*: This introduction is shorter than might have been expected, because in asking authors from a diversity of perspectives to contribute to the volume, I undertook not to situate their work within a polemic of my own. Nevertheless an introduction had to be written, but it is difficult to place the authors within a historical perspective without slanting the account in some way. I circulated a draft of the introduction to all the authors and I have incorporated their comments in this final version as fully as I can. I apologize to the authors if I have misrepresented their views but thank them for entrusting their work to my editorial control.

REFERENCES

Anyon, R. et al. 1996. Native American oral traditions and archaeology. *Society for American Archaeology Bulletin* 14(2): 14–16.

Barker, P. 1982. *Techniques of Archaeological Excavation*. London: Batsford.

Barrett, J. 1987. Fields of discourse: reconstituting a social archaeology. *Critique of Anthropology* 7: 5–16.

Binford, L. 1977. *For Theory Building in Archaeology*. New York: Academic Press.

Childe, V. G. 1936. *Man Makes Himself*. London: Collins.

Clarke, D. 1970. *Beaker Pottery of Great Britain and Ireland*. Cambridge: Cambridge University Press.

Clarke, D. 1973. Archaeology: the loss of innocence. *Antiquity* 47: 6–18.

Craib, I. 1998. *Experiencing Identity*. London: Sage.

Donald, M. 1991. *Origins of the Modern Mind*. Cambridge, MA: Harvard University Press.

Doran, J. and F. Hodson 1975. *Mathematics and Computers in Archaeology*. Edinburgh: Edinburgh University Press.

Galison, P. 1997. *Image and Logic: A Material Culture of Microphysics*. Chicago: University of Chicago Press.

Geertz, C. 1973. *The Interpretation of Cultures*. New York: Basic Books.

Gero, J. 1996. Archaeological practice and gendered encounters with field data. In R. P. Wright (ed.), *Gender and Archaeology*, 251–80. Philadelphia: University of Pennsylvania Press.

Hodder, I. 1991. *Archaeological Theory in Europe: The Last Three Decades*. London: Routledge.

Hodder, I. 1992. *Theory and Practice in Archaeology*. London: Routledge.

Johnson, M. 1999. *Archaeological Theory: An Introduction*. Oxford: Blackwell.

Lampeter Archaeology Workshop 1997. Relativism, objectivity and the politics of the past. *Archaeological Dialogues* 4: 164–98.

Langford, R. 1983. Our heritage – your playground. *Australian Archaeology* 16: 1–6.

Merleau-Ponty, M. 1962. *Phenomenology of Perception*. Atlantic Highlands, NJ: Humanities Press.

Merriman, N. 1991. *Beyond the Glass Case*. Leicester: Leicester University Press.

Miller, D. 1982. Structures and strategies: an aspect of the relationship between social hierarchy and cultural change. In I. Hodder (ed.), *Symbolic and Structural Archaeology*, 89–98. Cambridge: Cambridge University Press.

Preucel, R. and I. Hodder (eds) 1996. *Contemporary Archaeology in Theory*. Oxford: Blackwell.

Renfrew, C. 1994. Towards a cognitive archaeology. In C. Renfrew and E. B. W. Zubrow (eds), *The Ancient Mind, Elements of Cognitive Archaeology*, 3–12. Cambridge: Cambridge University Press.

Renfrew, C. and K. L. Cooke 1979. *Transformations: Mathematical Approaches to Culture Change*. New York: Academic Press.

Schiffer, M. B. 1995. *Behavioral Archaeology: First Principles*. Salt Lake City: University of Utah Press.

Schiffer, M. B. 1999. *The Material Life of Human Beings*. London: Routledge.

Shanks, M. and C. Tilley 1987. *Reconstructing Archaeology*. Cambridge: Cambridge University Press.

Skibo, J., W. Walker, and A. Nielsen (eds) 1995. *Expanding Archaeology*. Salt Lake City: University of Utah Press.

Spector, J.D. 1994. *What this Awl Means: Feminist Archaeology at a Wahpeton Dakota Village*. St. Paul: Minnesota Historical Society Press.

Thomas, J. 1996. *Time, Culture and Identity*. Cambridge: Cambridge University Press.

Tilley, C. 1994. *The Phenomenology of Landscape*. London: Berg.

Ucko, P. 1995. *Theory in Archaeology: A World Perspective*. Oxford: Routledge.

Whitley, D.S. 1998. *Reader in Archaeological Theory: Post-processual and Cognitive Approaches*. London: Routledge.

Wylie, A. 1989. Archaeological cables and tacking. *Philosophy of the Social Sciences* 19: 1–18.

Yoffee, N. and A. Sherratt 1993. *Archaeological Theory: Who Sets the Agenda?* Cambridge: Cambridge University Press.

# 2

# Behavioral Archaeology

## Toward a New Synthesis

## Vincent M. LaMotta and Michael B. Schiffer

### Introduction

Behavioral archaeology is commonly equated with the study of the formation processes of the archaeological record and with the reconstruction of the cultural past through behavioral inferences. Although not inaccurate, such a characterization incompletely describes the goals of the program. In this chapter, we present a general framework for *explaining* behavioral variability at a number of scales, thereby dispelling the myth that behavioral archaeologists are concerned only with *reconstructing* past behavior. Drawing on a growing corpus of literature – by behavioralists and others – we lay the methodological foundations for a behavioral archaeology geared toward explanation, and then present case studies that illustrate the development and application of explanatory theory. We suggest that explanations for many of the same types of processes of interest to processualist, postprocessualist, Marxist, and selectionist archaeologists – once reformulated in appropriate units of analysis – also can be furnished by principles of behavioral archaeology.

### Background

Behavioral archaeology is different from many other social sciences, including other branches of archaeology, in that it is based on the study of interactions between people and material objects ("behavior"). Behavioralists seek to develop appropriate method and theory for studying and explaining all forms of variation in human social life in terms of behavior. Among the first principles of the program is the conviction that variation in the form and arrangement of artifacts, architecture, and cultural deposits in living systems and in the archaeological record is *most directly* the product of human behavior (controlling for non-cultural formation processes), and not of some second-order analytical construct like "culture," mental states, or adaptive imperatives (Walker et al. 1995). For the behavioralist, then, virtually any aspect of human life is open to scientific scrutiny and explanation so long as research questions can be framed in terms of people–object interactions. Thus, many traditional questions of social scientists, as well as the corresponding units of analysis, need to be reformulated in terms amenable to study within a behavioral framework. Indeed, the provision of such an alternative behavioral lexicon for studying human social life has been among the primary goals of behavioral archaeologists.

Reid et al. (1974; see also Reid et al. 1975; Reid 1995; Schiffer 1995a: ch. 1) first crafted behavioral archaeology as an explicit program at the University of Arizona in the early 1970s. Though originally an outgrowth of the "new" (processual) archaeology developed by Binford (1962, 1965, 1968) and others (e.g. Deetz 1965; Hill 1970; Longacre 1970), behavioralists promoted an expanded archaeology that would overcome the many methodological and theoretical failings of early processualism.

To behavioralists, the irreducible core of archaeology is simply "the study of material objects . . . in order to describe and *explain* human behavior" (Reid et al. 1975: 864, emphasis added). In the 1970s, this definition shifted the focus of explanation away from the adaptationist concerns of processualism and toward the explanation of behavioral variation at many scales. Importantly, *behaviorally* defined units of analysis and explanation can be designed to transcend or cross-cut the temporal and spatial boundaries that circumscribe the "cultural systems" studied by processualists. Thus, behavioral archaeologists established a science of human behavior grounded in nomothetic statements about people–object interactions under specified boundary conditions – ranging from highly specific to highly general.

In their seminal statements, Reid et al. (1974, 1975) offered four research strategies to provide focus for a discipline that appeared to be reconfiguring into a new behavioral science with diverse research agendas (figure 2.1).

Strategies 2 and 3 are the theoretical workhorses, the areas of comparative research for developing general principles that could be applied

| Material Items | | |
| --- | --- | --- |
| | Past | Present |
| **Human Behavior** Past | 1. Prehistoric, historical and classical archaeologies | 2. Ethnoarchaeology and experimental archaeology |
| Present | 3. Study of long-term behavioral change | 4. Modern material culture studies |

**Figure 2.1**   The four strategies of behavioral archaeology (adapted from Reid 1995)

in explaining specific cases of behavioral variation in prehistoric (strategy 1) or modern (strategy 4) contexts. Three decades of research within strategy 2, encompassing ethnoarchaeology and experimental archaeology, has resulted in the development of countless experimental laws pertaining to diverse processes of human behavior, from the use of pottery and groundstone tools, to the deposition of ceremonial trash and human remains. An important feature of this nomothetic research is the construction of "behavioral contexts" – analytical units that specify the boundaries (e.g. material, behavioral, social, ecological parameters) of a process within which a general principle of behavior is applicable (Walker and LaMotta 1995; Walker et al. 1995). As shown below, behavioral contexts play a critical role in the use of nomothetic statements about behavior in idiographic research.

Clearly, behavioral archaeology was, and still is, much more than an extension of the processualist agenda. Behavioral archaeologists not only departed stridently from "new" archaeologists in their treatment of evidence from the archaeological record, but also questioned the explanatory potential of early processual theory. It was argued that new archaeologists had adopted simplistic conceptions of inference and upon these built inadequate methods for reconstructing past behavior, conflating traces of formation processes with traces of the "cultural" processes of interest (Schiffer 1976; Sullivan 1978). To remedy these problems, behavioralists formulated new models of inference (Dean 1978; Schiffer 1976: ch. 2; Sullivan 1978) and insisted on the need to investigate formation processes (Reid 1985; Schiffer 1972, 1976, 1983, 1985, 1987), seen as the major source of uncontrolled variables. As a result, formation-process research – conducted by behavioralists, "new" archaeologists, and many others – has been among the program's most visible and prolific products. Behavioral archaeologists also challenged the explanatory frameworks adopted by processualists, charging that the new archaeology's all-purpose causes – population pressure, environmental change and stress, and various cybernetic processes – were, for purposes of explaining behavioral and organizational variation and change, small improvements over those of culture history (Schiffer 1976: 2). Instead, Schiffer (1975a, 1976: 2–3) urged archaeologists to develop new behavioral theories, models, and experimental laws by drawing on the methods of strategy 2 of behavioral archaeology, and by exploiting the archaeological record itself (strategy 3) as the most appropriate source of evidence on long-term change processes. After twenty-plus years of behavioral research, we are now in a position to synthesize a methodological and theoretical framework for achieving these goals.

Apparently, one message that many archaeologists take from these early critiques is that behavioral archaeologists are atheoretical inductivists, hostile to explanation and to the construction of "social theory."[1] Others surmise that behavioralists are concerned solely, or at least primarily, with the discovery of "universal" laws of human behavior – i.e. principles that are true in *all* times and in *all* places (e.g. Flannery 1973; McGuire 1995; O'Brien and Holland 1995; cf. Wylie 1995). In fact, both beliefs are incorrect. Behavioralists have repeatedly called for the building, not borrowing, of explanatory theory, and they have devoted much effort to the construction of such theory in recent years (see below). Even in the 1970s and 1980s, behavioralists offered some formulations akin to social theory (e.g. McGuire and Schiffer 1983; Rathje and McCarthy 1977; Schiffer 1979), and c-transforms[2] and correlates[3] can themselves constitute social theory in certain research contexts (LaMotta 1999; Schiffer 1988; Tani 1995). The behavioral approach may appear to be inductivist because it proposes to construct "social" theories on the basis of regularities in observed or inferred interactions between people and objects. By privileging people–object interactions, however, behavioralists seek to redirect the construction of social theory across the human sciences: behavioral science can be neither behavioral nor scientific unless it also attends to artifacts (Schiffer 1995b: 23; see also Schiffer and Miller 1999b; Walker et al. 1995). Lastly, although the discovery of truly "universal" principles of behavior is among the program's goals, many examples in this chapter demonstrate that behavioralists are committed to building explanatory theory that operates anywhere along the continuum from general to specific.

The new behavioral theories might not look much like the old social theories, however. Theories borrowed from other social sciences often rest on untested premises about human behavior, and usually employ different and often incompatible (i.e. non-behavioral) units of analysis. Behavioral theories, therefore, require new ways of thinking about and researching human life that at first might seem quite alien.

In the following section we provide an outline for the types of explanatory questions that currently face behavioralists, and later furnish a discussion of behavioral method and theory necessary for addressing these questions rigorously. We conclude with several case studies that illustrate how behavioral theory can explain variation and change at several scales, ranging from discrete person–object interactions to the organizational structure of behavioral systems.


## Objectives: explaining behavior at different scales

What exactly is it that behavioralists are trying to *explain*? By "explanation" we mean subsuming empirical phenomena under nomothetic statements (i.e. explanatory, social, or behavioral theory) and empirical generalizations that specify regularities in behavioral processes at various scales, statements that operate within explicitly and concretely defined boundary conditions (see below, "Behavioral contexts"). It is convenient to recognize three scales of human behavioral variation, each of which poses a slightly different set of explanatory challenges:

(1)   *Interaction scale*, which is focused on regularity and variation in discrete person–object interactions. This area of research is geared toward understanding the specific processes whereby visual, tactile, acoustic, and chemical interactions occur between and among people and artifacts, and how such interactions underlie variation and change in larger-scale behavioral processes (e.g. see below, "Communication"). At this level of inquiry, if nowhere else, "universal" principles of behavior – i.e. regularities that inhere in *all* interactions – might be discovered.

(2)   *Activity scale*, in which synchronic variation, and diachronic change, in activities performed by individuals, households, or task groups is examined. An activity consists of the patterned behavior of one or more material (possibly human) elements (Schiffer 1992: 78). Materials, energy, and information are processed and potentially modified in the course of an activity. Alternative behaviors can develop for the performance of the same basic task, and such patterns of synchronic variation in activity performance may change through time. These are among the processes that behavioralists seek to explain at this scale. Sub-

stantial explanatory research at the activity scale has already been conducted by archaeologists and has yielded, for example, many principles for explaining variation and change in the design and use of artifacts and architectural spaces (see "Technology" below).

(3) *Systemic scale*, at which level synchronic variation, and diachronic change, in the organization of one or more behavioral systems are explained. A "behavioral system" is a set of patterned activities that articulate a human group with the physical world and with other behavioral systems (Schiffer 1979, 1992); for example, a household, community, institution, regional system, or nation-state can each be modeled as a behavioral system. Variations in the organization of activities, and in the networks of material, energy, and information flows among these activities (termed "linkages"), are some of the behavioral phenomena scrutinized at this scale. How, for example, do patterned networks of activities develop within a society or "behavioral system?" How are patterned flows of materials, energy, and information established among different activities and human actors? How are change processes initiated from within a behavioral system and how do such changes spread? Additionally, many processual questions, when reformulated in behavioral terms, can be accommodated at this scale of analysis (see below, "The 'big' questions").

By positing three scales of behavioral analysis, we emphasize that each requires a different set of explanatory principles. Although explanations for lower-order behavioral phenomena will likely contribute to explanations for high-order processes, we expect that higher scales will entail emergent properties that may not be fully reducible to lower-order principles. For example, long-term change in the organization of activities in a community (systemic scale) may not be explained efficiently by the same principles used to explicate the behavior of individuals participating in discrete activities (activity scale). Nonetheless, explanations for such higher-order phenomena can still be behavioral without being reductionist.

Finally, it is important to note that, in seeking principles of behavioral regularity and change at all scales, behavioral archaeologists do not posit, a priori, a single exogenous mechanism or set of mechanisms that drives or determines behavioral processes. Because the scientific study of human behavior is still in its infancy, the imposition of such a set of causal principles would be premature and self-limiting. Thus, at present we favor the application and *empirical testing* of a wide array of explanatory frameworks regarding behavioral variation and change, and reject the notion that explanation in archaeology must proceed from a *single* high-level social or cultural theory.

## Foundations: method and theory

In this section we discuss fundamental definitions and units of analysis, including a materialist definition of human behavior, an analytical methodology grounded in the study of artifact life histories in comparative behavioral contexts, and a material-behavioral model for describing and explaining change processes in activities and in behavioral systems.

### Behavior

Behavioral archaeologists define the basic unit of analysis – human behavior – precisely as the interaction of one or more living individuals with elements of the material world (Reid et al. 1974, 1975). As a unit of analysis, "behavior" includes both people and objects (Walker et al. 1995). This analytical focus on both the material (artifact) and organismal (people) aspects of behavior distinguishes behavioral archaeology from other theoretical perspectives founded on purely *organismal* conceptions of behavior (*sensu* Walker et al. 1995: 5–8). In organismal perspectives, an analytical barrier divides the animate organism from the inanimate world of material objects, and explanations for actions of the human organism are generally framed in terms of changing external variables ("the environment") or internal states ("ideology," "values," "attitudes," or "intentions"). Behavioralists do not argue that changes in environmental variables are uninvolved in behavioral change (e.g. see Reid 1978), nor do they dispute that people's knowledge affects their behavior (e.g. see Schiffer and Miller 1999b; Walker 1998b). Nonetheless, we conceive of behavior – when defined to include both people and objects – as a phenomenon that mediates all ecological, social, and cognitive processes; through behavior the *potential* impact of extrabehavioral phenomena on life processes is made *manifest*. Behavioralists, therefore, are not concerned with explaining the behavior of the organism as a process somehow distinct from the world of artifacts. Furthermore, artifacts define the boundaries of behavior in a fashion that is useful analytically, facilitating cross-cultural comparisons and the discovery of behavioral principles. To study behavior in a fashion that recognizes the centrality of artifacts in human interactions, we utilize a framework that focuses on regularities and variability in activities – for example, in the making, using, reusing, breaking, and disposal of objects.

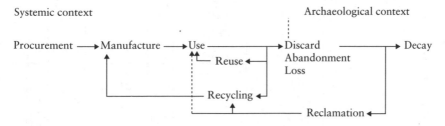

Systemic context                                               Archaeological context

**Figure 2.2** A generalized artifact life history (adapted from Schiffer 1976: 46)

## Life histories and behavioral chains

At the core of behavioral methodology lies the life history concept. An artifact's life history is the sequence of behaviors (i.e. interactions and activities) that lead from the procurement of raw materials and manufacture of that object, through various stages of use, reuse and/or recycling, to the eventual discard or abandonment of the object in the archaeological record – with the possibility of multiple cycles of manufacture, use and recycling, and of reclamation, reuse and discard (figure 2.2).

Life histories play a key role in building inferences about past behaviors and behavioral systems from their archaeological remains (Binford 1968: 21–2; Schiffer 1975b, 1976: 44–9, 1987: 13–15; Shipman 1981; Zedeño 1997; cf. *chaîne opératoire* [see Sellet 1993]), and for defining units of analysis and comparison in cross-cultural research (Walker and LaMotta 1995). For either purpose, a flow model or behavioral chain (Schiffer 1975b) can be constructed for any given artifact class in a behavioral system (see table 2.1). A complete behavioral chain for a ceramic cooking jar, maize, or a ritual fetish, for instance, would describe *all* of the interactions that typically occur in the life histories of these objects; the energy sources (including human social units) involved in each activity; additional artifacts used (conjoined elements); location, time, frequency, and order of activities; and each activity's material output (i.e. actual and potential contributions to the archaeological record). Values for some of these variables may be supplied by cross-cultural, ethnographic, or historic data, while others must be inferred from the archaeological record itself. It is seldom necessary or possible to construct a complete behavioral chain incorporating *all* life-history activities. Rather, behavioral chain *segments*, representing activities within a specific "behavioral context" (see below), are more typically constructed. Behavioral chain segments allow the researcher to infer the

**Table 2.1** A behavioral chain segment for maize in Hopi subsistence activities (ca. AD 1900). A complete behavioral chain for Hopi maize would need to incorporate activities in other behavioral contexts, e.g. including many ritual and ceremonial uses for maize that do not involve its consumption as food

| ACTIVITY | ENERGY SOURCES | | CONJOINED ELEMENTS | TIME AND FREQUENCY | LOCATION | OUTPUTS | INTERSECTIONS | |
| --- | --- | --- | --- | --- | --- | --- | --- | --- |
| | SOCIAL UNITS | NON-HUMAN | | | | | ADDITIONS | DELETIONS |
| HARVEST | ABLE VILLAGERS OF BOTH SEXES 3, 4 | | BASKETS 4 | SEVERAL DAYS IN SEPTEMBER 4 | FIELDS OF H.H. 3, 4 | STALKS, WASTED OR UNHARVESTED MAIZE | | |
| TRANSPORT | ABLE VILLAGERS OF BOTH SEXES 3, 4 | | BASKETS, BLANKETS 3, 4 | ONCE IN SEPTEMBER | FROM FIELDS TO ROOF OF H.H. AREA | POLLEN | | |
| HUSK | WOMEN OF H.H. AND OTHER FEMALES 3, 4 | | WOODEN OR BONE PEG 6 | ONE OR SEVERAL DAYS IN SEPTEMBER | ON ROOF OF H.H. AREA 3, 4 | POLLEN | | HUSKS |
| DRY | | SUNLIGHT 4 | ROOF OF H.H. AREA 4 | SEVERAL DAYS IN SEPTEMBER | ON ROOF OF H.H. AREA 3, 4 | POLLEN | | |
| TRANSPORT | WOMEN OF H.H. | | BASKETS | ONCE IN SEPTEMBER | FROM H.H. AREA TO STOREROOM | OCCASIONAL KERNELS, POLLEN | | |
| STORAGE | | | STOREROOM 3, 4, 6 | 1 TO 100 WEEKS 6 | STOREROOM 3, 4, 6 | OCCASIONAL KERNELS, POLLEN | | |
| TRANSPORT | WOMEN OF H.H. | | BASKETS | SEVERAL MORNINGS WEEKLY | FROM STOREROOM TO HABITATION ROOM | | | |
| REMOVE KERNELS | WOMEN OF H.H. 3 | | SHORT STICK, YUCCA BASKET 3 | SEVERAL MORNINGS WEEKLY | HABITATION ROOM | OCCASIONAL KERNELS, POLLEN | | |
| COARSE GRIND | WOMEN OF H.H. 1 | | MEALING BIN, STICK, COARSE MANO AND METATE, YUCCA BASKET 1, 2 | SEVERAL MORNINGS WEEKLY | HABITATION ROOM 1 | WASTED KERNELS AND MEAL POLLEN | | COBS |

| | WOMEN OF H.H. / WIND | YUCCA BASKET 3 | SEVERAL MORNINGS WEEKLY | OUTSIDE OF STRUCTURE | CHAFF | WATER, OTHER INGREDIENTS / OTHER FOODS |
|---|---|---|---|---|---|---|
| REMOVE CHAFF | WOMEN OF H.H. / WIND | YUCCA BASKET 3 | SEVERAL MORNINGS WEEKLY | OUTSIDE OF STRUCTURE | CHAFF | WATER, OTHER INGREDIENTS |
| MEDIUM GRIND | WOMEN OF H.H. 1 | MEALING BIN, STICK, MEDIUM MANO AND METATE, BOWL 1, 2 | SEVERAL MORNINGS WEEKLY | HABITATION ROOM 1 | WASTED MEAL | |
| FINE GRIND | WOMEN OF H.H. 1 | MEALING BIN, FINE MANO AND METATE STICK, BOWL 1, 2 | SEVERAL MORNINGS WEEKLY | HABITATION ROOM 1 | WASTED MEAL | |
| TRANSPORT | WOMEN OF H.H. | BOWLS 2 | SEVERAL MORNINGS WEEKLY | HABITATION ROOM TO STOREROOM | WASTED MEAL | |
| STORAGE | | BOWLS 2 | SEVERAL DAYS TO A WEEK | STOREROOM | WASTED MEAL | |
| TRANSPORT | WOMEN OF H.H. | BOWLS 2 | TWICE DAILY | STOREROOM TO HABITATION ROOM | WASTED MEAL | |
| MAKE DUMPLINGS | WOMEN OF H.H. / FIRE | COOKING JAR, BOWL | TWICE DAILY | HABITATION ROOM | WASTED MEAL | |
| COOK | FIRE | JUNIPER TWIGS, COOKING JAR, FIRE PIT 6 | TWICE DAILY 3 | HABITATION ROOM | SPILLAGE-WASTE | |
| SERVE | WOMEN OF H.H. | SERVING BOWLS, COOKING JARS, LADLES 5 | TWICE DAILY 3 | HABITATION ROOM | SPILLAGE-WASTE | |
| EAT | ENTIRE H.H. | BOWLS 5 | TWICE DAILY 3 | HABITATION ROOM | WASTE | OTHER FOODS |
| DIGEST TRANSPORT | ENTIRE H.H. | | ALMOST CONTINUOUSLY | LOCATIONS OF H.H. MEMBERS | | |
| DEFECATE DISCARD | ENTIRE H.H. | A BROAD LEAF | ONCE DAILY | AWAY FROM OCCUPIED ROOMS | A BROAD LEAF, RESIDUES | |

H.H. Household

Key: 1 Bartlett (1933)  3 Beaglehole (1937)  5 Turner and Lofgren (1966)
2 Bartlett (1936)  4 Stephen (1936)  6 Whiting (1939)
Source: From Schiffer 1975b.

types of activities that might have been responsible for the formation of a specific archaeological deposit by comparing the formal, spatial, associational, and quantitative properties (*sensu* Rathje and Schiffer 1982: 64–5) of that archaeological assemblage with predictions generated for hypothetical output assemblages from each activity in the behavioral chain (e.g. see Magers 1975). Beyond reconstruction, however, behavioral chain models also supply many of the relevant variables (such as type of activity, social group, conjoined elements, frequency, location, and outputs), and their associated values, that may be used to define the boundary conditions or "behavioral context" of a general principle or experimental law.

## Behavioral contexts

A *behavioral context*, the locus of a "process," is a problem-specific unit of analysis (Walker et al. 1995: 4). Such units bring together for examination and comparison behavioral interactions that share certain characteristics – termed *critical variables* – that are relevant to the research question(s) at hand (Walker and LaMotta 1995). Behavioral contexts are particularly useful as exploratory tools: First, the researcher tentatively specifies a principle, or experimental law, that explains regularities or variation in a limited set of behavioral observations. Next, one would draw together a wider array of cases documenting broadly similar behaviors in order to define more precisely the boundary conditions of the process described by the tentative explanatory principle. In some instances, a behavioral context may incorporate behaviors with high spatiotemporal contiguity (similar to a "cultural context" as traditionally defined), but for other research questions behaviors drawn from apparently dissimilar societies in diverse times and places are brought together (possibly including ethnographic, historical, ethnoarchaeological, and/or archaeological cases). The specific historical or "cultural" circumstances within which these behavioral observations are "embedded," and upon which they are seemingly contingent, are irrelevant *so long as* variation in those contingencies does not affect the values of critical variables.

Boundary conditions, defined by particular values for a set of critical variables, delimit the behavioral context of an explanatory principle. The number and types of critical variables are specific to the research question. Critical variables can include the specific form of the behavioral interaction, the segment(s) of the behavioral chain(s) of the relevant artifacts, the type and scale of behavioral component (i.e. "social group")

| | Examples of Critical Variables | | | |
|---|---|---|---|---|
| | *Behavioral component* | *Behavioral chain segment(s)* | *Type of artifact* | *Specific interaction* |
| Values | individual | materials procurement | ceramic jar | dig up raw clay |
| | household | manufacture | bone awl | grind long bones |
| | ritual sodality | use | corn cob | use to asperse with water |
| | matrilineal clan | abandonment | ritual structure | dismantle and burn roof |

**Figure 2.3**    Examples of critical variables and associated values

involved, and, for some questions, the relationship of the behavior (via "linkage factors," see below) to other activities in the behavioral system (see figure 2.3 for examples). We note that a similar comparative methodology – based on *cross-species* comparisons of critical variables – has been applied by behavioral ecologists to develop principles, specific and general, for explaining variation in some aspects of animal morphology, behavior, and social organization (e.g. Krebs and Davies 1993: ch. 2). For example, a "niche" could be modeled as a behavioral context within which an experimental law of adaptive behavior is operative.

A hypothetical example serves to illustrate the definition and use of a behavioral context, and to distinguish this comparative method from ethnographic analogy and the direct historical approach (see also Skibo 1992: ch. 2). Suppose a behavioralist were interested in the spatial differentiation of disposal behaviors involving worn-out ceremonial artifacts (e.g. see Walker 1995). Based on a limited number of empirical observations derived from archaeological fieldwork in the Pueblo Southwest, for instance, one might hypothesize that objects used in ceremonial activities were disposed of in locations apart from disposal areas used for domestic trash – for example, in specialized ceremonial middens, shrines, cemeteries, or abandoned ritual rooms. To test the generality of this behavioral principle, one would draw together examples from diverse ethnographic and archaeological cases to document other instances of disposal of ceremonial and domestic objects. One would then observe the spatial distribution of those disposal activities as values were allowed to vary for other critical variables, such as the size and type of the social group owning the objects and performing the disposal, degree of specialization among ritual practitioners, and location and context of use. Hypothetically, the archaeologist might find that the spatially differential disposal of ceremonial and domestic objects occurs when the ceremonial objects are used in rituals performed by specialized priests in non-localized ritual sodalities, but not when the locus of ritual use is restricted to the household or domestic unit. These critical variables and their associated values – greatly oversimplified here – describe the behavioral context to which this hypothetical principle applies. Of course, this would be only the first step in the process of explaining this behavioral pattern, and the researcher would want to test other hypotheses by observing what effects changes in other variables might have on the spatial properties of such disposal behaviors.

The behavioral context approach, employing carefully defined critical variables and associated values, can be contrasted with analogical and direct historical comparisons. Behavioral contexts differ from ethnographic analogy in how the comparative context is defined, and in the methods used to establish the boundaries of that comparison. Traditionally, comparisons between archaeological and ethnographic cases are based on broad similarities between the "cultures" under study – e.g. their regional affiliation or general level of sociopolitical "complexity." Determinants for similarities or differences in specific behavior(s) are generally sought *not* in the critical variables employed in behavioral contexts, but in overarching characteristics of the societies or cultures (or their environments); hence, the use of simple analogical reasoning – an "inference that if two or more things agree with one another in some respects they will probably agree in others" (Merriam-Webster 1985: 82; see also Salmon 1982: 61). Thus, the hypothesis-test procedure used to define the boundaries of a behavioral context is characteristically absent from many examples of "ethnographic analogy." Direct historical analogy, in which similarities between two or more behavioral systems are simply asserted based on the historical and genetic relatedness of the groups involved, employs a comparative logic that is even less rigorous. For example, in certain research contexts a behavioralist *might* attempt to explain prehistoric ritual disposal behaviors of prehistoric Pueblo groups by examining the determinants of variation in those behaviors among, for example, their modern Hopi and Zuni descendants. However, even assuming historical continuity in behavioral patterns, this narrowly defined behavioral context permits only limited testing of the effects of other critical variables on the behaviors in question, and provides only one (idiographic) level of explanation of those behaviors. The behavioral researcher is more likely to look to other, unrelated groups to define a broader behavioral context through which to identify a more general principle of behavior.

Behavioral contexts permit a great deal of flexibility in the design of research, while ensuring that cross-cultural comparisons and the behavioral principles derived from them are based on comparable units of analysis (critical variables) that are defined clearly and concretely. When comparative research is structured in this fashion, many of the pitfalls associated with the use of ethnoarchaeological data or of ethnographic "analogy" can be avoided (e.g. see Binford 1985; Cordell et al. 1987; Dunnell 1996: 115; Gould 1978b, 1980, 1985; O'Brien and Holland 1995; Schiffer 1978; 1995a: ch. 14; Watson 1982; Wylie 1995).

## Activities and behavioral systems

Having defined "behavior" above, we now explore some other units of analysis. The framework for analyzing activity change outlined by Schiffer (1979, 1992) provides our main point of departure for this discussion. This framework serves as a springboard for formulating nomothetic questions about behavioral change at the activity and systemic scales, and for suggesting appropriate lines of research for answering them.

We begin with a model in which the "social system" or "culture" – a common unit of analysis among archaeologists – is recast in behavioral terms. A *behavioral system*, then, is a set of patterned behaviors that articulates a human group with the physical world around it and with other semi-independent behavioral systems. A behavioral system includes people and *only* those elements of the material world with which they actually (i.e. physically, visually, chemically, acoustically) interact. Such a system is comprised of *activities* – patterned behaviors that process matter, energy, and information. Any activity is linked directly to one or more other activities in the behavioral system through the exchange of matter, energy, and information – the nature, direction, rates, and other constant or variable characteristics of these transfers (termed *linkages*)

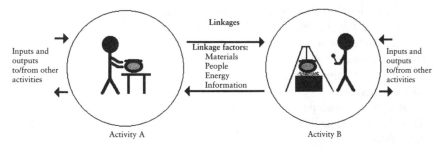

**Figure 2.4**   Element, energy, and information flows ("linkages") between activities

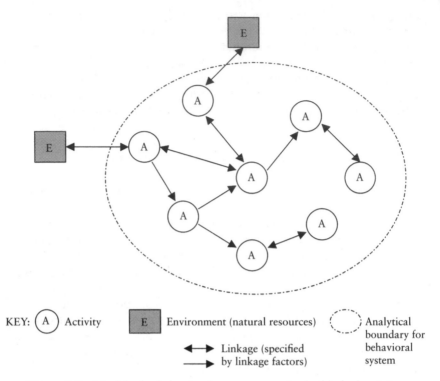

KEY: (A) Activity    [E] Environment (natural resources)    (⸝⸏) Analytical boundary for behavioral system

◀▬▶ Linkage (specified
▬▶ by linkage factors)

**Figure 2.5**    Model of a behavioral system comprised of linked activites

being specified by *linkage factors*[4] (see figure 2.4). Flows of matter, energy, and information establish patterned relationships among activities, leading to varying degrees of interdependence – direct or indirect, strong or weak – among all activities in a behavioral system (see figure 2.5).

A behavioral archaeologist seeking to explain change in an activity would look *first* to changes in directly and closely linked activities and to proximate variation in linkage factors, and *second* to the structure of interdependent activities within the system to identify more distant sources of change. Although behavioral change processes may be initiated by "external" phenomena (e.g. climatic change, immigration), the nature, extent, and persistence of change within the behavioral system is strongly determined by the structure of linkages among activities within that system.

Certainly, not all behavioral change is initiated by variation in inputs from the environment or from external behavioral systems. Explaining how change processes are initiated from within a behavioral system, and understanding how such change processes spread to other activity contexts, has been – and will continue to be – a major topic of behavioral research.

We propose that change processes are often initiated and spread through alterations in linkage factors between activities. The substitution of one activity for another, for instance, is likely to involve a change in inputs and outputs (linkage factors), possibly causing subsequent changes in other activities with which the replaced activity was formerly linked. Activity substitution or change may result from the replacement in an activity of one or more elements (people or materials) with functionally non-equivalent counterparts. Elements possess specific formal and behavioral properties – *performance characteristics* – that are crucial to that element's interactions in a specific activity. If the performance characteristics of a substituted element differ from those of the element it replaced, the fit between the substituted element and the activity may be sufficiently imperfect to alter activity performance, possibly leading to changes in linkage factors and far-reaching behavioral changes.

The box overleaf shows a simple example to illustrate the use of the model. The point of this example is to demonstrate that linkage factors provide a useful framework for examining change processes among related activities. The change in performance characteristics of a single artifact type can result in far-reaching behavioral change; however, the direction and extent of such changes largely depend on how activities are linked with each other.

Research both on the processes through which activity and element change may be initiated, and on human responses to technology and activity change, is being pursued rigorously by behavioral archaeologists. Within the context of activity performance, human responses to element substitutions and to changes in linked activities depend (1) on how those changes modify linkage factors (inputs) for the activity in question; (2) on which linkage factors (outputs) for that activity are prioritized; (3) on the technological and behavioral compromises that can or must be made to offset changes in linkage factors and in activity performance; and (4) on the availability and interpretation of feedback from activity performance. For example, behavioralists have addressed many of these issues while developing method and theory for understanding human interactions with artifacts during design, manufacture, and use (see below, "Technology").

We currently suggest four broad families of behavioral processes that might initiate element and activity change, and cause modifications in the nature, structure, and organization of activities within a behavioral

Suppose, for heuristic purposes, we are confronted with a behavioral system comprised of only three activities:

A   Food procurement through fishing
B   Food preparation and consumption
C   Pottery making

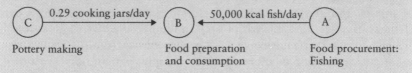

These activities are linked to each other via flows of people, artifacts, energy, and information – of which linkage factors we will consider only a few for this example. Let us assume that this behavioral system consists of a single behavioral component – a large (25-person) extended family living on an isolated Pacific island. Food procurement (activity A) consists initially of fishing alone. Fishermen in our behavioral system employ modern rod-and-reel technology, acquired through trade, to catch fish at a rate of 15 fish/day. Activity A is thus linked to activity B, food processing and consumption, by a linkage factor specified as 50,000 kcal fish/day (input) – sufficient to feed our 25 people. Food processing (activity B) involves the stewing of fish in ceramic cooking jars, which break or wear out at a rate of about 2 jars/week. Activity B is therefore linked to activity C (pottery making) by a linkage factor of 0.29 jars/day (input).

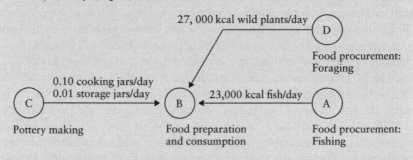

Next, suppose that most of our fishermen's rods-and-reels break or wear out and cannot be replaced, perhaps due to the vicissitudes of trade relations (i.e. there is a change in linkage factors with respect to the input of new rods-and-reels for activity A). For a time, at least, they are replaced with simple cane fishing poles which do not possess the same performance characteristics as rod-and-reel. As a result of this element substitution, activity A can only obtain fish at a rate of 7 per day, changing its linkage factor with activity B (input of 23,000 kcal fish/day – insufficient nourishment for the population). This modification in linkage factors between activities A and B requires that some behavioral change occur so that the basic caloric needs of the community can be met. One possible solution might involve the initiation of new food procurement activities focused on wild plant foods. This would create a new activity (D, foraging) linked to activity B via an input of 27,000 kcal/day of wild plant foods. Although this new activity would allow the community to meet its food needs, it would also introduce a new element (plant foods) with new performance characteristics into activity B. If preparation requirements for this food differ substantially from those for fish, information flows between activities B and C might stimulate potters to develop ceramic vessels with performance characteristics appropriate for cooking these new foods. Linkage factors from activity C to B, then, might change as well. Obviously, many other behavioral changes might occur as linked activities are compromised by changes in linkage factors.

system. We note that these processes are not all mutually exclusive and that additional processes will be recognized in the future.

First, element and activity change can be caused by massive and rapid changes in performance characteristics of elements. For example, disease epidemics, leading to morbidity and mortality, can alter the performance characteristics of human, plant, and animal elements in activities and often lead to widespread behavioral change and even structural modification of societies, community reorganization, and large-scale migration.

Second, as noted above, changes in input from activities that directly articulate a behavioral system with natural resources may have profound effects on that behavioral system. Such altered inputs may arise from changes in the natural environment *or* from changes in the extractive activities themselves (or both), and for this reason researchers must be careful to specify the exact linkage factors and change processes at work.

Third, technological experimentation historically has led to repeated episodes of technological and behavioral change. Technological modifications (experiments) at the design and manufacture stages may produce elements with new performance characteristics (inventions) and – if these new artifacts are widely adopted for use – possibly lead to significant activity change (see below, "Technology"). Importantly, the adoption of new technologies often entails *unforeseen* ramifications and/or *unpredicted* byproducts which may contribute through activity linkages to widespread behavioral change.

Fourth, we recognize that for some research questions it is useful to examine change processes from the perspective of individual actors and/or behavioral components ("social groups"). Many questions about "social power," the relationship(s) between structure and agency, or political economy – when phrased in behavioral terms – can be addressed from such a perspective within the activity analysis framework (e.g. Adams 1996; Cameron 1999; Nielsen 1995; Nielsen and Walker 1998; Walker 1998b; Walker and Lucero 1997). The capacity of individuals or groups to maintain, alter, or redirect the flows of people, materials, information, and energy among linked activities is certainly one aspect of behavior that is pertinent to such research. What are the change processes involved? How are such processes initiated? And, what circumstances (behavioral contexts) enable some groups or individuals to modify linkage factors more effectively than others? This is an area where much new research is needed. Nonetheless, we tentatively suggest several behavioral processes through which such changes might be effected (see below, "Formation processes of the archaeological record"). Two aspects of these processes merit attention: (1) changes initiated by the physical modification of elements during manufacture or use (including the destruction of objects or people), and (2) changes initiated by information (visual, acoustic, chemical, physical) furnished by an activity occurring at any point in an object's life history; i.e. activities entail the emission of information (via linkage factors) that may affect the subsequent behavior(s) of the recipients of the information, and it is likely that some change processes are initiated by variation in such linkage factors (see below, "Communication"). A consideration of such processes, their origins, and effects from the perspective of individual people, behavioral components, or sectors provides one approach for behaviorally researching subjects like power and political economy.

Lastly, in explaining behavioral change at activity and systemic scales, it should be evident that we do not adopt, a priori, the cybernetic or adaptive assumptions underlying models of behavior and social systems found, for example, in applications of systems theory, functionalism, or cultural ecology (*contra* McGuire 1995: 165). Although these theories may explain certain aspects of behavioral systems under some conditions, we recognize many change processes not explained by such models. Behavioral explanations for change processes must account for variation in the types of activities from which such processes are initiated, and in the linkage factors by which they are spread to other activities.

## The case studies

Although the work of constructing a methodological and theoretical framework for an explanatory behavioral archaeology has begun, the real work now begins – that of applying this framework to prehistoric, historic, and modern cases of behavioral variation and change. Nonetheless, this skeletal framework already demonstrates much potential for exploring new areas of human life in a behavioral fashion, and for re-examining some of the more traditional concerns of behavioral archaeology from a new, explanation-oriented perspective. To illustrate, we furnish discussions of a number of research areas that are currently being pursued by behavioralists. Some topics may seem familiar ("Technology," and "Formation processes of the archaeological record"); others enter realms not previously explored by behavioralists ("Communication," and "The 'big' questions"). Although we have arranged these topical discussions in approximate order by increasing scale of behavioral complexity, several scales of behavioral phenomena are in fact addressed under each topic.

## Communication

The communication of information is a critical aspect of all human behaviors. Information cues interactions and contributes to the forward motion of activities; moreover, information flows – via linkage factors – establish cohesion and coordination among a behavioral system's activities. It is widely recognized by archaeologists that artifacts play significant roles in human communication (e.g. Wobst 1977). In seeking to apply this insight, many archaeologists have adopted conventional theories of communication from the social sciences and humanities (for examples, see Littlejohn 1991). This is regrettable because these theories marginalize artifacts; however, an alternative behavioral theory now exists.

This theory is built on an uncommonly broad view of communication: the transmission of information among people and artifacts within and between activities. In constructing the theory, Schiffer and Miller (1999a, 1999b) argue that conventional theories of communication are flawed because they tacitly adopt symbolic language as the paradigm for all human communication. This move constrains the kinds of questions that investigators can ask about information transfers, and results in a misplaced focus on meaning and symbol, neither of which are behavioral phenomena (see also Gell 1998). We now summarize briefly arguments in favor a theory of communication not grounded in language.

The language paradigm enforces a concern with the person who originates a communicative performance; he or she is often called the "sender." Investigators attempt to scrutinize the sender's intent and interpret the symbols being employed. In contrast, Schiffer and Miller argue that analyses should be oriented with respect to the receiver, focused on his or her response to the information acquired from performances of other interactors. Importantly, in this behavioral framework the investigator can treat *any* human performance as a receiver's response.

Language-based formulations also marginalize "non-verbal" communication modes, such as tactile (mechanical), visual (including most artifacts as well as gestures and postures), and chemical (based on taste and smell). Schiffer and Miller maintain that information obtained through any communication mode is capable of cuing a receiver's response. Thus, privileging the verbal mode skews our understanding of how people actually secure the information that they act on in everyday activities. The antidote is to shed a priori assumptions about the importance of specific communication modes – verbal or non-verbal – and to investigate, in particular instances of communication, which modes actually supply the receiver with response-cuing information.

Conventional theories of communication recognize only two roles, sender and receiver. In eliminating the "two-body" constraint, Schiffer and Miller posit three roles: sender, emitter, and receiver. The sender, which is always inferred by the receiver (and so can be "supernatural"), imparts information by modifying the properties of the second interactor, the emitter, just as a potter paints the surface of a bowl. It is the emitter's performances – e.g. a pot's decoration performing visually – that the receiver senses and which provide him/her with information through inference. In everyday activities, receivers acquire much consequential information from artifacts, making sundry inferences about senders and responding accordingly. That this account resembles the process of archaeological inference is no accident: the new communication theory generalizes behavioral models of inference to all instances of human communication (Schiffer and Miller 1999b: ch. 4). In certain analyses, the investigator may wish to collapse the three roles into two, but the three-role model is the more general one.

Another significant flaw in extant communication theories is that they permit only people to play communicative roles. Yet, in everyday life humans acquire consequential information from the performances of plants, rocks, animals, and artifacts, and they infer the actions of non-material senders such as "spirits." The behavioral theory of communication, however, operates within a behavioral context that is sufficiently broad to incorporate interactions of this kind as well. This theory permits interactors of every kind to play any role so long as they have the requisite performance characteristics (e.g. a receiver must have a sensory apparatus and be capable of responding). This move forces the investigator to ascertain, in each case of communication, from which interactors – whether people or not – the receiver obtained information.

The behavioral theory reorients the study of human communication by emphasizing the need to explain receiver responses. In so doing, the investigator models the relational knowledge that is keyed in by the receiver in a specific communication context – defined by an activity occurring in a place. Such relational knowledge, examples of which are called *correlons*, has been acquired by the receiver through genetic and ontogenetic hard-wiring and by participation in life history activities. In brief, many correlons probably resemble experimental laws and empirical generalizations relating sender behavior to variation in emitter performances. The processes whereby the receiver builds (learns) correlons, and determines their boundary conditions, may be likened to the construction of behavioral contexts by the analyst seeking to delimit the boundaries of a principle of human behavior (see above); here, however, events and observations in a person's life history furnish a testing ground for establishing the validity and boundaries of a correlon (in contrast to the more specific body of cases used by the analyst to establish boundaries for a behavioral generalization). The explanation of a receiver response requires the investigator to invoke the consequential performances of emitters as well as the correlons that have come into play in that context. The task ahead for behavioralists, and it is an enormous one, is to develop scientific methodology for modeling correlons. However, we contend that correlons can in principle be modeled rigorously (for some suggestions, see Schiffer and Miller 1999b: 83–8); after all, correlons are grounded in the materiality of a person's biology and life-history activities (for another artifact-based theory of communication, see Thomas 1996).

Although behavioral research on communication has so far been focused at the interaction scale (i.e. on the workings of discrete person–object interactions), we are optimistic that work on the role of communication in behavioral processes at higher scales, i.e. within activities and between activities in a behavioral system, will develop apace (e.g. see Schiffer and Skibo 1997 on the impact of feedback from artifact performance on artifact design activities). In subsequent examples, we point to instances where such research on communication and information flows might prove useful.

## Technology

As stated, artifacts and technologies are a critical focus for behavioral research at all scales. Studies of technologies usually begin with inferences about specific activities in an artifact's life history. Countless correlates as well as c-transforms and n-transforms facilitate these studies, which treat all kinds of technological materials. Low-level inferences about life-history activities, now prevalent across the discipline, furnish a foundation for building higher-level inferences about social and behavioral phenomena affected by and affecting the technologies being studied (Rathje and Schiffer 1982: chs 4 and 10; Sheets 1975). For example, inferences about migration (J. L. Adams 1994; Lyons 1999) and exchange (Zedeño 1994) can be founded on technological studies, which enable archaeologists now to answer many traditional culture-historical questions with unaccustomed rigor (Stark 1998).

Behavioralists also build theories for explaining technological variability and change. These theories can be divided into three groups, which are defined with respect to the stages in a technology's history: invention, commercialization, and adoption. Traditionally, archaeologists conflate these stages, making it impossible to formulate research questions in behavioral terms. Theories of invention account for aspects of inventive activities; commercialization theories seek to understand the processes whereby product types are designed and brought to market by entrepreneurs, manufacturers, and artisans; and theories of adoption explain the acquisition behavior of consumers – individuals and behavioral components (such as companies, churches, and polities). Explaining variability and change in each stage requires different sets of theories, depending on the scale of the behavioral context under investigation.

## Invention

Behavioral theories of inventive activities are in their infancy. One model accounts for increases in the kinds and frequencies of inventive activities in relation to a particular artifact type in a behavioral system. The "stimulated variation" model (Schiffer 1996) was crafted to foster dialog on invention processes between behavioral and selectionist archaeologists (for the latter's views, see O'Brien et al. 1998); the model, which operates within a very generalized behavioral context, seeks the causes of inventive spurts in an artifact's selective environment – i.e. the activities linked to those of its life history. For example, if the potters in a community, who make their wares by the coil-and-scrape technique, are unable to keep up with demand for their products (i.e. meet the level of output dictated by linkage factors with other activities), they might experiment with ways to speed up production (holding constant the size of the labor pool). Experiments might include throwing off the hump, using the fast wheel or molds, or altering vessel designs to streamline the hand-building process. The stimulated variation model stresses that invention does not entail adoption: after the period of experimentation, the potters might reject all of these inventions.

Hayden (1998) has developed a model to explain the invention of a number of prestige technologies. This model suggests that every human society having in excess of 200–300 members potentially provides the appropriate demographic and economic conditions (behavioral context) in which a small number of "aggrandizers" can emerge. Where resources are concentrated and abundant, permitting the accumulation of "surpluses," aggrandizers may be able to divert flows of people (labor) and resources into inventive activities. Such projects often result in the invention of new technologies (e.g. metallurgy, ceramics, and ocean-going vessels), some of which might be widely adopted.

## Commercialization

Commercialization involves the transformation of technological prototypes into manufacturable products that are made available to consumers. An important component of commercialization is the design process.

Behavioral theories of design account for the formal properties of artifacts attributable to an artisan's behavior during materials procurement and manufacture activities (i.e. technical choices). Many investigators have offered models for the design of particular technologies, such as chipped stone (Hayden et al. 1996; Kuhn 1994), ground stone (J. L. Adams 1994; Horsfall 1987), and vernacular architecture (McGuire and Schiffer 1983), sometimes drawing inspiration from design theories – not always very behavioral – in other disciplines. Building on these efforts, Schiffer and Skibo (1997) constructed a fully behavioral, general theory of design whose behavioral context is the life history of any artifact type in any society.

This theory rests on the premise that an artisan's behaviors, which determine a given artifact's design, are responsive to that artifact's performances in activities along its entire behavioral chain. In principle, then, specific interactions in any activity, from procurement of raw materials to discard, can affect an artifact's design so long as the artisan has information about the conduct of those activities (communicated via linkage factors) and the "ideal" performance characteristics required. In practice, however, a great many other factors affect the extent that ideal performance characteristics, appropriate for all activities in an artifact's behavioral chain, are actually weighted in the design process. Among the intervening factors that the investigator needs to consider are the social heterogeneity of the artifact's behavioral chain, which in extreme cases can impede information flow from "downstream" activities, especially in industrial societies; compromises in performance characteristics necessitated by technical choices having polar effects (lots of sand temper strengthens a pot's thermal shock resistance but also decreases its resistance to impacts); learning/teaching frameworks, which accommodate everything from individual variation to a society's "technological style" (Lechtman 1977); and differences in social power and negotiation outcomes among participants in behavioral chain activities, which can tilt technical choices in favor of one group at the expense of others. Schiffer and Skibo's (1997) behavioral theory of design obviously requires a great deal of information about an artifact's behavioral chain activities, but it promises archaeologists the ability to construct rigorous and testable explanations for the artisan's decisions.

## Adoption

Adoption processes have been of considerable interest to behavioralists. Adoption models help one to understand patterns of what culture historians, geographers, and economists called "diffusion." Economic anthropologists also study adoption processes, but employ the term "consumption" to denote product-acquisition behavior (e.g. Wilk 1996). Historical archaeologists have long been interested in adoption processes, on scales ranging from households to regions (e.g. South 1977; Spencer-Wood 1987), and many of their models are quite behavioral.

The most general behavioral formulation is that consumers, which can be individuals, task groups, and so forth, differentially acquire products whose performance characteristics are better suited to specific activities – current and anticipated – than are alternative products (McGuire and Schiffer 1983; Schiffer and Skibo 1987; Schiffer 1995b). The investigator assesses the performance characteristics of alternative products by means of a "performance matrix." In constructing a performance matrix, one lists pertinent activities and the values of contextually relevant performance characteristics for the products being compared (for examples, see Schiffer and Skibo 1987; Schiffer 1995b: 29–31). Performance matrices enable the investigator to readily display patterns of compromise in the products' performance characteristics and thereby offer explanations for why one was adopted over alternatives.

Other general principles relate adoption patterns to the life histories of individuals (biological variation and social-role changes) and the developmental cycles of behavioral components, especially households. For example, Rathje and Schiffer (1982: 78–80) maintain that age and sex differences among individuals – which often entail participation in differing suites of activities – lead to variation in acquisition behavior. Similarly, individual differences in social roles, income, and wealth also contribute to varied acquisition (and disposal) patterns (e.g. Schiffer et al. 1981).

Archaeologists have built many behavioral models applying to particular adoption processes. Among the earliest were Binford's formulations about "curated" technologies and the kinds of toolkits adopted by mobile task groups (e.g. Binford 1973, 1979; for a review, see Nelson 1991). The hypothesis that mobility puts severe constraints on the technologies adopted by mobile task groups, capable of influencing performance characteristics such as maintainability and reliability (e.g. Bleed 1986), has been widely accepted.

In a recent work, Schiffer (1995b: 32–3) advanced the "Imelda Marcos" hypothesis to explain some instances of product acquisition by individuals and behavioral components. The hypothesis, which operates within a very generalized behavioral context, is that "the investment of resources in an activity, to enhance its performance, leads to an increase in unifunctional [i.e. highly specialized] artifacts" (Schiffer 1995b: 33). Thus, households that often perform car-repair activities at home are apt to acquire many specialized car-repair tools. One obvious corollary of the Imelda Marcos hypothesis is that wealthier behavioral components (especially households, corporations, and communities) can enhance many activities, and thus add countless artifacts and/or people of restricted function to their inventories (Schiffer 1995b: 32).

Rathje's Le Projet du Garbage has contributed many general hypotheses about consumption processes (see Rathje and Murphy 1992). Among the most fascinating is the counterintuitive finding, a tentative law of waste, that when the price of a basic commodity – e.g. red meat or sugar – undergoes a short-term increase, more of it is wasted (percentage-wise) by consumers. This comes about because people substitute products that, although they still contain the basic commodity (e.g. beef), exhibit unfamiliar performance characteristics in preparation and consumption activities. Thus, during the beef shortage in the spring of 1973, Americans bought cuts of beef as well as other beef-containing products that they had not previously consumed, and which they apparently did not know how to prepare well. During the shortage, households wasted beef at a rate three times that found for non-shortage months (Rathje and Murphy 1992: 61–3). Although this tentative law was derived from empirical observations in a market-based subsistence economy, it may well be applicable within a more generalized behavioral context.

In studying technology today we are fortunate that, over the past few decades, archaeologists of every theoretical persuasion have furnished countless experimental laws upon which we can now build new theories for explaining technological variability and change. A key behavioral insight is that many theories are needed for explaining aspects of each stage of a technology's history: invention, commercialization, and adoption. We expect rapid progress in this area because interest in theories of technology is becoming widespread across the discipline.

## Formation processes of the archaeological record

Eventually, most technologies, people, and other material elements wear out, break, die, or otherwise come to be deposited in the archaeological record. While questions about the design and use of artifacts are important, archaeologists must also explain *why* and *how* objects come to be removed from activities in a behavioral system and enter the archaeological record by way of cultural deposition. *Explanations* for variability in cultural deposition, a relatively underdeveloped area of research, can be framed in terms outlined by behavioralists in over two decades of formation process studies. Although formation process research remains critical and necessary for developing better inferences, here we focus on how such research may also help to illuminate the organizational aspects of, and changes in, past behavioral systems.

Behavioral archaeologists have long insisted that the archaeological record is a transformed or distorted reflection of past behavioral systems (Reid 1985; Schiffer 1976, 1983, 1985, 1987). We maintain that the transformative view of formation processes is necessary so long as researchers continue to build inferences on unrealistic and untested assumptions about the processes that created that record. In other research contexts, however, depositional behaviors, principally discard and abandonment, need not be considered as processes that only obscure the material traces of other, "more interesting" activities. Rather, depositional behaviors can and should be studied in their own right within an explicitly anthropological frame of reference (LaMotta 1999). Since these behaviors are conditioned and constrained by the same kinds of material and social relations (linkage factors) that impinge on all forms of human activity, the construction of theory to explain variation in depositional behavior should be a high priority for archaeologists (Tani 1995). Further, cultural deposition often involves more than the passive output of expended materials from a behavioral system; deposition may be linked to other activities via outputs of materials, information, and energy – linkages through which it may "act back" on the behavioral system and initiate change processes (see Rathje 1995; Walker et al. 1995). This discussion builds on these ideas and points to ways in which c-transforms (which stipulate how cultural materials are transformed from systemic to archaeological context via human behavior) can be used to explore behavioral processes at a variety of scales.

The study of cultural deposition (and its counterpart, curation) has been recognized for some time as a potentially valuable tool for examining variation in the organization of activities and behavioral systems (e.g. Binford 1977, 1978, 1979, 1980; Reid 1985; Schiffer 1985). With hindsight it is clear that some of the early studies were based on assumptions about the determinants of depositional behaviors that might not be as general as was believed (LaMotta and Schiffer 1999). Many scholars offered economic or "least effort" models to explain variation in, for example, which objects would be abandoned or curated if the owner were to undertake a long-distance residence move (e.g. Schiffer 1985). Such a model has been applied widely in the interpretation of assemblages left, for example, on house floors around the time of structure abandonment. However, archaeologists need to define carefully the boundary conditions, or behavioral context, within which an economic principle adequately explains depositional variation. For example, such a model might explain patterns of artifact deposition under circumstances of residence relocation, but even then the relative energy expenditures associated with artifact curation (and transport) or deposition (and then replacement) behaviors will be conditioned by the linkage factors associated with the abandonment event and with subsequent relocation-related activities. Since linkage factors vary on a case-by-case basis, the researcher must have an understanding of those factors before invoking a least-effort explanation for a specific depositional event. Additionally, ethnographic and archaeological studies clearly demonstrate that there are many discard and abandonment processes – especially among sedentary and semi-sedentary peoples – that are not explained by a least-effort model (e.g. LaMotta and Schiffer 1999; Walker 1995; see also Gould 1978a: 831). Additional explanatory frameworks, sensitive to depositional processes in other behavioral contexts, need to be developed. Moreover, it must recognized that because depositional behaviors occur in diverse behavioral contexts, archaeologists need to develop methods for matching appropriate explanatory theories to the cultural deposits under study (e.g. Montgomery 1993; Walker 1998b).

We turn our attention now to the development of several alternative models for explaining variation in discard and abandonment behaviors. Several critical variables need to be scrutinized for defining relevant behavioral contexts, including (1) the location in which a particular object was deposited, (2) the types of objects deposited together, (3) the life-history stage(s) when an object or architectural space entered the archaeological record, and (4) the types of activities that effect depositional events. These behavioral phenomena all beg for explanation. Clearly, *much* more focused ethnoarchaeological research is needed to discern all the factors that structure these and other aspects of depositional behaviors (but see Binford 1978; Gould 1978a; Hayden and Cannon 1983; papers in Cameron and Tomka 1993; papers in Staski and Sutro 1991). We suggest focusing initially on those activities directly linked to discard and/or abandonment behaviors via flows of people, artifacts, energy, and information (described in terms of linkage factors). General questions that must be asked in pursuing these lines of research include (1) To which other activities are depositional activities linked? (2) How does deposition, which entails the removal of elements from activities, affect linkage factors and the performance of linked activities? How do depositional behaviors contribute to stability, or initiate change processes, with respect to the structure and organization of activities and flows of material and information in a behavioral system? We provide a few tentative examples, drawn from ethnographic and archaeological research, that illustrate how such questions might lead to the explanation of depositional behaviors and, ultimately, to insights into a behavioral system's organization.

Cultural deposition is not always the casual byproduct of waste-generating activities. People may remove one or more object(s) or architectural spaces from a behavioral system to alter the performance and organization of activities, and to redirect flows of materials, people, energy, and information among activities. Such depositional behaviors can initiate profound changes in activity performance and, through activity linkages, produce widespread behavioral change. Strategies employed by sixteenth- and seventeenth-century Franciscan missionaries for spreading Catholicism among natives of the American Southwest provide apt examples. To destroy Pueblo religious practices, Franciscans burned and buried religious paraphernalia and ceremonial rooms, and killed native priests (e.g. Brew 1949; Dozier 1970: 47–52; Nequatewa 1994: 33–6). By destroying and redirecting these objects and people into the archaeological record, missionaries initiated change processes in native ritual activities that did effect significant, if temporary, alterations in religious practices. In the process, archaeological deposits consisting of discarded (and/or cached) religious paraphernalia, abandoned ceremonial rooms, and maltreated human remains would have been created (e.g. Kidder 1958: 232–40; Smith 1972: 59–67). Behaviors such as these would be especially disruptive in behavioral contexts wherein activity performance depends on objects or people with performance characteristics that cannot be reproduced easily (if at all) by replacement elements (e.g. ritual activities performed with unique paraphernalia or by specialists with esoteric knowledge).

People might also initiate changes in activities and in linkage factors by creating a specific, visually (and/or acoustically) salient event centered on discard or abandonment activities. Such events might furnish to receivers information about the individuals responsible for the depositional act and about the latter's relationship(s) to the receivers or to the larger community (or even to "the cosmos"). This type of model has been used commonly (if often implicitly) in the interpretation of mortuary deposition: archaeologists hypothesize that treatment of the corpse and the associated deposition of funerary artifacts conveyed information about the deceased person's social roles in life, indicated a particular construction of the deceased's former identity, and/or imparted information to receivers about the mourners and their social and economic roles in the community (e.g. Cannon 1989; McGuire 1992: ch. 7; Peebles and Kus 1977; Shanks and Tilley 1982). Presumably, some such visual performances involving cultural deposition would cue subsequent interactions between the survivors and between the social groups to which they belonged (Klandrud and LaMotta 1999). Before employing such a model, one must ask: Who would have viewed the depositional event? What specific information were the receivers likely to have obtained by that event? And, how would that information be disseminated into other linked activities and possibly lead to changes in activity performance and in linkage factors among those activities? Since all depositional behaviors can convey information visually, we suggest that such questions are pertinent not only for mortuary contexts but for all other discard and abandonment behaviors as well. We also recognize that these questions are not currently easy to answer, especially in prehistoric settings, but we are confident that attention to the spatial location of depositional events and to the properties of objects and assemblages, combined with further research on the roles of artifacts in communication, will begin to supply the necessary correlates and c-transforms.

It is also apparent that people may *use* an artifact by depositing it in the archaeological record, paradoxical though this may seem to the archaeologist. An example helps to elucidate this behavioral phenomenon: in some historic Pueblo societies in the American Southwest, spaces below the ground surface serve as conduits to the supernatural and natural realms (e.g. Parsons 1939: 217, 309–11). People alter the behavior of supernatural entities, or of natural phenomena such as rain clouds and game animals, by sending artifacts through this conduit (i.e. by modifying linkage factors with activities involving supernaturals and forces of nature). The Hopi, for example, bury prayer sticks, clay figurines, or vessels of water, sending them as offerings to influence the activities of rain-cloud spirits (*katsinam*) and other (super)natural forces (e.g. Hieb 1979: 580; Parsons 1939: 270–85; Stephen 1936: 824–9; Titiev 1944: 147–8). Hopi also sacrifice eagles and other birds, burying them in formal graves in cemeteries (Fewkes 1897; Voth 1912: 108). The transformation of these birds from systemic to archaeological context facilitates their journey to the realm of the rain spirits whom they are to petition, with offerings, for rain (Bradfield 1995: 255–6; Stephen 1936: 569). In these and many other cross-cultural examples, depositional behaviors modify the linkage factors tying human activities to the "otherworldly" activities of natural and supernatural actors. Clearly, such depositional behaviors involve more than just the casual disposal of expended materials. The recognition that the breakage and burial of an artifact may represent a "use" for that object is a significant step towards explaining variation in some depositional behaviors – in a proximal fashion at least.

Lastly, recent research suggests that under some conditions earlier events, or sequences of events, in the life history of an object (i.e. an artifact, person, animal, or architectural space) may condition that object for a particular type of deposition or discard. This is often the case for elements used in ritual or ceremony. For example, the manufacture of ceremonial items or spaces is sometimes accompanied by activities that bring objects, animals, or ritual structures into the social realm by formally naming them and by performing other *rites de passage* typically associated with the birth and naming of human beings (for Pueblo examples, see Fewkes 1900a, 1900b; Parsons 1939: 454; Stephen 1936: 151, 719–21; Voth 1912: 105–9). These ritual acts set apart, or singularize (*sensu* Kopytoff 1986; Walker 1995), these objects, spaces, and ritual animals from domestic structures and subsistence fauna, and typically set them on life-history courses that involve ritualized uses and a ritualized abandonment or discard. Research in the prehistoric American Southwest, for example, has demonstrated that there was sometimes a non-random relationship between (inferred) structure use and subsequent abandonment mode. Walker et al. (2000) and Wilshusen (1986, 1988) observed correlations between the location, size, and suite of internal features found in Anasazi pit houses and pueblo rooms, on the one hand, and the treatment of those rooms at abandonment, on the other (see also Cameron 1991). Large structures with complex, formalized suites of internal features (inferred to have been used in rituals), sometimes placed in plazas and set apart from blocks of domestic structures, tend to have been burned at abandonment – in contrast to smaller structures with more typical "domestic" features, which were burned rarely. Human remains and/or worn-out ritual artifacts also seem to have been preferentially deposited in such structures during, or after, abandonment. These and other cross-cultural examples suggest a general principle of abandonment: use of an architectural space for ritual activities predisposes that structure to be abandoned in a fashion that differentiates it from other types of structures. The challenge that lies ahead is to explain *how* linkages and linkage factors established during use condition abandonment activities. One way to approach this problem is to incorporate other critical variables (e.g. size and type of the behavioral component using and abandoning the structure; types of activities to which abandonment activities are linked; and the linkage factors connecting these events) to define additional (more specific) behavioral contexts in which variants of this general principle apply (for the most general formulation of this principle, see Walker 1995).

Walker's (1995) ethnoarchaeological and cross-cultural research also identified important general patterns in the disposal of portable items that had been used in ritual activities. He found that such items, when broken or worn out ("ceremonial trash"), tended to be disposed of in ways that distinguished them from domestic trash. Ritually used items were often deposited in areas spatially separate from domestic trash dumps, and tended to be burned, broken, and/or buried at the point of disposal. Importantly, he found that the spatial differentiation of ritual disposal facilities can result in the aggregation of ceremonial trash in concentrated deposits, such as that found in Jewish *genizahs*. Thus, aggregates of objects that follow broadly similar life histories prior to discard (at least in terms of ritual uses) tend to be discarded together physically and/or through similar discard behaviors. These ethnoarchaeological findings have important implications for identifying and interpreting ritual deposits in archaeological contexts (e.g. Walker et al. 2000). Walker (1995), LaMotta (1996), Karunaratne (1997), and Strand (1998), for example, working in the prehistoric American Southwest, were able to identify an aggregate of object types and faunal species that seems to have been preferentially discarded in abandoned ceremonial structures. These associations, combined with the location of discard, provide compelling arguments for inferring that these objects were members of a ritual aggregate. Explanations for the differential disposal of portable objects, like those for the abandonment of architectural spaces, must account for variation in linkage factors that conditions depositional activities. For example, one explanation for a behavior such as the singularized discard of ceremonial trash is that it restricts the flow of visual information from those activities. Indeed, the burning or burial of worn-out ritual sacra may, in some contexts, prevent detailed information about the formal properties of these objects from being acquired by non-specialists, thereby precluding the unsanctioned replication of artifacts used for interacting with the supernatural. This is only one possible explanation that must be tested with additional data, and we have omitted consideration of many relevant linkage factors for the sake of brevity. Nonetheless, this approach indicates one method for explaining variation in ritual behaviors, including deposition, that is based firmly on the study of people–object interactions.

The foregoing discussion of formation process research, and the new directions we envision for such work, may seem like a departure from earlier behavioralist writings on the subject (e.g. Reid 1985; Schiffer 1976, 1983, 1987). We emphasize, however, that research on formation processes must continue for the purpose of refining behavioral inferences from archaeological deposits. What we propose here is that archaeologists also work toward more contextualized understandings of depositional behaviors – i.e. investigate their linkages to other activities in a behavioral system – to facilitate explanation. Although we have discussed several factors that may condition variation in depositional behaviors, this list is surely incomplete. Additional research holds great promise for unraveling and explaining depositional behaviors, for illuminating the structural relationships within behavioral systems that govern variation in cultural deposition, *and* for making sense of the material patterns that those behaviors create in the archaeological record. Cultural formation processes, especially discard and abandonment, are behavioral phenomena that need to be explained, not just distorting processes to be controlled.

## The 'big' questions

In the Preface to *Behavioral Archeology*, Schiffer (1976: ix) acknowledged that the reader would not find in that book any "ready-made explanations" for the big issues in archaeology, such as the adoption of agriculture and the development of "civilization." Rather, he suggested that the book might be of interest if the reader were "concerned to ask these important questions in new ways and to devise more appropriate strategies for answering them" (see also Schiffer 1995a: 235).

To date, behavioralists have seldom engaged these same questions (but see Nielsen 1995), perhaps reluctant to tackle them before having an adequate corpus of behavioral method and theory. Although that corpus of principles remains modest, we believe that questions about some of these phenomena can now be formulated in behavioral terms. In this section, then, we indicate avenues for constructing behavioral explanations for the "origins" of agriculture and the development of complex societies. We emphasize that each formulation is merely one of many possible behavioral approaches to the problem; our examples are intended to be illustrative of the method and its theoretical possibilities rather than definitive statements. We frame both discussions in terms of two questions: (1) how can the process(es) of interest be defined in terms of behavior; and (2) what are the boundary conditions on the general principle(s) that describe that behavioral process (or processes)? We provide detailed discussions for the first question, and point to ways in which the second might be addressed fully in a more substantial analysis.

## The *"origins" of agriculture*

In this brief exercise, we demonstrate that by reformulating the question of agricultural "origins" in behavioral terms, it is possible to employ extant behavioral theory to suggest promising lines of empirical research. Many believe that the most important feature of early agriculture is the development of domesticated plants and animals. As Rindos (1984) and others remind us, domestication is simply the expectable consequence of persistent human meddling in the lives of other species. That being the case, we need to focus on the "meddling," defining it behaviorally so that we can discern which behavioral theories are relevant. Once that is done, it should be possible to posit the general factors that might lead people to adopt agricultural activities.

The examples in this discussion are based on sexually reproducing plants, but our formulations should also apply, with little modification, to other plant and animal species. We focus on the biological life histories of plants, paying careful attention to the intersection of those life histories with human activities.

The genetically determined life history of a sexually reproducing plant can be divided into a number of behaviorally relevant stages, such as germination, growth to sexual maturity, production of seeds, and seed dispersal. Humans can intervene at any stage, but when people meddle consistently in pre-harvest stages of many plants, we tend to label those groups as "agriculturalists." However, we should not forget that, on a plant-by-plant basis, the extent of human meddling lies on a continuum.

Every human activity occurring in the cultural life history of plants, collected or farmed, involves technologies. In wild-plant collecting activities, a host of technologies can take part, such as digging sticks, baskets, knives, pounding stones, and hearths; there may also be technologies for transport and storage. Farmed plants also tend to involve a large array of pre-harvest technologies, which can include tools for clearing and preparing fields, weeding, pest reduction, and irrigation. Many additional technologies – from specialized architecture to milling stones to pottery – often participate in post-harvest activities of cultivars such as crop transport, seed storage, shelling, winnowing, grinding, cooking, and serving. We suggest, then, that one way to frame the problem of farming "origins" is as a question about the differential adoption of plant-manipulation behaviors and technologies. To wit, why do people begin consistently to adopt particular behavioral strategies and associated technologies for interacting with plants during pre-harvest stages in the life histories of plants?

In seeking answers to this question, we should find that extant behavioral theories about technological variability and change (see above) are applicable. To explain the adoption of a technology, the investigator assesses its performance characteristics in relation to alternative technologies in relevant activities. A complete analysis of any one case would require us to construct detailed performance matrices for technological alternatives in specific collecting and farming activities – far beyond our needs in this paper. For heuristic purposes we suggest that investigators assess the general performance characteristics of technology aggregates – i.e. sets of artifacts used for plant manipulation – in sequential behavioral systems undergoing the transition from hunting and gathering to farming. Our expectation is that one will find overarching patterns in compromises among general performance characteristics such as the amount of edible product harvestable per unit time or harvesting area, and the effort needed to make, use, and maintain plant-manipulation technologies, especially those employed in pre-harvest activities.

Directing our attention to the performance characteristics of food-related technologies should enable us to explain specific sequences of change, including cases where farming technologies are not adopted. Thus, we suggest that a profitable way to research the origins of agriculture is to compare the performance characteristics of the technologies that pre- and post-agricultural societies adopt for meddling in the lives of plants and animals.

We also suggest that effort be devoted to defining the behavioral context(s) within which this process of technological adoption occurs. Ethnographically and archaeologically, there appears to be a wide range of variation in the conditions under which people opt for agricultural strategies: in the specific technologies employed, in the relative contributions of farmed and foraged resources, and so forth. We suspect that this variation simply reflects a fairly wide range of permissible values for the critical variables that define this behavioral context (alternatively, it indicates that there is some flexibility in the mix of critical variables that have some bearing on the operation of this process in different cases). Researchers might profitably employ the methods discussed earlier to identify and define the general boundaries on this process – at least some of which already have been researched in detail (e.g. Boserup 1981)

## The development of complex societies

As archaeologists embraced, in the 1980s and 1990s, "multicausal" explanations for the development of complex societies (e.g. Redman

1978), it became unclear how one could construct any non-trivial generalizations from the increasing welter of causal factors discerned in specific studies. We suggest two solutions to this problem: one employing organizational theory having a behavioral emphasis, the second focusing on recurrent "growth processes." Research then needs to be directed toward defining the behavioral contexts within which these processes are initiated and spread.

Let us first address the question, What phenomena are encompassed by the term "complex society?" Many archaeologists, drawing on neo-evolutionary formulations, believe that a complex society is one having a state political organization, a military apparatus under state control, marked social classes or at least a prominent elite, many occupational specialists, and so on. Regardless of which trait list one uses, complex society is at best a polythetic category, in that many exemplars do not possess every trait. Clearly, "complex society" subsumes an enormous amount of organizational and behavioral variation.

That the category of complex society obscures much variability is troubling to behavioralists who, above all, privilege the explanation of variability. Thus, the complex society category appears to be somewhat arbitrary, overly inclusive, and lacks a convincing theoretical warrant or a behavioral basis. An obvious move for the behavioralist is to point to the possibility that variability in societal complexity can be modeled as one or more continua (McGuire 1983; Rathje and Schiffer 1982: ch. 3).

Although a dramatic improvement over stage models, treating complexity as a continuum still obscures variability in the character of complexity. For example, two societies that are judged to be equally complex on the basis of some quantitative scale (e.g. size of population integrated, number of levels in the political or settlement hierarchy, degree of urbanization) could still differ appreciably in their mix of political, religious, military, and commercial developments. Apparently, variation in societal complexity is irreducibly multidimensional (see Crumley's [1979] concept of "heterarchy"). Thus, we eschew overarching conceptions of complexity in favor of formulations that are sensitive to variability that has a behavioral basis – i.e. can be phrased in terms of people–artifact interactions.

To highlight this variability, we propose that any complex society (however defined) is the product of differentially developed institutions and sectors. An institution is a large-scale behavioral component having a bureaucratic – i.e. hierarchical – structure (Rathje and Schiffer 1982: 47). Concretely, an institution is a domain of related activities, organized on a supra-household level, in any part of society, such as government, churches, the army, universities, labor unions, and professional sports. Institutions, which can be modeled as specialized behavioral systems, establish dedicated places and structures for their activities, and regulate flows of people, objects, energy, and information between and among these places and others. The operation of an institution depends on that system's connections, via linkage factors, to outside activities and to other institutions. The investigator can create horizontal groupings of functionally similar institutions, which can be called sectors, such as political, military, commercial, industrial, transportation, educational, and religious sectors. We suggest that the differential development of sectors (and the specific institutions that comprise them) is the most significant axis of behavioral variability in complex societies. If this kind of variation is of interest, then a priority for future research is to identify the factors that contributed to each society's unique mix of sectoral developments.

Identifying these case-specific factors rests on the recognition that as institutions (organizations) arise and become more complex they facilitate interactions of people and artifacts at ever-increasing scales and rates. Thus, institutions in a sector enable the management of activities – the flow of people and artifacts through space and their interactions. As people–artifact interactions become more intense and differentiated, institutions change, becoming more complex or failing. Failure may ensue when an institution can no longer process materials, people, energy, or information at rates demanded by linkage factors that connect the institution with activities providing input or receiving output. In such cases, new linkages may be established between the latter activities and other functionally similar institutions within the sector that are better able to meet demands established by increasing rates of material, energy, or information transfer. For example, a two-person partnership can manage a small company that makes and sells craft items in a local market. But if that company expands production dramatically and begins selling in a national market, more people and more kinds of occupational specialists – e.g. managers, designers, artisans, marketers, accountants, shipping clerks, janitors – will be required. Continued growth in production might eventually yield the modern multinational corporation with perhaps a dozen levels of decision-making and thousands of different occupational specialists. To explain fully the differential development of sectors in a specific society, then, we must chart the course of projects and activities that have contributed to the expansion of the institutions making up each sector. That is, we must identify changes in what institutions are actually doing: it is people–artifact interactions, in concrete activities, that establish the basic parameters for organizational development.

Although development of the specific institutions making up each sector and of the sectors themselves can vary somewhat independently, sometimes development in one sector stimulates growth in others. In the United States, for example, the political sector grew enormously in the twentieth century, taking on new activities such as taxing income, providing welfare, managing national parks and forests, and cleaning up the environment, partly in response to the activities of greatly expanded industrial and commercial sectors. The nature and extent of inter-sectoral linkages and changes in them over time are, of course, empirical questions to be answered anew in each study.

For the behavioralist, development involves more than the growth of organization – the widening and deepening of bureaucracy and the multiplication of occupational specialists. Indeed, a concomitant of development, regardless of sector, is the proliferation of artifacts. For example, the specialists who perform new behavioral roles – activity-specific behavior patterns (Schiffer 1992: 132) – do so most likely with new kinds of artifacts. Thus, when a modern organization adds a janitorial staff, it also acquires a host of specialized maintenance artifacts, from commercial vacuum cleaners and floor polishers to toilet-cleaning brushes and detergents, as well as dedicated places having furnishings appropriate for the activities they contain (e.g. janitor's store-room or closet). A host of new artifacts may also take part in maintaining hierarchy and in advertising social roles. As organizations develop, they come to occupy more and larger structures to house their activities, which also advertise their apparent success and importance.

If development is as much a process of adding artifacts as it is of adding new occupational specialists and levels of decision-making, then archaeologists ought to be identifying and studying the general processes that contribute to inventory expansion, enrichment, and change. Such questions can be handled by behavioral theories regarding artifact adoption. Clearly, an understanding of these adoption processes can enable us to better appreciate the material dimension of growth. But there is more: these processes themselves, working within and across sectors, are also motors of development. We single out two "growth processes" for brief discussion. Both processes focus on people–artifact interactions, at the scales of individuals and behavioral components (including households), that stimulate demand for new products. Meeting such demands causes further development of various sectors.

The first growth process is the Simmel process, which maintains systems of class grading in socially mobile, market-based societies

(McCracken 1988: 40–1; Schiffer 1976: 189–91). In such societies that lack sumptuary rules, it is possible for people to purchase artifacts that indicate membership in a superordinate class. As upper-class artifacts become widespread in subordinate classes, their ability to communicate information about social differentiation is impaired. In response, members of the superordinate class find new artifacts that can advertise their class affiliation less ambiguously. The Simmel process (named for sociologist Georg Simmel who first studied it) creates an incessant demand for new artifacts and for new technologies to produce them. This, in turn, contributes to complexity by the proliferation and growth of organizations that make new products and by the expansion of trade and transportation activities. Growth in these sectors can as well stimulate growth in the political sector. We submit that the Simmel growth process, resting ultimately on specific kinds of people–artifact interactions, is an important contributor to the development of institutions and sectors, especially in the United States during the past two centuries.

A second growth process is based on the Imelda Marcos hypothesis. Recall that when people (and behavioral components) invest resources to enhance the performance of activities, there is an increase in specialized artifacts (Schiffer 1995b: 33). The demands thus created for innumerable specialized artifacts are a significant fillip to the development of manufacturing, trading, and transportation organizations, in commercial and industrial sectors, that can supply them. Political institutions, in turn, grow as they take on the expanded regulatory and taxation activities that greater commerce creates.

The Simmel and Imelda Marcos growth processes exemplify the kinds of general processes that can contribute, incrementally, to the development of institutions and sectors in complex societies. The task ahead is to delineate additional processes and discern their influence on the developmental patterns of specific complex societies. We expect that there will be dozens – perhaps hundreds – of similar growth processes, all of them based on concrete people–artifact interactions. It is the operation of these processes, mediated by case-specific contingencies, that account for increases – and variation – in complexity. We note that these growth processes are in principle reversible, and so can also account for reductions in complexity.

A significant challenge that lies ahead is the determination of behavioral-context boundaries for the operation of each growth process. What are the critical variables for a particular growth process, and how do changing values for these variables alter the operation of that process? Understanding these boundary conditions and threshold values will allow the analyst to narrow down the range of processes likely to come into play in any given case. Unlike the adoption of agricultural strategies – defined by one or a few closely related processes – the emergence of complexity in institutional organizations is a much more generalized phenomenon that may involve many different growth processes, and variable mixes of processes, on a case-by-case basis. We encourage researchers to explore this variability by constructing general principles that describe growth processes, and then by testing the boundaries on those principles by constructing behavioral contexts with differing combinations of critical variables and associated values. Explanations for complexity based on principles derived in such a fashion will engage, rather than conflate, the enormous variation evident in this phenomenon of organizational complexity.

## *Discussion*

In the final analysis, the behavioral perspective enables the investigator to demystify a "big" question, turning it into many concrete ones having a behavioral basis and thereby rendering it researchable. In the case of agricultural "origins," the new questions focus on pinpointing the conditions (behavioral contexts) under which people adopt technologies for meddling in the life histories of plants and animals. In the study of complex societies, emphasis is placed on ascertaining the behavioral factors that influence the differential development of institutions and sectors and on identifying specific growth processes that contribute to greater complexity. In neither case are we attempting to explain a singular event (e.g. becoming farmers) or a transition between abstractions (e.g. a shift from tribe or chiefdom to state). Rather, effort is devoted to formulating questions about behavioral variability and change, conceived as people–artifact interactions in activities. And, in both cases, existing behavioral theories can apparently help the investigator to design research for answering the new questions; even so, the creation of many new behavioral theories will also be required.

## Conclusion

During slightly more than two decades as an explicit program, behavioral archaeology can count many accomplishments, from putting archaeological inference on a solid footing to producing countless correlates, c-transforms, and n-transforms through experimental archaeology and ethnoarchaeology. In this essay we have taken the opportunity to call attention as well to the program's theory-building efforts.

Although behavioral archaeology is a coherent and well-integrated program, it has little orthodoxy. For some practitioners, especially those who tackle evolutionary or postprocessual kinds of questions, behavioral archaeology simply supplies rigorous methodology. For others, the behavioral perspective furnishes a starting point for building new social theories, which serve archaeologists in their attempts to study technological variability and change, cultural deposition, ritual and religion, communication, and so on. Because behavioralists have recently placed a higher priority on the creation of social theory, we anticipate that efforts along those lines will expand in the decades ahead in directions that it would be foolhardy to predict. Above all, behavioral archaeology does not rule in or out specific subject matters a priori. Indeed, the program encourages the investigation of any phenomena that can be rendered in behavioral terms – i.e. people–artifact interactions in activities.

## NOTES

We are greatly indebted to the following individuals for their patience, endurance, and constructive criticism in the course of reading several earlier versions of this chapter: E. Charles Adams, Margaret Beck, P. Jeffrey Brantingham, Nancy Daly, Janet Griffitts, Cory Harris, Kacy Hollenback, Sarah Klandrud, Billie Krebs, William Longacre, Patrick Lyons, Arthur MacWilliams, Julia Meyers, Joanne Newcomb, William Rathje, James Skibo, Jennifer Strand, William Walker, and M. Nieves Zedeño. All illustrations by Vincent LaMotta except table 2.1 (by Charles Sternberg) and figure 2.5 (by Sarah Klandrud).

1 By "social theory" we mean any and all nomothetic formulations for explaining variability and change in behavior, culture, or society (cf. Schiffer 1988). Throughout this chapter, we use the term "behavioral theory" to characterize such general principles based on people–object interactions.
2 Principles that permit an investigator to specify the ways in which a cultural system deposits materials that may be observed archaeologically, e.g. by specifying system outputs, discard rates, discard locations, loss probabilities, or burial practices (see Schiffer 1987: ch. 4, 1995a: ch. 2).
3 Principles that relate behavioral or organizational variables to variation in the form, frequency, associations, and spatial distribution of material objects in a living behavioral system (see Schiffer 1995a: ch. 2).
4 Previously called "coupling parameters" (Schiffer, 1979, 1992: ch. 4).

REFERENCES

Adams, E. Charles 1996. Understanding aggregation in the Homol'ovi pueblos: scalar stress and social power. In E. Charles Adams (ed.), *River of Change: Prehistory of the Middle Little Colorado River Valley, Arizona*, 1–14. Arizona State Museum Archaeological Series 185. Tucson: Arizona State Museum.

Adams, Jenny L. 1994. The development of prehistoric grinding technology in the Point of Pines area, East Central Arizona. Ph.D. Dissertation, University of Arizona. Ann Arbor: University Microfilms.

Bartlett, Katherine 1933. Pueblo milling stones of the Flagstaff region and their relation to others in the Southwest. *Museum of Northern Arizona, Bulletin* no. 3, Flagstaff: Museum of Northern Arizona Press.

Bartlett, Katherine 1936. The utilization of maize among the ancient pueblos. *University of New Mexico, Bulletin* no. 269, Albuquerque: University of New Mexico Press.

Beaglehole, Ernest 1937. *Notes on Hopi Economic Life*. Yale University, Publications in Anthropology no. 15, New Haven: Yale University Press.

Binford, Lewis R. 1962. Archaeology as anthropology. *American Antiquity* 28: 217–25.

Binford, Lewis R. 1965. Archaeological systematics and the study of culture process. *American Antiquity* 31: 203–10.

Binford, Lewis R. 1968. Archeological perspectives. In Sally R. and Lewis R. Binford (eds), *New Perspectives in Archeology*, 5–32. Chicago: Aldine.

Binford, Lewis R. 1973. Interassemblage variability – the Mousterian and the "functional" argument. In Colin Renfrew (ed.), *The Explanation of Culture Change: Models in Prehistory*, 227–53. London: Duckworth.

Binford, Lewis R. 1977. Forty-seven trips: a case study in the character of archaeological formation processes. In R. V. S. Wright (ed.), *Stone Tools as Cultural Markers*, 24–36. Canberra: Australian Institute of Aboriginal Studies.

Binford, Lewis R. 1978. Dimensional analysis of behavior and site structure: learning from an Eskimo hunting stand. *American Antiquity* 43: 330–61.

Binford, Lewis R. 1979. Organization and formation processes: looking at curated technologies. *Journal of Anthropological Research* 35: 255–73.

Binford, Lewis R. 1980. Willow smoke and dogs' tails: hunter-gatherer settlement systems and archaeological site formation. *American Antiquity* 45: 4–20.

Binford, Lewis R. 1985. "Brand X" versus the recommended product. *American Antiquity* 50: 580–90.

Bleed, Peter 1986. The optimal design of hunting weapons: maintainability or reliability. *American Antiquity* 51: 737–47.

Boserup, Ester 1981. *Population and Technological Change: A Study of Long-Term Trends*. Chicago: University of Chicago Press.

Bradfield, Richard M. 1995. *An Interpretation of Hopi Culture*. Duffield, Derbyshire, UK: published by the author.

Brew, John O. 1949. Part I. The history of Awatovi. In Ross G. Montgomery,

Watson Smith, and John O. Brew, *Franciscan Awatovi: The Excavation and Conjectural Reconstruction of a 17th-Century Spanish Mission Establishment at a Hopi Indian Town in Northeastern Arizona,* 3–46. Papers of the Peabody Museum of American Archaeology and Ethnology 36, Cambridge, MA: Harvard University, Peabody Museum of American Archaeology and Ethnology.

Cameron, Catherine M. 1991. Structure abandonment in villages. *Archaeological Method and Theory* 3: 155–94.

Cameron, Catherine M. 1999. *Hopi Dwellings: Architecture at Orayvi.* Tucson: University of Arizona Press.

Cameron, Catherine M. and Steve A. Tomka (eds) 1993. *Abandonment of Settlements and Regions: Ethnoarchaeological and Archaeological Approaches.* Cambridge: Cambridge University Press.

Cannon, Aubrey 1989. The historical dimension in mortuary expressions of status and sentiment. *Current Anthropology* 30: 437–58.

Cordell, Linda S., Steadman Upham, and Sharon L. Brock 1987. Obscuring cultural patterns in the archaeological record: a discussion from Southwestern archaeology. *American Antiquity* 52: 565–77.

Crumley, Carole L. 1979. Three locational models: an epistemological assessment for anthropology and archaeology. *Advances in Archaeological Method and Theory* 2: 141–73.

Dean, Jeffrey S. 1978. Independent dating in archaeological analysis. *Advances in Archaeological Method and Theory* 1: 223–55.

Deetz, James F. 1965. *The Dynamics of Stylistic Change in Arikara Ceramics.* University of Illinois Studies in Anthropology no. 4. Urbana: University of Illinois.

Dozier, Edward P. 1970. *The Pueblo Indians of North America.* Prospect Hills, IL: Waveland Press.

Dunnell, Robert C. 1996. Style and function: a fundamental dichotomy. In Michael J. O'Brien (ed.), *Evolutionary Archaeology: Theory and Application,* 112–22. Salt Lake City: University of Utah Press. Originally published in *American Antiquity* 43 (1978): 192–202.

Fewkes, J. Walter 1897. The sacrificial element in Hopi worship. *Journal of American Folklore* 10: 187–210.

Fewkes, J. Walter 1900a. Property rights in eagles among the Hopi. *American Anthropologist* (new series) 2: 690–707.

Fewkes, J. Walter 1900b. Tusayan flute and snake ceremonies. In *Nineteenth Annual Report of the Bureau of American Ethnology, 1897–98, Part 2,* 957–1011. Washington DC: Government Printing Office.

Flannery, Kent V. 1973. Archaeology with a capital "S." In C.L. Redman (ed.), *Research and Theory in Current Archaeology,* 47–53. New York: Wiley.

Gell, Alfred 1998. *Art and Agency: An Anthropological Theory.* Oxford: Oxford University Press.

Gould, Richard A. 1978a: The anthropology of human residues. *American Anthropologist* 80: 815–35.

Gould, Richard A. 1978b. Beyond analogy in ethnoarchaeology. In Richard A. Gould (ed.), *Explorations in Ethnoarchaeology*, 249–93. Albuquerque: University of New Mexico Press.

Gould, Richard A. 1980. *Living Archaeology*. Cambridge: Cambridge University Press.

Gould, Richard A. 1985. The empiricist strikes back. *American Antiquity* 50: 639–44.

Hayden, Brian 1998. Practical and prestige technologies: the evolution of material systems. *Journal of Archaeological Method and Theory* 5: 1–55.

Hayden, Brian and Aubrey Cannon 1983. Where the garbage goes: refuse disposal in the Maya Highlands. *Journal of Anthropological Archaeology* 2: 117–63.

Hayden, Brian, Nora Franco, and Jim Spafford 1996. Evaluating lithic strategies and design criteria. In George H. Odell (ed.), *Stone Tools: Theoretical Insights into Human Prehistory*, 9–45. New York: Plenum.

Hieb, Louis A. 1979. Hopi world view. In Alfonso Ortiz (ed.), *Handbook of North American Indians, Volume 9: Southwest*, 577–80. Washington DC: Smithsonian Institution.

Hill, James N. 1970. *Broken K Pueblo: Prehistoric Social Organization in the American Southwest*. University of Arizona, Anthropological Papers, no. 18, Tucson: University of Arizona Press.

Horsfall, Gayel A. 1987. Design theory and grinding stones. In Brian Hayden (ed.), *Lithic Studies among the Contemporary Highland Maya*, 332–7. Tucson: University of Arizona Press.

Karunaratne, Priyantha 1997. Variability of ritual spaces and abandonment deposits as expressed in the archaeological record: a study on Pueblo IV villages in the Homol'ovi region. M.A. Thesis, Department of Anthropology, University of Arizona, Tucson.

Kidder, Alfred V. 1958. *Pecos, New Mexico: Archaeological Notes*. Papers of the Robert S. Peabody Foundation for Archaeology 5, Andover, MA: Phillips Academy.

Klandrud, Sarah E. and Vincent M. LaMotta 1999. Sex- and age-specific patterns of mortuary deposition in late Prehistoric Western Pueblos. Paper presented at the 64th Annual Meeting of the Society for American Archaeology, Chicago.

Kopytoff, Igor 1986. The cultural biography of things: commoditization as process. In Arjun Appadurai (ed.), *The Social Life of Things: Commodities in Cultural Perspective*, 64–94. Cambridge: Cambridge University Press.

Krebs, J. R. and N. B. Davies 1993. *An Introduction to Behavioural Ecology*, 3rd edn. London: Blackwell Scientific Publications.

Kuhn, Steven L. 1994. A formal approach to the design and assembly of mobile toolkits. *American Antiquity* 59: 426–42.

LaMotta, Vincent M. 1996. The use of disarticulated human remains in abandonment ritual at Homol'ovi. M.A. report, Department of Anthropology, University of Arizona, Tucson.

LaMotta, Vincent M. 1999. Depositional contexts as units of analysis and inference. Paper presented at the 64th Annual Meeting of the Society for American Archaeology, Chicago.

LaMotta, Vincent M. and Michael B. Schiffer 1999. Formation processes of house floor assemblages. In Penelope Allison (ed.), *The Archaeology of Household Activities*, 19–29. London: Routledge.

Lechtman, Heather 1977. Style in technology: some early thoughts. In H. Lechtman and R. Merrill (eds), *Material Culture: Styles, Organization, and Dynamics of Technology*, 3–20. St Paul: West Publishers.

Littlejohn, Stephen W. 1991. *Theories of Human Communication*. Belmont, CA: Wadsworth.

Longacre, William A. 1970. *Archaeology as Anthropology: A Case Study*. University of Arizona, Anthropological Papers, no. 17, Tucson: University of Arizona Press.

Lyons, Patrick D. 1999. New perspectives on Hay Hollow Valley and the upper Little Colorado: the view from Homol'ovi. Paper presented at the 64th Annual Meeting of the Society for American Archaeology, Chicago.

McCracken, Grant D. 1988. *Culture and Consumption: New Approaches to the Symbolic Character of Consumer Goods and Activities*. Bloomington: Indiana University Press.

McGuire, Randall H. 1983. Breaking down cultural complexity: inequality and heterogeneity. *Advances in Archaeological Method and Theory* 6: 91–142.

McGuire, Randall H. 1992. *A Marxist Archaeology*. San Diego: Academic Press.

McGuire, Randall H. 1995. Behavioral archaeology: reflections of a prodigal son. In James M. Skibo, William H. Walker, and Axel E. Nielsen (eds), *Expanding Archaeology*, 162–77. Salt Lake City: University of Utah Press.

McGuire, Randall H. and Michael B. Schiffer 1983. A theory of architectural design. *Journal of Anthropological Archaeology* 2: 277–303.

Magers, Pamela 1975. The cotton industry at Antelope House. *The Kiva* 41: 39–47.

Merriam-Webster 1985. *Webster's Ninth New Collegiate Dictionary*. Springfield, MA: Merriam-Webster Inc.

Montgomery, Barbara K. 1993. Ceramic analysis as a tool for discovering processes of pueblo abandonment. In Catherine M. Cameron and Steve A. Tomka (eds), *Abandonment of Settlements and Regions: Ethnoarchaeological and Archaeological Approaches*, 157–64. Cambridge: Cambridge University Press.

Nelson, Margaret C. 1991. The study of technological organization. *Archaeological Method and Theory* 3: 57–100.

Nequatewa, Edmund 1994. *Truth of a Hopi: Stories Relating to the Origin, Myths, and Clan Histories of the Hopi*. Flagstaff: Northland Publishing in cooperation with the Museum of Northern Arizona. Originally published in 1936, *Museum of Northern Arizona Bulletin* no. 8, Flagstaff: Museum of Northern Arizona.

Nielsen, Axel E. 1995. Architectural performance and the reproduction of social power. In James M. Skibo, William H. Walker, and Axel E. Nielsen (eds), *Expanding Archaeology*, 47–66. Salt Lake City: University of Utah Press.

Nielsen, Axel E. and William H. Walker 1998. Ritual conquest and political domination in the Inka Empire: a case study from Quebrada de Humahuaca. Paper presented at the 63rd Annual Meeting of the Society for American Archaeology, Seattle.

O'Brien, Michael J. and Thomas D. Holland 1995. Behavioral archaeology and the extended phenotype. In James M. Skibo, William H. Walker, and Axel E. Nielsen (eds), *Expanding Archaeology*, 143–61. Salt Lake City: University of Utah Press.

O'Brien, Michael J., R. Lee Lyman, and Robert D. Leonard 1998. Basic incompatibilities between evolutionary and behavioral archaeology. *American Antiquity* 63: 485–98.

Parsons, Elsie Clews 1939. *Pueblo Indian Religion*. 2 vols. Chicago: University of Chicago Press.

Peebles, Christopher and Susan Kus 1977. Some archaeological correlates of ranked societies. *American Antiquity* 42: 421–48.

Rathje, William L. 1995. Forever separate realities. In James M. Skibo, William H. Walker, and Axel E. Nielsen (eds), *Expanding Archaeology*, 36–46. Salt Lake City: University of Utah Press.

Rathje, William L. and Michael McCarthy 1977. Regularity and variability in contemporary garbage. In Stanley South (ed.), *Research Strategies in Historical Archaeology*, 261–86. New York: Academic Press.

Rathje, William L. and Cullen Murphy 1992. *Rubbish! The Archaeology of Garbage*. New York: HarperCollins.

Rathje, William L. and Michael B. Schiffer 1982. *Archaeology*. New York: Harcourt Brace Jovanovich.

Redman, Charles L. 1978. *The Rise of Civilization: From Early Farmers to Urban Society in the Ancient Near East*. San Francisco: W. H. Freeman.

Reid, J. Jefferson 1978. Response to stress at Grasshopper Pueblo, Arizona. In Paul Grebinger (ed.), *Discovering Past Behavior: Experiments in the Archaeology of the American Southwest*, 195–213. New York: Gordon and Breach.

Reid, J. Jefferson 1985. Formation processes for the practical prehistorian. In R.S. Dickens, Jr. and H.T. Ward (eds), *Structure and Process in Southeastern Archaeology*, 11–33. Tuscaloosa, AL: University of Alabama Press.

Reid, J. Jefferson 1995. Four strategies after twenty years: a return to basics. In James M. Skibo, William H. Walker, and Axel E. Nielsen (eds), *Expanding Archaeology*, 15–21. Salt Lake City: University of Utah Press.

Reid, J. Jefferson, William L. Rathje, and Michael B. Schiffer 1974. Expanding archaeology. *American Antiquity* 39: 125–6.

Reid, J. Jefferson, Michael B. Schiffer, and William L. Rathje 1975. Behavioral archaeology: four strategies. *American Anthropologist* 77: 836–48.

Rindos, David 1984. *The Origins of Agriculture: An Evolutionary Perspective.* New York: Academic Press.

Salmon, Merrilee H. 1982. *Philosophy and Archaeology.* New York: Academic Press.

Schiffer, Michael B. 1972. Archaeological context and systemic context. *American Antiquity* 37: 156–65.

Schiffer, Michael B. 1975a. Archaeology as behavioral science. *American Anthropologist* 77: 836–48.

Schiffer, Michael B. 1975b. Behavioral chain analysis: activities, organization, and the use of space. Chapters in the prehistory of Eastern Arizona, IV. *Fieldiana: Anthropology* 65: 103–19.

Schiffer, Michael B. 1976. *Behavioral Archeology.* New York: Academic Press.

Schiffer, Michael B. 1978. Methodological issues in ethnoarchaeology. In R. A. Gould (ed.), *Explorations in Ethnoarchaeology*, 229–47. Albuquerque: University of New Mexico Press.

Schiffer, Michael B. 1979. A preliminary consideration of behavioral change. In Colin Renfrew and Kenneth Cooke (eds), *Transformations: Mathematical Approaches to Culture Change*, 353–68. New York: Academic Press.

Schiffer, Michael B. 1983. Toward the identification of formation processes. *American Antiquity* 48: 675–706.

Schiffer, Michael B. 1985. Is there a "Pompeii" premise in archaeology? *Journal of Archaeological Research* 41: 18–41.

Schiffer, Michael B. 1987. *Formation Processes of the Archaeological Record.* Albuquerque: University of New Mexico Press.

Schiffer, Michael B. 1988. The structure of archaeological theory. *American Antiquity* 53: 461–85.

Schiffer, Michael B. 1992. *Technological Perspectives on Behavioral Change.* Tucson: University of Arizona Press.

Schiffer, Michael B. 1995a. *Behavioral Archaeology: First Principles.* Salt Lake City: University of Utah Press.

Schiffer, Michael B. 1995b. Social theory and history in behavioral archaeology. In James M. Skibo, William H. Walker, and Axel E. Nielsen (eds), *Expanding Archaeology*, 22–35. Salt Lake City: University of Utah Press.

Schiffer, Michael B. 1996. Some relationships between behavioral and evolutionary archaeologies. *American Antiquity* 61: 643–62.

Schiffer, Michael B. and Andrea R. Miller 1999a. A behavioral theory of meaning. In James M. Skibo and Gary Feinman (eds), *Pottery and People: A Dynamic Interaction*, 199–217. Salt Lake City: University of Utah Press.

Schiffer, Michael B. and Andrea R. Miller 1999b. *The Material Life of Human Beings: Artifacts, Behavior, and Communication.* London: Routledge.

Schiffer, Michael B. and James M. Skibo 1987. Theory and experiment in the study of technological change. *Current Anthropology* 28: 595–622.

Schiffer, Michael B. and James M. Skibo 1997. The explanation of artifact variability. *American Antiquity* 62: 27–50.

Schiffer, Michael B., T. E. Downing, and M. McCarthy 1981. Waste not, want not: an ethnoarchaeological study of reuse in Tucson, Arizona. In R. A. Gould and M. B. Schiffer (eds), *Modern Material Culture: The Archaeology of Us*, 67–86. New York: Academic Press.

Sellet, F. 1993. Chaîne opératoire: the concept and its application. *Lithic Technology* 1: 106–12.

Shanks, Michael and Christopher Tilley 1982. Ideology, symbolic power and ritual communication: a reinterpretation of neolithic mortuary practices. In Ian Hodder (ed.), *Symbolic and Structural Archaeology*, 129–54. Cambridge: Cambrige University Press.

Sheets, Payson 1975. Behavioral analysis and the structure of a prehistoric industry. *Current Anthropology* 16: 369–91.

Shipman, Pat 1981. *Life History of a Fossil: An Introduction to Taphonomy and Paleoecology*. Cambridge, MA: Harvard University Press.

Skibo, James M. 1992. *Pottery Function: A Use-Alteration Perspective*. New York: Plenum.

Smith, Watson 1972. *Prehistoric Kivas of Antelope Mesa, Northeastern Arizona*. Papers of the Peabody Museum of Archaeology and Ethnology 39(1), Cambridge, MA: Harvard University, Peabody Museum of Archaeology and Ethnology.

South, Stanley 1977. *Method and Theory in Historical Archaeology*. New York: Academic Press.

Spencer-Wood, Suzanne (ed.) 1987. *Consumer Choice in Historical Archaeology*. New York: Plenum.

Stark, Miriam (ed.) 1998. *The Archaeology of Social Boundaries*. Washington, D.C.: Smithsonian Institution Press.

Staski, Edward and Livingston D. Sutro (eds) 1991. *The Ethnoarchaeology of Refuse Disposal*. Anthropological Research Papers no. 42, Tempe: Arizona State University.

Stephen, Alexander M. 1936. *The Hopi Journal of Alexander M. Stephen*, ed. Elsie Clews Parsons. 2 vols. New York: Columbia University Press.

Strand, Jennifer G. 1998. An analysis of the Homol'ovi fauna with emphasis on ritual behavior. Ph.D. Dissertation, Department of Anthropology, University of Arizona. Ann Arbor: University Microfilms Inc.

Sullivan, Alan P. 1978. Inference and evidence in archaeology: a discussion of the conceptual problems. *Advances in Archaeological Method and Theory* 1: 183–222.

Tani, Masakazu 1995. Beyond the identification of formation processes: behavioral inference based on traces left by cultural formation processes. *Journal of Archaeological Method and Theory* 2: 231–52.

Thomas, Julian 1996. *Time, Culture and Identity*. London: Routledge.

Titiev, Mischa 1944. *Old Oraibi: A Study of the Hopi Indians of Third Mesa*. Papers of the Peabody Museum of American Archaeology and Ethnology 22(1), Cambridge, MA: Harvard University.

Turner, Christy G. II, and Laurel Lofgren 1966. Household size of prehistoric Western Pueblo Indians. *Southwestern Journal of Anthropology* 22: 117–32.

Voth, H.R. 1912. Brief miscellaneous Hopi papers. *Field Columbian Museum, Anthropological Series* 11: 90–149.

Walker, William H. 1995. Ceremonial trash? In James M. Skibo, William H. Walker, and Axel E. Nielsen (eds), *Expanding Archaeology*, 67–79. Salt Lake City: University of Utah Press.

Walker, William H. 1998a. Prehistoric ritual and object life histories. Paper presented at the 63rd Annual Meeting of the Society for American Archaeology, Seattle.

Walker, William H. 1998b. Where are the witches of prehistory? *Journal of Archaeological Method and Theory* 5: 245–308.

Walker, William H. and Vincent M. LaMotta 1995. Life histories as units of analysis. Paper presented at the 60th Annual Meeting of the Society for American Archaeology, Minneapolis.

Walker, William H. and Lisa Lucero 1997. The prehistoric pathways of ritual agents. Paper presented at the 62nd Annual Meeting of the Society for American Archaeology, Nashville.

Walker, William H., Vincent M. LaMotta, and E. Charles Adams 2000. Katsinas and kiva abandonment at Homol'ovi: a deposit-oriented perspective on religion in Southwest prehistory. In M. Hegmon (ed.), *The Archaeology of Regional Interaction: Religion, Warfare, and Exchange across the American Southwest and Beyond*, 341–60. Boulder, CO: University Press of Colorado.

Walker, William H., James M. Skibo, and Axel E. Nielsen 1995. Introduction: expanding archaeology. In James M. Skibo, William H. Walker, and Axel E. Nielsen (eds), *Expanding Archaeology*, 1–12. Salt Lake City: University of Utah Press.

Watson, Patty Jo 1982. Review of *Living Archaeology*, by Richard A. Gould. *American Antiquity* 47: 445–8.

Whiting, Alfred E. 1939. Ethnobotany of the Hopi. *Museum of Northern Arizona, Bulletin* no. 15, Flagstaff: Museum of Northern Arizona.

Wilk, Richard R. 1996. *Economies and Cultures: Foundations of Economic Anthropology*. Boulder, CO: Westview Press.

Wilshusen, Richard H. 1986. The relationship between abandonment mode and ritual use in Pueblo I Anasazi Protokivas. *Journal of Field Archaeology* 13: 245–54.

Wilshusen, Richard H. 1988. The abandonment of structures. In E. Blinman, C.J. Phagan, and R.H. Wilshusen (eds), *Dolores Archaeological Program Supporting Studies: Additive and Reductive Technologies*, 673–702. Denver: Bureau of Reclamation, Engineering and Research Center.

Wobst, H. Martin 1977. Stylistic behavior and information exchange. In C.E. Cleland (ed.), *Papers for the Director: Research Essays in Honor of James B. Griffin*, 317–34. University of Michigan, Museum of Anthropology, Anthropological Papers, no. 61, Ann Arbor: University of Michigan.

Wylie, Alison 1995. An expanded behavioral archaeology: transformation and redefinition. In James M. Skibo, William H. Walker, and Axel E. Nielsen (eds), *Expanding Archaeology*, 198–209. Salt Lake City: University of Utah Press.

Zedeño, Maria Nieves 1994. *Sourcing Prehistoric Ceramics at Chodistaas*

*Pueblo, Arizona: The Circulation of People and Pots in the Grasshopper Region.* University of Arizona, Anthropological Papers, no. 58, Tucson: University of Arizona Press.

Zedeño, Maria Nieves 1997. Landscapes, land use, and the history of territory formation: an example from the Puebloan Southwest. *Journal of Archaeological Method and Theory* 4: 67–103.

# 3

# Evolutionary Archaeology

## *Robert D. Leonard*

Archaeology has long been pre-eminently a discipline unto itself . . . Divorce from the biological sciences has been uncontested and amicable. Anthropology has been able to provide the grounds for the divorce by providing expert testimony on how humans are totally unlike the rest of creation. And, in providing itself with the justification of its own existence, it has provided the rest of biology with defenses for continued belief in the fundamental difference between our own species and the rest of the animal kingdom. In a rather rare instance of interdisciplinary cooperation, anthropology has been able to provide biology with all the reasons necessary to maintain an unquestioned and unquestioning acceptance of the incommensurability of one species with all others. One might expect a critical mind to note the self-serving nature of the argument and question it on those grounds if no other.

David Rindos, 1989

## Evolution and archaeology

Evolutionary archaeology (EA) had its origins in the late 1970s and 1980s when a small group of individuals sought to break down the barrier Rindos refers to between human evolution and the evolution of the rest of organic life by bringing Darwinian theory to archaeology (Braun 1990; Dunnell 1978a, 1978b, 1978c, 1980, 1982, 1989; Leonard

1989; Leonard and Jones 1987; Meltzer 1981; O'Brien and Holland 1990; Rindos 1984, 1985, 1986, 1989). Of course archaeologists had long discussed evolution before that time, and used a few evolutionary terms, but they discussed it in ways that had nothing to do with the evolution spoken of by Darwin (1859). Evolutionary Archaeologists refer to these early evolutionary efforts as *Cultural Evolution* in order to minimize confusion and maintain this important distinction between Darwinian and non-Darwinian thought. Leslie White, one of the great Cultural Evolutionary thinkers in anthropology, noted that Darwinian theory waś absent in Cultural Evolution in the following quote:

> It would be most gratifying to be able to report, in a paper commemorating the publication of *The Origin of Species*, that cultural anthropologists had borrowed the concept of evolution from Darwin and that they had employed this concept to establish and enrich their science. Unfortunately, we are unable to make such a report. On the contrary, we must point out that the theory of evolution was introduced into cultural anthropology independently of Darwin and, indeed, of biology in general. (1959a: 106)

The evolution White referred to was the progressivist evolutionary theories of Herbert Spencer (1857, 1860, 1876), Lewis Henry Morgan (1877), and Edward B. Tylor (1865, 1871). The work of these three men, whom White called "the three great pioneers of cultural evolutionism" (1959a: 107), provided the intellectual framework for White's evolutionary perspective that proved so prominent in the middle of the twentieth century, as well as today. While 1959 may seem a long time ago, the revolutionary movement first called the New Archaeology was about to emerge at the time, and White's student Lewis R. Binford was its main architect (e.g. Binford 1962, 1968, 1973; Binford and Binford 1966). Building upon the work of White (1943, 1945, 1959a, 1959b), Sahlins and Service (Sahlins and Service 1960; Service 1962), among other writers, the New Archaeology emerged as processual archaeology – likely the dominant intellectual movement in archaeology as we begin the new millennium. This New Archaeology had evolutionary aspirations, but it is clear that they were not founded upon Darwinian theory (see Dunnell 1980 for this discussion).

Returning to the quote by White, there are two ways to view his statement. First, if one sees the evolution of humanity as *unique* with respect to other forms of life, as Rindos implied many do, this was no loss. Darwinian theory was irrelevant, a different theory was needed, and was built – Cultural Evolution. Ultimately, it became what is called processual archaeology today. However, if one rejects the position that humans are unique, and largely immune to the effects of Darwinian processes, the lack of a Darwinian perspective in archaeology was a great setback, as while Darwinian evolution has dramatically increased our knowledge of life on earth, it has not until recently been employed to unravel the riddle of the evolution of humanity – particularly the evolution of human behavior. To Evolutionary Archaeologists, this is a tragedy. To us, the archaeological record is nothing but a record of the evolution of human behavior, yet several generations of archaeologists have turned their back on the incredible knowledge-generating machine of Darwinian evolutionary theory. To us, this loss is not unlike the loss that would have come to the physical sciences had physicists turned their back on Einstein's Theory of General Relativity.

The last twenty years have seen an emergence of Darwinian theory in archaeology – but this has not been without a struggle (see, for examples, criticisms in Bettinger et al. 1996; Boone 1998; Boone and Smith 1998; Broughton and O'Connell 1999; Cullen 1993; Lake 1997; Schiffer 1996; C. S. Spencer 1997). And in the process, Darwinian theory has been changed in subtle, yet important ways. The processes of history that did not let Darwin fully build his theory to incorporate humankind are now not so strong (e.g. the power of the church), and a new consideration of the archaeological record demands that a bit of tinkering had to be accomplished to bring Darwinian evolution to the human past. This might seem a new heresy to some, but archaeology has much to offer to the general theory of evolution.

## What is Darwinian theory?

Darwinian theory, if it is anything, is simple. As a theory – here used as a set of instructions about how to learn about the organic world – it is easier to understand than it is to learn how to set the clock on a VCR. Operationalizing it is a craft, like that of a carpenter who cuts rafters for a house or a baker who makes a loaf of bread. It must be learned, and most of us can learn it with varying degrees of proficiency. Yet, there is perhaps no other grand idea so misunderstood – and not just by religious fundamentalists. Anthropologists and archaeologists are some of the worst culprits. Many confound it with either the progressivist evolutionary ideas of Spencer, Tylor, and Morgan, or their more recent proponents Leslie White and Lewis R. Binford, what we call Cultural Evolutionism. Why do prominent anthropologists and archaeologists make this mistake? The answer is that they have not taken the time to learn the difference – they mistakenly believe that they know what Darwinian evolution is, and would find White's statement above astonishing. Others make the naturalistic fallacy, fearing that the explanatory power of evolutionary theory will be brought into moral realms. Others mistakenly believe that Darwinian theory reduces the complexity of human existence to understandings writ completely in terms of "guts and gonads."

These criticisms are misplaced, and would simply not exist if archaeologists would make the effort to understand Darwinian theory. So, let's get to the nuts and bolts. At its core, Darwinian theory states: (1) there is variation in organisms; (2) there is transmission of that variation, or inheritance; and (3) some variants do better in certain circumstances than other variants. This third component is the process of natural selection – the differential persistence of variation. These rules are simple, like the rules to the game of chess. Yet like chess, there are an infinite number of outcomes that can be produced by applying the rules during the course of a game. Applied to human behavior and the archaeological record, these simple rules can be used to help us understand the complexity of our behavior in the same way we can use the rules of chess to understand the outcome of a specific game.

To introduce the concept of evolution to my introductory anthropology classes I often ask them to look around the room at each other.

"Do you see differences in how each other looks?" I ask.

A few mutter affirmation while scanning their fellow classmates. "That is *variation*. Differences in height, weight, skin color, eye color, etc."

"Do you look more like your parents and grandparents than you do each other?" A few more catch on and nod or mutter affirmatively. "That is the product of genetic *transmission*, or inheritance."

They nod again.

"You are here today because *certain* characteristics that your ancestors possessed were favorable in specific environments, and as a consequence your ancestors had more offspring than others who lacked those characteristics. That is *natural selection*. As a whole these three facts constitute the basics of Darwinian evolution."

This simple lesson usually works. Students see variation, inheritance, and natural selection and how it operates – and that it has operated on their ancestors to shape them. Yet, this is only part of the story. How does this perspective deal with the evolution of human behavior as expressed in the archaeological record? Put simply, it does not. The connection to behavior and the archaeological record is made quite simply by employing the concept of phenotype. Biologist Ernst Mayr defines the phenotype as: "The totality of characteristics of an individual" (1982: 959).

In other words, the phenotype is all aspects of us, behavioral and physical, and it is the phenotype upon which natural selection operates. We unfold as individuals as our genetic structures dictate, yet the final package – our phenotype – is shaped both by our genes and by our environment – both physical and social. My particular phenotype consists of, among other things, genetically determined brown hair, brown eyes, and an environmentally influenced nutritional regime that made me 6 inches taller and 40 pounds heavier than my father. My phenotype also consists of behavioral traits that are influenced even more directly by the environment, including bifocals, sunscreen when I am in the field, a 1996 Chevy pickup, and a genuine affection for the music of Pink Floyd. Thus, we all have unique phenotypes, as do all life forms, yet we may also share a wide variety of individual characteristics. The sources of variation for many of these heavily environmentally determined characteristics are history, chance, and human behavior played out on top of the genotypic instructions.

To illustrate the evolution of the behavioral part of our phenotype, I ask my students "do you behave differently from each other?" They, of course, recognize that they do. They also recognize that some of their behavior has a genetic component, our brains being the product of the operation of natural selection that has operated on our ancestors for millions of years. This genetic component may establish our individual capacities for learning, influence our choices of mates, our patterns of reproduction, and aptitudes for, say, music or athletics. Students also know that much of their behavior is learned, and largely independent of any genetic influence. Importantly, learning is the greatest variation-generating component of our phenotype.

We learn behavior through a process that is called *cultural transmission*. Cultural transmission is not only *vertical* through our parents, but also *oblique*, from other elders, and *horizontal*, from our peers. I learned how to use a hammer from my father, to tell time from my grandmother, and about Pink Floyd from my friends. When we learn in this manner, what we learn is the product of a shared intellectual tradition, that is, *homologous*. Some of our behavior is more than simply learned, it is *invented*. Sometimes it is invented over and over again, without transmission. For example, stone tools, pottery, the wheel, all have been invented and reinvented a number of times, without cultural transmission occurring. These kinds of traits are called *analogous* traits, but more regarding these in a moment. Importantly the invention or generation of variation and transmission – both genetic and cultural – creates the phenotype that natural selection acts upon in a specific selective environment.

Evolutionary psychologists and human evolutionary ecologists have proposed a number of models of the specifics of the cultural transmission process. Yet much work remains to be done, and we may be as far from understanding cultural transmission as Darwin was from understanding the mechanism of inheritance we now know to be genetic. Darwin saw variation, knew natural selection operated on it, but had no idea how information was transmitted intergenerationally. Yet the theory of evolution was still operational, just as the carpenter can cut rafters with no knowledge of pure geometry, and the baker can make fine bread without knowing the chemistry of yeast.

Evolutionary archaeologists, for the most part, leave the study of mechanisms of transmission in the capable hands of the evolutionary psychologists and human evolutionary ecologists, among others (Best and Pocklington 1999; Cavalli-Sforza and Feldman 1981; Dawkins 1976, 1982, 1989, 1996; Dennett 1990; Dretske 1989; Dugatkin 1997; Durham 1990, 1991, 1992; Flinn 1997; Goodenough 1995; Lynch 1996; Lynch and Baker 1993, 1994; Lynch et al. 1989; Richerson and Boyd 1992; Wilkins 1998). These researchers are interested not only in how transmission happens, but also in what constitutes the units of transmission. Much current work focuses on the concept of *memes* (Dawkins 1976), minimal units of information that are transmitted.

With respect to transmission in the past, memes were ultimately translated into technology, leaving us an empirical record of cultural transmission (Neiman 1995). Therefore, it is first and foremost archaeologists who "see" transmission in the past. For it is archaeologists, and only archaeologists, who have in their intellectual domain several million years of the hard parts of the human phenotype, the archaeological record. That record transcends all continents, and indeed the earth itself – there is now an archaeological record on Earth's moon and every planet probed by our technology. The archaeological record is a record of variation, transmission, and differential persistence of that variation as the product of the operation of natural selection and chance. As a consequence, the record of human evolution can be written only by archaeologists or by those working closely with them.

Biological anthropologists may of course write evolutionary narratives of morphological changes in the human skeletal structure, but it is only archaeologists who can address the interaction between that biological structure and the technologies that, through time, constituted an ever-larger component of the human phenotype.

In sum, this evolutionary view outlined above requires only a few assumptions, but assumptions that are critical and unassailable if Darwinian theory is to be made operational. These assumptions are:

1 Humans are life forms.
2 Natural selection operates on phenotypes, making evolution in part a phenotypic phenomenon.
3 Behavior is part of the human phenotype, and it is transmitted partially through learning.
4 Technology is the product of human behavior, and consequently a component of the human phenotype.
5 The differential persistence of behavior will be reflected by the differential replication of technology through time.

As a logical consequence of making these assumptions, both human behavioral and technological change can be understood in Darwinian terms.

## Evolutionary Archaeology

To bring Darwinian theory to the archaeological record we need a concept that allows us to deal with the success not only of individuals, but of components of phenotypes, e.g. artifacts. George T. Jones and I have proposed the concept of *replicative success* to serve this purpose. "All traits, whether material or behavioral, have distributions in time and space, and all traits have what can be termed replicative success, or differential persistence through time" (Leonard and Jones 1987: 214).

This concept is important, but people don't always understand the complementary positions of the reproductive success of individuals, and the replicative success of artifacts. Although contemporary criticisms that conflate the two exist, I cite J. O. Brew's historic work (1946: 59) criticizing the zeal with which archaeologists extended the phylogenetic metaphor to ceramic change in the American Southwest. His objection was that pottery types are not organisms and do not reproduce. Brew writes: "we still are faced with the fact that, with the exception of skeletal material, the objects and concepts of archaeology are not living organisms or parts of living organisms. Consequently, their development is not properly represented by a classificatory technique based upon the genetic relationships of living organisms."

Not surprisingly given the early date of his criticism, evolutionary archaeologists appreciate Brew's comment for the simple reason that it allows us to show why he and more contemporary archaeologists make a mistake by confounding reproductive success with replicative success. Leonard and Jones (1987: 215) stated that in one way it is difficult not to appreciate Brew's comment, "but just the same, we must ask if the skeletal material Brew refers to, or even the parts of living organisms, reproduces in a manner identical to that of an individual. It does not."

At a public presentation in Chicago in 1999, George T. Jones and I stated that we would like to add that

> the objects of archaeology *were* parts of living organisms. Behavior and technology *are* components of the human phenotype. This fact is undeniable, and the recognition of it is an important part of bringing Darwinian theory to archaeology. To deny it takes us out of the scientific evolution game completely, and implies as well that those interested in the evolution of animal behavior in general also need a new paradigm.

While Brew and others are correct in asserting that "pot sherds don't breed," they miss the point. Of course pot sherds do not reproduce (any more than birds' nests and beaver dams do) but pottery is part of the human phenotype (i.e. is part of our behavior), exhibits variation (e.g. different aplastic inclusions in the clay, called temper), is replicated as part of the transmission process (is copied), and has differential replicative success in varying environments (e.g. glazes may influence ceramic durability in certain situations). Further, if a ceramic technology enhances the reproductive success(es) of the person or group of persons using it (e.g. they are able to gain nutritional benefits through cooking), it is an adaptation and understandable in evolutionary terms. Here we must carefully distinguish between the processualist use of the term "adaptation" and its evolutionary meaning. To a processualist, an adaptation is any behavior that has a function in an environment. To an evolutionist, it is a phenotypic feature that has been modified over time by natural selection so that it serves an important evolutionary function. An adaptation is best determined if there is an arguably causal relation between increased replication and increased reproduction, but this is not always possible, as will be discussed below. Where there is no demonstrable relation between increased replication and increased reproduction, increased replication must be understood in terms of chance, history, and drift. Likewise, increased reproduction must be understood in terms of other traits than that currently under investigation, as it is clearly other technologies that are influencing increased reproduction. In sum, both replication and reproduction need to be understood in both evolutionary and historical terms.

## Technologies as adaptations

Everyone recognizes the major competitive advantages of antibiotics, agriculture, the crossbow, the wheel, or nuclear weapons, for example, as well as their evolutionary implications as adaptations at certain times and places. It is more difficult, however, to imagine how a small advantage in technology can yield major evolutionary effects. The advantages of the more mundane technologies of life – say, doorknobs, eggbeaters, whisks and nutcrackers – are much harder to understand and appreciate.

Let's look at it a couple of ways. First, go into your kitchen and find every piece of technology that can open cans or bottles, and examine them, paying particular attention to any differences you can find. I have an assortment of church keys of different lengths and shapes, as well as a variety of types of can openers where one turns the handle and a blade cuts the lid off of the can. On the other end invariably is a bottle opener – its existence almost an afterthought. The products of manufacture are of differing materials and grades, the cutting blades and handles of varying shapes and angles. I also have a variety of gimme bottle openers from liquor stores – adding up to a virtual plethora of technologies. If I'm away from the kitchen, I also have my Swiss army knife or the interior lock on the door of my truck that will open bottles. I suppose I could find a rock or concrete block if I needed to. I am sure that you have as many, or can think of as many if not more, options.

For you and me, efficiency would appear to matter little when we are going to open only one or two cans or bottles. Yet, I'm sure that you routinely use the same opening technology rather than alternatives because one works particularly well in a given situation. One opener works better in the kitchen, a second at the grill in the back yard, a third at a picnic, and yet a fourth on an extended camping trip. This is despite the fact that *any* opening technology would probably suffice, as we are likely opening only a few bottles or cans whenever we use a particular opener. Energy savings would be small for each individual event, that is, each bottle or can opened, yet would surely add up over the course of a lifetime, consuming energy that could be used for other purposes, theoretically including reproduction and our potential investment in off-spring. While this example may seem trivial, the important point is that whether or not we realize it, natural selection has driven us to make these kinds of decisions regarding efficiency and technology – *even* mundane can-and-bottle-opening technology.

In situations where one needs to open many bottles, a technology that works most efficiently, i.e. opens the most bottles, without mechanical failure or human fatigue, should be preferred. To illustrate this point, let us go to my favorite neighborhood bar to conduct an experiment. We persuade two bartenders of equal talent to use different tools to open bottles for the evening. We arrive at 8:00 p.m., and the bar closes at 2:00 a.m. As it is a busy bar, the bartenders immediately go to work, competing for customers and tips. Bartender A uses technology A, and is able to process an average of 6 beers per minute. Each beer sold results in a return of, on average, 10 cents in terms of a tip. Six beers opened a minute returns 60 cents in tips a minute, $36 an hour, and $216 by closing time. Not bad for one evening's work.

Bartender B using technology B is not quite so efficient. Rather than opening and selling 6 beers per minute, Bartender B can only process 5 beers per minute (17 percent less efficient than Bartender A). Tips are the same, so Bartender B receives 50 cents a minute, $30 hour, and $180 by closing time. Not bad, but differences in technological efficiency increased Bartender A's return by $36 for the night, no small sum. Our friendly bartenders agreed to extend our experiment for the rest of the year, and assuming each worked 259 more days (a standard work year in the United States is 260), Bartender A would have earned $9,360 dollars more than Bartender B by tax time.

As the result of our experiment, Bartender B has been unable to adequately feed and clothe his family, and his mortgage and car payments have gone unpaid for several months. His wife has left him, creditors are at the door, his dog is eyeing him hungrily, and all because he used a bottle opening technology that was only 17 percent less efficient than Bartender A, who is now driving a Cadillac, with a pretty and pregnant wife at his side.

Let us look at this another way. Rather than money, let us consider technological efficiency that increases the birthrate (as well as explains Bartender A's budding reproductive success). We start with a society that has 100 people and a yearly rate of growth of 1 percent in a stable environment. After 100 years have passed (the blink of an eye to an archaeologist) the society would have approximately 270 members at a 1 percent rate of growth. Let us say that a second society of 100 members lives in the neighborhood during this time period. A more efficient technology results in this second society having a 2 percent growth rate, rather than the 1 percent growth rate of the first group. After 100 years, this second society would have grown to 724 members, nearly three times the size of the first group, with only a 1 percent difference in growth. In sum, a slight technological improvement that impacts growth rates may allow one group of individuals to ultimately out-compete the other. What is interesting about this is the fact that the members of the two societies may not even know what has transpired, let alone the reasons for it. This example demonstrates that subtle differences in technology that affect rates of growth may have major evolutionary implications. Furthermore, that technological difference should be visible in the archaeological record.

For an example in prehistory, contemplate the evolutionary advantage accrued to *Homo habilis* individuals 2.4 million years ago in the Rift Valley of Africa when broken pieces of basalt and chert turned our ancestors' grasping hands into highly efficient cutting implements. What tremendous degree of increased efficiency accrued when the sharp edge of a stone allowed for the rapid processing of meat, skin, and bone? One hundred percent? One thousand percent? Any tailor, homeowner, carpenter, cook, or mechanic who has tried to complete a simple task without the appropriate tool would probably argue for the latter. With this increased efficiency, *Homo habilis* groups using the technology would certainly out-reproduce and out-compete groups without it. These simple pieces of chipped stone set the stage for early hominid expansion into non-tropical niches of the globe, providing both the means and the population numbers necessary to accomplish the expansion.

Determining that a technology is actually an adaptation is at times straightforward, but more often difficult. With respect to the bottle-opening technology, it would be fairly simple. One would first measure the reproductive success of those individuals using each technology. If there is a correlation between a particular technology and reproduction, one then makes a logical argument that it is that technology (as opposed to some other technology) that resulted in increased reproduction. This argument would be supported by experimental evidence, or performance studies of the technology in action (e.g. our productivity analyses of our bartenders in action).

Our argument about technology as an adaptation, then, is based first on a correlation, second on the logical argument regarding the nature of that correlation, and finally on our performance studies. If necessary, we can also support our argument by evidence as to the rates at which technology changes. Adaptations tend to spread rapidly, and can be conceptualized as functional replacements. For example, typewriters have been nearly completely replaced by computers, quite rapidly. Alternatively, non-adaptations tend to have what are called *lenticular* distributions through time (Neiman 1993), where they slowly gain popularity, rise to a maximum, and decline at approximately the same rate at which they grew. With the *Homo habilis* example, the existence of the correlation between tool use and geographic radiation is well known, as are the performance characteristics of stone tools. An argument regarding the nature of this relationship is made, resulting in the hypothesis that natural selection favored stone-tool users, and as such, *Homo habilis* choppers are adaptations. This *hypothesis* is so well supported that it is broadly considered a *conclusion* rather than a hypothesis, and is considered an *explanation* of hominid radiations as well.

One argument made against EA by a group of researchers who share a research perspective called Evolutionary Ecology (EE) is that while examples with such deep time depth may work, the rate at which the world is changing today clearly illustrates that invention and replication occur much faster than does reproduction. As a consequence, they believe, changes in technology we are seeing today are not evolution, but a mere product of phenotypic *plasticity* or flexibility of human behavior (Boone and Smith 1998). That technological change today occurs much faster than reproduction is, in one sense, undeniable. The last twenty years have brought tremendous changes in our lives. Everyday items that come to mind include the personal computer, the fax machine, cell phones, and the Internet and World Wide Web. These years have brought about an information revolution perhaps surpassing that of the invention of the printing press.

Many proponents of EE also argue that our minds are the product of millions of years of evolution whereby natural selection has shaped our behavior within certain limits, or constraints. Boone and Smith put it this way: "Evolutionary ecologists tend to focus on strategic phenotypic response and assume that the trait under study has been designed by natural selection to have sufficient phenotypic plasticity to track environmental variation optimally . . . Hence, they do not equate phenotypic variation with evolutionary change; instead they attribute it to evolved capacities for adaptive variation" (Boone and Smith 1998: S145).

To the EE program, then, most if not all contemporary behavior is operating within the rules dictated by natural selection operating in the past. Concomitantly, most if not all technological change now is simply phenotypic plasticity.

I both agree and disagree with this perspective. I agree that replication is faster than reproduction. I agree that the human phenotype is incredibly plastic. I agree that our minds and behavior have been shaped by millions of years of evolution. All of this is, to me, undeniable given that overwhelming evidence exists that supports each of these propositions. To my knowledge, no researcher working within the EA research program doubts any of these propositions.

Two conclusions drawn by these critics, however, put them into an intellectual dilemma that I believe restricts their program unnecessarily.

First, these arguments are ostensibly *presentist*, in terms of interpreting the past in terms of the present, rather than seeing the past and the present as the product of the same ongoing evolutionary processes. To me, this is a misconstrual of evolution, with very odd consequences that result from looking at a mere snapshot of time – *now*. If evolution is viewed in this manner, by all appearances any variation or change that we see in this particular slice of time (or any particular slice of time for that matter) that we are now operating in is simply plastic – within the realms of our evolved status. As an unfortunate consequence, the "first" *Homo erectus* to use fire was only exhibiting behavior that would have been considered "plastic" if those following the EE program had the good fortune to observe the behavior (hopefully from the safe perspective of a well-fortified time machine). This would not have been, in the EE program, part of an evolutionary process. This is contrary to the widely accepted conclusion that fire is an incredible human adaptation that allowed tremendous population growth and geographic expansion. The EE program logically leads us to this unfortunate perspective.

But let us consider this example in still more detail. If that *Homo erectus* individual who first used fire had not used it effectively, or if it had not been culturally transmitted to others, it would only have been what I will call a *potential* adaptation, not a *realized* one. Human prehistory and history would never have been the same, and you and I would very likely not be here, let alone be considering these issues.

In other words, what may appear plastic from the present day, or even for the past several thousand years, may actually be (1) truly plastic, (2) a *realized* adaptation at an early stage of its adoption, or (3) a *potential* adaptation that may become adaptive under certain conditions that may never be realized.

So how do we discern the difference? With respect to outcome 1, identifying plasticity is relatively straightforward in many biological situations. For example, if relatively acid soil produces blue petals in petunias, while alkaline soil produces pink petals, phenotypic plasticity is easily identified. The attribute color is plastic, a function of soil pH. However, determining what is plastic and what is a product of evolution with respect to human behavior is much more problematic, if not at times impossible.

Outcome 2 seems problematic at first glance, but ultimately can be dealt with in a manner consistent with how adaptations are identified above. Remember, our argument about technology as an adaptation is based first on a correlation, second on the logical argument regarding the nature of that correlation, and finally on our performance studies. We can also support our argument by evidence as to the rates at which technology changes. How does this relate to a realized adaptation at the early stage of adoption? It does, but in a different way than might be expected.

Given how evolutionary theory is currently structured, time is the ultimate criterion by which the correlation between adoption of a technology and reproduction are measured. That is, if fitness is increased across generations as a result of the adoption of a technology, an argument for adaptation can be made. But what if we don't have time, or if time cannot readily be measured? Here we may turn to what I call the *Theory of Evolutionary Relativity*, where, as in Einstein's General Theory of Relativity, time and space become one under certain conditions.

For example, if one were to evaluate the hypothesis that the adoption of personal computers should bring an on average increase in reproductive success to those individuals utilizing the technology, we may not have sufficient time depth available to see the diachronic effects in one population, and ascertain whether or not the changes we see are meaningful, as is customary in most biological applications. We do, however, have space, a whole wide world of it, and can potentially see ripples in increased reproduction as this technology is replicated and spreads over space rather than through time. There must be, of course, a logical argument tying technology to the spatial correlation. Ultimately, with sufficient time, conclusions based on observations of space may be evaluated, if necessary.

We next turn to our performance studies to provide independent evaluation of any hypotheses based on space. That is, if we see increased replication across space, associated with evidence for subtle changes in reproduction, and our performance studies indicate that the technology being used should lead to enhanced reproduction in that environment, it is to my mind a reasonable hypothesis to posit that a particular technology is indeed an adaptation. In other words, evolution is very likely occurring as we speak. Of course, we are not necessarily restricted to evolution as it is occurring, as this procedure is applicable for any time period.

Arguments related to outcome 3 rely for the most part on performance studies, and may well speak to technologies well known, and technologies that had tremendous potential to influence evolutionary change we will never know about, that were lost to the vagaries of history. While we of course cannot speak of the unknown technologies with adaptive potential, the list of well-known technologies that could have had impacts but did not is infinite: Thomas Jefferson's wonderful plow that he called the *Mouldboard of Least Resistance*, the Osborne computer, and, with a little imagination, the Betamax VCR. All the "best" designs of their times, we have no idea where agriculture, computing, or video display technology would be now if we had followed that evolutionary path history disallowed.

After considering all options, we can see that assuming the possibility of _only_ outcome 1, the EE proponents have placed themselves in what seems to me an unnecessary intellectual bind. They assume the most difficult position to empirically demonstrate, and ignore the other two possibilities that are, in fact, much easier to demonstrate.

There is also one more reason not to assume phenotypic plasticity, and the general halt of perceivable evolution. As noted above, EE proponents assume that our potential and capacities were shaped over the last million years, primarily ending at the end of the Pleistocene. Above, I argued that this perspective is _presentist_ with respect to the past. Unfortunately, it is also _presentist_ with respect to the future. Rather than arguing that evolution has slowed if not stopped, we have every reason to believe that it is increasing, perhaps at an exponential rate. Archaeologists and biological anthropologists well know how technology and humanity co-evolved, marking major physiological and behavioral changes concurrently with technological ones throughout the Pleistocene. Yet, when human population growth and technological change are greater than they have ever been, why does the EE program wish for us to assume that human evolution has slowed, if not stopped?

The year 1999 brought us a world population of 6 billion people. Millions of years of evolution gave us the world's first billion people in 1804 according to United Nations estimates. Two billion people were reached in only the next 123 years, by 1927. Three billion were reached only thirty-three years later in 1960. By 1974, fourteen years later, our population had reached 4 billion. At the same time, technology has proceeded to change, evolve if you will, at similar rates. Human evolution has stopped? Is this technological change _mere_ plasticity without direct reproductive consequences as a product of natural selection? I think not.

Yet, despite these major changes, the other side of human behavior as adaptation is that not all behavior offers such a reproductive advantage. Furthermore, this kind of behavior may be understood in evolutionary terms as well. Let us take a familiar example. Bartender A's bottle opener may have had a red handle, while the bottle opener of Bartender B may have had a green one. While these may have helped the bartenders identify their own tools, there is no advantage conveyed because of the color itself – any other color would suffice. These kinds of traits, sometimes called stylistic traits by Evolutionary Archaeologists, owe their existence to the vagaries of chance and history. They are subject to the evolutionary process called drift, and are not directly under the influence of natural selection. This concept is difficult to understand, and I present an example to help clarify it.

## An archaeological example from northern Mexico

While archaeologists have been working in parts of the North American Southwest for over 100 years, our knowledge drops off at the border of Mexico and the United States (Phillips 1989). Much is known about sites north of the border, and many are familiar with such famous sites as Chaco Canyon and Mesa Verde. South of the border lies another large important site called Paquimé (formerly known as Casas Grandes) (see map and figure 3.1), which dates to 1275–1400 (Dean and Ravesloot 1993). Farther to the south lies the extremely well-known archaeological region of the Valley of Mexico. Virtually every question asked of the archaeological record of the area is influenced in one way or another

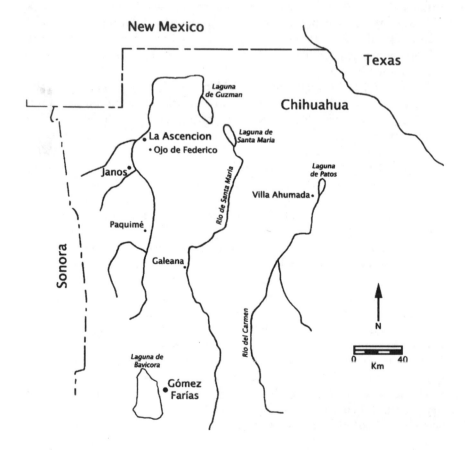

**Figure 3.1** Paquimé (formerly known as Casas Grandes) (photo: Tom Baker)

**Figure 3.2**   Casas Grandes ceramics from the Maxwell Museum, University of New Mexico

by how one views the relationships – expressed in similarities and differences – between the prehistoric inhabitants of the two areas. In other words, every interpretation of the area is based somehow in understanding what the similarities and differences among the archaeological records mean. But how do we measure similarities and differences? And what do they mean regarding cultural interactions? And how does this relate to evolutionary change in human behavior?

Let us consider the ceramics of North Mexico from the perspective of an Evolutionary Archaeologist. Chris VanPool, Marcel Harmon, Todd VanPool, and I, all of the University of New Mexico, are examining these pots with evolutionary theory as a framework for understanding. While our results are preliminary, they nevertheless lead us to some important evolutionary conclusions. Many of the ceramics of northern Mexico are quite beautiful polychromes that have a variety of complex motifs and icons (figure 3.2). The motifs and icons on these vessels likely convey complex information about group affiliation and individual identity (Wiessner 1983). That is, they have purpose. Yet, the image itself is a product of chance and history, as there is nothing inherent in that image itself that brings an evolutionary advantage. Importantly, they are all the product of intellectual traditions that cross-cut space and time. As beautiful as these pots are, they are also tools. Di Peso states: "Many of the beautifully painted polychrome vessels were smudged and soiled by cooking grease and food stains, demonstrating that these, along with the culinary wares, were used to ferment, cook, and serve, while others of equal grace were used as funeral furniture, to store foods, and even to line fire hearths" (Di Peso et al. 1974: 532–3). As tools, those that are more effective tools than others offer a competitive advantage to the people using them, as did the bottle openers in the example above.

With respect to the functional attributes, we have a number of ideas to be evaluated. For example, many of the pots are polished and painted around the lip. Chris VanPool has proposed that this trait might be functional, as polished and painted rims reduce spillage (Rice 1987). Reduced spillage is a clear evolutionary advantage. This aspect of our research is just beginning, and we need to understand how small differences in technology may have led to major changes in reproduction.

Charles Di Peso, the excavator of Paquimé, proposed perhaps the most widely used hypothetical relationships between the types based upon similarities (figure 3.3). People learned these traditions from each other, and they changed through time. Cultural transmission is implied because learning was involved, and change in both functional and neutral traits was used to monitor how ceramic assemblages changed through time.

Archaeologists working in the area have proposed a number of competing ideas about these relationships (Leonard et al. 1999):

1   The Casas Grandes ceramic tradition is related to the Puebloan traditions of the prehistoric American Southwest (Bandelier 1892; Brand 1933, 1935; Chapman 1923; Kidder 1924; Robles 1929).

2   The Casas Grandes ceramic tradition is related to the Toltec (we now know Di Peso's chronology was in error (Dean and Ravesloot 1993) – the extant tradition at the time of Paquimé was actually the Aztec, not Toltec, tradition of Mesoamerica (Di Peso et al. 1974).

3   The Casas Grandes ceramic tradition is a specific derivative of the Classic Mimbres (Sayles 1936a, 1936b).

4   The Casas Grandes ceramic tradition grew out of the more general Mogollon tradition of southern New Mexico and Arizona (LeBlanc 1986; Lister 1953).

5   The Casas Grandes ceramic tradition is related to the "Lower Gila style" from southern New Mexico and Arizona (Kidder 1916).

6   The Casas Grandes ceramic tradition is related to the Little Colorado red ware tradition (Amsden 1928; Sauer and Brand 1931).

7   The Casas Grandes ceramic tradition is unique (Carey 1931; Hewett 1908).

8   The Casas Grandes ceramic tradition is related to both the pueblos of the prehistoric American Southwest and the Aztecs of Mesoamerica.

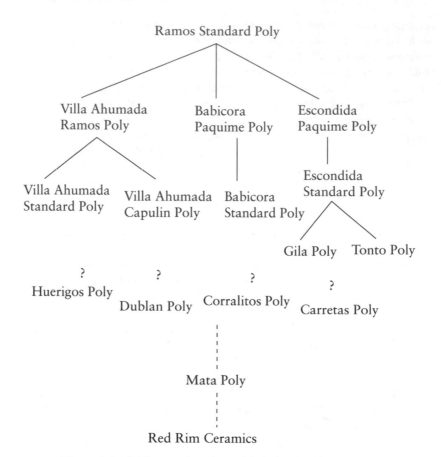

**Figure 3.3**   Di Peso (1974) hypothesized type relationships

This previous work can now guide us as a set of ideas that we can use as hypotheses regarding prehistoric cultural transmission and interaction. Evolutionary theory, however, demands that we use the concept of similarity in a different manner than that used by these researchers. Not all similarities are the product of the same processes. As noted briefly above, evolutionary theory recognizes homologous and analogous similarity (Lyman and O'Brien 1998; O'Brien and Lyman 2000a, 2000b, 2000c). Homologous similarity is the product of historical relatedness. Analogous similarity is the product of similar responses to similar conditions, or evolutionary convergence.

To confuse the two confounds the processes underlying observed change, meaning that we ultimately will have little or no knowledge of

either, and will be unable to explain their manifestations in the archaeological record. To presume homology where only analogy exists is to
presume historic relatedness where there is none. To presume analogy
where homology exists is to deny a historic relationship. To us, this is a
very important archaeological matter – and not just to evolutionary
archaeologists. To put it simply, we must identify homology and analogy
whenever we are interested in *any* kind of human interaction or behavior in the past.

In our consideration of the northern Mexico ceramics, we therefore
need to know which similarities are homologous and which are analogous
to ascertain the flow of cultural information. To help us solve this knotty
problem, evolutionary archaeologists make a distinction between technologies under the direct operation of natural selection and those that are
not (Dunnell 1978a, 1978b, 1978c; Meltzer 1981; Neiman 1995). Similarities in the former may be either homologous or analogous. Similarities
in the latter, however, are more often likely to be homologous. For
example, a ceramic tempering agent that allows for thinner walled ceramics that allow corn to be processed more efficiently, and with greater
nutrition that allows more people to be fed using less fuel, has direct consequences in terms of reproduction, and is, as a consequence, under selection. The symbols used to decorate these pots are unlikely to be under
selection, however, and their presence is most likely the result of a historical, or homologous relationship, and their distribution through time
subject to drift. By drift we mean change that is independent of the operation of selection, fading in and out of popularity with the passing of time,
like contemporary dress and hairstyles.

Both temper and the symbols used to decorate the pots may, of course,
be part of an intellectual tradition, but the ceramic tempering agent may
well emerge in different times and places as a product of convergence.
We assumed that "plumed serpents," "macaws," "snakes," and other
decorations have little such potential to simply be convergent. They
instead reflect cultural transmission and history. As a consequence, we
focused on decoration in order to maximize the probability that the
similarities we see are the product of historical relatedness.

To conduct our analysis of northern Mexico ceramics, we examined
103 whole pots, recording the presence and absence of 88 different
design attributes (see list overleaf). We also recorded classic type descriptions. These ceramics came from a variety of regions in the American
Southwest and northern Mexico.

As O'Brien and Lyman (2000a, 2000b, 2000c) suggest, similarities
of homologous traits and intellectual lineages can be illustrated by
building a phylogenetic tree (figure 3.4, pp. 88–9 below). What this tree

## Preliminary recorded design attributes

| | |
|---|---|
| Band | Running Squares with Dots |
| BI Division | Cross |
| Quad Division | Heart |
| Human Effigy | Rectangles Checkered |
| Badger Effigy | Squiggle lines |
| Bird Effigy | Parallel Hatching |
| Macaw Effigy | Perpendicular Hatching |
| Owl Effigy | Diagonal Hatching |
| Turtle Effigy | Serpent |
| Fish Effigy | Wing Serpent |
| Snake Effigy | Macaw |
| Ribbon Band | Macaw 2 |
| Snake Band | Turkey |
| Triangle | Bird |
| Triangle with Lines | Textile |
| Triangle with Dots | F Motif |
| Decorated Triangles | S Motif |
| Interlocking Triangles | Chevron |
| Square | Kilted Dancer |
| Scroll | Fish |
| Interlocking Scrolls | Ticking |
| Interlocking Steps | WingFeather |
| Steps | Eye Style 1 |
| Crosshatched Step | Eye Style 2 |
| Squared Scroll | Diamond Eyes |
| Interlocking Squared Scrolls | Almond Eyes |
| Filled Shape | Glasses |
| Negative Shape | Facial Marking T-Shape |
| Balanced Lines | Death Teeth |
| Arrow | Stacking Triangles |
| Square with Dot | V with V |
| Checkerboard | Incised Lines |
| Checkerboard with Dots | Incised Ticking |
| Circle with Dot | Incised Cross |
| Circle | Incised Scroll |
| Running Checkerboard with Dots | Incised Step |
| Running Checkerboard | Incised Band |
| Running Circles | Incised Triangle |
| Running Squares | Incised Macaw |
| Running Dots | Corrugated |
| Running Squares | Finger Punched |

is, in sum, is a hypothesized historical lineage. As such, it purports to measure the direction and flow of culturally transmitted ideas through time and across space in the region. Individual branches on the tree represent individual pots. They are coded on the far right, and they are color coded by DiPeso's types; e.g. Ramos Polychrome. Different clusters of pots can be seen as hypotheses regarding historical relatedness – participation to greater or lesser degrees in shared intellectual traditions.

As can be seen, the traditional types can be found in different clusters, suggesting that many pots identified as belonging to the same types actually more closely resemble pots belonging to different types! We suggest that the reason for this is that the traditional types confound homologous and analogous similarity by being based on some combination of design elements, paste composition, or surface treatment, among other characteristics. As the types are constructed using a mix of historically related and convergent traits together, the types may not measure historical relatedness as well as they could.

Among the many things to be learned from this tree, we found Cluster 7 to be quite interesting, suggesting cultural transmission between the Classic Mimbres, the later Northern Mexico traditions, and the Hohokam and Salado traditions to the north as well. Figure 3.5 shows the table of shared attributes across all clusters. Notice that Cluster 7 (identified in figure 3.4) is characterized by bands, decorated triangles, filled shapes, negative shapes, parallel hatchures, triangles, and triangles with hatching (summarized in table 3.1, p. 92). The probability of these seven traits clustering on three different regional ceramic types (Mimbres, Salado, and Casas Grandes) is improbably low given that we recorded 88 different design elements. Ultimately the clusters depicted in figures 3.4 and 3.5 will be evaluated by using the archaeological methodologies of occurrence and frequency seriation. If we are indeed constructing historical lineages, battleship-shaped or lenticular curves will ultimately provide additional insights into the reliability of our conclusions.

Returning to the eight hypotheses referred to above, we now find support for propositions 3 and 5 and no support for proposition 7. (The evaluation of hypotheses 1, 2, 4, 6, and 8 await further analysis.) That is, the Casas Grandes ceramic tradition is not unique, and cultural transmission between the individuals living during the Classic Mimbres period of southern New Mexico persisted at least in part through time to the North Mexico Casas Grandes tradition as well as the "Lower Gila style" of southern New Mexico and Arizona.

Additional analyses are needed to evaluate these conclusions, and ultimately we may well be shown to be wrong. This is not a weakness in our theory, but a strength that comes with using the epistemology of

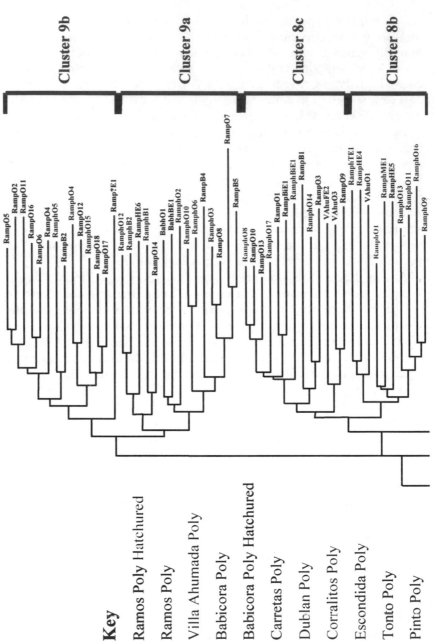

**Key**

Ramos Poly Hatchured

Ramos Poly

Villa Ahumada Poly

Babicora Poly

Babicora Poly Hatchured

Carretas Poly

Dublan Poly

Corralitos Poly

Escondida Poly

Tonto Poly

Pinto Poly

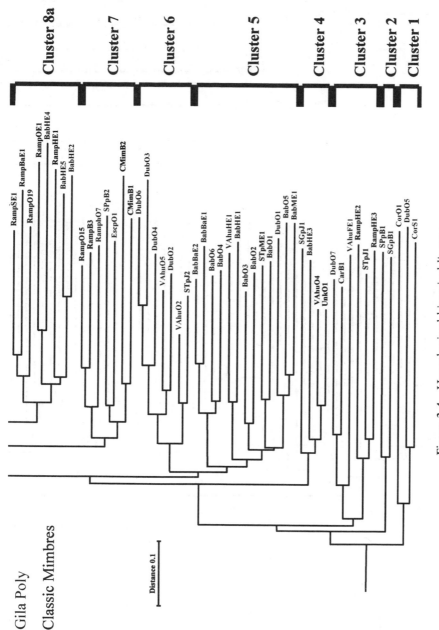

Figure 3.4 Hypothesized historical lineage

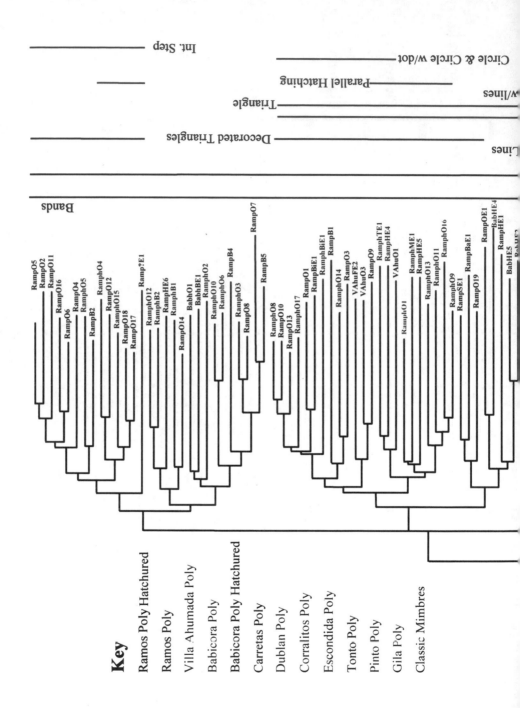

Key

Ramos Poly Hatchured

Ramos Poly

Villa Ahumada Poly

Babicora Poly

Babicora Poly Hatchured

Carretas Poly

Dublan Poly

Corralitos Poly

Escondida Poly

Tonto Poly

Pinto Poly

Gila Poly

Classic Mimbres

Int. Step

Circle & Circle w/dot

Parallel Hatching

w/lines

Triangle

Decorated Triangles

Lines

Bands

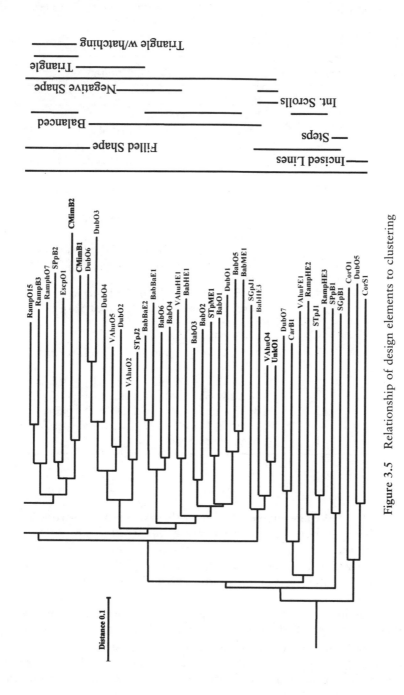

Figure 3.5 Relationship of design elements to clustering

**Table 3.1**   Shared attributes summary table

| Cluster | Number of pots | Shared attributes |
|---|---|---|
| 1 | 3 | Band; Incised Lines |
| 2 | 2 | Band; Filled Shape; Steps |
| 3 | 6 | Band; Balanced Lines; Filled Shape |
| 4 | 4 | Band; Decorated Triangle; Filled Shape; Interlocking Square Scroll; Negative Shape; Triangle |
| 5 | 13 | Band; Balanced Lines; Decorated Triangle; Filled Shape; Triangle |
| 6 | 7 | Band; Balanced Lines; Negative Shape; Triangle; Triangle with Lines |
| 7 | 6 | Band; Decorated Triangle; Filled Shape; Negative Shape; Parallel Hatching; Triangle; Triangle with Hatching |
| 8a | 14 | Band; Filled Shape; Parallel Hatching |
| 8b | 14 | Band; Decorated Triangle; Filled Shape; Interlocking Steps |
| 8 total | 28 | Band; Filled Shape |
| 9a | 8 | Band; Bi-Division; Filled Shape; Ticking; Triangle |
| 9b | 10 | Band; Circle; Decorated Triangle; Filled Shape; Negative Shape; Parallel Hatching; Triangle |
| 9c | 13 | Band; Circle; Circle with Dots; Decorated Triangle; Filled Shape; Negative Shape; Triangle |
| 9 total | 31 | Band; Filled Shape; Triangle |

science. We used Darwinian evolutionary theory to generate propositions – hypotheses – about the past that we as well as others may evaluate. These propositions may or may not stand the test of time, but the powerful theoretical structure behind them will allow others a means of evaluation, and a strict set of rules to follow to conduct such an evaluation.

Many more propositions of a different sort must be forthcoming for evaluation as well. While this example focused on cultural transmission, style, homology, and drift, much more work needs to be done with these materials regarding function, analogy, and the operation of natural selection – the full evolutionary application – which is, of course, beyond the scope of this short essay.

## Conclusions

As all readers of this book know by now, the word "theory" means different things to different authors in this volume. To Evolutionary Archaeologists theory is a set of rules to follow in order to understand the world around us. To many others, theory seems to be any set of abstractions people wish to use at any one time to learn. While evolutionary theory does change as we gain more knowledge of the world around us, the change is remarkably slow and tends to be minor. Evolutionary Archaeologists are simply seeking to bring, for the first time, the most productive set of rules ever used to understand life on earth to the human past – Darwinian theory. In the world of EA, not every good idea or abstraction constitutes theory. One consequence of this is that many people play by the same rules, and can thus easily build upon, understand, and evaluate each other's work. Importantly, the intellectual product is cumulative, and cross-cultural.

In conclusion, I very much hope this simple piece provides the basics by which one can understand how evolutionary theory is put into practice. As with chess, one must know the rules in order to play the game.

Your move.

### REFERENCES

Amsden, M. 1928. *Archaeological Reconnaissance in Sonora*. Southwest Museum Papers 1. Los Angeles: Southwest Museum.

Bandelier, A. F. 1892. *Final Report of Investigations among the Indians of the Southwestern United States, Carried on Mainly in the Years from 1880 to 1885*. Papers of the Archaeological Institute of America IV. Cambridge, MA: John Wilson and Son.

Best, M. L. and R. Pocklington 1999. Meaning as use: transmission fidelity and evolution in NetNews. *Journal of Theoretical Biology* 196(3): 389–95.

Bettinger, R. L., R. Boyd, and P. J. Richerson 1996. Style, function, and cultural evolutionary processes. In H. D. G. Maschner (ed.), *Darwinian Archaeologies*, 133–64. New York: Plenum Press.

Binford, L. R. 1962. Archaeology as anthropology. *American Antiquity* 28(2): 217–25.

Binford, L. R. 1968. Archaeological perspectives. In S. R. Binford and L. R. Binford (eds), *New Perspectives in Archaeology*, 5–32. New York: Aldine.

Binford, L. R. 1973. Interassemblage variability – the Mousterian and the functional argument. In C. Renfrew (ed.), *The Explanation of Cultural Change*, 227–54. London: Duckworth.

Binford, L.R. and S.R. Binford 1966. A preliminary analysis of functional variability in the Mousterian of the Levallois Facies. In J.D. Clark and F.C. Howell
(eds), *Recent Studies in Paleoanthropology*, 238–95. *American Anthropologist* 68(2). Washington DC: American Anthropological Association.

Boone, J.L. 1998. Comment on Lyman and O'Brien's "The Goals of Evolutionary
Archaeology: History and Explanation". *Current Anthropology* 39: 631–2.

Boone, J.L. and E.A. Smith 1998. Is it evolution yet? A critique of "Evolutionary Archeology." *Current Anthropology* 39(Supplement): S141–S173.

Brand, D.D. 1933. The historical geography of Northwestern Chihuahua.
Dissertation, University of California.

Brand, D.D. 1935. The distribution of pottery types in Northwest Mexico.
*American Anthropologist* 37: 287–305.

Braun, D.P. 1990. Selection and evolution in non-hierarchical organization.
In Steadman Upham (ed.) *The Evolution of Political Systems*. Cambridge:
Cambridge University Press.

Brew, J.O. 1946. *Archaeology of Alkali Ridge, Southeastern Utah*. Cambridge,
MA: Peabody Museum of American Archaeology and Ethnology.

Broughton, J.M. and J.F. O'Connell 1999. On evolutionary ecology, selectionist archaeology, and behavioral archaeology. *American Antiquity* 64(1):
153–65.

Carey, H.A. 1931. An analysis of the Northwestern Chihuahua culture.
*American Anthropologist* 33: 325–74.

Cavalli-Sforza, L.L. and M.W. Feldman 1981. *Cultural Transmission and
Evolution*. Princeton: Princeton University Press.

Chapman, K.M. 1923. Casas Grandes pottery. *Art and Archaeology* 16: 34.

Cullen, B. 1993. The Darwinian resurgence and the cultural virus critique.
*Cambridge Archaeological Journal* 3(2): 179–202.

Darwin, C. 1859. *On the Origin of Species by Means of Natural Selection, or
the Preservation of Favoured Races in the Struggle for Life*. London: John
Murray.

Dawkins, R. 1976. *The Selfish Gene*. Oxford: Oxford University Press.

Dawkins, R. 1982. *The Extended Phenotype: The Gene as the Unit of Selection*.
Oxford: W.H. Freeman.

Dawkins, R. 1989. *The Selfish Gene*, new edn. Oxford: Oxford University Press.

Dawkins, R. 1996. *Climbing Mount Improbable*. New York: W.W. Norton.

Dean, J. and John C. Ravesloot 1993. The chronology of cultural interaction in
the Gran Chichimeca. In A.I. Woosley and J.C. Ravesloot (eds), *Culture and
Contact: Charles C. Di Peso's Gran Chichimeca*. Albuquerque: University of
New Mexico Press.

Dennett, D.C. 1990. Memes and the exploitation of imagination. *Journal of
Aesthetics and Art Criticism* 48(2): 127–35.

Di Peso, C.C., J.B. Rinaldo, and G.J. Fenner 1974. *Casas Grandes: A Fallen
Trading Center of the Gran Chichimeca*. Dragoon, AZ: Amerind Foundation.

Dretske, F. 1989. *Explaining Behavior: Reasons in a World of Causes*. Cambridge, MA: MIT Press.

Dugatkin, L.A. 1997. The evolution of cooperation: four paths to the evolution
and maintenance of cooperative behavior. *Bioscience* 47(6): 355–62.

Dunnell, R.C. 1978a. Archaeological potential of anthropological and scientific models of function. In R.C. Dunnell and E.S. Hall (eds), *Archaeological Essays in Honor of Irving B. Rouse*, 41–73. The Hague: Mouton.

Dunnell, R.C. 1978b. Natural selection, scale, and cultural evolution: some preliminary considerations. Paper to 77th Annual Meeting of the American Anthropological Association, Los Angeles.

Dunnell, R.C. 1978c. Style and function: a fundamental dichotomy. *American Antiquity* 43(2): 192–202.

Dunnell, R.C. 1980. Evolutionary theory and archaeology. In M.B. Schiffer (ed.), *Advances in Archaeological Method and Theory*, 35–99. New York: Academic Press.

Dunnell, R.C. 1982. Science, social science, and common sense: the agonizing dilemma of modern archaeology. *Journal of Anthropological Research* 38(1): 1–25.

Dunnell, R.C. 1989. Aspects of the application of evolutionary theory in archaeology. In C.C. Lamberg-Karlovsky (ed.), *Archaeological Thought in America*, 35–49. Cambridge: Cambridge University Press.

Durham, W.H. 1990. Advances in evolutionary culture theory. *Annual Review of Anthropology* 19: 187–210.

Durham, W.H. 1991. *Coevolution: Genes, Culture, and Human Diversity*. Stanford: Stanford University Press.

Durham, W.H. 1992. Applications of evolutionary culture theory. *Annual Review of Anthropology* 21: 331–55.

Flinn, M.V. 1997. Culture and the evolution of social learning. *Evolution and Human Behavior* 18: 23–67.

Goodenough, O.R. 1995. Mind viruses: culture, evolution and the puzzle of altruism. *Social Science Information* 34(2): 287–320.

Hewett, E.L. 1908. *Les Communautés anciennes dans le Désert Américain*. Geneva: Librairie Kundig.

Kidder, A.V. 1916. The pottery of the Casas Grandes District, Chihuahua. In *Holmes Anniversary Volume*. Washington DC: Smithsonian Institution.

Kidder, A.V. 1924. *An Introduction to the Study of Southwestern Archaeology*. New Haven, CT: Yale University Press.

Lake, M. 1997. Darwinian archaeology: an "ism" for our times? *Antiquity* 71: 1086–8.

LeBlanc, S.A. 1986. Aspects of Southwestern prehistory: A.D. 900–1400. In F.J. Mathien and R.H. McGuire (eds), *Ripples in the Chichimec Sea: New Considerations of Southwestern-Mesoamerican Interactions*. Carbondale and Edwardsville, IL: Center for Archaeological Investigations and Southern Illinois University Press.

Leonard, R.D. 1989. Resource specialization, population growth, and agricultural production in the American Southwest. *American Antiquity* 54(3): 491–503.

Leonard, R.D. and G.T. Jones 1987. Elements of an inclusive evolutionary model for archaeology. *Journal of Anthropological Archaeology* 6: 199–219.

Leonard, R.D., C. VanPool, M. Harmon, and T. VanPool 1999. Intellectual traditions in Northern Mexico ceramics. Paper to Il Conferencia de Arqueologia de la Frontera, Casas Grandes, Chihuahua, 25–26 June.

Lister, R.H. 1953. Excavations in Cave Valley, Chihuahua, Mexico: a preliminary note. *American Antiquity* 2: 166–9.

Lyman, R.L. and M.J. O'Brien 1998. The goals of evolutionary archaeology: history and explanation. *Current Anthropology* 39: 615–52.

Lynch, A. 1996. *Thought Contagion: How Belief Spreads Through Society*. New York: Basic Books.

Lynch, A. and A.J. Baker 1993. A population memetics approach to cultural evolution in Chaffinch song: meme diversity within populations. *American Naturalist* 141: 597–620.

Lynch, A. and A.J. Baker 1994. A population memetics approach to cultural evolution in Chaffinch song: differentiation among populations. *Evolution* 48: 351–9.

Lynch, A., G.M. Plunkett, A.J. Baker, and P.F. Jenkins 1989. A model of cultural evolution of Chaffinch song derived with the meme concept. *American Naturalist* 133: 634–53.

Mayr, E. 1982. *The Growth of Biological Thought: Diversity, Evolution, and Inheritance*. Cambridge, MA: Harvard University Press.

Meltzer, D.J. 1981. A study of style and function in a class of tools. *Journal of Field Archaeology* 8: 313–26.

Morgan, L.H. 1877. *Ancient Society*. New York: Holt.

Neiman, F.D. 1993. What makes the seriation clock tick? Temporal dynamics of style under drift. Paper to 58th Annual Meeting of the Society for American Archaeology, St Louis.

Neiman, F.D. 1995. Stylistic variation in evolutionary perspective: inferences from decorative diversity and interassemblage distance in Illinois woodland ceramic assemblages. *American Antiquity* 60: 7–36.

O'Brien, M.J. and T.D. Holland 1990. Variation, selection, and the archaeological record. In M.B. Schiffer (ed.), *Archaeological Method and Theory*, vol. 2, 31–79. Tucson: University of Arizona Press.

O'Brien, M.J. and R.L. Lyman 2000a. *Applying Evolutionary Archaeology: A Systematic Approach*. New York: Plenum Press.

O'Brien, M.J. and R.L. Lyman 2000b. Darwinian evolutionism is applicable to historical archaeology. *International Journal of Historical Archaeology* 4: 71–112.

O'Brien, M.J. and R.L. Lyman 2000c. Evolutionary archaeology: reconstructing and explaining historical lineages. In M.B. Schiffer (ed.), *Explorations in Social Theory*. Salt Lake City: University of Utah Press.

Phillips, D.A., Jr. 1989. Prehistory of Chihuahua and Sonora, Mexico. *Journal of World Prehistory* 3(4): 373–401.

Rice, P.M. 1987. *Pottery Analysis: A Sourcebook*. Chicago: University of Chicago Press.

Richerson, P.J. and R. Boyd 1992. Cultural inheritance and evolutionary ecology. In E.A. Smith and B. Winterhalder (ed.), *Evolutionary Ecology and Human Behavior*, 61–94. New York: Aldine De Gruyter.

Rindos, D. 1984. *The Origins of Agriculture: An Evolutionary Perspective*. New York: Academic Press.

Rindos, D. 1985. Darwinian selection, symbolic variation, and the evolution of culture. *Current Anthropology* 26(1): 65–88.

Rindos, D. 1986. The evolution of the capacity for culture: sociobiology, structuralism, and cultural selectionism. *Current Anthropology* 27(4): 315–32.

Rindos, D. 1989. Undirected variation and the Darwinian explanation of cultural change. In M.B. Schiffer (ed.), *Archaeological Method and Theory*, vol. 1, 1–45. Tucson: University of Arizona Press.

Robles, C.A. 1929. *La Region Arqueologica de Casas Grandes, Chihuahua*. Mexico, D.F.: Imprenta Nunez.

Sahlins, M. and E. Service (eds) 1960. *Evolution and Culture*. Ann Arbor: University of Michigan Press.

Sauer, C. and D. Brand 1931. *Pueblo Sites in Southeastern Arizona*. University of California Publications in Geography 3, no. 7. Berkeley: University of California Press.

Sayles, E.B. 1936a. *An Archaeological Survey of Chihuahua, Mexico*. Medallion Papers XXII. Globe, AZ: Gila Pueblo.

Sayles, E.B. 1936b. *Some Southwestern Pottery Types*. Medallion Papers XXI. Globe, AZ: Gila Pueblo.

Schiffer, M.B. 1996. Some relationships between behavioral and evolutionary archaeologies. *American Antiquity* 61: 643–62.

Service, E. 1962. *Primitive Social Organization*. New York: Random House.

Spencer, C.S. 1997. Evolutionary approaches in archaeology. *Journal of Archaeological Research* 5(3): 209–64.

Spencer, H. 1857. Progress: its laws and causes. *Westminster Review* 67: 445–85.

Spencer, H. 1860. The social organism. *Westminster Review* 17: 90–121.

Spencer, H. 1876. *Principles of Sociology*. New York: D. Appleton.

Tylor, E.B. 1865. *Researches into the Early History of Mankind and the Development of Civilization*. London: J. Murray.

Tylor, E.B. 1871. *Primitive Culture: Researchers into the Development of Mythology, Philosophy, Religion, Language, Art and Custom*. London: J. Murray.

White, L. 1943. Energy and the evolution of culture. *American Anthropologist* 45: 335–56.

White, L. 1945. Diffusion versus evolution: an anti-evolutionist fallacy. *American Anthropologist* 47: 339–56.

White, L. (ed.) 1959a. *The Concept of Evolution in Anthropology: Evolution and Anthropology: A Centennial Appraisal*. Washington DC: Anthropological Society of Washington.

White, L. 1959b. *The Evolution of Culture*. New York: McGraw Hill.

Wiessner, P. 1983. Style and social information in Kalahari San projectile points. *American Antiquity* 48(2): 253–76.

Wilkins, J.S. 1998. What's in a meme? Reflections from the perspective of the history and philosophy of evolutionary biology. *Journal of Memetics – Evolutionary Models of Information Transmission* (*http://www.cpm.mmu.ac.uk/jom-emit/1998/vol2/wilkins_js.html*) 2.

# 4

# Archaeological Theory and Theories of Cognitive Evolution

## Steven Mithen

### Introduction

Archaeologists should always be seeking to extend the domain of their discipline – exploring how new aspects of the past can be examined, and how the past has a bearing on further aspects of the present than have been previously considered. The emergence of cognitive archaeology in the 1980s is one example of how new issues began to be addressed, often by archaeologists coming from radically different paradigmatic positions but concurring that we neglect past minds at our peril. Yet it should not just be past minds that are of interest to us: the evidence from the archaeological record has a key bearing on understanding the nature of the modern mind.

In this chapter I will examine selected issues in cognitive evolution as a means to explore the role of archaeology in understanding both past and present minds. A key argument will be that archaeologists need to make greater efforts to engage with the theories, data, and ideas within the cognitive sciences. There have, of course, been very significant recent developments in this regard, exemplified by the volumes edited by Mellars and Gibson (1996) and by Renfrew and Scarre (1998), both of which derived from interdisciplinary meetings involving archaeologists, anthropologists, and cognitive scientists. Noble and Davidson (1996) and myself (Mithen 1996c) have sought to synthesize evidence and data from archaeology with that from various branches of psychology. Such work has forged an opportunity for greater engagement between these disciplines which must be grasped by further investments of time and resources by archaeologists in building theory regarding cognitive evolution.

## Grasping the nettle of cognitive evolution

This is an important time for archaeology as cognitive scientists have recently become much more willing to pay attention to archaeological evidence and ideas when seeking to understand the nature and evolution of the mind. They have been persuaded to do so partly by archaeologists themselves, such as by organizing the conferences and editing the volumes referred to above. Hence there is now an opportunity for archaeologists to play a substantial role in the interdisciplinary studies of cognitive evolution and this is a nettle that we must grasp. Archaeologists must not only contribute data and ideas for the evaluation of theories generated within the cognitive sciences; we must play an equal role in setting the agenda for studying cognitive evolution. We must generate our share of the theory.

This opportunity for interdisciplinary engagement is significant because until recently cognitive scientists have, in general, neglected archaeological evidence and theory in their arguments about cognitive evolution. One notable exception was Merlin Donald's (1991) excellent volume, *Origins of the Modern Mind*, which set a model for how archaeological evidence can be integrated with that from cognitive science. But many other studies have effectively ignored archaeological data. As I will explain below, theories regarding cognitive evolution put forward by Cosmides and Tooby (1994; Tooby and Cosmides 1992), Miller (1998), and Boyd and Richerson (1996) are all seriously weakened by their neglect of archaeological evidence as a means to support, test, or evaluate their theories.

By making this accusation of neglect, I am not suggesting that the degree of scholarship shown by these writers is any worse than that of archaeologists who have neglected to address and draw upon relevant areas of cognitive science when writing about the past. There are certainly many cases of this within my own work which, with the benefit of hindsight, I can readily identify. The main problem we all face is that of artificial disciplinary boundaries created by the history of our subjects and the nature of our institutions.

There are signs of change within the current literature, showing that archaeological evidence is gaining a more prominent and appropriate place within interdisciplinary studies on cognitive evolution. I have, for instance, just received a newly published book entitled *The Mathematical Brain* by Brian Butterworth (1999), the distinguished cognitive neuroscientist. This book addresses why and how the brain is so effective at using numbers. There is a significant amount of text devoted to archaeological evidence which is invoked not just for curiosity's sake but as a key element of Butterworth's argument. And he uses this evidence in a sophisticated fashion, quite aware of the difficulties involved in its interpretation. Edited books listed under the rubric of cognitive sciences are more frequently carrying papers by archaeologists, or have papers which draw upon archaeological evidence in a substantive manner. Examples include those recent books concerning social learning in mammals (Box and Gibson 1999), the nature of consciousness (Hameroff et al. 1999), understanding other minds (Baron-Cohen et al. 2000), and about Piaget, evolution, and development (Langer and Killen 1998). Conversely, psychologists are appreciating that it is important for them to publish within archaeological journals and to have their work recognized and discussed by archaeologists (e.g. Humphrey 1998). Consequently, from an archaeologist's perspective there are very positive developments in the study of cognitive evolution. But archaeologists still need to devote more time and resources to this area, and to further demonstrate that archaeological evidence and archaeological theories must not be neglected. While this will be to the benefit of the study of cognitive evolution in general, it will be of particular benefit to archaeologists themselves, as an explicit reference to the nature of past mentality is an essential element of archaeological interpretation. We must seek to make those references as rigorous and well-informed as possible.

To illustrate how archaeologists can engage with current theories of cognitive evolution, and what benefits might accrue to our interpretations, I will examine three key issues in cognitive evolution – mental modularity, sexual selection, and the extended mind – and briefly comment on some further issues of particular relevance to archaeologists. These three key issues are ones that I have myself addressed in recent research and which appear to me as having the potential to resolve longstanding problems of archaeological interpretation. While my own interest with these issues relates specifically to Palaeolithic archaeology, they are also of relevance to archaeological theory in general and have direct bearing on the problems discussed by archaeologists studying later prehistory and the historic periods.

## Mental modularity

Mental modularity is one of the major issues in the study of how the mind works and how it came into being. In essence this notion argues that the mind is constituted of multiple, self-contained modules, each devoted to a different function. Beyond such a simple characterization, notions of modularity come in a vast array of different forms, some quite incompatible with others. Fodor (1983) argued, for instance, that perceptual processes are heavily modularized, and as such are in complete contrast to central processes (i.e. those concerned with thought). Gardner (1983) provided another take on modularity by invoking multiple intelligences in the human mind, such as those concerned with music, logic, and social interaction. During the last decade arguments regarding mental modularity have been favored by those adopting an explicitly evolutionary perspective on the mind, most notably by Cosmides and Tooby (1994), and by Pinker (1997).

Cosmides and Tooby (1987, 1994; Tooby and Cosmides 1992) have been the main proponents of the view that the modern human mind is constituted by a series of mental modules, each "designed" by natural selection to solve one specific adaptive problem that hunter-gatherers faced in the Pleistocene – problems such as choosing mates, finding food, and avoiding danger. Such arguments were expressed, however, with minimal reference to any specific archaeological, fossil or palaeoenvironmental data and interpretation, and professed notions about "environments of evolutionary adaptedness" that appear simplistic to many palaeoanthropologists (e.g. Foley 1996). Although the 1970s and 1980s had seen ardent debates about past lifestyles – hunting or scavenging in the Plio-Pleistocene, cultures or tool-kits in the Mousterian, simple or complex hunter-gatherers in the Mesolithic – evolutionary psychologists ignored these completely and presented the past as if it were appropriate to project the !Kung back into 3 million years of prehistory.

One can certainly have sympathy with their position and excuse their neglect – no "outsider" would have found the debates within archaeology of the 1980s conducive to extra study while wrestling with the debates within one's own discipline. Neither Binfordian-like polemics nor postmodernist Shanks and Tilleyite hermeneutic introspection have been very helpful to our discipline's reception into the wider world of scholarly debate. Nevertheless, it was the case that Tooby and Cosmides (1992) explicitly argued for conceptual integration between disciplines as the means to understand the modern mind, but then omitted to include archaeology in their considerations.

Although the credibility of Cosmides and Tooby's extreme position regarding mental modularity has yet to be established, it seems quite impossible to question the notion that minds are modular in some respects – there is simply too much evidence deriving from too wide a variety of disciplines for this to be dismissed. This leaves us with a question: Why should archaeologists concern themselves with the arguments about the origin, nature, and extent of mental modularity?

There are three reasons. The first relates to the understanding of the modern mind. Some evolutionary psychologists claim that the mental modules which exist today would have been selected during human evolution. Hence the mind today remains adapted for life in the Pleistocene, and this may account for much of the maladaptive behavior we see in the modern world – people living in urban, industrialized, sedentary communities but still thinking like mobile hunter-gatherers and/or acting in strict self interest to maximize their inclusive fitness. Two classic examples of this are the proposed reality of the "Cinderella syndrome" (step-parents are more likely to harm children than are biological parents, Wilson and Daly 1997) and the mental attraction of people towards sweet and fatty foods which are deleterious to health today. Such attraction, however, is likely to have been a useful adaptation to Pleistocene environments when such foodstuffs were particularly scarce and nutritious.

If one were to accept the argument that a substantial amount of our thought processes remained molded to a Pleistocene hunter-gatherer existence (and it certainly has some grain of truth in it, though probably a rather small grain), then to identify quite what modules may be present requires us to understand more fully the selective pressures which acted on the hominid mind. So here is a real opportunity for archaeologists to use their ability at reconstructing the past to contribute toward understanding the world today.

. A second reason for engaging with the debates about mental modularity is to help evaluate the basic question: does the archaeological record support the notion that human mentality evolved in a modular fashion? This is a question I have addressed (Mithen 1996c), and for which I reached a positive answer for much of human evolution, but found that strict modularity is quite incompatible with the evidence for the Upper Palaeolithic/Later Stone Age. That evidence strongly supports the notion that interaction between mental modules (or cognitive domains as I prefer to call them) was the major evolutionary development during the latter stages of cognitive evolution. This argument, therefore, questions the strong modularity thesis put forward by

Cosmides and Tooby, while it supports ideas from other psychologists who are, like myself (Mithen 1996c), sympathetic to a modularity position but believe that modularity by itself is insufficient to explain how minds develop/evolve and function (e.g. Karmiloff-Smith 1992; Carey and Spelke 1994).

## Mental modularity and the Neanderthal mind

A third reason for archaeologists to engage with the debates about mental modularity concerns our direct interest in reconstructing the past. Consider, for instance, our understanding of the Neanderthals. As evidence about these people has accumulated during the last thirty years, more and more paradoxes and contradictions have emerged which appear unresolvable by our current theoretical approaches. On the one hand detailed studies of their technology showed that it often displayed considerable technical skill, easily equivalent to that of modern humans, while on the other hand developments in absolute dating showed that technical innovations were even scarcer during the Middle Palaeolithic than previously believed – quite different from modern humans. Similarly, while the anatomical evidence for a linguistic capacity accumulated, evidence for language-mediated behavior remained resolutely absent (for reviews of this evidence see Stringer and Gamble 1993; Mellars 1996). As a result some of the debate about the Neanderthal mind has become rather stale and stymied, continuing to rehearse old arguments about language and its relative complexity, or the possibility of acculturation (e.g. Mellars 1991; D'Errico et al. 1998). By turning to new ideas, such as the notion of mental modularity, new theories and new perspectives on the Neanderthal mind can be developed (e.g. Mithen 1996a, 1996b). My own arguments have suggested that those apparent contradictions in past behavior are no such thing but precisely what one should expect from a "domain-specific" human mentality.

Whether my own arguments are right, wrong, or somewhere between the two, is not my immediate concern in this chapter. That is simply to argue that by looking toward ideas about mental modularity, archaeologists can find ways to reinvigorate old debates, find new ways to interpret their data, and possibly find the key concepts required for understanding the past. Precisely the same can be argued for the next issue in cognitive evolution I will consider: sexual selection.

## Sexual selection, mate choice, and cognition

Geoffrey Miller (1998, 1999) has been one of the foremost proponents of the role of sexual selection in human evolution. In essence, sexual selection concerns mate choice: Those individuals who possess characteristics which are attractive to members of the opposite sex will be chosen as reproductive partners; if those characteristics have some genetic basis they will flourish in future generations. Even if they have no genetic basis they are still likely to flourish among species – such as humans (past and present) – that can evaluate the pros and cons of different types of behavior. Sexual selection is the accepted means by which particularly extravagant traits have evolved in the biological world, such as the peacock's tail, the antlers of the extinct giant elk, and various parts of human anatomy which are involved in sexual attraction (Zahavi and Zahavi 1997).

Miller (1998) has made a strong argument that the most extravagant entity of the biological world – the human brain – is also a product of sexual selection. Rather than its having evolved because bigger brains could process more information, Miller claims that the key feature of a bigger brain is its ability to come up with creative and novel behavior. He argues that neophilia, the love of novelty, is the most important feature of the human mind and claims that:

> in modern society, human neophilia is the foundation of the art, music, television, film, publishing, drug, travel, pornography, fashion, and research interests, which account for a substantial proportion of the global economy. Before such entertainment industries amused us, we had to amuse each other on the African savannah, and our neophilia may have demanded ever more creative displays from our mates. This hypothesis can explain the mysterious cultural capacities that are universally and uniquely developed in humans such as language, music, dance, art, humour, intellectual creativity, and innovative sexual play. (Miller 1998: 116).

Miller's proposal is that those individuals within early hominid society who were able to engage in creative and novel behavior were particularly attractive to members of the opposite sex and hence were selected as mates. As a consequence those traits of creative thinking and bigger brains proliferated in future generations. This is an intriguing argument and whether it is right or wrong is again not my immediate concern. That is simply to stress that archaeologists need to pay attention to Miller's theory, to evaluate it with archaeological evidence, and to consider whether it may indeed help us to understand encephalization and the appearance of art and creative behavior. It is perhaps unfortunate that Miller himself did not consider whether the archaeological evidence supports his theory, especially as discussions about Plio-Pleistocene behavior and the origin of art have been so prominent within the recent literature (e.g. Bednarik 1992, 1995; Marshack 1997; Mithen 1996b).

Whether or not Miller's specific arguments are correct, the stress he has laid on mate choice and sexual selection in cognitive and cultural evolution may be of considerable value in developing archaeological theory and interpretation. Camilla Power (1999) has drawn upon these themes when attempting to explain the origin of art, which she believes relates to the appearance of ochre in Middle Stone Age deposits of southern Africa. She has argued that the "forces of sexual selection drove the elaboration of cosmetic body-paint traditions through factors of competition between female ritual coalitions and male mate choice for cosmetically decorated females" (Power 1999: 109). Although such arguments appear to rely excessively upon ethnographic analogy with recent Khosian San practices, there has been a substantial effort by Power, Watts, and Knight to evaluate such ideas by using the archaeology evidence (Knight et al. 1995; Power and Watts 1997; Watts 1999).

## Sexual selection and Acheulian handaxes

Further archaeological problems may be illuminated by a greater concern with sexual selection. One whole suite of these concerns that strange entity, the handaxe. Why do so many handaxes appear to have been overdesigned with an excessive amount of fine flake removal to create levels of symmetry which seem quite unnecessary for their use as butchery instruments? Why were some handaxes made too large for adequate manipulation? Why were so many discarded when in a pristine condition? How are these intriguing features of handaxes related to each other?

Together with Marek Kohn I have suggested that these features of handaxes can be explained by recognizing that these artifacts (or at least some of them) were themselves products of sexual selection (Kohn and Mithen 1999). Following Miller's (1998) strong argument about the role of sexual selection in human evolution, we have argued that mate selection during the Middle Pleistocene was partly based upon the criteria of material culture. The ability to make a fine symmetrical handaxe displayed one's ability at planning, one's state of good health, one's knowledge of resources – all features attractive to members of the opposite sex when selecting mates. In other words, handaxes were means of displaying "good genes," just as is the case for the tails of peacocks, the canines of primates, and the antlers of stags.

The symmetry of handaxes was also significant in this game of mate choice. By the Middle Pleistocene, the evolved state of human perception was such that symmetry was positively valued. As has been established for several species today, including humans, both males and females use the criteria of symmetry in the morphology of members of the opposite sex when selecting mates (e.g. for swallows, Møller 1990; primates, Manning and Chamberlain 1993; humans, Thornhill and Gangstad 1996). This is because there is a strong relationship between the extent of symmetry and the genetic and physical health of the individual (Parsons 1992). In our view, the symmetry of handaxes was a means of exploiting the perceptual biases of the opposite sex (Kohn and Mithen 1999). Hence those individuals who were able to make fine, symmetrical handaxes were preferentially selected as mates, leading to the persistence of this technology within society. According to our argument it was only when the costs of reproduction imposed on females by encephalization became such that they required male provisioning for themselves and their offspring that the criteria for mate selection changed. At that time we see the replacement of an Acheulian technology by one concerned with more efficient big-game hunting, epitomized by the manufacture of levallois points.

We would not want to suggest that the sexual selection argument can resolve all the outstanding problems of handaxes; it is readily evident that any explanation for their form and persistence in the archaeological record will need to invoke many variables, including raw materials, functional activities, and human mobility patterns. Nevertheless, by viewing handaxes from the new perspective of sexual selection and making explicit reference to the cognitive processes involved in mate choice during human evolution, a solution to certain outstanding problems concerning these artifacts may be found. Moreover, by doing so archaeologists will contribute to the broader interdisciplinary debates regarding the significance of sexual selection in molding the modern mind and modern world.


## The extended mind


One of the key issues in the philosophy of mind is the mind/body problem. Put in stark terms, one can simply ask whether the mind is reducible to the brain and ultimately to the firing of neurones and the chemistry of neurotransmitters. Some would argue that such reductionism is fatal to gaining any profound understanding of human mentality. With the advent of brain scanning, and the remarkable pictures of brain activity it generates, much of the recent literature has slipped into the assumption that understanding how the brain works will indeed explain the modern mind (e.g. Carter 1998). But in some circles the notion that the mind is dependent upon much more than brain matter has recently gained considerable ground and generated ideas and debates with which archaeologists should engage.

This is particularly evident in the work of the philosopher Andy Clark (1996). He argues that our brains are not so different from the "fragmented, special-purpose, action-oriented organs of other animals and autonomous robots" (1996: 180) – in other words, the highly modular type of organs that Cosmides and Tooby would favor, as described above. The reason why humans are so much more intelligent, however, is that we have an ability to dissipate reasoning: "to diffuse achieved knowledge and practical wisdom through complex social structures, and to reduce the loads on individual brains in complex webs of linguistic, social, political, and institutional constraints" (Clark 1996: 180). As an archaeologist I would be quick to add material culture as one more medium by which the mind has been extended into the world outside of brain and body. Hence, for Clark, that entity we call mind is constituted by the brain plus these "chunks of external scaffolding" (1996: 180). This coupling of the human organism with an external entity has been termed by Clark and Chalmers (1998) as "active externalism."

The notion of the extended mind also has a prominent place in social anthropology, where it seems to have developed quite independently from philosophy (at least I can find no citation of each other's work). Gell (1998: 222), for instance, has argued that we should "consider 'persons' not as bounded biological organisms, but use this label to apply to all the objects and/or events in the milieu from which agency or personhood can be abducted."

Of the three issues I have covered in this chapter, this notion of the extended mind has, I believe, the greatest potential for aiding our understanding of both the archaeological record and cognitive evolution. At a very coarse level it seems to offer a means to understand how behavior and thought can have changed so radically long after modern brain dimensions, and most probably brain organization, had been reached more than 200,000 years ago. Although the evolution of the brain may have come to an end, that of the mind has continued – and is continuing – as this is partly constituted by the material culture, the social, economic, and political institutions which we create and which remain in flux. In this regard, therefore, we should not see major cultural developments such as the appearance of ice age cave paintings, the first domesticated plants, or the emergence of the internet, simply as products of evolving minds – these objects, institutions, and activities are as much the causes, and indeed the very substances, of evolving, extended minds.

In this regard material culture plays a similar role to that of language in structuring and creating thought (Mithen 1998a). Dennett (1997) has described words as tools for thought, while Clark (1996, 1998) has explained how public language allows conceptual spaces to be created and explored that are no longer part of a single mind/brain. Material culture is likely to be far more potent than utterances at doing this because unlike those utterances, artifacts endure in space and time. In this regard, therefore, cognitive evolution must be intimately entwined with the evolution of material culture.

There has been some adoption of the idea of active externalism within cognitive archaeology. The significance of this was first explained by Donald (1991), who characterized some of the art objects of the Upper Palaeolithic as externalized memory. This is more profound than simply describing them as aide-memoires, a notion that had been present for many years. Donald explained that we should consider these objects literally as external storage devices, a notion that has since been further explored within the volume edited by Renfrew and Scarre (1998). Unfortunately neither Donald's work, nor much of that in Renfrew and Scarre, has been grounded as thoroughly as one would wish in the philosophy of active externalism – but the potential for developments in this regard has clearly been established.

### The extended mind and religious thought

My own interest in the extended mind has concerned the evolution, persistence, and transmission of religious ideas and the art of the Upper Palaeolithic (Mithen 1997, 1998c). The pervasiveness and peculiarity of religious ideas within human societies offer immense challenges to archaeologists of all persuasions. We cannot fail to recognize that any adequate understanding of past societies must encompass reference to their religious ideologies. Equally we must accept the immense difficulties, which perhaps cannot be overcome, of reconstructing those ideologies. The problems posed by the study of prehistoric religion are particularly pressing to those archaeologists, like myself, who favor viewing the human mind from an evolutionary perspective, as (unlike abilities at rational decision-making, mate selection, or tool manufacture) any evolutionary rationale for believing in ghosts, Gods, and life after death – let alone devoting time and energy to the worship of these – is quite lacking.

This, however, actually holds the key to understanding the significance of the material culture items which play a pervasive, probably universal, role in religious ideologies. To explain this we must briefly return to the notion of mental modularity. A good case can be made that within the human mind there are modules/cognitive domains/intelligences which relate to understanding other humans, other species, material objects, and indeed the majority of "real" entities in the world (Mithen 1996c). These would have been put in place by natural selection and provide us with an intuitive knowledge of the world that develops within our minds rather than requires learning. Hence when we hear about some aspect of a social relationship (Joe is Mary's partner, but Mary has started sleeping with Pete who is also Joe's best friend) we can easily, and correctly, imagine many other aspects of those relationships (e.g. how Pete might behave toward Joe). Knowledge about social relationships has a natural home within the mind, where it becomes naturally embellished with our intuitive knowledge of human social behavior (Boyer 1994). And because of this, such ideas and stories are easily transmitted from person to person because we all share the same base of intuitive knowledge, which acts as a mental anchor for those ideas.

Religious ideas have no natural home in the mind. There is no evidence that they came into existence until very late in human evolution and I have previously argued that they are a product of cognitive fluidity (Mithen 1996c, 1997). Indeed I think that they are what S. J. Gould has referred to as an evolutionary spandrel – they have no evolutionary value and come "for free" as a by-product of other cognitive adaptations. But once present they provide an excellent medium for individuals to exploit when securing their own power base within a society. The problem with religious ideas, such as those about supernatural beings, is not only with thinking them oneself, but also with transmitting them to another individual. Try, for instance, having the Christian concept of the Holy Trinity, or the Aboriginal concept of an Ancestral Being explained to you, or if you understand them, try explaining them to somebody else. The problem is that we lack any evolved mental anchors for those entities that have no actual existence in the world – entities such as invisible beings, those which can change their shape at will, those which perform miracles, those which are neither born nor die.

So how is it that those entities become memorable, transmitted, and indeed shared to a sufficient degree that religious institutions are formed? Boyer (1994) has suggested that they are often hitched onto intuitive knowledge by taking on some human-like qualities – the gods of ancient Greece, for instance, get jealous and squabble. But another means to achieve this has been by externalizing these concepts from the mind and representing them in material culture. Hence, rather than having a shared biologically based anchor in our brains that allows the persistence and transmission of religious ideas, we have adopted material anchors in the form of either abstract or naturalistic depictions. The mind has simply been extended into the material world to extend the range of concepts that it can think about – to explore new conceptual spaces. Leach (1976: 173) had argued that we convert religious ideas into material objects to give them relative permanence so that they can be subjected to operations which are beyond the capacity of the mind. He ought to have said: which are beyond the capacity of our brains, as those objects are part of the very substance of our minds.

This extension of the mind, the coupling with material objects, is essential not only for thought about supernatural beings, but for thought about all concepts that are counterintuitive – in other words, those concepts that the brain has not been designed to think about by natural selection. One whole suite of these is found in science – the study of sub-atomic particles, the origins of the universe, and the nature of consciousness is dependent upon externalizing ideas into material culture, whether that is formal mathematical notion, jottings, or physical depictions. Perhaps the most telling example is that of Watson and Crick using their 3D models to unravel the structure of DNA. Such models were like the cave paintings of half-human/half-animal beings on the walls of ice age caves – not a mere supplement to the brain of one individual but an integral part of an extended mind.

## Further issues of cognitive evolution

In this chapter I have so far considered just three issues regarding cognitive evolution – issues which have a direct bearing upon our archaeological studies and with which archaeologists should become further engaged. There are, however, numerous other issues of this nature, some of which I will now briefly consider to further highlight how there is both a need and an opportunity for more archaeological theory about cognitive evolution.

## The evolution of language

This is perhaps the aspect of cognitive evolution which is best known to archaeologists due to the attention it has recently received (e.g. Davidson 1991; Mellars 1991; Schepartz 1993; Bickerton 1995; Dunbar 1996; Noble and Davidson 1996; Hurford et al. 1998), a substantial amount of which has come from archaeologists and anthropologists. It is noticeable, however, that the major theories about the evolution of language, such as the "gossip" theory of Dunbar (1996), and the non-syntactical proto-language theory of Bickerton (1995), have made scant reference to archaeological evidence for past behavior and thought. To my mind the major dilemma that we face is that referred to above: While the anatomical evidence for an early (i.e. pre-250,000 BP) evolution of spoken language has become substantial, there continues to be an absence of any unambiguous evidence for language-mediated behavior in the pre-Upper Palaeolithic archaeological record. My own attempt at resolving this has been to suggest that right up until the Upper Palaeolithic language remained a social language alone, having no impact on the material culture of the archaeological record (Mithen 1996c). But this is not wholly convincing (to be generous) and some serious archaeological theory about the nature of proto-language must be a priority for those concerned with cognitive evolution.

## The evolution of a theory of mind

The foundation for complex social interaction is the ability to "read" other people's minds – to appreciate that they may have knowledge, ideas, and feelings quite different from one's own. This is frequently referred to as having a "theory of mind," although there are several different theories for what a theory of mind actually is (Carruthers and Smith 1996). There is some debate as to whether chimpanzees, our closest living relatives, have a theory of mind (Povinelli 1996) – their relatively complex social interactions may simply arise from their being extremely clever "behaviorists" rather than mind-readers (Whiten 1996b). Even if chimpanzees do have some form of a theory of mind, there can be little doubt that this is substantially less complex than that of modern humans. Consequently the latter must have evolved sometime after 6 million years ago, the time when we shared a common ancestor with the chimpanzee. As the theory of mind is one of our most important cognitive assets, understanding its evolutionary origins is a key undertaking for scientists from several disciplines, and archaeologists must play a role in this task. It would seem likely that the evolution of a theory of mind is related to that of language (Smith 1996), and most probably related to the substantial encephalization that occurred after 600,000 years ago (Mithen 2000). Yet this begs the question about those hominid species and societies which dispersed from Africa soon after 2 million years ago and made handaxes. Could these handaxes have been constructed by species without a sophisticated theory of mind? Archaeologists need to pay substantial attention to this issue.

## The evolution of life history and its social and cognitive implications

There have been substantial developments in our understanding of the evolution of human life history which have been used to address the nature of early human society (e.g. Key and Aiello 1999; Key 2000). The key issues are why humans – in contrast to other primates – have long post-menopausal lifespans and extended childhoods, with the latter involving fetal rates of brain growth for a year after birth and a substantial adolescent growth spurt. These life-history characteristics are fundamentally related to human anatomy, partly as a means to enable humans to have both large brains and a bipedal gait – the latter requiring a narrow pelvis and hence constraining the size of the brain at birth. Most attention has been placed on the life-history consequences of having a large brain, but Key (2000) argues that the evolution of large female body size at the Austalopithecine/Homo transition is at least as significant in the evolution of a distinctively modern human life history.

While there has been substantial discussion about the social consequences of these anatomical and life-history characteristics, largely focusing on the aspect of provisioning and support for pregnant and nursing females, there has been limited consideration of their cognitive implications. These must be substantial. Just as with newborn infants today, the major period of neural networking occurs in the first few years after birth and is heavily influenced by the social and cultural context of that infant (Changeux 1997). Bogin (1997) has argued that the key feature of childhood is the shift in the care of offspring away from the mother alone to other group members, and there are strong arguments that older females would have played a substantial role in this (Hawkes et al.'s 1997 "Grandmothering hypothesis"). Hence this shift would have substantially changed the patterns of cultural transmission within early human society and the trajectory of cognitive development within the child. As Key (2000) suggests, the emergence of childhood at the Australopithecine/Homo transition seems to have been a necessary precondition for the evolution of modern human cognition.

Issues about childhood and cognitive development become particularly pertinent when we consider the Neanderthals. If the demographic patterns proposed by Trinkaus (1995) are correct, then Neanderthal children would have been developing in contexts in which people over 35 years of age would have been extremely rare and hence male provisioning and care of offspring may have become substantially more important. Again, this would influence the paths along which cultural information was transmitted and the cultural context of the child at critical times of neural networking. Moreover, Neanderthal children may simply have needed to become nutritionally independent much earlier than their anatomically modern human counterparts. At present archaeologists have paid limited attention to these issues of childhood and cognitive development in premodern human society. They seem to be areas very much in need of further attention and ripe for the construction of archaeological theory and for integrated studies with anthropology and developmental psychology.

### Sex differences in cognition

The claim that cognitive differences between the sexes have an evolutionary basis – and are therefore biologically based – has been largely ignored by archaeologists. This is surprising in light of the development of gender archaeology. There is substantial experimental and observational evidence to support this claim, especially in the area of visual-spatial skills (Silverman and Eals 1992; Falk 1993) and mathematics (Geary 1996). As Gilchrist (1999) has argued, feminist archaeologists must engage their studies with those of cognition and move beyond the knee-jerk rejection of any biologically based claim regarding sex/gender differences in cognition. Moreover, the explanations being offered by evolutionary psychologists for claimed sex differences in cognition invoke models of Pleistocene hunter-gatherer lifestyles which few archaeologists would support today (e.g. the Isaac home base/food-sharing model for the Plio-Pleistocene). Here therefore, is an area of study which requires an archaeological input, and one with which archaeologists should engage for the further development of gender archaeology.

## Social learning and cultural transmission

The patterns and products of cultural change in human society depend upon the nature of social learning. That itself is dependent upon various attributes of the human mind, and an understanding of the evolved cognitive basis of social learning is a prerequisite for understanding cultural change – whether we are dealing with early prehistory or the modern day. There are several different approaches to this topic currently being discussed by various types of cognitive scientists, all of which make some reference to the archaeological record. Each of these approaches has attracted the interest of one or more archaeologist (e.g. Lake 1998; Mithen 1994; Shennan 1996), but the absence of substantial informed archaeological knowledge within these discussions is a point of weakness.

As an example one can consider the arguments put forward by Boyd and Richerson (1996) to explain why within animals in general culture is common but cultural evolution is rare. By that they mean that whereas many animal groups display particular socially learnt patterns of behavior, epitomized by the various tool-using traditions of chimpanzees, only among humans does one see a cumulative cultural change through time. They explain this by drawing on Tomasello et al.'s (1993) claim that chimpanzees (and by implication all non-human animals) lack the ability for observation learning, or imitation. Hence once the ability to imitate has evolved, culture begins to change, and accumulate through time. As I have argued (Mithen 1999), this cannot be correct: the Acheulean assemblages of the Middle Pleistocene clearly demonstrate abilities at imitation by the strong similarities in many handaxes, but there is no evidence for cultural accumulation through time of the type that Boyd and Richerson would expect once imitation is present.

This particular issue about imitation and culture change is just one aspect of a long debate about different types of social learning, the definition and recognition of imitation, and in what ways monkey, ape, and human social learning are different from each other (e.g. Visalberghi and Fragaszy 1990; Whiten and Ham 1992; Whiten 1996a; Parker 1996). As I have tried to show, these debates are of considerable significance for archaeologists, possibly allowing new approaches to old problems (e.g. that of the Clactonian and Acheulian, Mithen 1994). There is a need for archaeology to contribute to such debates. Psychologists are inevitably prone to jump from the chimpanzee mind (assumed to be the same as that of the 6 million-year-old common ancestor) to that of modern humans, assuming that just one vital ingredient needs adding (e.g. language, theory of mind). The archaeological record shows that cognitive evolution has not been a single track affair: there are several other types of human-like minds that must be accounted for and explained. By just focusing on those species alive on the planet today, we get a very narrow view of the diversity of human-like and ape-like minds that have evolved during the last 6 million years.

A further area of research with which archaeologists must engage is that which has invoked "memes" as units of cultural transmission (Blackmore 1999). Personally I find the concept of the meme to be rather vacuous, reliant on an ill-founded analogy with genes and units of biological transmission. But this notion has gained serious attention, principally from distinguished biologists and philosophers (e.g. Dawkins 1976, 1999; Dennett 1995), and archaeologists need to engage in the evaluation of this concept, as indeed has been partly undertaken by Lake (1998). While the notion of memes may have limited value for understanding culture in modern humans, it may be useful for understanding some of the seemingly non-functional and spatially restricted aspects of early technology, such as the twisted ovates described by White (1998).

### Human creativity

A further aspect of cognitive evolution that can both contribute toward, and benefit from, more archaeological theory is that about human creativity. As I argued within a recently edited volume about creativity in human evolution and prehistory (Mithen 1998b), this topic has been discussed by cognitive scientists with limited reference to the evidence from the archaeological record. Such reference is required to gain a more informed understanding of how and when a capacity for creative thought evolved, and indeed of quite what we mean by creative thought.

## Conclusion

While I have structured this chapter around several different aspects of cognitive evolution, all of these aspects are intimately related to each other. The evolution of language, of theory of mind, and of life history can no more be understood in isolation from each other than can the nature of modularity, sex differences in cognition, and sexually selected attributes – mental or material. Yet some division of this type is necessary to get to grips with the problems we face: trying to study the evolution of cognition as a whole is too overwhelming a task.

My aim in this chapter has been to demonstrate that archaeologists can and must play a role in the discussions and debates about cognitive evolution. We must do this for two reasons. First, because an explicit reference to the mentality of past humans is an essential element of archaeological interpretation and our studies of the past can benefit by drawing more substantially on cognitive science. Second, archaeologists have a unique contribution to make to the interdisciplinary study of cognitive evolution. My impression is that there is a considerable willingness from all branches of cognitive science to draw upon archaeological data and theory at present, and that many of the key issues currently being discussed within the cognitive sciences are particularly pertinent to archaeological concerns.

Archaeological theory about cognitive evolution, and indeed about premodern human societies in general, is a particularly exciting area of growth at present, as reflected in books such as that edited by Steele and Shennan (1996). This is a radical change of affairs from a decade ago when archaeological theory appeared synonymous with later prehistory and Palaeolithic studies were effectively ignored within books aspiring to cater for archaeological theory as a whole (e.g. Shanks and Tilley 1987). Moreover, cognitive evolution should not be of interest to Palaeolithic archaeologists alone. Archaeologists working in all periods need to make explicit reference to how the mind works. As this is partly dependent upon its evolutionary history, those issues I have discussed in this chapter, most notably those about modularity, sexual selection, and the extended mind, should be pervasive in the archaeological theories and interpretations relating to all periods of the human past.

REFERENCES

Baron-Cohen, S., H. Tager Flusberg, and D. Cohen (eds) 2000. *Understanding Other Minds: Perspectives from Autism and Cognitive Neuroscience*. Oxford: Oxford University Press.
Bednarik, R. G. 1992. Palaeoart and archaeological myths. *Cambridge Archeological Journal* 2: 27–57.
Bednarik, R. G. 1995. Concept mediated marking in the Lower Palaeolithic. *Current Anthropology* 36: 605–17.
Bickerton, D. 1995. *Language and Human Behaviour*. London: London University Press.
Blackmore, S. 1999. *The Meme Machine*. Oxford: Oxford University Press.

Bogin, B. 1997. Evolutionary hypotheses for human childhood. *Yearbook of Physical Anthropology* 40: 63–89.

Box, H. and K. Gibson (eds) 1999. *Social Learning in Mammals*. Cambridge: Cambridge University Press.

Boyd, R. and P.J. Richerson. 1996. Why culture is common but cultural evolution is rare. In W.G. Runciman, J.M. Smith, and R.I.M. Dunbar (eds), *Evolution of Social Behaviour Patterns in Primates and Man*, 77–95. Oxford: Oxford University Press.

Boyer, P. 1994. *The Naturalness of Religious Ideas: A Cognitive Theory of Religion*. Berkeley: University of California Press.

Butterworth, B. 1999. *The Mathematical Brain*. London: Macmillan.

Carey, S. and E. Spelke 1994. Domain specific knowledge and conceptual change. In L.A. Hirschfeld and S.A. Gelman (eds), *Mapping the Mind: Domain Specificity in Cognition and Culture*, 169–200. Cambridge: Cambridge University Press.

Carruthers, P. and P.K. Smith 1996. *Theories of Theories of Mind*. Cambridge: Cambridge University Press.

Carter, R. 1998. *Mapping the Mind*. London: Weidenfeld and Nicolson.

Changeux, J.-P. 1997. *Neuronal Man: The Biology of Mind*. Princeton: Princeton University Press.

Clark, A. 1996. *Being There: Putting Brain, Body and World Together Again*. Cambridge, MA: MIT Press.

Clark, A. 1998. Magic words: how language augments human computation. In P. Carruthers and J. Boucher (eds), *Language and Thought: Interdisciplinary Themes*, 162–84. Cambridge: Cambridge University Press.

Clark, A. and D. Chalmers 1998. The extended mind. *Analysis* 58: 7–19.

Cosmides, L. and J. Tooby 1987. From evolution to behaviour: evolutionary psychology as the missing link. In J. Dupré (ed.), *The Latest on the Best: Essays on Evolution and Optimality*, 277–307. Cambridge MA: MIT Press.

Cosmides, L. and J. Tooby 1994. Origins of domain specificity: the evolution of functional organization. In L.A. Hirschfeld and S.A. Gelman (eds), *Mapping the Mind: Domain Specificity in Cognition and Culture*, 85–117. Cambridge: Cambridge University Press.

Davidson, I. 1991. The archaeology of language origins: a review. *Antiquity* 65: 39–48.

Dawkins, R. 1976. *The Selfish Gene*. Oxford: Oxford University Press.

Dawkins, R. 1999. Foreword. In S. Blackmore, *The Meme Machine*, vii–xvii. Oxford: Oxford University Press.

Dennett, D. 1995. *Darwin's Dangerous Idea*. Harmondsworth: Penguin Books.

Dennett, D. 1997. How to do other things with words. In J. Preston (ed.), *Thought and Language*, 219–37. Cambridge: Cambridge University Press.

D'Errico, F., J. Zilhaõ, M. Julien, D. Baffier, and J. Pelegrin 1998. Neanderthal acculturation in western Europe? A critical review of the evidence and its interpretation. *Current Anthropology* 39: 1–45.

Donald, M. 1991. *Origins of the Modern Mind*. Cambridge, MA: Harvard University Press.

Dunbar, R. 1996. *Grooming, Gossip and the Evolution of Language*. London: Faber and Faber.

Falk, D. 1993. Sex differences in visuospatial skills: implications for hominid evolution. In K.R. Gibson and T. Ingold (eds), *Tools, Language and Cognition in Human Behaviour*, 216–29. Oxford: Oxford University Press.

Fodor, J. 1983. *The Modularity of Mind*. Cambridge, MA: MIT Press.

Foley, R. 1996. An evolutionary and chronological framework for human social behaviour. In W.G. Runciman, J.M. Smith, and R.I.M. Dunbar (eds), *Evolution of Social Behaviour Patterns in Primates and Man*, 95–119. Oxford: Oxford University Press.

Gardner, H. 1983. *Frames of Mind: The Fairy of Multiple Intelligences*. New York: Basic Books.

Geary, D.C. 1996. Sexual selection and sex differences in mathematical abilities. *Behavioural and Brain Sciences* 19: 229–84.

Gell, A. 1998. *Art and Agency: An Anthropological Theory*. Oxford: Oxford University Press.

Gilchrist, R. 1999. *Gender and Archaeology: Contesting the Past*. London: Routledge.

Hameroff, S.R., A.W. Kaszniak, and D.S. Chalmers 1999. *Toward a Science of Consciousness III*. Cambridge, MA: MIT Press.

Hawkes, K., J.F. O'Connell, and N.G. Blurton-Jones 1997. Hadza women time allocation, offspring provisioning and the evolution of long post-menopausal lifespans. *Current Anthropology* 38: 551–77.

Humphrey, N. 1998. Cave art, autism, and the evolution of the human mind. *Cambridge Archaeological Journal* 8(2): 165–91.

Hurford, J.R., M. Studdert-Kennedy, and C. Knight (eds) 1998. *Approaches to the Evolution of Language*. Cambridge: Cambridge University Press.

Karmiloff-Smith, A. 1992. *Beyond Modularity: A Developmental Perspective on Cognitive Science*. Cambridge, MA: MIT Press.

Key, C. 2000. The evolution of human life history. *World Archaeology* 31: 329–50.

Key, C. and L. Aiello 1999. The evolution of social organisation. In R. Dunbar, C. Knight, and C. Power (eds), *The Evolution of Culture*, 15–34. Edinburgh: Edinburgh University Press.

Knight, C., C. Power, and I. Watts. 1995. The human symbolic revolution: a Darwinian account. *Cambridge Archaeological Journal* 5(1): 75–114.

Kohn, M. and S. Mithen. 1999. Handaxes: products of sexual selection? *Antiquity* 73: 518–26.

Lake, M. 1998. Digging for memes: the role of material objects in cultural evolution. In C. Renfrew and C. Scarre (eds), *Cognition and Material Culture: The Archaeology of Symbolic Storage*, 77–88. Cambridge: McDonald Institute.

Langer, J. and M. Killen 1998. *Piaget, Evolution, and Development*. London: Lawrence Erlbaum.

Leach, E. 1976. *Culture and Communication*. Cambridge: Cambridge University Press.

Manning, J.T. and A.T. Chamberlain 1993. Fluctuating asymmetry, sexual selection and canine teeth in primates. *Proceedings of the Royal Society of London,* Series B, 251: 83–7.

Marshack, A. 1997. The Berekhat ram figurine. *Antiquity* 71: 327–37.

Mellars, P. 1991. Cognitive changes in the emergence of modern humans. *Cambridge Archaeological Journal* 1(1): 63–76.

Mellars, P. 1996. *The Neanderthal Legacy: An Archaeological Perspective from Western Europe.* Princeton: Princeton University Press.

Mellars, P. and K. Gibson 1996. *Modelling the Early Human Mind.* Cambridge: McDonald Institute.

Miller, G. F. 1998. How mate choice shaped human culture. In C. Crawford and D. L. Krebs (eds), *Handbook of Evolutionary Psychology,* 87–129. Mahwah, NJ: Lawrence Erlbaum.

Miller, G. F. 1999. Sexual selection for cultural displays. In R. Dunbar, C. Knight, and C. Power (eds), *The Evolution of Culture,* 71–92. Edinburgh: Edinburgh University Press.

Mithen, S. J. 1994. Technology and society during the Middle Pleistocene. *Cambridge Archaeological Journal* 4(1): 3–33.

Mithen, S. J. 1996a. Domain specific intelligence and the Neanderthal mind. In P. Mellars and K. Gibson (eds), *Modelling the Early Human Mind,* 666–9. Cambridge: McDonald Institute.

Mithen, S. J. 1996b. On Early Palaeolithic "concept mediated marks", mental modularity and the origins of art. *Current Anthropology* 37: 666–70.

Mithen, S. J. 1996c. *The Prehistory of the Mind.* London: Thames and Hudson.

Mithen, S. J. 1997. Cognitive archaeology, evolutionary psychology and cultural transmission, with particular reference to religious ideas. In C. M. Barton and G. A. Clark (eds), *Rediscovering Darwin: Evolutionary Theory in Archaeological Explanation,* 67–75. Arlington, VA: American Anthropological Association.

Mithen, S. J. 1998a. A creative explosion? Theory of mind, language and the disembodied mind of the Upper Palaeolithic. In S. Mithen (ed.), *Creativity in Human Evolution and Prehistory,* 165–86. London: Routledge.

Mithen, S. J. (ed.) 1998b. *Creativity in Human Evolution and Prehistory.* London: Routledge.

Mithen, S. J. 1998c. The supernatural beings of prehistory and the external storage of religious ideas. In C. Renfrew and C. Scarre (eds), *Cognition and Material Culture: The Archaeology of Symbolic Storage,* 97–107. Cambridge: McDonald Institute.

Mithen, S. J. 1999. Social learning and cultural change: a view from the Stone Age. In H. Box and K. Gibson (eds), *Social Learning in Mammals.* Cambridge: Cambridge University Press.

Mithen, S. J. 2000. Palaeoanthropological perspective on the evolution of a theory of mind. In S. Baron-Cohen, H. Tager Flusberg, and D. Cohen (eds), *Understanding Other Minds: Perspectives from Autism and Cognitive Neuroscience,* 488–502. Oxford: Oxford University Press.

Møller, A. P. 1990. Fluctuating asymmetry in male sexual ornaments may reliably reveal male quality. *Animal Behaviour* 40: 1185–7.

Noble, W. and I. Davidson. 1996. *Human Evolution, Language and Mind: A Psychological and Archaeological Inquiry*. Cambridge: Cambridge University Press.

Parker, S.T. 1996. Apprenticeship in tool-mediated extractive foraging: the origins of imitation, teaching and self-awareness in great apes. In A.E. Russon, K.A. Bard, and S.T. Parker (eds), *Reaching into Thought: The Minds of the Great Apes*, 348–71. Cambridge: Cambridge University Press.

Parsons, P.A. 1992. Fluctuating asymmetry: a biological monitor of environmental and genomic stress. *Heredity* 68: 361–4.

Pinker, S. 1997. *How the Mind Works*. Harmondsworth: Allen Lane/Penguin Press.

Povinelli, D. 1996. Chimpanzee theory of mind? The long road to strong inference. In P. Carruthers and P.K. Smith (eds), *Theories of Theories of Mind*, 293–330. Cambridge: Cambridge University Press.

Power, C. 1999. Beauty magic: the origins of art. In R. Dunbar, C. Knight, and C. Power (eds), *The Evolution of Culture*, 92–112. Edinburgh: Edinburgh University Press.

Power, C. and I. Watts 1997. Female strategies and collective behaviour: the archaeology of earliest *Homo sapiens sapiens*. In J. Steele and S. Shennan (eds), *The Archaeology of Human Ancestry: Power, Sex and Tradition*, 306–31. London: Routledge.

Renfrew, C. and C. Scarre 1998. *Cognition and Material Culture: The Archaeology of Symbolic Storage*. Cambridge: McDonald Institute.

Schepartz, L.A. 1993. Language and modern human origins. *Yearbook of Physical Anthropology* 36: 91–126.

Shanks, M. and C. Tilley 1987. *Reconstructing Archeology*. Cambridge: Cambridge University Press.

Shennan, S. 1996. Cultural transmission and cultural change. In R.W. Preucel and I. Hodder (eds), *Contemporary Archaeology in Theory: A Reader*, 282–96. Oxford: Blackwell.

Silverman, I. and M. Eals 1992. Sex differences in spatial abilities: evolutionary theory and data. In J.H. Barkow, L. Cosmides, and J. Tooby (eds), *The Adapted Mind: Evolutionary Psychology and the Generation of Culture*, 533–49. Oxford: Oxford University Press.

Smith, P.K. 1996. Language and the evolution of mind-reading. In P. Carruthers and P.K. Smith (eds), *Theories of Theories of Mind*, 344–55. Cambridge: Cambridge University Press.

Steele, J. and S. Shennan (eds) 1996. *The Archaeology of Human Ancestry*. London: Routledge.

Stringer, C. and C. Gamble 1993. *In search of the Neanderthals*. London: Thames and Hudson.

Thornhill, R. and S. Gangestad 1996. The evolution of human sexuality. *Trends in Ecology and Evolution* 11: 98–102.

Tomasello, M., A.C. Kruger, and H.H. Ratner 1993. Cultural learning. *Behavioral and Brain Sciences* 16: 495–552.

Tooby, J. and L. Cosmides 1992. The psychological foundations of culture. In

J.H. Barkow, L. Cosmides, and J. Tooby (eds), *The Adapted Mind: Evolutionary Psychology and the Generation of Culture*, 19–137. Oxford: Oxford University Press.

Trinkaus, E. 1995. Neanderthal mortality patterns. *Journal of Archaeological Science* 22: 121–42.

Visalberghi, E. and D.M. Fragaszy 1990. Do monkeys ape? In S.T. Parker and K.R. Gibson (eds), *Language and Intelligence in Monkeys and Apes: Comparative Developmental Perspectives*, 247–73. Cambridge: Cambridge University Press.

Watts, I. 1999. Origin of symbolic culture. In R. Dunbar, C. Knight, and C. Power (eds), *The Evolution of Culture*, 113–47. Edinburgh: Edinburgh University Press.

White, M. 1998. Twisted ovate bifaces in the British Lower Palaeolithic; some observations and implications. In N. Ashton, F. Healey, and P. Pettitt (eds), *Stone Age Archaeology*, 98–105. Oxford : Oxbow Books. Monograph 102.

Whiten, A. 1996a. Imitation, pretense, and mind-reading: secondary representation in comparative primatology and developmental psychology? In A.E. Russon, K.A. Bard, and S.T. Parker (eds), *Reaching into Thought: The Minds of the Great Apes*, 300–25. Cambridge: Cambridge University Press.

Whiten, A. 1996b. When does smart behaviour-reading become mind-reading? In P. Carruthers and P.K. Smith (eds), *Theories of Theories of Mind*, 277–93. Cambridge: Cambridge University Press.

Whiten, A. and R. Ham 1992. On the nature and evolution of imitation in the animal kingdom: reappraisal of a century of research. In P.J.B. Slater, J.S. Rosenblatt, C. Beer, and M. Milinski (eds), *Advances in the Study of Behaviour*, vol. 21, 239–83. New York: Academic Press.

Wilson, M. and M. Daly 1997. Relationship-specific social psychological adaptations. In G.R. Book (ed.), *Characterization of Human Psychological Adaptations*, CIBA Foundations Symposium 208, 253–69. Chichester: John Wiley.

Zahavi, A. and A. Zahavi 1997. *The Handicap Principle*. New York: Oxford University Press.

# 5

# Symbol before Concept
## Material Engagement and the Early Development of Society

## *Colin Renfrew*

### Introduction: the cognitive dimension

Any survey of archaeological theory today must acknowledge the wide range of sources of inspiration which are available to the contemporary theorist in our field. Nearly twenty years ago, when discussions were underway which led to the subsequent formation in the United Kingdom of the Theoretical Archaeology Group, and to the annual TAG conferences which ensued, the situation seemed very different. The initial impact of early processual archaeology, then still termed "New Archaeology," had been felt, and with it came a range of writings in the philosophy of science, but most of the concerns of interpretive archaeology (not yet denominated "postprocessual") had not been clearly formulated, nor the canons of postmodernist thought assimilated.

Reviewing the literature available one may certainly be impressed by its diversity, and at the variety of fields of experience now being subjected to systematic scrutiny and investigation. One of the strengths of recent work, I believe, is the extent to which human perception, experience, and thought, often at the individual level, are being brought into serious consideration. The experience of the individual, whether the prehistoric agent or the modern investigator, is currently the focus of consideration, and this emphasis upon personal experience gives much current writing a somewhat "existential" flavor.

Elsewhere (Renfrew 1994; 1998a) I indicated my dissatisfaction that cognitive issues had been insufficiently addressed by the early, functional–processual phase of processual archaeology. But concern has been expressed by a number of recent commentators that some of the discussions conducted under the banner of "postprocessual" archaeology, now often termed "interpretive" archaeology (Hodder et al. 1995), have lacked a coherent and explicit logical framework which would permit critical analysis or evaluation in the light of further data. Although more recent works in the now well-established interpretive tradition certainly invoke an impressive, at times even eclectic, array of intellectual sources, they do not entirely answer the criticisms which have been levelled (e.g. Renfrew 1989), in which the relativism of some current interpretive approaches was stressed. Often today the individual observer offers an interpretation of the archaeological finds made in a specific context but does so without at the same time seeking to address the inherent problem of making the relevance of these views both clear and acceptable to a different observer who may be undertaking the task of interpreting the same finds from the same context. Objectivity has long since been rejected as an attainable goal, but the task of replacing it with some procedures for reaching a commonly agreed view is rarely undertaken in the present permissive atmosphere of unbridled individualism.

Paradoxically there persists an underlying assumption among "postprocessual" archaeologists that the interpretations offered in relation to one context under study are of some wider interest, and might somehow be relevant to interpretations made in relation to a different context. Such may indeed be the case, and the assumption has indeed been a general one among processual archaeologists. But this assumption, when examined, runs directly counter to the particularistic doctrines of most interpretive archaeologists. Certainly it is often made without any consideration of the framework of inference which would be needed to make this possible, or of the extent to which such a view would explicitly contradict the initial programmatic statements with their emphasis upon specific context and their rejection of the comparative frameworks of the processual approach. There would seem to be contradictions or even confusions here in the general "interpretive" approach.

These considerations – that is to say both an admiration for the broad range of problems now being tackled, and yet a puzzlement at what seems the paucity of the underlying epistemological framework – have led me to stress the importance and value of the strong and sustained tradition of ongoing work (e.g. Marcus and Flannery 1996; Earle 1997; Feinman and Marcus 1998) which can be situated, at least from the epistemological standpoint, broadly within the processual tradition, and yet which does indeed deal explicitly with cognitive and symbolic matters. Its aspiration is to make the underlying reasoning as explicit as possible and it sees no objection in doing so within an inferential framework which would aspire to be coherent when seen from the standpoint of the philosophy of science. This I have referred to as the cognitive–processual approach (Renfrew 1994; Renfrew and Bahn 1996: ch. 10). It is not the purpose here to reiterate those arguments, and still less to relive some of the by now rather wearisome "processual" versus "postprocessual" disputes of the past decade. I would, however, like to underline one particular issue, that of generalization and the explanation of long-term change, and then to argue that archaeology should not forget or overlook the opportunities offered by its ongoing engagement with material things.

## On generalization and long-term change

One of the criticisms frequently leveled at early processual archaeology by critics working within the postprocessual tendency, in the context of the alleged "scientism" of the processualists, was the concern of these for cross-cultural comparisons and often for generalization which inevitably reached across the spatial and temporal boundaries of individual archaeological contexts and specific social groups. By contrast a contextual approach was argued, whereby the specific features of the particular case under study would be elucidated and emphasized, so that the interpretive process could proceed with as rich an information base as possible. No one, I think, has ever questioned the merits of a holistic and contextual approach, and the point is in that sense well taken. This is particularly relevant when the relationship between symbol and referent is under consideration. It is well understood that the relationship between signifier and thing signified is often largely an arbitrary one, and any inference as to meaning based upon material culture must indeed be undertaken with as full a consideration as possible of the cultural context understood in terms of its temporal and spatial position and its immediate antecedents.

But the interpretive discussion here is, on closer examination, generally found to be replete with implied generalizations, which frequently remain hidden. Indeed it would not be an exaggeration to assert that most interpretive analyses in the postprocessual tradition are based upon concealed generalizations (even if limited in their scope) about material culture. In nearly every case some wider significance is claimed for the analysis, going beyond the specific case study under consideration. The reader who has taken seriously the critique of generalization as practiced within the conventions of processual archaeology is inclined to enquire precisely where this wider interest resides. In many cases, as noted above, there is the implied claim (no doubt often an entirely valid one) that the interpretive case study does have a wider relevance beyond its specific context in space and time. I feel strongly that this point should be recognized and analyzed more carefully, for the rhetoric of much interpretive or postprocessual archaeology is often expressive in its hostility to certain kinds of generalization. Yet the significance of most case studies is clearly often felt to reside in their wider applicability and relevance. This point, if it is accepted, hints at a lacuna in many theories of interpretive or postprocessual archaeology as it is widely understood and advocated, which deserves to be investigated.

Of course one of the criticisms often leveled at the generalizing approaches of processual archaeology is that they often thereby are seen to be lacking in humanity and in an adequate respect for the individual human as a significant agent in history. That argument may however embody a confusion of scale. For it is possible to work at the micro level (that of the individual) or at the macro level (that of the society). Although the two are indeed interrelated, they should not be confused. The standpoint of methodological individualism (Bell 1994) is one of the approaches available which facilitates analysis and the transition between the two levels of explanation.

In this chapter I should like to return once again to the concern that one of the legitimate objectives of archaeology and of prehistory is the explanation of long-term change. Such explanation, for events extending over several and sometimes many generations, has clearly to deal with a range of factors, some of which operate beyond the individual and the local. Here as elsewhere considerations of context may indeed be necessary, but they are unlikely to be sufficient to explain a more general phenomenon.

## The social life of things

Fifteen years ago I had the privilege of attending a symposium whose discussions were published under the title *The Social Life of Things* (Appadurai 1986). The volume had a considerable impact, not least in the field of economic anthropology, and was recently followed by a further symposium. It became clear then that the impact of the stock markets of Southeast Asia upon rural production, even in remote areas, was so pervasive that such "non-things" as stock futures and derivatives were now the focus of explanatory attention, and the allure of the object itself and the power of palpable material symbols were no longer at the forefront of study (van Binsbergen and Geschiere forthcoming). The experience did, however, lead me to feel more clearly than before that some of the lessons of the first symposium have not yet been assimilated by archaeologists. With the current emphasis within archaeological theory upon what might be termed *existential* issues, ultimately dealing with descriptive aspects of life within a synchronic time frame and a specific spatial context (as noted above), the potential explanatory role of the changing human engagement with material things has been insufficiently exploited.

In the sections which follow, and drawing upon my paper for the second symposium (Renfrew forthcoming), I should like to indicate areas of archaeological theory which have been widely neglected in recent years. It seems indeed paradoxical that archaeology, which could after all be defined (in its narrowest focus) as the study of ancient things and has indeed sometimes been defined as the science of material culture, should overlook the significance of things. The reason, however, is not far to seek. Archaeologists have in general been so concerned with the fragmentary condition of the archaeological record that their aim has been to understand more fully how that record was formed. One major approach has therefore been taphonomic: the C-transforms and N-transforms of Schiffer (1976) constituting an excellent example. It is to Ian Hodder (1982a: 212; 1982b: 4) that we owe an early indication of the active role of material culture, that it is not merely reflective of the social realities but in part constitutive of them. But with few exceptions (notably Miller 1987 and, in relation to the British Neolithic, Thomas 1991) these insights have not been carried much further, and the potential for *explaining* change through this active role has not yet been exploited. It is the purpose of the present chapter to argue that when this neglected field of archaeological theory and practice is further developed we may gain several new insights into the nature of culture change. The first section relates to the understanding of the so-called "human revolution."

## The sapient paradox

In recent works which discuss the origins of "mind," and the crucial evolutionary developments which led to the emergence of human societies as we know them, it is often asserted that there was one decisive moment (or period) in which the "human revolution" took place (Mellars and Gibson 1996). It is often asserted, rather than demonstrated, that with the emergence of our own species *Homo sapiens sapiens*, perhaps 150,000 years ago in Africa and certainly by 40,000 years ago in Europe, there came about not only physically modern humans, but the formulation of fully developed language as we know it, of more sophisticated material culture, and the emergence also of fully human self-consciousness. It should be stressed, however, that after this momentous conjuncture (if such it was), looking at the question broadly and at a distance, there were few decisive happenings in human existence for another 30,000 years. Hunter-gatherer communities peopled much of the earth – what the biologists term an adaptive radiation. But there were few other profound and long-lasting changes, at any rate when the picture is perceived in very general terms, until the end of the Pleistocene period.

Why was this? Why did subsequent change – the cultural trajectories that in many parts of the world later led to the development of complex societies – come so slowly? The central theme of this chapter is that it was human *engagement* with the material world which turns out to have been the decisive process.

Language may well have been fully developed in all humans by 40,000 years ago. And words are indeed symbols, the most flexible of symbols by which reality can be conceived, represented, and communicated. But language itself does not seem to have made all that much difference. Hunter-gatherer societies, with a few exceptions, seem to have been conservative – adaptive certainly but not often innovative. Words and narratives there may have been, but until humans became more interactively involved with the material substance of the world, until they began to act upon the world in a range of new ways, using a wider range of materials, not very much changed. And it was when some of these materials themselves took on, or were led to take on, symbolic power that the process of engagement became a powerful driving force for social and economic change.

We may discern at least two crucial episodes in this process, prior to the development of writing, which as Merlin Donald has shown (Donald 1991), ultimately came to offer the most flexible and significant form of "external symbolic storage." But he and others have overlooked a series of fundamental developments before the inception of writing became possible (see Renfrew and Zubrow 1994; Renfrew 1998a). In the first episode the development of sedentary society allowed a much more varied relationship with the material world to develop. In the second, the emergence of certain materials as embodying wealth and prestige led to fundamental changes in the nature of human culture and society.

In an earlier essay (Renfrew 1996) I have sought to show how strange it is, on the conventional view of the "human revolution," as indicated above, that the new genotype producing the new phenotype *Homo sapiens sapiens* did not at once produce a whole new range of interesting behavior patterns. What, then, was so novel about this new species? Usually when a new species emerges it develops the new behavior patterns by which we recognize it. Here we may speak of the "praktotype" from the word *praxis*, referring to activity and behavior. In retrospect we may regard this new human animal as a very special one, when we survey its achievements over the forty or so millennia since its appearance in Europe, or the hundred or more since its initial emergence in Africa. But why is it only in the past ten millennia that we see strikingly new behavior patterns – constructions, innovations, inventions – which are changing the world?

My answer is that the true human revolution came only much later, with the emergence of a way of life which permitted a much greater engagement between the human animal and the world in which we live. Human culture become more substantive, more material. We came to use the world in new ways, and become involved with it in new ways. I suggest that the key to this new embodiment, this new materialization, may have been sedentism.

## A *hypostatic view*

Hominids learnt to make tools way back in the time of *Homo habilis*, and this step has rightly been hailed by anthropologists as a crucial step by which a new kind of engagement with the world could be effected. Clearly many other species use the substance of the world for their own purposes. Not just for food, but in many cases for shelter, for example by the elaborate constructions of the termite ants or the bower birds. But by the time of *Homo erectus* the deliberate artifact, the handaxe, has reached a sophistication matched by no other species. Often the raw material had first to be procured from a distance, and the artifact carefully shaped, using techniques which were passed down over the centuries and millennia, no doubt through a process of mimesis. With the emergence of *Homo sapiens sapiens* came a greater range and sophistication of tool-kits, such as are seen in the Upper Palaeolithic blade industries of Europe.

That this was a sophisticated animal may be inferred from the likelihood that well-developed language abilities had emerged before the dispersals of ca. 70,000 years ago. It is documented by the exceptionally sophisticated Franco-Cantabrian cave art which is seen in Europe (but only in Europe) during the late Pleistocene period.

Despite all that, however, hunter-gatherer societies in Palaeolithic times showed only a limited range of behaviors. Indeed if we look at hunter-gatherer societies down to the present day, it is possible to argue much the same point, although in the past 5,000 or 10,000 years some may have developed more elaborate behaviors than were seen in the Pleistocene period. Certainly one can point to impressive village settlements of hunter-gatherer-fisher communities with a complex pattern of behavior (I am thinking notably of the potlatch of the communities of the North American northwest coast). But the most sophisticated of these appear to have been sedentary communities, albeit with a hunter-gatherer-fisher economy.

I would argue that it was the development of a sedentary way of life (which, among other things, is of course dependent upon a steady food supply) that opened the way to a more complex way of life, and that it did so through a process of "substantialization." This is where the old "mind" versus "matter" dichotomy breaks down. The mistake made by commentators who focus exclusively upon the "mind" is that they emphasize the potential for rich symbolic behavior without indicating that the ultimate criterion is the praxis in the material world. This supposed potential only reaches fulfillment when mind and matter come together in a new material behavior. To deal with these issues properly requires what one may term a *hypostatic* approach which transcends the mind/matter dichotomy (even if such terminology recalls medieval theological debates about the essence of the Holy Trinity). My approach in this chapter is that in many cases it is not correct to assume that mind precedes practice, or that concept precedes material symbol. As we shall see, symbols are not always just the reflection or "materialization" (DeMarrais et al. 1996) of pre-existing concepts. The substantive engagement process brings the two forward together.

## Symbol before concept

It is widely agreed that what distinguishes humankind most obviously from other species is the ability to use symbols. Ernst Cassirer (1944: 26) defined man as *animal symbolicum*, and all that we learn supports the validity of that definition. Words, of course, are symbols and the definition embraces speech and language. But there is also non-verbal communication and symbol can precede language, as the dance of the bees (indicating direction and distance) exemplifies.

Here I want to make the point that material culture can have its own active role, as Hodder (1986) has emphasized, and that there are categories of "symbol" which are not adequately described by the formulation:

X represents Y in C (where C is the context)

which is the usual definition of the symbol X, the signifier representing Y as signified. I want to draw attention to a range of cases where the material *thing* which does indeed work as a symbol, that is to say has a symbolic role, is not representing something else but is itself active. We might call it a *constitutive symbol*.

The philosopher John Searle, in *The Construction of Social Reality*, has drawn attention to the key role of what he terms "institutional facts," which are realities by which society is governed (1995: 31ff). As he puts it:

> Some rules regulate antecedently existing activities . . . However some rules do not merely regulate; they also create the very possibility of certain activities. Thus the rules of chess do not regulate an antecedently existing activity . . . Rather the rules of chess create the very possibility of playing chess. The rules are *constitutive* of chess in the sense that playing chess is constituted in part by acting in accord with the rules. (1995: 27)

The institutional facts to which Searle refers and which are the building blocks of society include such social realities as marriage, kingship, property, value, law, and so forth. Most of these are concepts which are formulated in words and which are best expressed by words – that is how Searle sees it, and philosophers operate with words. Searle draws attention to what he terms the self-referentiality of many social concepts, and he takes "money" as a prime example. But the point I wish to stress today is that in some cases – and money is a very good example – the material reality, the material symbol, takes precedence. The concept is meaningless without the actual substance (or at least in the case of money it was for many centuries, until further systems of rules allowed promissory notes to become formalized as paper money, then as equities and bank cheques, and now as electronic transactions). In an early society you could not have money unless you had valuables to serve as money, and the valuables (the material) preceded the concept (money).

Some material symbols, then, are constitutive in their material reality. They are not disembodied verbal concepts, or not initially. They have an indissoluble reality of substance: they are substantive. The symbol (in its real, actual substance) actually precedes the concept. Or, if that is almost claiming too much, they are self-referential. The symbol cannot exist without the substance, and the material reality of the substance precedes the symbolic role which is ascribed to it when it comes to embody such an institutional fact. If this discussion seems rather abstract, a first example is given below, and others will follow.

It is my argument here that this process lies at the nub of the development of human societies. Moreover, in non-literate societies it is material symbols which play a central role by allowing the emergence and development of institutional facts. Some classes of institutional fact may well be a feature of all human societies. Affinal kinship relations – including the institution of marriage or something like it – seem to be a feature of all human societies (and indeed one could argue that enduring pair-bonding among many other species hints at something like it more widely). But I shall argue that other kinds of material symbol are not generally a feature of mobile hunter-gatherer societies. It is not until the emergence of sedentary societies (usually in conjunction with food production) that the process of the human engagement with the material world takes on a new form and permits the development of new modes of interaction with the material world permitting the ascription of (symbolic) meaning to material objects.

This, I will argue, is the solution of the Sapient Paradox – why so little that was truly and radically novel accompanied the emergence of our own species *Homo sapiens sapiens*, despite what we can now recognize as its enormous inherent potential to undergo and initiate radical change.

## The crucial nexus: toward inequality and power

In many societies of the Old World, and possibly of the New World, one may seek to identify a crucial nexus of symbolic concepts for which the above remarks are highly relevant. The nexus is less obvious than another more prominent configuration, the power nexus, which is very widely recognized as central to the existence of non-egalitarian societies in which the exercise of power is of paramount significance. Such is the case in those polities which are generally recognized as state societies. There the exercise of power and the institutionalization of power are generally regarded as defining criteria. The institutions of power generally involve elaborate symbolism which accompanies a wide range of institutional facts, including kingship itself, the various offices of state, and the mutual obligations of ruler and ruled. There is a symbolism associated with military force which allows its effective exercise without the frequent outbreak of open conflict. The role of material symbols in all these areas remains to be analyzed with thoroughness.

Here, however, I would like to stress a different nexus: the interrelationship between at least four crucial concepts, three of which are undoubtedly symbolic and of the kind described above where the material reality has to accompany or precede the concept. The symbol is not simply a projection of an antecedent concept, but in its substantive reality is constitutive of the concept. The configuration is as in the diagram.

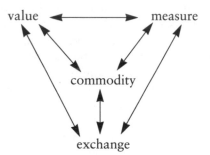

Value and measure are both primary concepts of this kind. Commodity perhaps depends upon the pre-existence of both, and also on the prior reality of exchange (since individual objects can be exchanged without any notion of commodity, but the notion of goods as commodities is difficult to conceive without the possibility of their changing hands).

## Measure

In drawing attention to the special case of the Indus Valley stone cubes, I have elsewhere sought to show (Renfrew 1982) that from direct archaeological observation and inference one may establish that in the Indus Valley civilization there was in operation a procedure equivalent to that which we would describe as *weighing*, with a system of counting by *standard units* of weight. The further inference is that the practice of weighing has a utilitarian purpose which is to establish some sort of equivalence between what is being weighed on the left and what is being weighed on the right, and that (if the enterprise is to be more than vacuous) two different materials are involved. This brings us close to the notion of equivalence between different materials in terms of measured parameters. This allows the notion of quantifying such equivalencies, and does not in itself necessitate exchange. But it is easy to see that the quantification of equivalencies will fit easily with notions of value and with the practice of exchange.

The essential point here, in terms of the earlier discussion, is that "weight" can have no meaning in a disembodied sense. Only material things have weight and the concept has no meaning without experience of these. The substantive reality precedes any notion of quantifying it or of standardizing it by balancing a standard object (the "weight") against other objects.

The same observation applies to any form of measurement. The phenomenon (extension, volume) pre-exists its measure. Any standard of measure, by which X may be compared with Y (which now therefore enters the symbolic domain) is secondary to the substantive realities. Obviously this applies as much to measure of extension as to weight, of time as to volume (whether liquid or dry), of temperature as to field intensity.

## Value

Value is one of the most elusive of concepts. Ultimately value is clearly ascribed. Nothing is "of value" unless it is "valued." As I have pointed out in relation to the earliest known goldworking and the Copper Age site of Varna in Bulgaria, the notion of intrinsic value amounts to an institutionalized fact (Renfrew 1986). It is indeed the case that in many cultures particular materials are singled out and considered to be of value.

We are familiar in our own society with the notion of the "intrinsic" value of gold and diamonds. In prehispanic Mexico turquoise and macaw feathers were highly esteemed – and, as in China, jade (Clark 1986). It seems clear, however, that none of these things could be coveted (and thus valued) without their inherent qualities being noticed and admired. The material becomes the "valuable" only when it is noticed.

This discussion applies to prestige materials and commodities, and does not directly extend to what Marx described as the "use value" of everyday things and commodities. Here a different argument needs to be developed. Clearly an edible material is useful in that it may be eaten. But that it is valuable must depend on other possibilities, and in particular the potential for exchange. The concept of "value" generally implies some measure of "agreed value" as determined between individuals: it is a social concept. Underlying the ascription is the notion of K amount of X being worth L amount of Y. The equivalence again brings us to the notion of X as equivalent to (in some sense may stand for) Y, and we discover again that the potential exchange interaction implies a symbolic relationship, or what stands close to one.

To return to "valuables," their value may be ascribed, but it is inseparable from their substantive and material existence. (This is not the place for a long disquisition on value: Some individual objects acquire their "value" exclusively from their history, for instance a lock of Napoleon's hair. That is a different case and depends upon other symbolic constructs.)

The development of systems of value is an interesting feature in the emergence of most, or perhaps all, complex societies. What will interest us further below is that such systems may rarely be seen among egalitarian societies, including most hunter-gatherer societies.


## Commodity

Commodity is clearly a symbolic concept at one remove from the range of possible specific instances: wheat, maize, olives, wool, linen, perfumed oil, computer chip, refrigerator, television set, or whatever. But in its initial sense it relates to substances (the first six on the above list) rather than to manufactured and assembled products (the last three). It refers to a material whose quantity may be measured, which may have a definite value, and which may be exchanged. Its central position in the nexus is evident.


## Exchange

"Exchange" is, like "value" and "measure" but unlike "commodity," a verb as well as a noun. As we have noted, it implies a transaction between two agents, with some notion of balance or equivalence between what is given and what is received. To set up an exchange therefore creates the relationship "X balances Y," which is very close to the defining relationship of a symbol: "X stands for Y." There is something special about this homology, just as there is in the substitution which operates in the metaphor where "X replaces Y."

It may be that, in dealing with this nexus, we should not characterize the various equivalencies as "symbolic" so much as "catallactic" (i.e.
pertaining to exchange). For the moment we will continue to proceed as
if the latter is subsumed within the former.

These relationships seem to be crucial to the growth and development
of most complex societies. I will illustrate in a moment with the prehistoric European case how the development of metallurgy brought forth
new kinds of valuables which permitted the development of many social
features and roles not previously prominent – the warrior, the craft specialist, the constitution of masculinity as seen in the European Iron Age
(and therefore of femininity also), the seafarer, the trader. In a way that
is often subtle, the notion of value (and sometimes the related notion of
prestige) had a part in most of these developments. In every case we can
see how the products of material culture and their evaluation were of
central significance.

This is a point which I made some years ago in relation to the emergence of complex society in the prehistoric Aegean:

> The interactions among the subsystems of the society take place chiefly at
> the level of the human individual since the subsystems of a culture are
> defined ultimately by the activities of individuals. It is the individual who
> equates wealth with prestige or social rank, for instance, or who forms for
> him- or herself a projection of the world where social roles and religious
> concepts both find a place . . . Underlying these expressions of social status,
> these mechanisms for enhancing reputation and self-satisfaction, is a
> *symbolic equivalence of social and material values*, an equivalence without
> which the multiplier effect could scarcely operate. The well-being which
> comes from the satisfaction of primary animal needs is no longer the chief
> human goal, but rather the satisfaction accruing from prestige, status and
> good reputation. These can sometimes be acquired and expressed though
> material goods. The material world is now the field for a symbolic
> competition. (Renfrew 1972: 496–8)

The emphasis here upon the individual is in some sense valid – the
approach is one of what is often termed "methodological individualism"
(Bell 1994) – but we should emphasize Searle's point that these symbolic
equivalencies are "institutional facts" which are valid for society as a
whole, not just for individuals. The symbols we are speaking of are in
that sense social products as well as cognitive ones.

This then is the central point of this chapter – that the crucial transi-
tions in prehistory were dependent upon the development of a series
of quite sophisticated concepts. Their sophistication is not, however,

instantly obvious today because they have by now become obvious to us, and are embedded within our own thinking. Indeed in a capitalist society, where money is the measure of everything, not just of wealth, to question the intrinsic worth of gold may seem close to a heresy. These distinctions are, however, crucial, and their emergence, and the far-reaching consequences of that emergence, can be seen in the archaeological record of prehistoric Europe and beyond.

## The European trajectory in the Bronze Age

The trajectory of cultural development in the European Bronze Age well exemplifies some of these points. In neolithic Britain the societies of the later neolithic had some degree of central organization capable of creating large monuments such as Stonehenge (Bradley 1993, 1998). But these were "group-oriented" societies, contrasting with the "individualizing" societies of the Early Bronze Age (Renfrew 1974), where the status of the individual came to be expressed in individual burial under a tumulus (burial mound) and with the accompaniment of sometimes rich gravegoods.

Although polished stone axes (sometimes of jade) and bracelets and pendants of shell must be regarded already during the neolithic as prestige goods (shells of the marine mollusc *Spondylus gaederopus* were traded over great distances), it was during the Copper Age of southeast Europe that high-prestige burials are first discerned in the cemetery of Varna (Renfrew 1986). Significantly the materials there include some innovations – the first appearance of gold ornaments on any scale anywhere in the world, and the use of copper as what appears to be a prestige commodity. These are, however, simply the beginnings during the Copper Age.

Two millennia later, at the onset of the Early Bronze Age in northwest Europe we see very clearly the use of a significant new artifact, the bronze dagger. It is here that a new nexus develops between bronze, weapons of war, and a masculine ethos which continued to develop over three millennia, leading first to the chiefly societies of the "Celtic" Iron Age, and subsequently to the chivalry of the medieval knights.

Paul Treherne (1995) has traced the emergence of masculine self-identity and the notion of the warrior's beauty during the Bronze Age. Here once again the metal weapons and the finery of the warrior are constitutive of these qualities, not merely reflective. The "materialization" of which DeMarrais et al. (1996) speak is not the embodiment in material culture of pre-existing concepts; it is a hypostatic union of idea and material. Without the bronze, without the weapons there would have been no Bronze Age warrior idea. I have tried to show (Renfrew 1998b) how the horse and chariot, and later the horse supporting the mounted warrior, formed elements of "cognitive constellations" which caught the imagination of the time, and are seen in models, carvings, and other representations during the Bronze Age (for the chariot) and the Iron Age (for the horseman).

We may see here how the sedentism of the European neolithic permitted the development of group-oriented societies, whose religious and ideological aspirations found expression in and were given shape by monuments. The shift toward individual prestige was accompanied by the nexus of value, commodity, and exchange discussed earlier, and by the specifically European nexus of bronze, weaponry, and masculinity, reinforced later by the chariot and then the cavalry. In these cases the symbolic role of these things is crucial, but the symbol did not reflect so much as constitute the perceived and conceptualized reality.

## Symbols, ritual, and religion

The role of the material symbol in the development of ritual and religion, touched upon earlier, is worth emphasizing. As noted above, Cauvin (1994) has rightly stressed the use of images – plastered skulls and clay effigies – in the religious life of the earliest sedentary societies of the Near East. The belief system we see there, and which was (with some transformations) carried to southeast Europe by the first farmers, may be described as *iconic*: it involved representations of human and/or divine forms. However, we should note that the power of the symbol in the religious field goes far beyond that.

In northwest Europe it is clear from the distribution of special sites, notably the henge monuments of the British Isles, that religious rituals of considerable intensity were carried out at special places. But the evidence is almost entirely aniconic. An almost puritanical reluctance to represent the human form prevails, and the spirals on the Irish neolithic monuments are the nearest one comes to the Mediterranean profusion of neolithic Greece or Malta.

The form of ritual and religious practice seen in Britain was as much shaped by constitutive material symbolism as that in southeast Europe, however. The burial monuments and chapels ("megalithic tombs") and the ritual monuments of neolithic Britain continue to impress, indeed to awe us, today, although we no longer have the narrative, the myth, to interpret them fully. But they well exemplify the points made by DeMarrais et al. (1996), by Earle (1997), and by Mithen (1998) concerning the importance for ritual and its wider appreciation and perpetuation of the material presence. By their works ye shall know them. Comparable remarks may be made about the great houses and kivas of the American Southwest, notably at Chaco Canyon. Again the belief system which took shape there was an aniconic one, but one whose compelling power was constituted as well as reflected by these great and indeed awe-inspiring structures. Such remarks are obviously pertinent also for the great religious centers of Mesoamerica. These are all testimony to the active and constituent role of material culture in the development of human society.

## Conclusion

The central thesis here, sketched out only in outline, attempts to grapple with the dilemma which faces much of today's archaeological theory: that it fails to give much insight into the processes of culture change, or to explain why these took place when and where they did. I argue that the "human revolution," that is to say the emergence of our own species, was not in itself followed very rapidly by decisive changes in the archaeological record. Many of these came only with the development of sedentism, which became widespread only in the Holocene period. In particular the new productive capacities made possible the production, on a deliberate basis, of commodities for exchange. New concepts of value developed and it was indeed these concepts of value which made possible the development of other aspects of human society, including the development of social hierarchies, and the sustained exercise of power.

They made possible also, or at least much easier and richer, the expression of other symbolic aspects of human existence, including more generalized concepts of gender and status. Some of these are indeed found in hunter-gatherer communities today, particularly in sedentary ones, but it was in the developed agricultural societies in the Old World and in the sedentary societies of the New World that they found more complete expression. Prehistoric archaeology has yet to exploit the insights offered by the study of the social lives of things, and by a fuller examination of the process of engagement by which human individuals and societies involve themselves more fully with the material world in constructing their own social realities.

REFERENCES

Appadurai, A. (ed.) 1986. *The Social Life of Things*. Cambridge: Cambridge University Press.
Bell, J. A. 1994. *Reconstructing Prehistory: Scientific Method in Archaeology*. Philadelphia, PA: Temple University Press.
Bradley, R. 1993. *Altering the Earth*. Edinburgh: Society of Antiquaries of Scotland.
Bradley, R. 1998. *The Significance of Monuments*. London: Routledge.
Cassirer, E. 1994. *An Essay of Man*. New Haven: Yale University Press.
Cauvin, J. 1994. *Naissance des divinités, naissance de l'agriculture*. Paris: CNRS.
Clark, J. G. D. 1986. *Symbols of Excellence: Precious Materials as Expressions of Status*. Cambridge: Cambridge University Press.
DeMarrais, E., L. J. Castillo, and T. Earle 1996. Ideology, materialization and power ideologies. *Current Anthropology* 37: 15–31.
Donald, M. 1991. *Origins of the Modern Mind: Three Stages in the Evolution of Culture and Cognition*. Cambridge, MA: Harvard University Press.
Earle, T. 1997. *How Chiefs Came to Power*. Stanford, CA: Stanford University Press.
Feinman, G. M. and J. Marcus (eds) 1998. *Archaic States*. Santa Fe: School of American Research.
Hodder, I. 1982a. *The Present Past*. London: Batsford.
Hodder, I. 1982b. Theoretical archaeology: a reactionary view. In I. Hodder (ed.), *Symbolic and Structural Archaeology*, 1–15. Cambridge: Cambridge University Press.
Hodder, I. 1986. *Reading the Past*. Cambridge: Cambridge University Press.
Hodder, I., M. Shanks, M. Alexandri, V. Buchli, J. Carman, J. Last, and G. Lucas 1995. *Interpreting Archaeology*. London: Routledge.
Marcus, J. and K. V. Flannery 1996. *Zapotec Civilisation: How Society Evolved in Mexico's Oaxaca Valley*. London: Thames and Hudson.
Mellars, P. A. and K. Gibson (eds) 1996. *Modelling the Early Human Mind*. Cambridge: McDonald Institute for Archaeological Research.
Miller, D. 1987. *Material Culture and Mass Consumption*. Oxford: Blackwell.
Mithen, S. 1998. The supernatural beings of prehistory and the external storage of religious ideas. In C. Renfrew and C. Scarre (eds), *Cognition and Material Culture: The Archaeology of Symbolic Storage*, 97–106. Cambridge: Cambridge University Press.
Renfrew, C. 1972. *The Emergence of Civilisation: The Cyclades and the Aegean in the Third Millennium BC*. London: Methuen.
Renfrew, C. 1974. Beyond a subsistence economy: the evolution of social organisation in prehistoric Europe. In C. B. Moore (ed.), *Reconstructing Complex Societies: An Archaeological Colloquium*, 69–95. Cambridge, MA: Supplement to the Bulletin of the American Schools of Oriental Research 20.
Renfrew, C. 1982. *Towards an Archaeology of Mind* (Inaugural Lecture). Cambridge: Cambridge University Press.

Renfrew, C. 1986. Varna and the emergence of wealth in prehistoric Europe. In A. Appadurai (ed.), *The Social Life of Things*, 141–68. Cambridge: Cambridge University Press.

Renfrew, C. 1989. Comments on "Archaeology into the 1990s." *Norwegian Archaeological Review* 22: 33–41.

Renfrew, C. 1994. Towards a cognitive archaeology. In C. Renfrew and E. B. W. Zubrow (eds), *The Ancient Mind: Elements of Cognitive Archaeology*, 3–12. Cambridge: Cambridge University Press.

Renfrew, C. 1996. The sapient behaviour paradox: how to test for potential? In P. A. Mellars and K. Gibson (eds), *Modelling the Early Human Mind*, 11–14. Cambridge: McDonald Institute for Archaeological Research.

Renfrew, C. 1998a. Mind and matter: cognitive archaeology and external symbolic storage. In C. Renfrew and C. Scarre (eds), *Cognition and Material Culture: The Archaeology of Symbolic Storage*, 1–6. Cambridge: Cambridge University Press.

Renfrew, C. 1998b. All the King's horses: assessing cognitive maps in later prehistoric Europe. In S. Mithen (ed.), *Creativity in Human Evolution and Prehistory*, 260–84. London: Routledge.

Renfrew, C. forthcoming. Archaeology and commodification: the role of things in societal transformation. In W. van Binsbergen and P. Geschiere (eds), *Commodification and Identity: Social Life of Things Revisited*.

Renfrew, C. and P. Bahn 1996. *Archaeology: Theories, Methods and Practice*, 2nd edn. London: Thames and Hudson.

Renfrew, C. and E. B. W. Zubrow (eds) 1994. *The Ancient Mind: Elements of Cognitive Archaeology*. Cambridge: Cambridge University Press.

Schiffer, M. 1976. *Behavioral Archaeology*. New York: Academic Press.

Searle, J. R. 1995. *The Construction of Social Reality*. Harmondsworth: Allen Lane/Penguin Press.

Thomas, J. 1991. *Rethinking the Neolithic*. Cambridge: Cambridge University Press.

Treherne, P. 1995. The warrior's beauty: the masculine body and self identity in Bronze Age Europe. *Journal of European Archaeology* 3(1): 105–44.

van Binsbergen, W. and P. Geschiere (eds) forthcoming. *Commodification and Identity: Social Life of Things Revisited*.

# 6

# Agency, the Duality of Structure, and the Problem of the Archaeological Record

## John C. Barrett

It is not enough to know the ensemble of relations as they exist at any given time as a given system. They must be known genetically, in the movement of their formation.

Antonio Gramsci

## Introduction

Agency entered archaeology as a theoretical concern during the 1980s. It did so partly as a critique of processual archaeology, and it also accompanied the growing interest in archaeologies of gender and the attempts to build more self-critical approaches to archaeological practice in general (e.g. Hodder 1982). This is understandable; agents are accepted as "knowledgeable" and this challenges archaeologies which treat people's actions as if they had been fully determined by external conditions. Agency is the means by which things are achieved. It therefore has the power to act and human agency operates knowledgeably and reflexively. Agents are therefore accepted as monitoring their own actions as well as the actions of others in the construction both of their world and of themselves culturally and socially. Agents do not appear upon the historical stage as a given, rather they make themselves within and through their own specific social and cultural conditions. The concern with agency therefore accepts the implications of the "double hermeneutic" in which the social sciences come to recognize that their knowledge of social conditions must also accommodate the subjective knowledges of those who actually made those conditions (Giddens 1982: 7). I should add immediately that this is not a call for "empathy" whereby the social scientist or indeed the archaeologist claims to think in the same way as those whom they study. Rather it is to accept the presence of knowledgeable agents within the operation of the social conditions which are before us.

It is not my intention to pursue the concept of agency through the literature of theoretical sociology. The task is too daunting and it would achieve little with reference to the aims of this volume. Instead I will argue the case that if archaeology is to employ the sociological literature then it must consider more fully that literature's implications for archaeological practice. Theory can operate in two ways: it can facilitate the formulation of ideas about certain conditions, where those ideas then demand some kind of empirical investigation, or it can orientate our ways of looking at and interpreting certain conditions. Either way theory must be embedded into the practices of our discipline and must withstand an evaluation of its adequacy in dealing with particular problems and interpreting particular conditions. Admittedly many theoretical formulations are relatively abstract, but this is simply a feature of the theory-building process. The point is not to be mesmerized by the elegance of the abstraction, but to critically evaluate the possibilities of its application. I therefore intend to do three things. First, review the main ground which sociological theory has mapped with reference to the ways archaeologists have attempted to deal with the issue of "society." Second, reconsider what the object of archaeological study should be. Third, draw out the implications of an object of study which includes the presence of human agency.

## Archaeology and society

Archaeologists approach their understanding of the past through the representational metaphor of an "archaeological record." In other words, archaeological remains are treated as a present-day representation of certain aspects of the past. This perception of the material-as-record has directed archaeological thinking along some very specific lines of inquiry. The material record of the past is regarded as partial; at any one time there were a lot of things going on which either left no surviving record, or left a record which is not open to our interpretation. Consequently, whilst anthropologists have been regarded as entering richly contextualized cultural settings in which to encounter people who continue to inhabit their own material universe, the archaeologist appears only to pick up a few uninhabited fragments of a universe long since discarded. There seems little point in archaeologists trying to become like anthropologists given this "poverty" of the former's record compared to the first-hand and detailed experiences available to the latter. But what the archaeological record lacks in contextual detail it gains in geographical breadth and historical depth. The broad spatial and temporal patterning visible in the material record seems to encourage analysis of the past at a similar scale, which explains the dominant archaeological interest in historical processes which operated over large areas and through long periods of time. This apparent difference in the empirical realities studied by archaeology compared with other branches of the social sciences such as anthropology also seems to question the extent to which archaeology and the social sciences can share common conceptual and theoretical categories.

One "strength" of archaeology is therefore conventionally regarded to be its ability to generalize in terms of large-scale spatial regularities and to trace long-term historical trends and their transformations. These "regularities" and "trends" are represented by the material remains which cumulatively form coherent patterns traceable over time and space, partial and fragmentary though those patterns may be. This cumulative analysis depends for its efficacy upon accepting that material categories, such as artifact or monument types, maintain the same value wherever they are encountered; the material is tediously repetitive, another type A brooch here, another type B pot there, and so the patterns coalesce. But what do these patterns represent? On one level they obviously represent the material regularities of physical survival, taphonomic processes for example resulting in a Palaeolithic period which is considered almost entirely with reference to stone tools and animal bone assemblages instead of utilized wooden objects. But on another level the observable patterns would seem to result from, and thus to represent, regularities in the organization of human behavior, where the regularity of humans' actions became fossilized in the regular form of a material trace. Observing the archaeological record thus, as the record of regularities of behavior which extended widely in space and deeply though time, archaeologists appear to be presented with an unambiguous "object of study," namely the characterization and understanding of normative behavior. But there is another way to understand the archaeological program, and it is this alternative which I intend to explore here.

Before we proceed however, and because these issues are fundamental to what will follow, let me stress that the metaphor of an "archaeological record" immediately poses the question "a record of what?" (Patrik 1985). The answer to this question formulates the archaeological program as a whole. The "what" is usually identified tautologically as "that which created the material record." The implication is that if we understand the formation of the record we will understand the operation of the past. The record is treated as a series of material patterns, each one of which can be characterized as a common corpus of forms and associations. The mechanisms which created each of these patterns are then discussed in general terms, that is, in terms of general processes which recurred over time and space giving rise to the material corpora (types of pots, buildings, burials, and plant remains, for example) and their internal systemic organization (settlement hierarchies, rich burials, and so forth). The material therefore appears to record normative processes, be they "natural" or behavioral. Both types of processes appear to have been geographically extensive and to have been long-lived, and the processes which determined human behavioral regularities are those which archaeology in particular seeks to understand.

In the early part of the twentieth century normative behavior was characterized culturally, a position classically associated with the work of Childe. The distribution of archaeological cultures was deemed to demarcate regions of commonly held conventions learnt by individuals in the process of becoming *social* beings. It was the existence of the social group which in some way determined the behavior of its members. The logic of this reasoning was generally taken for granted and the theoretical issues which it begged remained uninvestigated. Cultural behavior was therefore accepted as being "socially determined." Childe asserted that archaeology studied "the results of human behaviour, but not so much the instinctive behaviour, specific to *Homo sapiens* – that would be a subject for zoology – but the patterns of behaviours learned from, and distinctive of, human societies" (Childe 1956: 7). And elsewhere in that text Childe went on to cite his intellectual debt to Durkheim and to Marx.

It is important to notice the way Childe drew apart instinct as inherent to the species, and behavior as learnt from society. Notice also his reaffirmation that the materials studied were the *results* of human behavior. Society, for Childe, therefore appeared as something essential to humanity and from which its individual members learnt as a way of gaining their social rather than their biological identities. Society therefore appeared to have an existence which not only extended beyond the lifespan of the individual agent but also existed in some way outside that agent upon whom it acted. Presumably society was regarded as something which was entered at birth and in which the conventions of life were learnt. Society was quite simply an object. Childe also presented society as an organization whose operation facilitated the satisfaction of human needs through the steady improvement of its technological capabilities (Childe 1944), but within which a distinction – indeed a contradiction – could be drawn between technological and material activity on the one hand (the realm of science) and the ideological beliefs of a society's members on the other (Childe 1956: 159ff). Ideologies arose, as far as Childe was concerned, from the failure of a society's members to understand their own social world to the same extent to which they understood the material or "natural" world (Childe 1947: 1–5). Childe therefore drew a distinction between a practical mastery of material conditions, such as the physical knapping of a flint, and the ideological gloss or "delusions" which surrounded the execution of such technical competence. He also recognized that the consequences of certain actions need not have corresponded to the motivations and intentions of those who instigated them (Childe 1956: 171). However much we might now question the distinctions Childe imputed between the individual and society or between material conditions and their ideological representations, they did raise profound issues concerning historical processes. They also raised issues concerning the relationship between the historical agent and the archaeological observer, for Childe clearly believed that the observer, albeit from the perspective of their own times, could see more fully the nature of the actually existing conditions of the past than could the participant.

The move against cultural archaeology in the 1960s did not involve questioning the link between specific categories of material and behavioral norms, nor did it result in treating "society" as a particularly problematic category. Indeed it reasserted that societies could be treated as whole "things" but only inasmuch as those things were made up of parts, in the same way that a system is made up of subsystems. What was criticized was the tendency to treat all material variability as representative of behavioral norms *which were socially determined at the level of the social totality itself*. It also attempted to distinguish between style, as a way of doing things, and function, as the thing done, and it gave explanatory primacy to the latter. The material patterns in the record were certainly taken as representative of human behavior and this behavior was certainly regarded as being socially determined, but it was now argued that determination operated at the level of the subsystem. Consequently the material record had to be understood as resulting from human behavior situated in various subsystems. The role of each subsystem, what each actually did, was to contribute to the integration and stability of the entire system within its broader environmental context (Clark 1957: fig. 25; Binford 1962; Clarke 1968: 83ff; Renfrew 1984). Archaeologists could now consider the material record of "economic," "religious," and "social" behavior, and they could then proceed to analyze the interrelationship which had once operated between different subsystems. Ultimately the aim was the characterization of the systemic organization of a particular society. On a higher and a more general level it seemed reasonable to classify different social organizations into particular types and to seek the general logic by which such types functioned, as well as the logic of the historical processes which brought them into being or which transformed them. Throughout this reasoning runs the normally implicit assumption that the social system, situated within a particular environment and containing its own internal mechanisms for change, was the proper unit of analysis.

Processual archaeology therefore regards material categories as related to behavioral categories which were functionally determined by the social systemic contexts within which they operated. In understanding categories of behavior, primacy is given to the consequences of that behavior in functional terms, that is, to what it achieved either materially or in terms of social integration. Of secondary importance is the style of the action, the way it was executed, or the cultural disposition through which it was executed, all of which need be treated as "no more" than local color. The motivations for action are also regarded as beyond recovery but of lesser significance compared with what those actions achieved. There is an echo here of Childe's rationalism which sought to distinguish the ideological component of an action from its technical efficiency. Ethnoarchaeological fieldwork, for example, has not foregrounded the stories people tell about what they are doing but emphasized instead what they "actually" do, as if the storytelling is not part of that actuality whereas the physical consequences of people's actions are.

All this is familiar enough ground. So too is the criticism that all these approaches pay scant regard to the active participation of the inhabitants of the social system. Such inhabitants appear to have been fully determined by their conditions – social and environmental – and to have operated as "dopes" who simply followed the requirements of those conditions. According to cultural archaeology the people who created the culturally ordered worlds of the past did so as bearers of conventions and values learnt from their social contexts, and in the case of processual archaeology the outcomes of their actions were determined by the functional requirements of the social system. We must now find ways to allow human agency to bear its role in the creation of history, a challenge which will change the object of archaeological study.

## The object of study

The archaeological study of human society is deemed to be possible because extinct societies have left a material trace. Societies are treated as if they were real things which can be studied independently of the agencies which inhabited them. It is as if the extinct social totality could be conceived of as a series of rooms which existed whether or not they were inhabited; when the rooms were inhabited, however, their shape determined the behavior of the inhabitants, who in turn left behind a record of that behavior. The record is regarded as secure by us because it is unambiguously material and because it derives directly from the socially determined actions of people. In short, society wrote its identity upon the archaeological record through the actions of its members.

To *study* anything involves us in a process of objectification. The object of study must be defined, however provisionally, and a context for its analysis established. We remake the world through our study of it, where things which are taken to exist independently of us are defined with reference to our analytical program. These things are held in place by our definitions of them, and our knowledge of them is communicated by language and by representation; they do not appear in our discourses in an unmediated form, they appear in the forms by which we speak of them. In this way the world is constituted through our discursive practices, a process which makes an object of study out of our ways of looking at the world, of working on the world, and of talking about the world. This of course does not deny that there exists an external world beyond us, a world which we seek to know and upon which we can work, but our discourse makes the world available in terms of a particular perception. It also structures us as observers for it constructs a relationship between us and those things that we study. Our practices define the categories through which we will experience the world and they bestow values upon those categories as a consequence of our chosen methods of examination. In short, study involves not the revelation of the world as it is, but rather the building of an understanding which is achieved from a particular perspective.

It is hardly a radical proposition to state that the world does not reveal itself, but that we seek it out using traditions of observation and description. The active part played by the ways we frame the object of analysis, grounded as they are partly upon conventional social practices and partly upon our assumptions regarding the characteristics of the object of study, means that all forms of knowledge require self-critical evaluation. That evaluation must expose the ways the object has been formulated and the assumptions and values which are embodied in that objectification. Obviously this self-critical evaluation is yet another form of objectification, where the process of knowledge-building is turned into a thing to be studied. The significant point is that the process of objectification is a discursive practice where practitioners deliberately strike a position outside of, or in opposition to, that which has been selected for study. We will return to this point again. For the moment I want to propose that archaeology has built an object of analysis which is inadequate for our purposes.

## Human agency in history

One of theory's roles is to illuminate, and thus critically evaluate, those processes which are the object of study. Up until the early 1980s archaeological theory was directed towards the recognition of past social organizations through their material record. To reject social organization as the object of study demands a rebuilding of the theoretical program. This program must be realizable in practice, it must drive us towards a reworking of the intellectual and the physical means necessary to build new understandings of the conditions of history.

Current perceptions treat history as structured by the relationship between given conditions, including material conditions, conventions, values, systemic organization, and the subjective understandings, desires, motivations of agency, and its consequences. Stated thus the relationship echoes the classic dualism which has haunted the long struggle to build social theory, namely the relationship between "society" and "individual" or between "structure" and "agency." Archaeological practice seems to have been to accept the dualism as given, assuming that a real opposition existed historically between something called society and the agents whose actions and whose understandings were in some way determined by society. Yet the dualism is questionable; societies have never existed without the people who made the conditions of a given society possible, and these people were themselves social beings. Both "social conditions" and "social agency" are constructed through a relationship in which each has a presence in the other. Social facts must always include the actions of agents, and agents through their actions become categories of social being. Nonetheless, both we as outside observers of other social conditions, and the agents who reproduced their own social conditions, do at times create a distinction between external conditions, including social institutions and material environment, and the agent's subjective experiences of those conditions. Childe, as we have seen, did exactly this, and we must recognize our own role in constructing the analytical distinction between objective conditions and subjective awareness; it is not a given.

Giddens writes that "the basic domain of study of the social sciences, according to the theory of structuration, is neither the experience of the individual actor, nor the existence of any form of societal totality, but social practices ordered across time and space" (Giddens 1984: 2). The emphasis upon "practices ordered across time and space" is an attempt to transcend the analytical dualism separating subjective experience and social totality. Whether Giddens has been successful in reworking the fundamentals of social theory is now an issue of sustained critique (Holmwood and Stewart 1991; Mouzelis 1991, 1995) and my own treatment of Giddens's work is written in the light of my understanding of these critical works. Giddens has not only achieved a substantial output of publications, he has also stimulated a considerable secondary literature (cf. Cohen 1989; Clark, Modgil, and Modgil 1990; Bryant and Jary 1991). I do not intend to produce another summary of the theory of structuration; Mouzelis (1995: 118) has after all managed to do this in less than a page! Instead I want to think through the quote offered above in order to pave the way for a critical review of Giddens's concept of the "duality of structure" which I hope will be useful archaeologically.

The phrase "practices ordered across time and space" contains all the elements we will need to chart our way into the heart of Giddens's project. Practice necessarily requires the presence of an agent, the active participant, although reference to the agent is not necessarily reference to the individual. Certainly individuals act as agents and certainly agency operates through the bodies of individuals, but agency must also include the operation of collectivities extending beyond the individual's body and their own lifespan. A concern with agency therefore neither marks a return to the individual in history, nor a return to methodological individualism. The individual does not now become the basic unit of our analysis, nor are we primarily concerned with individual motivations, nor do we begin analysis with a consideration of an individual action, nor do we see societies as being nothing more than the cumulative product of individual actions.

Agency is always situated in structural conditions which facilitate its actions because agency requires a medium through which to work. Practice is therefore structured by the resources which are its medium and its outcome. These resources extend from material and symbolic resources to traditions of execution and expression. The effectiveness of the mobilization of such resources in practice depends partly upon the degree of control and knowledgeability exercised by the agent, partly upon the power of the agent over those resources, and partly upon the agent's expertise to communicate effectively. The structuring of practice is enabling, it empowers the agent because it facilitates effective action, it makes possible actions which are socially comprehensible and to various degrees are regarded as legitimate by the agent and by others. There is a twofold use of the concept of power in this context. The power to act, where power is defined positively as enabling, is distinguished from the traditional emphasis placed upon the more negative definition of power as domination, that is, power over something. Obviously the distinction is not sharply drawn but hopefully it will be clear that power-as-domination is likely to be linked quite directly with strategies of objectification because the thing to be dominated requires an initial definition as a thing, named and categorized.

Structures should not be regarded as simply constraining or determinate, but rather as a field of possibilities reproduced by the practices which occupy that field. The comparison often made is with language and talk, where language as a structure of communication is reproduced through the practical and inventive acts of talking. Language is both medium and outcome of the practice of talk. Social practices cannot therefore be explained as the product of structural conditions in the traditional terms of cause and effect any more than conversations can be explained as a consequence of grammar. Structural conditions are reproduced and transformed through the various outcomes, both intended and unintended, of the practices which they facilitate. This is what Giddens means by the "duality of structure"; the concept does not re-establish an opposition between structure and agency (the dualism which Giddens rejects), rather the duality is embedded in "the structural properties of a social system [which] are both medium and outcome of the practices they recursively organise" (Giddens 1984: 25). This duality necessarily occupies the passing of time, and given that we are concerned with embodied practices, it also occupies space.

The practices of agency are therefore structured inasmuch as agency vitalizes those structures, carrying them forward and transforming them through time and over space. The recursive relationship between structure and agency is crafted from the agents' abilities to monitor the conditions under which they act, a monitoring which is knowledgeable as to how to proceed, drawing as it does upon experience and upon pre-expectations to inform that agent about the conditions it confronts.

Significantly we must recognize that the range of such knowledge encompasses both the practical knowledge of knowing "how to go on" and the discursive knowledges which are brought to mind, objectified, and spoken about. This is to recognize both an ability to live in the world "as it is," recognizing its order to be so unremarkable that it "goes without saying" (cf. Bloch 1992), and the ability to stand apart from the world and examine it "objectively." The former needs emphasis – it is the embodied ability to inhabit the world, represented by the agents' security in their movement into the world, finding through their own embodied experiences a sense of place and of being. In this expression of the duality of structure the world remakes the body as the body works to claim a time and a place for itself (a "being-in-the-world"). The world is thus present in the sensuality of the body, and is transformed by the presence of the body's awareness of itself, its desires, and its actions.

The need to grasp the practical logic of such non-discursive knowledge and the need to distinguish it, if not actually rescue it, from our traditional academic obsessions with discursive knowledges is one issue which lies at the heart of the work of Pierre Bourdieu (1977, 1990). His task is hardly an easy one, for working in the tradition of an objective academic discourse Bourdieu seeks to evoke those practices which would never seek discursive expression. The fact that they are so expressed is a product of their appropriation by academic practice, which turns the embodied practices of others into the object of analysis. Bourdieu therefore seeks to express the logic of non-linguistic practice through language, demonstrating that by objectifying the practical discursively the anthropologist gains insights unavailable to the practitioner whilst simultaneously risking the loss of the very thing which these insights seek to capture. There is a certain irony in this intellectualized study of the embodied sensualities of others, though whether or not Bourdieu fully recognizes that irony is another matter (Jenkins 1992: 152ff).

One of the ways in which Bourdieu illustrates the nuanced and strategic components of practice, emphasizing that the competence of practice is not a matter of knowing the rules discursively but rather a practical mastery of knowing "how to go on," is with reference to the circulation of gifts. We "know" that gift-giving demands reciprocation, but the skill in executing the reciprocal act is a matter not simply of knowing what to return but of when to return it; it lies in knowing instinctively the "right moment" to avoid either disrespect or dishonor and instead enhance the status of the respondent. Reducing gift circulation to its rule would be to state merely what to return, whereas the practical skill lies in the timing. It is this practical skill which Bourdieu seeks to uncover

(Bourdieu 1990: 98ff). A consideration of gift circulation establishes not only the context of its practical mastery but also its materiality. Mauss's original essay on the gift explored the way human identities were carried in the value of the things circulating between people (Mauss 1970). But human identities are not only objectified in the things exchanged, they are also objectified in the labour of making those things in the first place. The artifact thus objectifies both the labour of craft production in the making of things, and the relationship between gift partners in the making of exchanges. Throughout these processes human agency can recognize itself becoming externalized in the materiality of its existence (Miller 1987). For Bourdieu therefore the effectiveness of the practice lies in its *tempo*. This is a practice which inhabits time, knowing the moment when to act as an expression of its skill, as well as the distances between the respondents; the circulation of gifts helps structure both. Archaeologists wedded to the analysis of a record will have little to contribute to the study of such practice, being able only to note a cumulative record of gift-giving in the final distribution of things deposited. The point however is not to recognize that an action has occurred because we find the record of that action, but to understand something of the performance of that action, the means of its execution, and its historical context.

The full significance of the materiality of practice is perhaps not fully enough recognized in Bourdieu's work. Bourdieu is obviously aware of the ways material culture is drawn strategically into the reproduction of social practices (cf. Bourdieu 1984), but the point which needs stressing is that practices make reference to conditions and values which are absent and that material conditions are part of the media which structure that referential process. We rely upon clues to guide our actions, finding a familiarity and security by recognizing our place in the world, and to this extent material conditions can be regarded as "both medium and outcome of the practices they recursively organise" (Giddens 1984: 25). Material conditions are therefore an active component of the structural properties of the social system. We know, for example, something of the way to enter and inhabit a place because the body is able to read and to act upon the signs of that place.

The practicality of life, lived as the embodiment of knowing how to move into the world, is therefore built with reference to the material components of that world rather than being merely recorded by them. At the same time practice draws upon memory, past experience, expectations and desires, and a communicative engagement with other co-inhabitants. Practices work on the material world, recognizing its malleability and resistances. Agents therefore recognize a coming into being of their own existence in an engagement with the remaking of the world itself. The *tempo* of practice, the feature emphasized by Bourdieu, is never an abstraction but is experienced, for example, by reference to the changing seasons, the movement of the sun, and by the service of food, where one temporal practice might mark out the timing of another. The development of commonly understood and habitual practices (Bourdieu's *habitus*) of what is possible and proper to the occasion, or of what pushes against the acceptable and transgresses convention, is gained by monitoring the reactions of others; practices are worked through with reference to interrelationships in a complex material universe and in the co-presence of others. The historical translation of values or of symbolic and material products from one field of practices to another, in the way for example a tomb may have facilitated death rituals as well as ancestral veneration, was achieved in part by the sharing of a common architectural frame of reference, where the tomb, for example, carried symbolic resources from one field (the corpse involved in burial rites) into the other (the venerated ancestral remains) (Barrett 1988b, 1994). Notice here the directionality involved in this transformation, where the corpse is carried *to* the tomb and the ancestral presence is drawn *from* the tomb. Notice also that the movement from one field to another describes a particular biography of agency in terms of a path through space and time and between places of different value. My point is simply that a theory of practice must understand the materiality of practice in order to explore how that materiality is engaged in the very structuring of practice. Materiality cannot be reduced merely to an archaeological record of the practices which once inhabited it. Consequently the archaeology of practice examines not the material traces of such practices but rather the material facilities which were inhabited. What point is there after all in the archaeological depiction of a building plan if one never understands what is involved in pushing open a door to enter a room?

Through the embodied and materially situated practices of the *habitus*, social practices appear "ordered across time and space." As we have seen, those practices are structured recursively through agency's empowered occupation of certain material and symbolic resources. We must now consider the distinction Giddens draws between *structure*, which is carried forward in situated practices, and the *social system* which describes the consequent patterning of those practices over time and space. The distinction is important. The arrangement of different fields of structured practices gives rise to a certain recognizable systemic patterning. We must be interested in the form of this pattern and in examining the systemic integration between certain fields in a particular historical case. Understanding each particular case of systemic integration must involve a return to an analysis of the structuring of social practices. It is at this point that Mouzelis (1991, 1995) detects Giddens's failure to adequately address mechanisms of systemic integration through the theory of structuration. Structuration theory, so Mouzelis asserts, addresses the local or micro situation concerning the practices of agency, where systemic integration arises as a direct consequence of the intercutting of different fields of social practice. However the theory does not say much about hierarchically ranked systems in which certain agents wield considerable power to act directly upon the lives of others. This issue is of central importance in the understanding of large-scale and hierarchical political systems which emerge in the complex interrelationship between localized practices and the vertical and widespread control achieved by political, economic, and military elites.

In the consideration of practice offered above I have placed emphasis upon actions which were constituted through non-discursively ordered forms of knowledge. Such forms of knowledge were reproduced as the practical recognition of an order in the world; they did not make either that order, or their own traditions of knowledge, objects of inquiry. Indeed their very effectiveness lay in the fact that the practitioner did not stand opposed to the world experienced but worked within it (Taylor 1993). Here practical knowledge was validated not by critical inquiry but by the simple empirical fact that it worked. But there were moments when practitioners stood apart from the world of their actions and looked in upon that world discursively. They objectified certain conditions as a strategy for acting upon them. Such moments of analysis may have arisen when things did not work, at moments of personal or social crisis, or at moments when political authorities sought to extend their authority, to objectify, and thus to act upon, the lives of others. In such situations the dominant social agents were akin to social theorists, formulating a ritual or a political theory of their own world in an attempt to control and analyse that world through their own actions. They ascribed an identity for others, objectifying such communities in the legislative schemes of political control. Hierarchically structured forms of systemic integration may therefore be expected to contain agents who objectify some aspects of the social system upon which they might then act.

Structure always reproduces, through its duality with agency, different qualities of knowledge which operate through different forms of social practice. The rather simple distinction in the modes of knowledge identified above, between forms of knowledge which work empirically as the sensuous affirmation of the given order of the world, and those which objectify the world discursively as something deemed worthy of explicit examination, also demarcates different forms of power. Bloch distinguishes between "psychological" and "anthropological" theories of cognition as a way of capturing this difference (Bloch 1985), and we need to investigate the ways the shift from practical knowledge to the latter schemes of objectification involve different levels of empowerment and operate toward achieving higher levels of systemic integration. In some cases we might see ritual practices as objectifying certain principles of social integration and thus understand more fully the ways ritual practices and ritual elites operated to secure systemic integration at the ideological level (Barrett 1991).

## Archaeological implications

*The social totality should not form the basic domain or unit of archaeological study.* In Childe's argument individuals learn from society. From our perspective, as individuals learn so they make society. Historically, social systems were continually brought into being, gaining their reality out of the systemic integration arising between different fields of social practice, but these were never closed systems, functioning as autonomous totalities (Friedman 1994). We must certainly trace the degrees of systemic integration between different fields of practice, but that is not the same thing as assuming closure within the bounds of a single social totality.

The emphasis upon practice negates attempts to divorce the mechanical, instrumental, or functional aspects of actions from the style of their execution. The cultural particulars which processual archaeology has tended to dismiss as being the superficial components of action now re-emerge as expressive of the ways the embodied presence of the agent found its place in, and acted effectively upon, its own world. Without such knowledge, organized either practically or discursively, effective action would not have been possible. The implications for archaeological practice are profound. For example, Childe distinguished the technical competence which harnessed physical properties from the unnecessary ideological delusions which accompanied the agent's knowledge of them (Childe 1956: 171). History, for Childe, included the steady development of that technical competence which, by its increasingly self-evident logic, stripped away the redundant ideology. However a history of practice cannot be treated in this way, for all the components of knowledge work to sustain and transmit that practice through time, including the style in which the practices were executed and the various symbolic guides which supported the reproduction of that knowledge. The histories of those performances which we characterize as *techno-logical* now become far more complex issues which are historically and culturally specific and which eschew the simple application of uniformitarian principles (Dobres and Hoffman 1999). The making of a copper axe was thus also the making of the agencies, knowledgeable and empowered, which converged upon that process. The subsequent development of the alloying of bronze was achieved as a transformation in that agency's practices and cannot be reduced to the decision merely to change the composition of the alloy.

At this point we would do well to abandon the concept of the archaeological record. Material conditions must be conceived as an element of the structural properties of a social system. Material conditions cannot be taken to have recursively organized the structural properties of the social system while at the same time forming a record of that system's existence. In the latter case, material conditions appear alienated from the very processes of which they were an active component. The material conditions oriented actions but they did so along a number of trajectories traced by the biographies of different groups of agents. Different agents may have arrived at the same place, but they will have seen it from a number of different perspectives which will have informed the ways in which they then acted at that place. Those actions may have left a material trace, but between the material conditions and the material trace stood the knowledgeablity of that agency. It is these inhabited conditions which the archaeologist must investigate. We can no longer follow Childe and treat material culture merely as the results of human behavior. Rather we should regard it as the material condition which necessarily and actively facilitated certain strategies of social practice. The historical significance of the material is therefore not represented by its form (the same categories of material do not have the same meaning wherever they are encountered) but lies in the diverse contexts of the social practices in which it was situated. It is important to note that this lays to rest once and for all the facile distinction often drawn between "environmental" conditions which supposedly acted as a stimulus on a human population, and "material culture" as the "extrasomatic" means of that population's adaptation to the environment. No such distinction may be erected between a pre-existing "natural" state and the subsequent creation of "cultural" conditions, and in its place the more complex and dynamic totality of an inhabited materiality now needs to be addressed.

Material conditions cannot simply be taken to represent the social system, and neither can they be taken as representing the knowledges mobilized by different groups of agents in their actions. Material conditions facilitated practice through the *tempo* and order with which that materiality was encountered and worked. Practices also modified the world according to certain schemes and certain strategies, traces of those material modifications being recoverable archaeologically. Different knowledges were deemed competent because they worked under given conditions. If we treat material residues as representing rather than having facilitated agency, or if we treat the residues of actions as the material manifestation of that agency's knowledge (or indeed of "the ideas in people's heads"), then we lose sight of the situated nature of practice over time and space. As a consequence, archaeological approaches concerned with representation will objectify knowledge in terms of a material pattern and treat that knowledge as if it were simply the expression of a series of rules which demanded application. A great deal of so-called "structural" archaeology can look just like this, where the pattern of material deposits is taken as representing the structural template which people were once supposed to have followed in their activities. There is little difference between Childe's concept of culture and reasoning such as this, and both are open to similar criticisms. Both objectify knowledge into rules, a move which in turn maintains the analytically false separation between "mind" and "body" and between "agent" and "society." Knowledge is made in the embodied practices, the performances, by which agents find a place for themselves in the world. By moving into the world, agents make both themselves and the social conditions of their time through those practices.

The archaeological program now looks very different from that to which we have grown accustomed. The material conditions we study cannot be explained with reference to a historically generative condition known as the social system because social systems were reproduced through people's inhabitation and working of that materiality. Consequently archaeology needs to investigate the historical realities of human agency, a confrontation with the lives of people and communities, rather than simply invest labour in the cataloging of material remains in the hope that the burgeoning catalog will someday represent something that we recognize as "the past." Beyond the accepted procedures of stratigraphic excavation no standard methodology can therefore be offered to realize this new archaeological program, and in its place we must develop ways of thinking and working to guide our historical inquiries.

We need to encounter the ways agencies worked within the structural conditions of their time. The archaeological understanding of any particular historical condition hinges, I would contend, upon the investigation of fundamental issues which operated at different levels of analysis. First, there is the definition of the *material structural conditions* which were variously inhabited, along with the *fields of social practice* which inhabited and reworked the material conditions. Second, there is the question of the *mechanisms of systemic integration* which linked different social fields.

*Material structural conditions* were the conditions of an agency's environment in terms of all its material facilities. Such structural conditions are not the same thing as the corpus of all contemporary physical conditions which archaeologists can assign to some arbitrary period. Such a compilation would be a pointless exercise. Rather, structural conditions were the *inhabited* conditions which acted partly as medium and partly as outcome of that agency's existence. They are therefore the spaces and facilities once inhabited by particular fields of social practice, and their definition is relative to our investigation of those various fields. *Fields* are the regions of time/space which were occupied by social actors engaged in particular tasks which were likely to have involved certain exchanges between those participants and to have effected transformations in the nature and the values of the materials involved (Barrett 1988a). Here we find both the remaking of the world and of categories of agency. These fields are not given to us as investigators, we do not dig them up, rather they are reconstituted through our own inquiries. Thus we might explore the annual cycles involved in the management, processing, storage, and consumption of plant and animal resources, or we might investigate the daily cycle of food preparation and consumption. In addition we might distinguish between fields such as these which were often reproduced through routine practice and those fields which were more formally and discursively organized, such as the ritual paths traced in burial rites.

The analysis proposed here operates by situating certain chosen fields of social practice within the material conditions which those fields once inhabited, thus constituting a "duality of structure." An archaeology of inhabitation differs from recent more phenomenological approaches because it does not begin analysis with an individual's reading or experience of certain material conditions (cf. Tilley 1994). The possibilities of such individual readings can certainly be accommodated in what I am proposing but I am more concerned to locate agency firmly in a field of productive relations than in the isolated presence of an individual's experience. This is not an archaeological program which is concerned with the abstract modeling of "social processes," but it is one whose objective is to confront the historically specific ways social practices may have operated within, and thus have transformed, certain given material conditions.

Our inquiry will now bring us to a more detailed level of analysis concerning the duality of structure which explores the ways particular fields of social practice were regionalized. Regionalization simply refers to the subdivisions of time/space within a particular field, a regionalization effected by the movement and the orientation of particular groups of people and by the physical intervention of paths, barriers, and doorways. Regionalization structured the field, providing sequences of activities or the focal points for action. It may have ranked participants, and in the experiences of those participants it distinguished such areas as "front" and "back" space. These terms are borrowed from Goffman (1969) and do no more than contrast areas open to view with those which were hidden, or the areas before the agent with those behind. All these terms are value-laden; regionalization and orientation, like the exchanges which took place, reproduced values through use. Those who inhabited these regions understood something of those values, their basis, and the means of their transformation. We might select here three themes as being of particular importance in the development of this approach.

First, the material context will have offered a series of *framing devices* and *focal points*. These may simply have enclosed particular spaces or have orientated actions toward a particular place. However, such devices will have done more than provide physical orientation or closure for a regionalized space; their fuller significance may have lain in the references they made to other places and to a wider horizon of values. We might consider here Hodder's analysis of the rooms at Catal Huyuk, the symbolism of which would have referenced a suite of cosmological values within which agents were situated and against which the activities taking place in those rooms were played out (Hodder 1987 and 1990). Such activities need not have made those values explicit, but rather have worked with them as a background of distantly located cosmological security. At other times, however, those references could have been foregrounded in a more explicit exegesis. In either case we must recognize that the range of interpretations and understandings of that cosmology may have been considerable, depending upon the experiences and expectations of the various practitioners, as well as upon various political attempts to close down that diversity toward a single authoritative reading.

Second, the material context will have offered a series of *paths* between regions, facilitating certain lines of access and perhaps foreclosing others. Again this was more than a material facility for movement; paths linked certain places rather than others, and the practice of movement linked those places in certain value-laden sequences allowing the practitioners to rework those values into their own biographies through the movement of their own bodies. Thus practice literally relived certain basic values of place, movement, and orientation in the way, for example, that the leaving of a house may have been a walk toward the rising sun at the opening of the day and a return to the building followed the path of the evening sun. The point of reference here was the body of the practitioner and this point is important. Later prehistoric round houses in Britain, for example, normally operated around the solar axis just described, but this was not a matter of a rule that "the house should face south-east towards the rising sun," rather it was framing a dual axis of easterly–westerly movement separated by time and presumably by the activities of the day (cf. Fitzpatrick 1994; Giles and Parker Pearson 1999). But not everyone may have experienced so clear a mapping of their day against this presumed cosmological norm, or they may have seen it otherwise as they faced out from the house to confront those who returned at the end of the day. This brings us back to the point I made earlier with reference to Bourdieu's discussion of the temporality of prac-tice. Archaeological analysis should not be about the mapping of a static spatial order as if it represented some cosmological or structural rule, but rather about considering the ways agencies found places for them-selves in the contexts of their own world. This point can be illustrated by continuing with my chosen example. At the time when round-house architecture had begun to work within the axis of movement already described, a number of cremation cemeteries in southern Britain devel-oped in which the cremated remains were deposited outside and to the south-east of circular burial mounds. But again it was not that these cemeteries "faced" south-east in a similar manner to the contemporary houses, but that the mourner's movement from funerary pyre to the site of burial was toward the mound and toward the setting of the sun. If a homology existed in the practices which inhabited the house and the cemetery then it was one which described the westwardly path of return, with each path structured by a different architectural frame and a dif-ferent dominant symbolism.

Third, the material context will have structured the various acts of exchange and *transformation*. Such actions will have been situated within particular regions of the field, whether it be the location of the funerary pyre just discussed, around the pottery kiln, or around the hearth for the cooking of food accompanied by the vessels used for its service and consumption. Situated at particular places and at the inter-section of different paths, these various acts and the objects which helped

facilitate them did not merely serve the material or the bodily requirements of the process but worked referentially to situate those actions
meaningfully.

The analytical process outlined above is designed to explore archaeologically the structuring of social practices. We have treated these practices as constituting fields of time/space which inhabited particular sets
of material structural conditions and we have considered the ways these
fields were regionalized in terms of the architecture of the fields, the
movements of agents within the field, and the transformative practices
which occurred. Throughout, the aim is to return us to the detail of
archaeological materials and to their historical interpretation with reference to the lives of people.

Social systems arose in history as a consequence of the distribution
of different fields of practice over time and space. However, *mechanisms
of systemic integration* involved more than this. Historically they will
have involved the transference and transformation of resources between
fields, where these resources could be conceived of as forms of "capital"
accumulated in one field of practice and reinvested in another. This
implies a degree of vertical differentiation between different fields
and thus between the agents who mediated such exchanges and those
excluded from them. These processes of systemic integration therefore
involved agents differentially empowered, for example as a ritual elite
may have mediated exchanges between the secular community and
the sacred. This vertical integration was taken a stage further when
certain agents were able to objectify the social system itself as a resource
upon which to act. Here we encounter the structuring of large-scale
and vertically ranked political systems within which certain elites
worked explicitly to define the conditions under which other forms
of agency could operate. The qualities of power in this case were
forms of domination which were mobilized to a certain extent through
discursive practices. We might expect to encounter increasing interest
in the explicit recording of forms of knowledge which monitored
and demarcated as legitimate the actions of those subjugated. It is
perhaps unsurprising that discourses on geography, ethnography, and
military strategy emerge at these particular points in history. The
technologies involved – forms of administrative, political, economic, and
military control for example (cf. Mann 1986) – required (indeed, still
require) massive capital investment. It becomes a central archaeological
concern to explore the ways such material structural conditions were
strategically controlled, and the extent of their reach into the fields of
social practice which were operating within the realm of their claimed
hegemony.

## Conclusion

The purpose of this contribution has been to get beyond a review of current theories of agency and offer a redesign for archaeological practices which is informed by those theories. Archaeologists are too often obsessed with what they perceive to be the weaknesses in their empirical data where those data are regarded as the fragmented and often inadequate record of the historical processes. The traditional presumption has been that we must treat the material recovered archaeologically as the consequence of past actions and processes, in other words as a record. It is my contention that theories of agency demand a reconceptualization of the relationship between material conditions and human practice which, drawing upon Giddens's "duality of structure," situate human agency within the structural conditions of its actions. From this perspective archaeologists must confront the ways agencies operated through the materials which have survived for our study, a confrontation which requires new ways of thinking about the significance of the material and new ways of writing these agencies of history into being (cf. Andrews, Barrett, and Lewis 2000). Field practices in archaeology are well designed to deal with the details of the recovered material conditions, a detail which is often abandoned in face of the need to write general histories of social processes. However, if we were to consider instead the ways agencies were created and transformed through their inhabitation of complex material conditions, archaeology would not only reaffirm the historical significance of the material details it recovers, but it would also contribute significantly to the development of the social theory which it has chosen to employ.

NOTE

I am grateful to those who have discussed this chapter with me, including Jane Downes, Kathryn Fewster, Danny Hind, and John Lewis. I am particularly grateful to Michael Tierney for his criticisms, which I know I have yet to address.

REFERENCES

Andrews, G., J. C. Barrett, and J. Lewis 2000. Interpretation not record: the practice of archaeology. *Antiquity* 74: 525–30.
Barrett, J. C. 1988a. Fields of discourse: reconstructing a social archaeology. *Critique of Anthropology* 7: 5–16.

Barrett, J.C. 1988b. The living, the dead and the ancestors: neolithic and early bronze age mortuary practices. In J.C. Barrett and I.A. Kinnes (eds), *The Archaeology of Context in the Neolithic and Bronze Age: Recent Trends*, 30–41. Sheffield: J.R. Collis.

Barrett, J.C. 1991. Towards an archaeology of ritual. In P. Garwood, D. Jennings, R. Skeates, and J. Toms (eds), *Sacred and Profane: Proceedings of a Conference on Archaeology, Ritual and Religion. Oxford, 1989*, 1–9. Oxford: Oxford University Committee for Archaeology.

Barrett, J.C. 1994. *Fragments from Antiquity: An Archaeology of Social Life in Britain, 2900–1200 BC.* Oxford: Blackwell.

Binford, L.R. 1962. Archaeology as anthropology. *American Antiquity* 28: 217–25.

Bloch, M. 1985. From cognition to ideology. In R. Fardon (ed.), *Power and Knowledge: Anthropological and Sociological Approaches*, 21–48. Edinburgh: Scottish Academic Press.

Bloch, M. 1992. What goes without saying: the conceptualisation of Zafimaniry society. In A. Kuper (ed.), *Conceptualizing Society*, 127–46. London: Routledge.

Bourdieu, P. 1977. *Outline of a Theory of Practice.* Cambridge: Cambridge University Press.

Bourdieu, P. 1984. *Distinction: A Social Critique of the Judgement of Taste.* London: Routledge and Kegan Paul.

Bourdieu, P. 1990. *The Logic of Practice.* Cambridge: Polity.

Bryant, C.G.A. and D. Jary 1991. *Giddens' Theory of Structuration: A Critical Appreciation.* London: Routledge.

Childe, V.G. 1944. *Progress and Archaeology.* London: Watts.

Childe, V.G. 1947. *History.* London: Cobbett Press.

Childe, V.G. 1956. *Piecing Together the Past.* London: Routledge and Kegan Paul.

Clark, J.G.D. 1957. *Archaeology and Society: Reconstructing the Prehistoric Past.* 3rd edn. London: Methuen.

Clark, J., C. Modgil, and S. Modgil (eds) 1990. *Anthony Giddens: Consensus and Controversy.* London: Falmer Press.

Clarke, D.L. 1968. *Analytical Archaeology.* London: Methuen.

Cohen, I.J. 1989. *Structuration Theory: Anthony Giddens and the Constitution of Social Life.* London: Macmillan.

Dobres, M.-A. and C.R. Hoffman (eds) 1999. *The Social Dynamics of Technology: Practice, Politics and World Views.* Washington: Smithsonian Institution Press.

Fitzpatrick, A. 1994. Outside in: the structure of an early Iron Age house at Dunston Park, Thatcham, Berkshire. In A. Fitzpatrick and E. Morris (eds), *The Iron Age in Wessex: Recent Work*, 86–72. Salisbury: Trust for Wessex Archaeology.

Friedman, J. 1994. *Cultural Identity and Global Process.* London: Sage.

Giddens, A. 1982. *Profiles and Critiques in Social Theory.* London: Macmillan.

Giddens, A. 1984. *The Constitution of Society.* Cambridge: Polity.

Giles, M. and M. Parker Pearson 1999. Learning to live in the Iron Age: dwelling and praxis. In B. Bevan (ed.), *Northern Exposure: Interpretative Devolution and the Iron Ages in Britain*, 21–231. Leicester: School of Archaeological Studies, University of Leicester.

Goffman, E. 1969. *The Representation of the Self in Everyday Life*. London: Penguin Books.

Hodder, I. (ed.) 1982. *Symbolic and Structural Archaeology*. Cambridge: Cambridge University Press.

Hodder, I. 1987. Contextual archaeology: an interpretation of Catal Huyuk and a discussion of the origins of agriculture. *Bulletin of the Institute of Archaeology* 24: 43–56.

Hodder, I. 1990. *The Domestication of Europe*. Oxford: Blackwell.

Holmwood, J. and A. Stewart 1991. *Explanation and Social Theory*. London: Macmillan.

Jenkins, R. 1992. *Pierre Bourdieu*. London: Routledge.

Mann, M. 1986. *The Sources of Social Power: Volume I, A History of Power from the Beginning to* AD *1760*. Cambridge: Cambridge University Press.

Mauss, M. 1970. *The Gift*. London: Cohen and West.

Miller, D. 1987. *Material Culture and Mass Consumption*. Oxford: Blackwell.

Mouzelis, N. 1991. *Back to Sociological Theory: The Construction of Social Orders*. London: Macmillan.

Mouzelis, N. 1995. *Sociological Theory: What Went Wrong?* London: Routledge.

Patrik, L. E. 1985. Is there an archaeological record? *Advances in Archaeological Method and Theory* 8: 27–62.

Renfrew, C. 1984. *Approaches to Social Archaeology*. Edinburgh: Edinburgh University Press.

Taylor, C. 1993. "To follow a rule . . ." In C. Calhoun, E. LiPuma, and M. Postone (eds), *Bourdieu: Critical Perspectives*, 45–60. Cambridge: Polity.

Tilley, C. 1994. *A Phenomenology of Landscape*. Oxford: Berg.

# 7

# Archaeologies of Place and Landscape

## *Julian Thomas*

### Introduction: duplicitous landscapes

The notion of a landscape archaeology is one that has a long history. From General Pitt Rivers' investigations in Cranborne Chase onward, the results of excavations have often been contextualized through the sustained interrogation of a defined area (Pitt Rivers 1887). This has sometimes enabled archaeologists to overcome a myopic focus on single sites. During the twentieth century, a predominantly British tradition of inquiry promoted the image of landscape as a palimpsest of material traces, an "assemblage of real-word features – natural, semi-natural and wholly artificial" which is available to us in the present (Roberts 1987: 79). Through field survey, documentary study, and cartographic analysis, as well as selective excavation, it has proved possible to prize apart the different phases of a landscape's development (Aston and Rowley 1974). However, as Barrett (1999: 26) argues, the end product of this kind of analysis is "a history of things that have been done to the land," which often seems quite remote from the past human lives that were lived in these places. In general, this branch of archaeology has been overwhelmingly empiricist, and it has only been in the past decade or so that landscape has emerged as an object of theoretical reflection within the discipline. But curiously, it has been in the course of this thematic discussion of landscape that archaeologists have been most willing to question some of the received norms of the discipline: period, sequence, identity, and objectivity. Moreover, it has been within this new form of landscape archaeology that some of the more radical experiments in writing about the past have been generated (e.g. Bender 1998; Edmonds 1999). In this contribution, I will suggest that any critical examination of the concept of landscape brings us face to face with the implication of archaeology in the conditions and ways of thinking of modernity. It is for this reason that it has provided the focus for some of the more lively debates over archaeological theory in recent years.

A significant inspiration for the development of a theoretically informed landscape archaeology has been the emergence of forms of human geography which have rejected the "spatial science" of the 1960s, opting instead to concentrate on culture and social relations, power and politics, identity and experience (e.g. Gregory and Urry 1985; Peet and Thrift 1989; Pile and Thrift 1995; Seamon and Mugerauer 1985). Within this very diverse set of approaches, a more distinct school of cultural geography can be identified (Cosgrove and Daniels 1988), which has drawn upon the work of theorists who have explicitly addressed the issue of landscape as a cultural phenomenon (Berger 1972; Williams 1973). For these thinkers the vision of landscape as an accumulated record of continuity and tradition, which gives us access to an authentic past, is an ideological one. It serves to conceal inequality and conflict (Daniels 1989: 196; Bender 1998: 33). Seeking harmony and authenticity, we may find only fragmentation and multiple encodings (Daniels and Cosgrove 1988: 8).

One reason for this is that landscape is a singularly complex and difficult concept. The word has multiple meanings, and its precise significance has shifted repeatedly in historic times. "Landscape" can mean the topography and land forms of a given region, or a terrain within which people dwell, or a fragment of the land which can be overseen from a single vantage point, and represented as such (Olwig 1993: 307; Ingold 1997: 29). Landscape can be an object, an experience, or a representation, and these different meanings frequently merge into one another (Lemaire 1997: 5). For this reason, it can refer simultaneously to a way of seeing the world which is specific to elite social groups, and to the inhabited lifeworld of a broader community (Daniels 1989: 206). Moreover, Hirsch (1995: 3) argues that any landscape which provides the context for human life necessarily incorporates a relationship between a lived reality and a potential for other ways of being, between the everyday and conditions which are metaphysical, imagined, or idealized. Every use of the term "landscape" brings a series of resonances with it, of alienation and liberation, sensuous experience and coercion, aspiration and inequality. The challenge of working with landscape is one of holding these elements in a productive tension rather than hoping to find a resolution (Daniels 1989: 217; Bender 1998: 38).

It is revealing to consider how and why these difficulties should have arisen. Contemporary western understandings of landscape are set within a distinctive conception of the world which developed during the birth of the modern era. In premodern Europe, no great ontological gulf was recognized between human beings and the rest of creation. All things were the products of God's handiwork, and all things could be the subjects of culture and cultivation (Hirsch 1995: 6; Jordanova 1989: 37; Olwig 1993: 313). The categorical separation of culture from nature, and of human beings from their environment, can be identified with the growth of instrumental reason, exemplified by the scientific revolution and the Enlightenment. This is the hallmark of what Martin Heidegger referred to as the "age of the world picture," an era in which the world comes to be conceived and grasped as an image that can be apprehended by humanity (Heidegger 1977: 129). In a sense, humanity has gradually usurped God in the modern era, assuming a position at the centre of creation. But instead of the creator, Man (*sic*) has become the arbitrator of reality, so that that which exists is that which has been brought before Man (Heidegger 1977: 130). In consequence, vision has become the dominant metaphor for the acquisition of knowledge, and observational science has gained a pre-eminent position in the definition of reality and truth. Object and subject have been split, so that Man becomes the active subject who observes a passive nature, the object of science. Furthermore, the valorization of human beings as the bearers of reason creates an imperative to construe nature as something which exists *for* them: at once a home and a store of resources (Zimmerman 1985: 250).

Defined as an object of investigation, nature is understood as being composed of a number of discrete entities or events (Ingold 1993: 154). These can be expected to operate in a lawlike and comprehensible fashion because, at a fundamental level, they all possess spatial extent and spatiotemporal motion. Forces, motion, and distance thus compose what Heidegger identifies as the "ground plan" of the Cartesian world-view, a set of assumptions which render all things amenable to investigation through a certain kind of mechanics, even before an analysis begins (Heidegger 1977: 119). In the modern west, then, human beings and nature have been positioned as separate and opposed entities. Both can be subjected to study, but as observing intelligences people appear to be self-evidently possessed of a mind and a soul, which exist outside of space and materiality. It is the combination of the conception of the world as image and object, and that of human beings as external observers, that provides the conditions for the creation of the modern western notion of landscape.

## Landscape art and the landscape idea

One of the most tangible manifestations of the modern worldview is landscape painting, which emerged in northern Italy and Flanders during the fifteenth century (Cosgrove 1984: 20). Indeed, the English word "landscape" comes from the Dutch, and originally referred to a particular kind of pictorial representation (Olwig 1993: 318). Cosgrove (1984) has linked the development of landscape painting to that of capitalism, implying that it is a way of seeing which exists under quite specific historical conditions. He argues that the linear perspective which was used by Brunelleschi and formalized by Alberti depends upon the conception of land as an alienable commodity. The realist representation of the world through perspective places the artist and the viewer outside of the frame, perceiving the land visually without immersion or engagement (Cosgrove 1984: 27). As John Berger puts it, a landscape painting is "not so much a framed window onto the world as a safe let into the wall, a safe into which the visible has been deposited" (1972: 109). Of course, those who commissioned these paintings were not the peasants who lived on the land, but the landowners who increasingly saw it as something to be measured, partitioned, and bought and sold at will. Landscape painting opens the world up to simultaneous perception, allowing visual pleasure to be taken without any form of reciprocation. As a phenomenon, it provides an indication that capitalism is itself a product of a modern sensibility, in which the things of the world are atomized and estranged from human involvement, as objects produced and consumed by subjects. Moreover, by visually appropriating the land in a specific manner, landscape painting had a series of significant effects, particularly in respect of the ways in which places were understood and physically transformed. Notions of the pastoral, of Arcadia, of the sublime, of scenery and of wilderness were promoted through the circulation of painterly imagery. This conditioned the interpretation of unfamiliar landscapes in the colonized world (Mugerauer 1985), and influenced the construction of parks and gardens, which were increasingly laid out around prospects and vistas (Hirsch 1995: 2).

Despite its close ties with landed capital, landscape painting has often been considered to embody ethical and aesthetic values. Although modernity has eventually seen the divine supplanted by Man, humanity first assumed the position of the deity's privileged interpreter. We should remember that the scientific revolution initially charged itself with revealing God's design in nature, an orientation that was only finally rooted out of natural science by the Darwinian theory of evolution. In a similar way, Ruskin believed that landscape art was a means by which the divine order which is manifested in nature could be reconstructed in the artwork: a kind of act of aesthetic piety (Fuller 1988: 16; Daniels and Cosgrove 1988: 5). Even as a form of representation, landscape appears to be complex and paradoxical.

The principal determinant of landscape art, though, is the look. As we have seen, vision has achieved a privileged status in the modern era, signifying the objective and dispassionate gathering of knowledge (Jay 1986: 187). I will argue below that this knowledge has often been conceived as a reconstruction or representation of an external reality within the mind. Consequently the gaze achieves the status of mediating between the inner and the outer world, the mind and materiality. It may be for this reason that the viewer is so often associated with reason and culture, while the viewed object takes on the characteristics of passive nature (Bender 1999: 31). In this sense, landscape art and empirical science are variations on a modern way of looking, which is also a power relation. It is a look which is disengaged but controlling, which assumes superiority, and which is gendered. Traditionally, it is the prerogative of the *flâneur*, the male metropolitan citizen, who is free to stroll the arcades of the modern city, "taking it all in." The *flâneur* glimpses shop windows, events, people, but is not involved with any of them. He "embodies the gaze of modernity which is both covetous and erotic" (Pollock 1988: 67). This gendered gaze is characteristically the way in which we look at landscape. Just as western painting defines men as the active producers and viewers of images, while women are passive objects of visual pleasure, so landscape is feminized (Ford 1991). The female body provides a series of metaphors for landscape and nature, and this promotes the impression that the land is a bounded and integrated entity (Best 1995: 184). Within archaeology such a sexualized way of looking is particularly troubling, since we habitually make use of a series of spatial technologies (GIS, satellite imagery, air photography) which seek to lay bare and penetrate the land. Archaeological understandings of landscape might thus be said to be voyeuristic and androcentric (Thomas 1993: 25).

Closely related to both perspective art and empirical natural science is the representation of land through cartography. Even more than landscape painting, maps can appeal to a status of objectivity, yet they represent a technology of power and knowledge (Harley 1988: 279; Smith 1998). Mapmaking has traditionally been a preserve of elite groups, who are literate, numerate, and empowered to carve the world up on paper. Maps are made and used by landowners, the military, the nobility and the bureaucracy, and are as notable for what they omit as for what they depict (Harley 1988: 287). What Don DeLillo describes in his novel *Underworld* as the "white spaces on the map" are locations which have been removed from view by hegemonic forces. From the papal line which defined Spanish and Portuguese spheres of influence in the New World to the Versailles peace agreement, maps have provided an instrument which renders the world malleable. Like other manifestations of the western gaze, cartography presents a distanced view as a dispassionate one, manipulating the world while at the same time dehumanizing it. Injustice and human suffering are not visible on any map. An important aspect of this manipulation has been the role of maps in the promotion and construction of national identity (Herb 1989). And just as maps depict the land in an orthographic, Cartesian fashion and delimit the nation states of the modern era, so too is the nation bound up with the concept of landscape. A landscape may be an area that was carved out by the national ancestors, but alternatively the archetypal landscape of a region (the German forest; the English downland; the American prairie) may be held to have nurtured the national spirit (Olwig 1993: 311; Lowenthal 1994). These ideas about the relationship between the land and the community, most forcefully expressed in the work of Friedrich Ratzel, were deeply influential in the formation of culture-historic archaeology. Developed into Gustav Kossinna's "settlement archaeological method" (Veit 1989) they betray a distinctive modernist preoccupation: the search backward through time to identify the origin of the nation and its primordial relationship with the land from which it sprang.

## Landscape, perception and being-in-the-world

If the dominant western perspective on landscape is one which is alienated, objectified, distanced, and dehumanized, one response might be to follow the "humanist geographers" (e.g. Tuan 1974) into an investigation of the human awareness and perception of space. By this means, we might hope to "put the people back" into the past. I would suggest that the recent concern with phenomenology in archaeology has sometimes been misconstrued as such a project (e.g. Jones 1998: 7). By arguing that perception is an activity in which human beings process sense data drawn from the environment, it seems possible to reintroduce the personal into the past while still holding on to the Cartesian world of measurable distances, velocities, and densities. Such an approach maintains that the world that is revealed to us in maps, diagrams, and air photographs approximates closely to empirical reality. It is in the first instance empty of meaning (Ingold 1992: 89), so that "space" is transformed into "place" through a human intervention. This means that archaeologists are at liberty to investigate past landscapes as aggregates of land forms, soil types, rainfall zones, and vegetation patterns in the first instance, only later turning to how these phenomena might have been *perceived* by past people. The implication is that through our objective, high-tech methodologies we have access to a stratum of reality which was unavailable to people in the past. Their perceptions of these landscapes would necessarily have been distorted and impoverished versions of a reality which we can more fully grasp.

All of this can only be entertained while we continue to rely upon the modernist divisions of mind and body, and subject and object. The notion of landscape perception is founded in the splitting of human beings into an inner and an outer person, so that information gathered in the outside world is internalized, and used to reconstruct a "mental picture" of the environment (Taylor 1993: 317). If this is the case, we arrive at a very harsh Cartesianism in which the human body inhabits a geometrical world of mere objects, and all meanings are events which take place in the metaphysical space of the mind. Banishing meaning from the material world, we have to hypothesize that language and symbols are means by which meanings produced inside one mind are transformed into something physical (an object or a sound), and then decoded by another mind using the same apparatus as it uses to perceive the world in general. This is what Tim Ingold calls the "building perspective," in which culture is imagined as "an arbitrary symbolic framework built on the surface of reality" (Ingold 1995: 66).

In an insightful discussion of these matters, Johnson (1998: 57) seeks to distinguish between "explicit" and "inherent" perceptions of the landscape. In the former, perception intercedes between an outer reality and an internalized mental image, while in the latter it is embedded in the lived experience of being within the land. This is rather akin to the notion of "direct perception" which Ingold (1998: 39) takes from the environmental psychologist J. J. Gibson. Direct perception is a process in which creatures get to know their surroundings through their complete bodily immersion in the world, finding out what affordances it can provide, rather than simply representing it in their minds. While I am in sympathy with both of these points of view, I would nonetheless reject the use of the term "perception" altogether, on the grounds that it inevitably carries a sense of subsidiarity or supplementarity. Instead, I would choose to talk of "disclosure" or "experience," which do not imply that our understanding of the world is somehow a failed attempt to come to terms with things as they really are.

Clearly, the model of perception as the construction of a mental picture is closely related to landscape as a way of representing the world. However, I would like to argue that while we cannot rid ourselves of this conception of landscape, another, parallel understanding is possible, based upon the relational and embedded way in which people conduct themselves in the world. Such a perspective would follow Ingold in arguing that nothing intervenes between ourselves and the world that we inhabit. Thinking is not something that happens in an interior space; it is part of our bodily immersion in the world. However, the world that we inhabit is not simply a set of meaningless physical objects: on the contrary, we encounter worldly things in their meaningfulness. We apprehend them *as* meanings, rather than as objective sense data. Putting this another way, the world in which we find ourselves is a horizon of intelligibility, a relational background which provides the context that enables anything that we focus upon to be rendered comprehensible. As a result, the condition of being-in-the-world is not simply a matter of being physically contained within a much larger entity; it is a relational involvement like being "in business" or "in love." It is "residing, dwelling, and being accustomed to a world" (Heidegger 1962: 79). Being-in-the-world involves an everyday way of "getting on with things" in which we skillfully negotiate and make sense of our surroundings, without having to think about them analytically for much of the time (Relph 1985: 16). But it is not something that we could extract ourselves from: there is no other way to be than in the world. Moreover, our involvement in a world is always presupposed in any comprehension of things: they only make sense because they have a background to stand out from.

## Reference and relationality

If the world is a horizon of intelligibility rather than a bare physical structure of objects and distances, it is important to consider the kind of spatiality that human beings experience. Lived space, as opposed to measured geometric space, is defined by the qualitative attributes of direction and closeness. Both of these are relationships, brought into being by a human presence. It is human concern, the way in which the disposition of material things *matters* to us, which grounds distance and directionality (Dreyfus 1991: 130). We can measure the distance between two objects, but only because we already make the qualitative distinction between "near" and "far." In this sense, mathematical or cartographic space is secondary to and derived from the everyday space that we inhabit. The feeling of being close to something is not simply a matter of physical location; it is constrained and facilitated by the accumulation of life experience, and by our relationships with other people (Dovey 1993: 250). To give an example: I may be in greater proximity to a house than is its owner, who may for the moment be absent, but through living in it over a period of years she has acquired a closeness to it that I do not have. What this means is that although people can only ever be in one place at a time, their dwelling *pervades* a much more extensive area (Heidegger 1971: 157). When we turn this insight onto the notion of landscape it is evident that people are knitted into a network of locales with which, through habitual and inconspicuous familiarity, they will have formed a kind of communion.

Furthermore, these locales will have the characteristic of being "places." A place is not just a thing or an entity. Place is a relational concept, since locations are always drawn to our attention through what happens there or through the things which we expect to find there (the hook on the wall is the place for the horse harness; the cupboard is where we keep the broom). A place is always the place *of* something (Heidegger 1962: 136). For this reason I reject the idea, already alluded to, that what is at first a formless space can be transformed into meaningful place. On the country, a place is always disclosed, or comes into focus, *as* a place. Prior to this we can have no awareness of it as any kind of non-place. My alternative conception of landscape is thus a network of related places, which have gradually been revealed through people's habitual activities and interactions, through the closeness and affinity that they have developed for some locations, and through the important events, festivals, calamities, and surprises which have drawn other spots to their attention, causing them to be remembered or incorporated into stories. Importantly, the series of places through which people's life histories are threaded help them to give account of their own identity. Our personal biographies are built up from located acts. So although we can say that landscapes are constructed out of the imbricated actions and experiences of people, those people are themselves constructed in and dispersed through their habituated landscape (Bachelard 1964: 8; Tilley 1996: 162).

While a represented landscape is an object or entity, a lived landscape is a set of relationships. A familiar example which demonstrates this point concerns Australian aboriginal landscapes, which represent networks through which the identities of people, ancestral beings, and places are continually produced and reproduced (Smith 1999: 190). It is very much in these terms that Gosden and Head (1994: 113–14) have argued that "social landscapes" represent systems of reference, in which each human action that is performed is intelligible in the context of other past and future acts. Landscape thus becomes the appropriate framework for investigating social life over the long term. By implication, each separate action (knapping a stone tool, or building a hearth) provides an opening into a nexus of implicit links which radiates outward from the momentary event that is discernible in the archaeological record. So while some archaeologists have argued that only the continuities of ecological development and adaptation can provide a context for human actions dispersed across time (Bailey 1981), Gosden and Head suggest that the lived landscape embodies human practices and dispositions as they are played out over the centuries.

## Embedded and multiple landscapes

In the western world, landscape is predominantly a visual term, which denotes something separate from ourselves. Despite this, we westerners inhabit experiential or relational landscapes, while in the non-western world there are many communities which have no sense of alienation from the land. Ethnographic studies have documented a variety of different ways in which people's embeddedness in the land can manifest itself. Given this diversity it would be unwise to impose any particular example onto the premodern European past in the form of an analogy. Instead, we should simply be aware of a range of possibilities which can inform our hypotheses about the past. For example, among the Australian Yolngu, it is believed that ancestral beings moved across the land in the Dreaming, and that they were eventually incorporated into the landscape, providing the distinctive character of significant places. Gaining a familiarity with the land is at the same time an acquisition of knowledge of the Dreaming, which still exists embodied in the land. People's movements along ancestral tracks and their experiences of places reproduce the Dreaming (Morphy 1995: 187). For many New Guinea communities, land is considered to embody ancestral energies, which are nurtured through human involvement (Tilley 1994: 58). Yet the full meanings of places and the energies that they contain may be socially restricted, and gaining knowledge of the landscape may be a means of cultivating social authority (Tilley 1994: 59). The Saami of northern Scandinavia understand the sacred sites that they use for sacrifices to be

imbued with spiritual forces (Mulk 1994: 125). These places are generally outstanding topographical features like mountain peaks, springs,
and rivers. At the risk of oversimplifying this material, each example
appears to present the landscape as in some sense animated, and involved
in a kind of reciprocity with human beings.

One particular way in which people's interconnection with the land
is often expressed is through the medium of kinship. This can take a
number of forms. Land may be connected with ancestry in various ways:
ancestors may have formed the land, or emerged out of it, or cleared the
wilderness and created fields and gardens (Toren 1995: 178). In each
case, the landscape provides a continuous reminder of the relationship
between the living and past generations, and consequently of lines of
descent and inheritance. The continued use of places through time draws
attention to the historically constituted connections which exist between
members of a community (Bender 1999: 36). At a more specific level,
the traces of human activity in the landscape may represent a source
of detailed information about kin relations. For instance, in western
Amazonia the pattern of houses and gardens gradually falling into decay
and decrepitude within the forest is recognized as a physical record of
residential history, which can be directly related to genealogical lore
(Gow 1995: 48). Over the generations the movements and fissioning of
households have produced a complex landscape, and movement through
it in the present is a means of recapitulating their histories. Similarly,
in the case of New Ireland, Küchler (1987: 249) has shown how the
mapping of the places in the landscape and kin relations may be more
or less congruent. If kinship is a means of expressing relationships among
human beings, it is instructive that it is so often embedded in landscape.
Land, place, people, and material substances may all be fundamentally
linked rather than constituting entirely separate classes of things.

This sense of the physical and symbolic interconnection of different
aspects of the social world chimes with recent landscape archaeologies
which have been at pains to break down any distinction between "ritual"
and "everyday" aspects of life. We have seen already that landscape
offers an integrating framework for archaeology, as a context which links
dispersed human acts. Significantly, such a framework can accommodate
activities that modern reason would tend to assign to separate categories.
The landscape is the familiar world within which people perform their
everyday tasks, but religious observances and other rituals are likely to
fit into and inform the mundane pattern. While contemporary westerners tend to seclude spiritual matters both spatially and temporally, it may
be more usual for ritualized conceptions of existence to permeate the
whole of people's lives (Edmonds 1999: 155–6). This lack of separation

between ritual and quotidian aspects of life has inspired Bender, Hamilton, and Tilley's (1997) work on the landscapes of Leskernick Hill, on Bodmin Moor in Cornwall. While the area surrounding Leskernick Hill is dotted with funerary cairns, stone circles, and stone rows, much of their fieldwork has concentrated on two settlements of circular stone houses which are Bronze Age in date. Bender, Hamilton, and Tilley argue that the stone which was used for the construction of both houses and monuments carried a deep symbolic charge (see also Tilley 1996). The houses incorporated large stones, significantly placed at the back of the building, while many of the "natural" stones in and around the settlements had been subtly altered and repositioned, joined together, enclosed, or exposed (Bender et al. 1997: 173). So there is no suggestion here of domestic spaces surrounded by separate "ritual landscapes" of ceremonial monuments. Instead, the settlements and their surroundings are filled with numerous shrines which extend ritual activity throughout the whole landscape. This dispersal of ritual across all of the spaces that people would have frequented, and by implication throughout much of their lives, suggests practices and beliefs which were engaged in by a whole community rather than monopolized by a few (Bender et al. 1997: 174).

We have suggested that lived landscapes are relational entities constituted by people in their engagement with the world. It follows from this that different people may experience and understand the same landscape in rather different ways (Bender 1998: 87). I do not mean to suggest by this that people possess some foundational uniqueness which provides them with an ability to see things differently. Rather, each person occupies a distinctive position in relation to their landscape. As a consequence of their gender, class, ethnicity, sexuality, age, cultural tradition and personal life history they are differentially located. So each person has a particular set of possibilities when it comes to presenting an account of their own landscape. Landscapes might thus be said to be multiple or fragmented. It is not simply that they are perceived differently: the same location may effectively be a different place for two different persons. This is particularly the case when people possess different cultural inheritances. Discussing the Cape York peninsula in Australia, Veronica Strang (1999) describes the utterly incompatible understandings of the land held by the aboriginal community and the Euro-Australian cattle herders. The Aborigines believe that every part of the landscape is distinctive and embodies ancestral beings from the Dreaming. Human lives extend between places of special spiritual potency which bring about birth and death. Personal and group identity, moral order, and social organization are all embedded in human relationships with the land.

However, for the inhabitants of the cattle stations the landscape is a hostile and dangerous wilderness. If the Aborigines see themselves as engaged in reciprocity with the land, the cattle herders are its adversaries. From a western capitalist viewpoint the land has to be overcome, controlled, enclosed, and used to produce wealth. The value of land is its financial worth, and the Aborigines are said to "do nothing" with the country, for they do not use it to accumulate income (Strang 1999: 212). These two communities do not simply have different mental images of the same landscape; they are engaged in different sets of lived relationships, even if they find themselves in the same physical space.

## Landscapes and monuments

Broadly speaking, the existence of a theoretical landscape archaeology is most clearly discernible in later prehistoric studies in Britain and Europe. Here, the earliest construction of ceremonial monuments at the start of the Neolithic has been connected with new experiences of place, and a closer identification between people and particular locations (Bradley 1998: 18). Similar lines of argument have been pursued in other contexts. Paul Taçon (1994: 126) has discussed Australian rock art as a means by which landscapes were socialized. Similarly, Gosden and Head (1994: 114) have speculated that the "transported landscapes" of the Pacific (which transformed island faunas and floras by introducing a range of new species) would have changed the spatial and temporal rhythms of human life. However, the investigation of prehistoric monuments has proved especially productive, since it offers the opportunity to study the details of architecture, mortuary activity, and depositional practices in the context of the surrounding topography. In some cases there may be a disjuncture between the site and its environs: Richard Bradley makes the interesting observation that the structural development of Stonehenge appears to have been more gradual than the social and cultural changes which overtook its landscape. The monument's connections with ritual, ancestry, and the past would have rendered it a force for social stability and the maintenance of tradition, which would need to be accommodated within changing political and economic circumstances (Bradley 1998: 100).

This concern with the place of monuments within lived landscapes is also demonstrated by a renewed interest in the implications of mobility (e.g. Whittle 1997). While chambered tombs and stone circles have often been identified as central places, implicitly assumed to have been located

**Figure 7.1**   Megalithic tomb at Loughcrew, County Meath

close to sedentary habitations, it seems that they may often have been constructed on routeways. Patterns of movement between and around monuments may have been important in the seasonal round practiced by prehistoric communities, and on a smaller scale they may also have been fundamental to the ways in which these sites were used. In her study of the passage-tomb cemetery at Loughcrew in Ireland, Shannon Frazer argues that the relatively distinct focal areas which surround the monuments might have held large gatherings of people (figure 7.1). The detail of the local topography is such that quite specific patterns of movement around the tombs would have been promoted. Indeed, the growth of the tomb group appears to have gradually elaborated upon the natural features of the hilltops, defining and constraining areas of congregation and setting up particular relationships between monuments and assemblies of people. Frazer's argument is that if these tombs and their use were instrumental in the maintenance of authority and traditions of knowledge, this reproduction could only have been secured in public, rather than exclusively within the secluded spaces of the tomb interiors (Frazer 1998: 209).

Frazer's account of Loughcrew suggests that the place itself was already marked out as sacred before the tombs began to be constructed. More generally, monuments may have been a means of reconfiguring or enhancing landscapes, rather than an imposition which negates the existing identity of a place. Bradley points to the similarity which often exists between monuments and their surrounding country, so that the structure becomes a microcosm of the landscape. Stone circles, as permeable monuments, would have allowed the relationships between people occupying the site, other monuments, and topographic features to have been appreciated (Bradley 1998: 121–2, 128). Equally important is the way in which Neolithic and Bronze Age monuments reorganize the materials of the landscape itself. Structures made of earth, wood, and stone present the substance of the land in unfamiliar ways, and it is conceivable that these elements had wider sets of meanings so that their use amounted to a symbolic re-engineering of the cosmos (Bender 1998: 49).

A number of recent studies have indicated that the materials used in monumental architecture and their configuration was anything but a matter of expediency. Colin Richards (1996b) suggests that in Neolithic Orkney houses, tombs and henges were all aspects of a single cosmological scheme which drew upon the natural forms of the land. This point is made more explicitly in his paper on the architecture of henge monuments, which draws out a series of connections between site location, ditch morphology, and orientation. What links all of these elements is water: human movement within and between the monuments involves crossing water or following the flow of rivers in the wider landscape (Richards 1996a: 329). Once again the monument becomes a context in which the relationships between people and land are clarified and dramatized. The use of specific materials that have quite particular meanings is also considered by Parker Pearson and Ramilisonina (1998), who hypothesize that timber monuments in later Neolithic Britain may have been used by the living, but that stone structures were the preserve of the dead. This argument has been criticized by Barrett and Fewster (1998) for its undue reliance on ethnographic analogy, but it does have the virtue of pointing to the way in which architecture builds meanings as well as things.

The evaluation of monuments in experiential terms, as parts of lived landscapes, has been a distinctive element in recent prehistoric archaeology. However, in the past few years a number of criticisms have begun to emerge. Both Meskell (1996: 6) and Hodder (1999: 13) have suggested that while these approaches are preoccupied with an encounter between a human body and a location, the bodies involved are anonymous and universal. Both authors argue that a concern with individual lives is the element which is missing. Hodder adds that archaeologies which concentrate on bodily practice often absolve themselves of any need to consider meaning or empathy with the past. The identification of specific meanings is rejected in favor of a focus on the practices which allowed meaning to be produced (Hodder 1999: 133–4). Frazer, for instance, holds that the search for the past meaning content of megalithic tombs is "a fruitless exercise" (Frazer 1998: 205). In its place she advocates a consideration of "the strategies by which narratives of place and biographies of the landscape itself are implicated in the making of the self and the perception of being *in* place" (Frazer 1998: 206). Frazer, and others like Barrett (1987), would suggest that the precise ways in which things or events are understood are likely to be multiple and fleeting, so that it will be impossible to arrive at a definitive reading which approximates to what "they" thought in the past. Hodder would probably counter (I think correctly) that an interpretation of past meaning-producing practices is still a meaning, and consequently that it is impossible to construct an understanding of the past which is meaning-free. This would require interpretation to operate at a level of meta-discourse which transcends the condition of language.

Coming toward the same issues from a different perspective, Layton and Ucko (1999: 12) suggest that prehistoric landscapes represent sets of "empty signs" which archaeologists attempt at their peril to fill with a "surrogate discourse." Their implication is that specific meanings probably were given to places and features in the past, but that we may be deluding ourselves if we imagine that we can gain access to them in the present. Cast in these terms, the case is unanswerable. However, I think that it is possible to propose an alternative approach to the meaning of landscape which is more fruitful. We have already concluded that landscapes are relational, and it would follow from this that people do not simply label places with meanings that they "think up." Meaning is produced in the dynamic working of the relationships between people, things, and places. What has been significant about the "phenomenology of landscape" (to use Tilley's phrase: Tilley 1994) is that it advocates an encounter between the archaeologist and the places and monuments that they study. This encounter may be real and physical, or imagined. But in either case what we are effectively doing is entering into the same set of material relationships in which people found themselves in the past, in order to produce our own interpretation. This interpretation may be what Layton and Ucko would dismiss as a "surrogate": I would prefer to describe it as an allegory, a present-day understanding which "stands for" the past meaning. We cannot "get at" a past meaning, and we certainly cannot get inside the heads of past people through an act of empathy. But we can put ourselves inside a set of material circumstances which were integral to a meaningful world in the past. *Contra* Layton and Ucko, these material circumstances do not merely reflect a past social reality. Using our own bodies as analogs for those of the past, we are seeking to "reanimate" a past world, and in the process to identify the ways in which it differed from our own.

While Brück (1998: 28) has a good point to make when she asks how a pregnant woman, or a child, or a disabled person might have negotiated the Dorset Cursus 5,000 years ago, I think it is incorrect to suggest that the bodies in recent postprocessual landscape archaeologies are "average" or universal. Rather, they are the bodies of late twentieth-century academics, because these are the only bodies which are distinguished by our "ownliness" – the only bodies that we can ever live through (Thomas forthcoming). Our engagement with the material traces of the past does not give us access to past experiences, but it provides a basis for understanding how far they may have been unlike our own. Frazer puts this rather well when she describes our practice as "inhabiting the archaeological landscape in the present" (Frazer 1998: 204), a phrase which echoes Ingold's (1993: 152) description of archaeology as the most recent form of dwelling on an ancient site.

## Conclusion

I have argued that there are two quite different understandings of the term "landscape": as a territory which can be apprehended visually, and as a set of relationships between people and places which provide the context for everyday conduct. In a more or less explicit way, archaeologists have recognized that landscape provides a framework for integrating many different forms of information and different aspects of human life. However, the landscapes to which they have been referring have generally been specular and objectified. Identifying the historical specificity of the landscape idea has opened up the conceptual space for a new kind of landscape archaeology. A new approach will still require that we identify and plot the traces of past activity in the countryside. But the uses to which these traces will be put will have to go beyond the reconstruction of economic regimes and speculations as to how the land may have been perceived by past people. In considering the ways in which the significance of the landscape gradually emerged, through practices of building, maintenance, tending, harvesting, and dwelling, we are constructing in the present an analogy for past worlds of meaning.

REFERENCES

Aston, M. and T. Rowley 1974. *Landscape Archaeology: An Introduction to Fieldwork Techniques on Post-Roman Landscapes*. Newton Abbot: David and Charles.

Bachelard, G. 1964. *The Poetics of Space*. Boston: Beacon Press.

Bailey, G. 1981. Concepts, time-scales and explanations in economic prehistory. In A. Sheridan and G. Bailey (eds), *Economic Archaeology*, 97–118. Oxford: British Archaeological Reports s96.

Barrett, J.C. 1987. Contextual archaeology. *Antiquity* 61: 468–73.

Barrett, J.C. 1999. Chronologies of landscape. In P. Ucko and R. Layton (eds), *The Archaeology and Anthropology of Landscape*, 21–30. London: Routledge.

Barrett, J.C. and K. Fewster 1998. Stonehenge: is the medium the message? *Antiquity* 72: 847–52.

Bender, B. 1998. *Stonehenge: Making Space*. London: Berg.

Bender, B. 1999. Subverting the western gaze: mapping alternative worlds. In P. Ucko and R. Layton (eds), *The Archaeology and Anthropology of Landscape*, 31–45. London: Routledge.

Bender, B., S. Hamilton, and C.Y. Tilley 1997. Leskernick: stone worlds; alternative narratives; nested landscapes. *Proceedings of the Prehistoric Society* 63: 147–78.

Berger, J. 1972. *Ways of Seeing*. Harmondsworth: Penguin.

Best, S. 1995. Sexualising space. In E. Grosz and E. Probyn (eds), *Sexy Bodies: The Strange Carnalities of Feminism*, 181–94. London: Routledge.

Bradley, R.J. 1998. *The Significance of Monuments*. London: Routledge.

Brück, J. 1998. In the footsteps of the ancestors: a review of Christopher Tilley's *A Phenomenology of Landscape: Places, Paths and Monuments*. *Archaeological Review from Cambridge* 15: 23–36.

Cosgrove, D. 1984. *Social Formation and Symbolic Landscape*. London: Croom Helm.

Cosgrove, D. and S. Daniels (eds) 1988. *The Iconography of Landscape*. Cambridge: Cambridge University Press.

Daniels, S. 1989. Marxism, culture, and the duplicity of landscape. In R. Peet and N. Thrift (eds), *New Models in Human Geography, Volume 2*, 196–220. London: Unwin Hyman.

Daniels, S. and D. Cosgrove 1988. Introduction: iconography and landscape. In D. Cosgrove and S. Daniels (eds), *The Iconography of Landscape*, 1–10. Cambridge: Cambridge University Press.

Dovey, K. 1993. Putting geometry in its place: towards a phenomenology of the design process. In D. Seamon (ed.), *Dwelling, Seeing and Designing*, 247–69. Albany: State University of New York Press.

Dreyfus, H. 1991. *Being-in-the-World: A Commentary on Heidegger's "Being and Time", Division 1*. Cambridge, MA: Massachusetts Institute of Technology Press.

Edmonds, M.R. 1999. *Ancestral Geographies of the Neolithic: Landscapes, Monuments and Memory*. London: Routledge.

Ford, S. 1991. Landscape revisited: a feminist reappraisal. In C. Philo (compiler), *New Words, New Worlds: Reconceptualising Social and Cultural Geography*, 151–5. Lampeter: Saint David's University College.

Frazer, S. 1998. The public forum and the space between: the materiality of social strategy in the Irish Neolithic. *Proceedings of the Prehistoric Society* 64: 203–24.

Fuller, P. 1988. The geography of mother nature. In D. Cosgrove and S. Daniels (eds), *The Iconography of Landscape*, 11–31. Cambridge: Cambridge University Press.

Gosden, C. and L. Head 1994. Landscape: a usefully ambiguous concept. *Archaeology in Oceania* 29: 113–16.

Gow, P. 1995. Land, people and paper in western Amazonia. In E. Hirsch and M. O'Hanlon (eds), *The Anthropology of Landscape*, 43–62. Oxford: Oxford University Press.

Gregory, C. and J. Urry 1985. *Social Relations and Spatial Structures*. London: Macmillan.

Harley, J.B. 1988. Maps, knowledge and power. In D. Cosgrove and S. Daniels (eds), *The Iconography of Landscape*, 277–312. Cambridge: Cambridge University Press.

Heidegger, M. 1962. *Being and Time*, tr. J. Macquarrie and E. Robinson. Oxford: Blackwell.

Heidegger, M. 1971. Building dwelling thinking. In M. Heidegger, *Poetry, Language, Thought*, 143–62. New York: Harper and Row.

Heidegger, M. 1977. The age of the world-picture. In M. Heidegger, *The Question Concerning Technology and Other Essays*, 115–54. New York: Harper and Row.

Herb, H. 1989. Persuasive cartography in *Geopolitik* and National Socialism. *Political Geography Quarterly* 8: 289–303.

Hirsch, E. 1995. Landscape: between place and space. In E. Hirsch and M. O'Hanlon (eds), *The Anthropology of Landscape*, 1–30. Oxford: Oxford University Press.

Hodder, I.R. 1999. *The Archaeological Process: An Introduction*. Oxford: Blackwell.

Ingold, T. 1992. Culture and the perception of the environment. In E. Croll and D. Parkin (eds), *Bush Base, Forest Farm*, 39–56. London: Routledge.

Ingold, T. 1993. The temporality of the landscape. *World Archaeology* 25: 152–74.

Ingold, T. 1995. Building, dwelling, living: how animals and people make themselves at home in the world. In S. Strathern (ed.), *Shifting Contexts: Transformations in Anthropological Knowledge*, 57–80. London: Routledge.

Ingold, T. 1997. The picture is not the terrain: maps, paintings and the dwelt-in world. *Archaeological Dialogues* 4: 29–31.

Ingold, T. 1998. From complementarity to obviation: on dissolving the boundaries between social and biological anthropology, archaeology and psychology. *Zeitschrift für Ethnologie* 123: 21–52.

Jay, M. 1986. In the empire of the gaze: Foucault and the denigration of vision in twentieth-century French thought. In D.C. Hoy (ed.), *Foucault: A Critical Reader*, 175–204. Oxford: Blackwell.

Johnson, R. 1998. Approaches to the perception of landscape. *Archaeological Dialogues* 5, 54–68.

Jones, C. 1998. Interpreting the perceptions of past people. *Archaeological Review from Cambridge* 15: 7–22.

Jordanova, L. 1989. *Sexual Visions: Images of Gender in Science and Medicine between the Eighteenth and Twentieth Centuries*. London: Harvester Wheatsheaf.

Küchler, S. 1987. Malangan: art and memory in a Melanesian society. *Man* 22: 238–55.

Layton, R. and P. Ucko 1999. Introduction: gazing at the landscape and encountering the environment. In P. Ucko and R. Layton (eds), *The Archaeology and Anthropology of Landscape*, 1–20. London: Routledge.

Lemaire, T. 1997. Archaeology between the invention and destruction of the landscape. *Archaeological Dialogues* 4: 5–21.

Lowenthal, D. 1994. European and English landscapes as national symbols. In D. Hooson (ed.), *Geography and National Identity*, 15–38. Oxford: Blackwell.

Meskell, L. 1996. The somatisation of archaeology: institutions, discourses, corporeality. *Norwegian Archaeological Review* 29: 1–16.

Morphy, H. 1995. Landscape and the reproduction of the ancestral past. In E. Hirsch and M. O'Hanlon (eds), *The Anthropology of Landscape*, 184–209. Oxford: Oxford University Press.

Mugerauer, R. 1985. Language and the emergence of the environment. In D. Seamon and R. Mugerauer (eds), *Dwelling, Place and Environment*, 51–70. New York: Columbia University Press.

Mulk, I.M. 1994. Sacrificial places and their meaning in Saami society. In D.L. Carmichael, J. Hubert, B. Reeves, and A. Schanche (eds), *Sacred Sites, Sacred Places*, 121–31. London: Routledge.

Olwig, K. 1993. Sexual cosmology: nation and landscape at the conceptual interstices of nature and culture; or what does landscape really mean? In B. Bender (ed.), *Landscape: Politics and Perspectives*, 307–43. Oxford: Berg.

Parker Pearson, M. and Ramilisonina 1998. Stonehenge for the ancestors: the stones pass on the message. *Antiquity* 72: 308–26.

Peet, R. and N. Thrift (eds) 1989. *New Models in Geography*. London: Unwin Hyman.

Pile, S. and N. Thrift (eds) 1995. *Mapping the Subject: Geographies of Cultural Transformation*. London: Routledge.

Pitt Rivers, A.L.F. 1887. *Excavations in Cranborne Chase near Rushmore, on the Borders of Dorset and Wilts., Vol. I*. Farnham: Privately printed.

Pollock, G. 1988. *Vision and Difference: Femininity, Feminism and the Histories of Art*. London: Routledge.

Relph, E. 1985. Geographical experiences and being-in-the-world: the phenomenological origins of geography. In D. Seamon and R. Mugerauer (eds), *Dwelling, Place and Environment*, 15–32. New York: Columbia University Press.

Richards, C.C. 1996a. Henges and water: towards an elemental understanding of monumentality and landscape in late Neolithic Britain. *Journal of Material Culture* 1: 313–36.

Richards, C.C. 1996b. Monuments as landscape: creating the centre of the world in late Neolithic Orkney. *World Archaeology* 28: 190–208.

Roberts, B.K. 1987. Landscape archaeology. In M. Wagstaff (ed.), *Landscape and Culture*, 77–95. Oxford: Blackwell.

Seamon, D. and R. Mugerauer 1985. *Dwelling, Place and Environment*. New York: Columbia University Press.

Smith, A. 1998. Landscapes of power in nineteenth century Ireland: archaeology and Ordnance Survey maps. *Archaeological Dialogues* 5: 69–84.

Smith, C. 1999. Ancestors, place and people: social landscapes in Aboriginal Australia. In P. Ucko and R. Layton (eds), *The Archaeology and Anthropology of Landscape*, 189–205. London: Routledge.

Strang, V. 1999. Competing perceptions of landscape in Kowanyama, north Queensland. In P. Ucko and R. Layton (eds), *The Archaeology and Anthropology of Landscape*, 206–18. London: Routledge.

Taçon, P. 1994. Socialising landscapes: the long-term implications of signs, symbols and marks on the land. *Archaeology in Oceania* 29: 117–29.

Taylor, C. 1993. Engaged agency and background in Heidegger. In C. Guignon (ed.), *The Cambridge Companion to Heidegger*, 317–36. Cambridge: Cambridge University Press.

Thomas, J.S. 1993. The politics of vision and the archaeologies of landscape. In B. Bender (ed.) *Landscape: Politics and Perspectives*, 19–48. Oxford: Berg.

Thomas, J.S. forthcoming. The great dark book: archaeology, experience and interpretation. In J.L. Bintliff (ed.), *The Blackwell Companion to Archaeology*. Oxford: Blackwell.

Tilley, C.Y. 1994. *A Phenomenology of Landscape: Places, Paths and Monuments*. Oxford: Berg.

Tilley, C.Y. 1996. The powers of rocks: topography and monument construction on Bodmin Moor. *World Archaeology* 28: 161–76.

Toren, C. 1995. Seeing the ancestral sites: transformations in Fijiian notions of the land. In E. Hirsch and M. O'Hanlon (eds), *The Anthropology of Landscape*, 163–83. Oxford: Oxford University Press.

Tuan, Y.F. 1974. Space and place: humanistic perspective. *Progress in Geography* 6: 211–52.

Veit, U. 1989. Ethnic concepts in prehistory: a case study on the relationship between cultural identity and archaeological objectivity. In S.J. Shennan (ed.),

*Archaeological Approaches to Cultural Identity*, 33–56. London: Unwin Hyman.

Whittle, A.W.R. 1997. Moving on and moving around: Neolithic settlement mobility. In P. Topping (ed.), *Neolithic Landscapes*, 14–22. Oxford: Oxbow.

Williams, R. 1973. *The Country and the City*. London: Paladin.

Zimmerman, M.E. 1985. The role of spiritual discipline in learning to dwell on earth. In D. Seamon and R. Mugerauer (eds), *Dwelling, Place and Environment*, 247–56. New York: Columbia University Press.

# 8

# Archaeologies of Identity

## *Lynn Meskell*

Do we *truly* need a *true* sex? With a persistence that borders on stubbornness, modern Western societies have answered in the affirmative. They have obstinately brought into play the question of a "true sex" in an order of things where one might have imagined that all that counted was the reality of the body and the intensity of its pleasures.

> Michel Foucault, *Herculine Barbin,*
> *Being the Recently Discovered Memoirs of*
> *a Nineteenth Century Hermaphrodite*

With these words Michel Foucault opened his famous study of sexual identity based on the memoirs of Herculine Barbin (Foucault 1980), also known as Alexina, Camille, and Abel. It is a brief and compelling account of the life of a hermaphrodite, but also an exposé of juridico-medical classifications and our cultural fascination with category. In the case of Herculine, those pronouncements had disastrous effects resulting in suicide. Apart from our current preoccupation in all matters sexual, the story of this Herculine is important for it belies the rigidity of Western taxonomizing, especially where it concerns identity, be it race, class, gender, or sexual preference. That rigidity necessitates that all individuals be neatly pigeonholed and categorized according to a set of predetermined labels. So too in our archaeological investigations we have concentrated on single-issue questions of identity, focusing singularly on gender or ethnicity, and have attempted to locate people from antiquity into a priori Western taxonomies: heterosexual/homosexual, male/female, elite/non-elite, etc. Archaeologists tend to concentrate on specific sets of issues that coalesce around topics like gender, age, or status, without interpolating other axes of identity, be they class, ethnicity, or sexual orientation for example, because this has been seen as too vast or complex a project. As Sarah Nelson (1997: 16) recently commented, whilst feminists have been discussing other variables such as ethnicity, sexual orientation, age, and the other ways people are categorized, "everything cannot be studied at once." This is where the generations divide. Being feminists, it is surely part of our project to open up the debate to all those vectors of difference by which individuals are named and subjectified. Following Sawicki (1991: 47), "theoretical pluralism makes possible the expansion of social ontology, a redefinition and redescription of experience from the perspectives of those who are more often simply objects of theory." Without such sensitivities we run the risk of doing interpretive violence in representing the people of the past and, by seamless extension, those imbricated in present-day struggles.

In this chapter I have two aims: the first is to present a third wave feminist outline of what an archaeology of identity might look like, moving beyond a simple position of identity politics. The second is to break the boundaries of identity categories themselves, blurring the crucial domains of identity formation, be they based on gender, sexuality, kin, politics, religion, or social systems. Only through deconstruction of the domains we see as "natural" or prediscursive can we truly approach an archaeology of difference – real cultural difference and contextuality.

## Identity issues: ethnicity, class, sex, etc.

Whilst examining identity in a holistic manner might represent one of the newest fields represented in this volume, single issue studies have been of great interest to archaeologists for the past few decades. Most scholars acknowledge that we all have a number of social identities which entail constant negotiation and organize our relationships to other individuals and groups within our social world (Craib 1998: 4–9), yet we often forget the subjective, inner world of the individual. It is not simply a matter of uncovering the top-down implementations of power that have effects on people or the "technologies of the self" that infer a disembodied force. Here the popular writings of Giddens, Foucault, and even Bourdieu often fall short of an archaeology of identity. Although some aspects of our identity are given to us as a starting point – our sex, class, ethnicity, etc. – this frames the self, it does not rigidly determine the sort of person we might become or our actions in the future. Understanding social identity often requires a metanarrative, just as awareness of individual selves requires that identity and life experience be inserted into that equation (Craib 1998: 28). In fact, there are two levels of operation: one is the broader social level in which identities are defined by formal associations or mores; the other is the individual or personal level where a person experiences many aspects of identity within a single subjectivity, fluid over the trajectories of life. The latter is more contingent, immediate, and operates at a greater frequency, whereas society's categories and constraints take longer to reformulate. But as the case of Herculine Barbin illustrates, those typologies of identity can change within the space of a few decades. The two levels operate in a recursive manner, with individuals playing important roles in the mechanisms of change.

Archaeological materials are deeply imbricated in political discourses and objectives (see papers in Meskell 1998b). It is the very materiality of our field – the historical depth of monuments and objects, their visibility in museums, their iconic value – that ultimately have residual potency in the contemporary imaginary. These objects can be mobilized and deployed in identity struggles, whereas anthropological ethnographies and theorizing cannot, despite their influence in scholarly circles. For so long in the shadow of anthropology, this unique aspect of the archaeological project should be of prime importance to a host of other disciplines, providing a rare opportunity to contribute to, rather than simply borrow from, the social sciences. The materiality of the past has long-term consequences in the lives of numerous generations, extending beyond a heuristic enterprise. Inequalities get reproduced, be they based on sexuality, religion, ethnicity, or other axes of difference. And it is the very tangibility and longevity of our data that are often at the source of those processes.

One obvious dimension has been the archaeological interest in ethnicity, ethnogenesis, and the related trajectories of politics and nationalism (see Emberling 1997 for a full summary). There has never been any consensus in terminology, and "ethnicity" has been used to denote the individual versus the group, the contents of an ethnic identity versus its instrumental expression, personal feelings versus the instrumental expression of identity, etc. (Banks 1996: 47). Ethnic identity is only one social determinate which can be cut across by status, occupation, gender, etc. that allows contact between groups. But it involves the social negotiation of difference and sameness, and it often entails larger tensions between individuals, the group, and the state. According to Emberling

(1997: 305) ethnic identity is not fundamentally hierarchical like class and status in either a Marxist or Weberian sense. It is a concept aligned to the construct of kinship, albeit larger than the group, clan, or lineage. Archaeologists have shown that ethnicity is not always synonymous with a single language, race, location, or material culture. Some markers are more telling than others, such as styles of food or household arrangements, rather than language or pottery for example. Studies from areas as diverse as Mesoamerica (e.g. Teotihuacan, Chichen Itzá, Kaminaljuyú) and Mesopotamia (e.g. Kultepe Kanesh) have shown the complexities of identifying ethnicity, enclaves, and cultural boundaries due to the processes of cultural assimilation or maintenance of differences (see Emberling 1997: 316–18). Michael Spence's work (1992) on Oaxacan-influenced material culture and social practices at Teotihuacan provides an excellent example of these complex valencies.

There has been a flood of volumes and papers which deal with these concepts as articulated in antiquity or as they have been deployed in modern settings (e.g. McGuire 1982; Marcus and Flannery 1983; Auger et al. 1987; Trigger 1989; Aldenderfer 1993; Brown 1994; Brumfiel and Fox 1994; Chapman 1994; Pollock and Lutz 1994; Baines 1996; Jones 1996). Nazi uses of archaeological materials to ground claims of ethnic superiority provide a particularly evocative and chilling example (Arnold 1990; Anthony 1995). Volumes on nationalism and the creation and maintenance of ethnic identities have traced developments over the past few centuries and demonstrate how archaeological accounts have been deeply imbricated (Kohl and Fawcett 1995; Trigger 1995; Díaz-Andreu and Champion 1996; Hamilakis 1996; Meskell 1998b). For example, Atatürk's creation of a modern, secular Turkish state drew on imagery and heritage claims from Sumerian Mesopotamia as well as the Hittites in an explicitly political manner to rebuild a nation. Indeed, some have claimed there is a positive and empowering aspect to studies of ethnicity (Rowlands 1994; Naccache 1998). In a climate of postcolonialism, indigenous archaeologists have also been called on to produce narratives to counter the hegemonic discourses of Western commentators (papers in Bond and Gilliam 1994; Gathercole and Lowenthal 1994; Shennan 1994; Meskell 1998b). The World Archaeology Congress has had a particularly influential role in these developments.

As is clearly seen in sociology, ethnicity and gender may reside at the forefront of interpretive debate. However, archaeology has had a long-standing interest in class and status (e.g. Peebles and Kus 1977; Tainter 1978; J. A. Brown 1981; Chapman et al. 1981; Chapman and Randsborg 1981; O'Shea 1984; Morris 1987, 1992; Lesko 1994; Wason 1994; Nordström 1996; Joyce 1996; S. Brown 1997; Meskell 1997). In

Weberian terms, class refers to a group of people who have in common a specific causal component of their life chances insofar as this component is represented exclusively by economic interests. He distinguished class from status, since the latter is based on a specific, positive or negative, social estimation of honor and styles of life. However, there is often a strong correlation between the two phenomena. Class theory in sociology, based on Marx and Weber, has been recently charged with constructing an oversocialized conception of human nature (Crompton 1995). From the 1960s onward there has been an active critique of the closed system where the social world is perceived as a cohesive totality, resistant to change and structured by a tightly arranged hierarchy of power (Bauman 1995: 77). Comparative studies of civilizations have demonstrated that no human population is confined within a single system, but rather in a multiplicity of only partly coalescing organizations, collectives, and systems. After the 1970s, discussion of these issues fragmented into structure/agency debates. Major players like Althusser, Foucault, and Bourdieu diffused the image of society as an implacable machine that serves to maintain inequality, power, and privilege (Touraine 1995: 85), and this vision has persisted in archaeological theorizing, particularly in mortuary studies (e.g. DeMarrais et al. 1996; Earle 1997; Kristiansen 1991).

The growing interest in rank within archaeology emerged out of a broader trend toward a social archaeology, largely stimulated by the work of Childe, Clarke, Renfrew, and the Cambridge school (e.g. Hodder, Miller, Tilley, Shanks). Following the work of Service and Fried, archaeologists in the United States, like Yoffee and Earle, pursued models derived from anthropology (particularly the big man, chiefdom, stratified society, and state typologies) to describe the evolution of complex society. Most of these archaeologists were aiming to identify institutionalized status inequality, i.e. any hierarchy of statuses that form part of social structure and extend beyond age, sex, individual characteristics, and intrafamilial roles (Wason 1994: 19). Another development stemmed from Marxist notions of class struggle and oppression and found its fullest expression in historical archaeology (e.g. Spriggs 1984; Paynter and McGuire 1991). From the 1980s, many archaeologists have been gripped by Giddensian structuration theory: the notion that modes of economic relationships are translated into non-economic social structures (Giddens 1981: 105, see also Giddens 1984). This approach implies that class relationships are actively structured, although Giddens has received serious criticism for undermining agency in his own writing (Craib 1992; Shilling and Mellor 1996). Similarly Bourdieu has been embraced by archaeologists as a social theorist who promises to dissolve the structure:agency dualism and for allowing agents some contribution to their construction in the world (Bourdieu 1977, 1987, 1998). However, many of the same criticisms could be leveled at Bourdieu, who still manages to perpetuate a top-down vision of class structure and identity, delimiting the possibilities for self-fashioning. In archaeology, the ground-breaking paper which re-envisioned class in relation to a host of other signifiers was Elizabeth Brumfiel's American Anthropological Association Distinguished Lecture on gender, class, and faction. Here she argued against the system-based (or ecosystem) approach in favor of an agent-centered one which acknowledges the dynamism of gendered, ethnic, and class interactions (Brumfiel 1992). She imputed that elites were not the only prime movers of change and that subordinate groups could affect the structure of hierarchy. From this position paper we can witness the nascent stirrings of a third wave feminist position which encompassed a range of identity markers allowing for hierarchies of difference in archaeological interpretation.

Approaches to other dimensions of identity that are burgeoning are those of age, the body, intimate relations (e.g. Gamble 1998; Lyons 1998; Meskell 1998c), and sexuality (see below). To date, studies of aging have largely referred to a focus upon children, though this is gradually being replaced by more nuanced readings of the lifecycle (papers in Gilchrist 2000). A recent study of Egyptian private life employs the lifecycle as a more relevant template from which we might apprehend Egyptian experience, rather than traditional, Western, and ultimately teleological categorizations (Meskell forthcoming). These vectors of inquiry are related to an engendered enterprise but are depicted as often being tangential to it since they do not explicitly target "women" per se.

Conceptualizing the body has recently provided a salient nexus for reconciling issues such as biological imperatives, cultural markers, personal embodiment and experience, diachronic diversity, and social difference. There has been a vast outpouring of case studies from prehistoric contexts (e.g. Shanks and Tilley 1982; Yates and Nordbladh 1990; Kus 1992; Marcus 1993; Thomas and Tilley 1993; Yates 1993; Shanks 1995; Knapp and Meskell 1997) to historically embedded examples (e.g. Bahrani 1996; Meskell 1996, 1998d, 1999; Robins 1996; Winter 1996; Joyce 1998, 2000a, 2001; Gilchrist 1997, 1999; Montserrat 1998; Osborne 1998a, 1998b). These studies suggest that archaeology as a discipline has much to offer other social sciences in being able to discuss the cultural specificities of corporeality, as well as a long temporal trajectory. Many of the initial studies drew heavily on Foucauldian notions of bodily inscription, that is, the literal marking of society upon the body of the individual. Social constructionism, largely influenced by poststructuralist theorizing, conceives bodies and identities as constructed through various disciplines and discourses. Following Craib (1998: 7), I would argue that in matters of agency and politics, identity is irreducible, it cannot be explained away. Foucauldian archaeology was followed in the 1990s by more contextual readings of embodiment on both cultural and individual levels, influenced by feminist and corporeal philosophies. Identity and experience are now perceived as being deeply implicated and grounded in the materiality of the body. Although there is social malleability, evident in the construction of bodily identity, there is also a material fixity which frames the individual, as there is with most strands of identity. Other related arenas of interest converge around subjectivity, selfhood, agency, emotionality, and the individual (Blake 1999; Meskell 1999; Tarlow 1999).

Explications of the body in all its sexed specificities prompted new discussions of sexuality in archaeology in the late 1990s (e.g. Montserrat 1996; Koloski-Ostrow and Lyons 1997; Robb 1997; Hollimon 2000; Joyce 2000a; Meskell 1999, 2000; McCafferty and McCafferty 1999). Generally, the field has been slow to recognize the interpretive potentials of this significant vector of identity. It was only in 1998 that the first session on sexuality was organized for the Society for American Archaeology meetings (Schmidt and Voss 2000). Sexuality is very much a historical construction which brings together a host of different biological and psychical possibilities, such as gender identity, bodily differences, reproductive capacities, needs, desires, and fantasies. These need not be linked together and in other cultures have not been (Weeks 1997: 15). It is variety, not uniformity, that is the norm. Like the other strands of identity discussed, "sexuality may be thought about, experienced and acted on differently according to age, class, ethnicity, physical ability, sexual orientation and preference, religion, and region" (Vance 1984: 17). For archaeologists it may be possible to pursue the subject of sexuality in a number of ways. Following Weeks (1997: 23) we might ask how is sexuality shaped and articulated by economic, social, and political structures; how and why has this domain come to be so central to Western culture given its various possibilities; what is the relationship between sex and power specifically in terms of class and race divisions? In addition, gendered archaeology has taken heterosexuality to be the normative category, although the rise of queer theory, and the enormous popularity of Judith Butler's writings, exposed this position as untenable (Claassen 1992a; Meskell 1996; Joyce 1996). In all our engagements with this volatile topic we have to recenter human agency, volition, and variability.

Archaeology in its current interpretive guise is enjoying a *frisson* of activity in the arena of identity. Made possible through the plurality of a postprocessual archaeology, the debate has been most ardently influenced by the recent outgrowth of gender and feminist archaeologies. It is for this reason that I will briefly chart the developments in this critical area of identity in archaeology.

## Gendered identities

In the 1980s gender archaeology emerged within the conceptual space of a postprocessual archaeology. It became *de rigueur* to critique the construction of knowledge within the field, especially those studies which claimed scientific objectivity. The first programmatic paper appeared in 1984 (Conkey and Spector 1984), although its real impact was felt in the 1990s when the validity of feminist perspectives gained widespread recognition. Reasons for this initial reluctance have been posited as the earlier positivist, hypothetico-deductive trends in processual archaeology, particularly in its American guise (Wylie 1991, 1992). The first volume devoted to gender and informed by feminist theory appeared as late as 1991 (Gero and Conkey 1991) and was influenced by long-standing feminist contributions in anthropology (see also Conkey and Gero 1997).

Like Wylie (1991) I see the course of gender archaeology as having taken several different turnings in the preceding two decades. She saw a tripartite development beginning with the critique of androcentrism, followed by the search for women and a fundamental reconceptualization: this was not an unfolding of stages but a parallel structuring (Joyce and Claassen 1997: 2). The first forays are best characterized as "finding women," which refers not only to those women of prehistory, but to female archaeologists who had been erased from our own historiographic record (e.g. Gero 1985; Nixon 1994). To remedy this came numerous volumes dedicated to eminent women of the past, many of whom were far from feminist in their own politics (e.g. Kathleen Kenyon, Harriet Boyd Hawes; see Reyman 1992; Parezo 1993; Claassen 1994; Schrire 1995). Extensive studies that highlighted equity issues in both academic and non-academic archaeologies underscored the glaring bias in regard to education, employment, publication, and academic seniority (Nelson et al. 1994). The inherent sexism involved in conducting fieldwork, central to both archaeology and anthropology (Gero and Root 1990), was another central issue. Similar concerns have continued into later writings (e.g. Gero 1996).

Feminist contributions then moved toward revisionist histories (Gilchrist 1991), recasting women as active agents, creating their own social realities and resisting domination in the process (e.g. Arnold 1991; Beaudry et al. 1991; Gero and Conkey 1991; Hodder 1991; Øvrevik 1991; Spencer-Wood 1991). This was particularly visible in prehistoric scenarios which had tacitly promoted a history of "mankind," characterized by "man the hunter" and similar stone-age *mentalités*. In the mid-1990s a series of contextual studies emerged, putting into practice theories of gender (e.g. Gibbs 1987; Robins 1993; Wall 1994; Gilchrist 1994; Spector 1994; Yentsch 1994). However, many were to remain implicitly studies of women. These concrete case studies were a marked departure from earlier position papers and critiques of androcentrism. With them came a flurry of edited books, often conference proceedings (e.g. Bertelsen et al. 1987; Walde and Willows 1991; Claassen 1992b; du Cros and Smith 1993; Kokkinidou and Nikolaidou 1993; Balm and Beck 1995; Wright 1996; Casey et al. 1998). Many of these 1990s studies have been firmly locked in the language of second wave feminism, reiterating the constant oppression of women, and *doing gender* as finding women, looking at women's clothes and hairstyles, and ignoring the complexities of sex, sexuality, ageing, status, ethnicity, thus eliding all possibilities of difference. Gender is only one social determinate in the hierarchy of identity issues. As Conkey and Gero ask:

> Why, despite the many new studies in the archaeology of gender, have most merely added gender as just another variable into an otherwise depersonalized view of the past? into an archaeological account in the passive voice? into a way of framing human life that distances and categorizes more than allowing our own positionalities to inform and generate engagements with the people of the past? We worry that the recent archaeological studies of gender have participated in narrowing the field rather than opening up our studies. (Conkey and Gero 1997: 425)

At the end of the 1990s archaeologists of gender have pursued third wave agendas, often implicitly, by interpolating factors such as age, sexual orientation, ethnicity (e.g. Claassen and Joyce 1997; Gilchrist 1997; Hollimon 1997; Joyce and Claassen 1997; Lesick 1997; Lesure 1997; Prezzano 1997; Rega 1997; Wilson 1997; Sweely 1999; Woodhouse-Beyer 1999). This has been a long overdue shift from the second wave feminist tenets of finding women, as a homogeneous group, at the cost of all others. Gender identity should be seen as a complex assortment of networks of signifying practices, varying for individuals over time, as it intersects with other networks of signifying practices located in such concepts as class and race. As Alison Wylie (1992: 59) commented almost a decade ago, "feminists can no longer assume substantial commonalities in the power held, exercised, or suffered by women *as women*; their own critical and empirical explorations make it clear that, even within a single society, the extent and kinds of power women exercise varies dramatically across class, race, and ethnic divisions, and also through the life cycles of individual women." The corollary of this could be found in contemporary masculinist theory, yet studies of social relations, masculinity (Knapp and Meskell 1997; Knapp 1998), or sexuality have not generally been construed as gender archaeology. There remains a considerable time lag in the recognition of these more nuanced engagements. *Ipso facto* gender remains the domain of women writing predominantly about women.

It is now axiomatic that our identities are fluid and mutable, under negotiation as we experience life, and open to manipulation if we have the opportunity. Life on the web has demonstrated that people will avidly change their gender and their sexual preferences when confronted with the opportunity afforded by anonymity (Turkle 1996; Porter 1997). People do not always perform as "men" or "women" and identities are not coherent or prior to the interactions through which they are constituted. Individuals are gendered through discursive daily practices: "gender is thus a process of becoming rather than a state of being" (Harvey and Gow 1994a: 8). This new concept of identity politics does not necessarily entail objective needs or political implications, but challenges the connections between identity and politics and positions identity as a factor in any political analysis. Thus, we can say that though gender is not natural, biological, universal, or essential, we can still claim that it is relevant because of its political ramifications. Here gender is defined in positional terms. In the past few decades we have been indelibly influenced, both in political and professional terms, by the sexual revolution, gay liberation, feminism and race-minority power (di Leonardo and Lancaster 1997). It must come as no surprise then that much work is suffused with those very concepts or that, in the least, contemporary theory has been influenced by those events.

Some would posit distinct problems with the use of contemporary identity terminologies to discuss the ancient past. For example, how do we reconceptualize "sex" in societies that do not conform to Western binary categories and how do we even begin to use the word "gender," itself founded on the discursive construction of biological sex versus culturally created gender? Additionally, in cultures such as Egypt there was no word for heterosexual or homosexual (Parkinson 1995), so how might we apprehend same-sex relations in that well-documented context? I would suggest that there are two projects that archaeologists could pursue. First, we can acknowledge that "homosexuality" is an aspect of identity with enormous contemporary valency and that it is entirely valid to examine similar engagements in the past, whilst acknowledging that there are cultural specificities which name and label practices and people in divergent ways (Foucault 1978, 1985, 1986). Second, we can acknowledge that "same-sex relations" may present a less loaded terminology and focus predominantly on the salient differences with which people name and construct their lived identities. Archaeologists might focus on the diverse ways people experience their lives without the constraining taxonomies with which modern Westerners have shackled themselves, i.e. that "homosexuality" did not exist as a typology prior to the late 1800s. But we should not let semantics impede us: language and culture do not necessarily constitute what is talked about. As Craib quips:

> I cannot talk about my liver without language, but it does not make any sense to say that my liver is constructed by language or culture . . . different societies might have different conceptions of the liver and its function and one might surmise that modern medical science has a very sophisticated concept of the liver – much more sophisticated, for example, than classical Greek society. However, it does not follow that my liver is more sophisticated than was Plato's liver. (1998: 109)

## Unnatural domains

I would like now to argue that it is not enough to provide a list of salient identity markers, we must interrogate the very foundations of our imposed categories and try to understand social domains in their cultural context. I suggest that archaeologists have been reticent in adopting a third wave feminist approach, whereby they would conduct complex analysis of identity in holistic terms, and this represents the first stumbling block. Without a recognition of the full spectrum of social difference and the specificities of operation, archaeologists cannot move on to further contextual understandings by deconstructing the "natural" categories we create and project. So I see that archaeology has a double project to fulfill. And the inspiration for this theorization has come from anthropology, specifically from the work by Sylvia Yanagisako and Carol Delaney (1995a), *Naturalizing Power*. Theirs is a provocative thesis which focuses attention on the domains in society that are crucial for the formation of people's identity – family, sexuality, race, nation, religion. They argue that we cannot assume a priori that what *we* consider as natural, no matter how institutionalized, is fundamental. They argue that

> [t]he verities on which identity – whether gender, sexual orientation, nationality, ethnicity, or religion – has traditionally been based no longer provide the answers, in part because of the contact and conflict between peoples and in part because the explanatory schemes upon which identity was based have been shown to rest not on the bedrock of fact but suspended in narratives of origin. (Yanagisako and Delaney 1995b: 1)

Whilst the false foundational premises of sex and gender have only recently been challenged in archaeology, this has rarely extended to other vectors of identity – whether it be sexuality or ethnicity. Archaeologists have found it difficult to extricate themselves from "naturalized power" in the discourses of identity that are fundamental to our own culture: thus we have construed gender in the past, for instance, as simplistically mirroring specific contemporary terms and agendas, or connoted sexuality as existing primarily in a modern European guise. The specificities of the ancient data, when studied contextually, challenge that normativity. Reciprocally, anthropologists and social sociologists might draw upon archaeology's provision of a deep temporal sequence in terms of cultural difference, often as it is mediated through the discursive production of material culture. This rich strata of evidence can only enhance, and contribute to, the complex picture already emerging of identity as having both contextual and embedded entanglements.

Anthropologists Yanagisako and Delaney ask: "what is more natural than sex?" Yet we can easily go about demonstrating the cultural diversity of approaches in specific contexts: understanding biology/reproduction is not necessarily correspondent with the obvious logical causality that we make. Consider David Schneider's work with the Yap, a group living in the Pacific, who recognize the linkage between sexual organs, intercourse, and reproduction in pigs, yet view human sexuality rather differently. After all, as they wisely point out, pigs are not people (Yanagisako and Delaney 1995b: 7). There are other ways of seeing and deploying similar knowledges. For ourselves,

> [g]ender definition and value have been inherent in the Western theory of procreation, but procreation is not just about the natural; it includes an ontological dimension. Because gender is at the heart of these socio-

religious systems it is not surprising that issues of gender and procreation – marriage, family, birth control, abortion, sexuality, homosexuality, new reproductive technologies – are at the centre of contemporary debates in our society, for new beliefs and practices are not just about the private, domestic domain, but challenge the entire cosmological order. (Yanagisako and Delaney 1995b: 9; see also Weeks 1997)

And much the same point could be directed at the ancient Egyptian evidence, specifically the domestic evidence at the New Kingdom site of Deir el Medina (ca. 1550–1070 BC; see Meskell 1998a) with its iconography of female sexuality, birth, children, ritual, and religion all existing harmoniously in a settlement context (Meskell 1999, 2000), and usually within the same room, signifying the necessary blurring of category and the linkage between identity and the cosmological order. What we see as natural exists largely within our own temporal and cultural borders, yet we take this as fixed and "natural" and thus transferable to ancient contexts. The elision of difference results in a predictably normative picture of the past that may bear little relation to ancient realities.

For a fuller explication of these processes of identity formation and social domains, archaeologists might look to anthropological case studies. Lila Abu-Lughod's influential studies of the Egyptian Bedouin suggest that formal institutional domains are not cross-culturally applicable and that coherent systems of meaning can exist in seemingly contradictory ways: the discourse of honor and shame is set beside the poetic discourse of vulnerability and attachment (Abu-Lughod 1991: 162; Abu-Lughod 1993). Although not wanting to infer lineage or stasis, I would posit that similar contradictory themes were interwoven in ancient Egyptian society: female sexuality, desire, and romantic freedoms could be easily juxtaposed with mothering, birth and domestic ritual, as well as sexual inequality, legal discrimination and harsh, sometimes misogynist, treatments of women in society (Meskell 1994, 1998a, 1999). Other societies, from the Pacific to Latin America, constellate sexuality and violence in ways Anglo-Americans find difficult to conceptualize or accept (Harvey and Gow 1994b). Love and desire can be predicated on socially sanctioned practices which threaten the physical integrity of the beloved. In essence we should relinquish our own desire for a coherent narrative structure of social identity and life experience.

Archaeologists might also draw on, and contribute to, recent feminist analyses of identity, specifically those which source individual (and gender) identity along multiple lines. The engendered subject occupies the site of multiple differences and thus multiple subjectivities (Moore

1994: 143). Drawing on the work of de Lauretis, Moore refers to this as a post-poststructuralist concept of subjectivity. De Lauretis (1986: 9) cites a body of emergent feminist writing that offers the concept of a multiple, shifting, and often self-contradictory identity – this entails "an identity made up of heterogeneous and heteronomous representations of gender, race and class, and often indeed across languages and cultures." Feminist musings on embodied subjectivity and the contradictory positions we assume as part of daily (gendered) negotiations are helpful for archaeologists examining the contradictions presented to us by the ancient data, particularly those related to intimate relations and sexed hierarchies of power and inequality. It is perhaps at this level that archaeologists can finally participate within wider gender debates about issues of representation and reality – offering the potentials of real interdisciplinarity.

The meanings of male and female are not always about natural or prediscursive difference, thus prompting us to explore the ways in which these meanings are connected with other inequalities, supposedly structured by other differences. Feminists have been committed to challenging the gender status quo and feminist anthropologists played a crucial role in situating ideologies of natural identities within structures of inequality. Research on gender already suggests that its construction doesn't always follow predetermined, "natural" patterns so that archaeological interpretations "will have to focus on the particularities of gender constructs, especially their symbolic and ideational dimensions, in specific contexts" (Wylie 1991: 49). We should further recognize that hierarchies of status and power come already embedded in symbolic systems which can only be revealed through contextually specific cultural practices (Yanagisako and Delaney 1995b: 10–11). So instead of structuring identity along single, unilinear lines as Nelson (1997: 16) would argue, we might consider revising the entire ontological basis of our investigations. Might it not be better to consider social lives in terms of the lifecycle rather than a list of social signifiers? To date we have followed the latter line of inquiry, reducing social relations to a simple set of separate identity politics. By considering the lifecycle we might more closely approximate the realities of social experience, since age and sex, sexuality and life course, ethnicity and class more often coalesce together and in indivisible ways. This is also part of the deconstruction of naturalism, a breaking down of the categories we hold as distinct.

Recent investigations at Deir el Medina, specifically the rich mortuary data (Meskell 1998c, 1999), suggest that sex cannot be singled out as the primary structuring principle since a host of factors were operative and subject to change within a matter of generations. In the poorer cemetery of the early-mid-Eighteenth Dynasty age and marital status seem to be the primary issues for structuring inequality, whereas sex was generally smoothed over. The burial wealth of males and females was basically commensurate at this lower socio-economic level. The spatial layout of this cemetery was based on the lifecycle: neonates were buried at the base of the slope, children further up, adolescents were buried mid-slope and adults were positioned at the top of the slope. In the wealthier cemetery the main distinction structuring tomb wealth was sex and to a lesser degree age. Men were buried with many times the burial wealth of their female counterparts. For the same cemetery in the Ramesside Period, some hundred years later, divisions on the basis of sex lessen and tombs begin to include a large number of family members and generations, suggesting a move to lineage-based burials. There is no children's cemetery and all family members tend to be incorporated into these multi-vaulted tombs. Nonetheless, male relatives continue to get the lion's share of funerary wealth and are featured more prominently in mortuary iconography and representations. The 400 tombs at Deir el Medina which span the entire New Kingdom provide a concrete example of the complexities of identity issues, which cannot be reduced to unidimensional analyses but must be made complex, rather than doing interpretive violence to the data – that is, privileging one dimension of difference because of our own political commitments.

This need for multidimensional analysis equally applies to the taxonomies that archaeologists regularly deploy, domains such as the domestic, religious or ritual, social and sexual spheres, etc. In the settlement at Deir el Medina we can also see the breakdown or blurring of categories. I have previously discussed the overlapping of domesticity, sexuality, and ritual life in Egyptian social life. The iconography of these households might strike us as contradictory: in rooms supposedly relating to women's space and birthing we had an example of a nude, female musician replete with several erotic signifiers (Meskell 2000). At first glance the woman depicted has all the visual cues we would associate with a male view of sexuality – possibly even prostitution. The workman Nebamun either painted this image himself or had it commissioned, and it occupied a prominent position, being immediately visible to anyone who entered the house. I remember wondering how the women of the house related to this example of erotica – was it pornographic, offensive, or even desirable for these women? It is easy for us to separate out such images as being sexual or pornographic because of contemporary labels and taxonomies (see Hunt 1993). Yet these initial reactions were gradually replaced by a sense of blurred boundaries and collapsed dichotomies, a sense that sexuality did not exist as a separate sphere;

there is no word for "sexuality" in Egyptian language. One is not designed heterosexual or homosexual either; there were names for practices rather than people (Parkinson 1995: 59). From the archaeological and iconographic data it appeared that what we term "sexuality" pervaded so many aspects of Egyptian social and ritual life that it was a truly embedded concept, free of many of the moralistic connotations we are familiar with. It proved unproductive to hold to Western categories when Egyptian ones were so culturally different and fundamental to a more contextual understanding of social dynamics. Judeo-Christian sentiments might radically erase the connections between family and sexuality, the sexualization of children, or the possibilities of sexuality in the next life – but the Egyptians had no such framework. The interstices of all these networks of identity and experience provide the really interesting terrain of ancient life.

Another dimension through which identity is formulated and established is that of what we construe as kin, usually as defined by anthropological theorizing. According to Yanagisako and Delaney, "any particular kinship system was thought to be a cultural elaboration of the biological facts of human reproduction, and anthropologists recognized that there were significant differences in how far these genealogical maps extended and how relations in them were classified" (1995b: 9–10). As a demonstration of a challenge to this normativity we might return to Egyptian kinship terminology, which extended to those of blood relation as well as unrelated peer groups. The term *sn* for "brother" is a salient example; it includes the relationship of brother, brother-in-law, brother's son, mother's brother, and sister's son (Robins 1979: 202). Much the same pattern exists for the female equivalent *snt* for "sister". Lovers frequently refer to themselves as brother and sister (Robins 1979: 203; McDowell 1999), which read literally has led to much confusion over Egyptian incest.

David Schneider famously critiqued the reduction of kinship to genealogy, arguing that kinship cannot be conflated simply with a biological infrastructure since the cultural dimension, terms, and practices vary widely from society to society (Weston 1995: 88). If we find it difficult to refigure kin outside our own Western terminologies then consider our own deconstruction of kinship as a domain. Our own notions of kinship are now being challenged by two powerful domains: new reproductive technologies and changing gender and sexual relationships (see Dolgin 1995; McKinnon 1995). Today we are effectively rewriting kin relations in social and legal spheres. This predicament underscores that nothing is natural (see Laqueur 1990), since science and sexuality have begun impinging on what many would posit were the most fundamental of human social relationships at the very nexus of individual identity.

In ancient contexts we can never be clear where one cultural domain ends and another begins. Take the example of the ancestor busts in Egypt, revered relatives who had become effective spirits in the next world (Demarée 1983; Friedman 1985, 1994). The boundaries are blurred between kinship, magic, and religion. These artifacts bridged the classic divide between the functioning objects of this world and the world beyond the grave. Even the concept of the object as a static artifact without agency in and of itself has been rendered suspect (Gell 1998: 134, 223). In a similar study Rosemary Joyce (2000b) has suggested that Mesoamerican heirloom valuables such as jades and costume ornaments were circulated for hundreds of years after their production, thus retaining residual memories and taking on new meanings for Classic Maya nobles. Here again artifacts become repositories of more than single meanings and histories, they become liminal pieces in the worlds of both living and dead. According to Yanagisako and Delaney, only culture makes the boundaries of domains seem natural, gives ideologies power, and makes hegemonies appear seamless. It might be more interesting to inquire how meanings migrate across domain boundaries and how specific actions are multiply constituted. How do we as archaeologists historicize our domains and trace their effects? We also have to interrogate what we have constructed as the facts of life, calling into question the constricting constructions of motherhood, the domain of kinship, the spheres of sexuality and religiosity for example. If the sacred is open to divergent readings then what is supposedly "natural" must be revisited. Anthropologists, and by extension archaeologists, have happily read across other people's cultural domains. In fact anthropology has shown us the inherent pitfalls of that approach, suggesting to those of us who study the past that we too have been guilty of projecting "natural" boundaries and categorizations onto unsuitable, very different cultural contexts. We cannot assume that in other societies cultural domains are structured like ours and expect the same analytic constellations and results. Contextual archaeology is premised on the recognition of local patterns of meanings-in-practice. But I would argue we have not taken it far enough. Archaeologists have been reticent to explore the full spectrum of social identity, either because they are wary of increased complexity in their analyses or due to their privileging of specific discourses of difference – predominantly gender-based inequality.

As a feminist I argue we need to democratize our struggles by giving equal respect to the claims of other minorities, resulting in a real theoretical pluralism which is in keeping with both third wave feminism as well as postprocessual or contextual archaeology. Extending this redescription further I have suggested we critique and explore the construction of ancient social domains, those which we have overlain from contemporary culture assuming that they are "natural" and fundamental due to our own institutionalization. Following Yanagisako and Delaney, these are generally the analytic domains of kinship, gender, politics, religion, and social systems. I have proposed that many of these domains are now being refigured in contemporary society and should similarly be interrogated more fully before application to archaeological or historical contexts. If we fail to push these questions further we risk an elision of difference, conflating ancient and modern experience in the process. Identity provides a salient case in point – as one of the most compelling issues of our day it is right that we focus on the social experiences of ancient people, yet what makes these questions so intriguing is how specific societies evoked such different responses prompted by categorical differences in their understandings and constructions of social domains. We should fight the temptation to elide history through the deep-seated conviction that what is "real" cannot, should not, be subject to change (Weston 1995: 90–1) and acknowledge that as cultural commentators we continually reinvent and romanticize the "real."

## NOTE

This chapter owes a substantial intellectual debt to the work of Sylvia Yanagisako and Carol Delaney in *Naturalizing Power*. It is not often that a single work impells us to re-envision our ways of seeing culture and category in ontological terms or to reframe the operationalizing of identities in a well-known context such as ancient Egypt. I would also like to thank Victor Buchli, Geoff Emberling, Ian Hodder, Rosemary Joyce, and Chris Gosden for reading and commenting on the piece. A special thanks to Alison Wylie for her close reading of the text and for her many insights.

## REFERENCES

Abu-Lughod, L. 1991. Writing against culture. In R. G. Fox (ed.), *Recapturing Anthropology: Working in the Present*, 137–62. Santa Fe: School of American Research Press.

Abu-Lughod, L. 1993. Islam and the gendered discourse of death. *International Journal of Middle Eastern Studies* 25: 187–205.

Aldenderfer, M. S. (ed.) 1993. *Domestic Architecture, Ethnicity and Complementarity in the South-Central Andes*. Iowa: University of Iowa Press.

Anthony, D. 1995. Nazi and eco-feminist prehistories: counter points in Indo-European archaeology. In P. Kohl and C. Fawcett (eds), *Nationalism, Politics and the Practice of Archaeology*, 82–96. Cambridge: Cambridge University Press.

Arnold, B. 1990. The past as propaganda: totalitarian archaeology in Nazi Germany. *Antiquity* 64: 464–78.

Arnold, B. 1991. The deposed Princess of Vix: the need for an engendered European prehistory. In D. Walde and N. Willows (eds), *The Archaeology of Gender*, 366–74. Calgary: University of Calgary.

Auger, R. et al. (eds) 1987. *Ethnicity and Culture*. Calgary: Archaeological Association at the University of Calgary.

Bahrani, Z. 1996. The Hellenization of Ishtar: nudity, fetishism, and the production of cultural differentiation in ancient art. *Oxford Art Journal* 19(2): 3–16.

Baines, J. 1996. Contextualizing Egyptian representations of society and ethnicity. In J.S. Cooper and G.M. Schwartz (eds), *The Study of the Ancient Near East in the 21st Century*, 339–84. Winona Lake, IN: Eisenbrauns.

Balm, J. and W. Beck (eds) 1995. *Gendered Archaeology: The Second Australian Women in Archaeology Conference*. Canberra: ANU Press.

Banks, M. 1996. *Ethnicity: Anthropological Constructions*. London: Routledge.

Bauman, Z. 1995. Sociology and postmodernity. In P. Joyce (ed.), *Class*, 74–83. Oxford: Oxford University Press.

Beaudry, M.C., L.J. Cook, and S.A. Mrozowski 1991. Artifacts and active voices: material culture as social discourse. In R.H. McGuire and R. Paynter (eds), *The Archaeology of Inequality*, 150–91. Oxford: Blackwell.

Bertelsen, R., A. Lillehammer, and J.-R. Naess (eds) 1987. *Were They All Men? An Examination of Sex Roles in Prehistoric Society*. Stavanger: Arkeologisk Museum i Stavanger.

Blake, E.C. 1999. Identity mapping in the Sardinian Bronze Age. *European Journal of Archaeology* 2(1): 55–75.

Bond, G.C. and A. Gilliam (eds) 1994. *Social Construction of the Past: Representation as Power*. London: Routledge.

Bourdieu, P. 1977. *Outline of a Theory of Practice*. Cambridge: Cambridge University Press.

Bourdieu, P. 1987. What makes a social class. *Berkeley Journal of Sociology* 22: 1–18.

Bourdieu, P. 1998. *Practical Reason: On the Theory of Action*. Cambridge: Polity.

Brown, J.A. 1981. The search for rank in prehistoric burials. In R. Chapman, I. Kinnes and K. Randsborg (eds), *The Archaeology of Death*, 25–37. Cambridge: Cambridge University Press.

Brown, K.S. 1994. Seeing stars: character and identity in the landscapes of modern Macedonia. *Antiquity* 68(261): 784–96.

Brown, S. 1997. "Ways of seeing" women in antiquity: an introduction to feminism in classical archaeology and art history. In A.O. Koloski-Ostrow and

C. L. Lyons (eds), *Naked Truths: Women, Sexuality, and Gender in Classical Art and Archaeology*, 12–42. London: Routledge.

Brumfiel, E. M. 1992. Distinguished Lecture in Archaeology. Breaking and entering the ecosystem – gender, class, and faction steal the show. *American Anthropologist* 94: 551–67.

Brumfiel, E. M. and J. W. Fox (eds) 1994. *Factional Competition and Political Development in the New World*. Cambridge: Cambridge University Press.

Casey, M. et al. (eds) 1998. *Redefining Archaeology: Feminist Perspectives*. Canberra: ANU Press.

Chapman, J. 1994. Destruction of a common heritage: the archaeology of war in Croatia, Bosnia and Hercegovina. *Antiquity* 68(258): 120–6.

Chapman, R. and K. Randsborg 1981. Approaches to the archaeology of death. In R. Chapman, I. Kinnes, and K. Randsborg (eds), *The Archaeology of Death*, 1–24. Cambridge: Cambridge University Press.

Chapman, R., I. Kinnes, and K. Randsborg (eds) 1981. *The Archaeology of Death*. Cambridge: Cambridge University Press.

Claassen, C. (ed.) 1992a. *Exploring Gender through Archaeology: Selected Papers from the 1991 Boone Conference*. Madison, WI: Prehistory Press.

Claassen, C. 1992b. Questioning gender: an introduction. In C. Claassen (ed.), *Exploring Gender through Archaeology: Selected Papers from the 1991 Boone Conference*, 1–9. Madison, WI: Prehistory Press.

Claassen, C. (ed.) 1994. *Women in Archaeology*. Philadelphia: University of Pennsylvania Press.

Claassen, C. and R. A. Joyce (eds) 1997. *Women in Prehistory: North America and Mesoamerica*. Philadelphia: University of Pennsylvania Press.

Conkey, M. W. and J. M. Gero 1997. Programme to practice: gender and feminism in archaeology. *Annual Review of Anthropology* 26: 411–37.

Conkey, M. W. and J. D. Spector 1984. Archaeology and the study of gender. *Advances in Archaeological Method and Theory* 7: 1–38.

Craib, I. 1992. *Anthony Giddens*. London: Routledge.

Craib, I. 1998. *Experiencing Identity*. London: Sage.

Crompton, R. 1995. The development of classical inheritance. In P. Joyce (ed.), *Class*, 43–55. Oxford: Oxford University Press.

de Lauretis, T. (ed.) 1986. *Feminist Studies/Critical Studies*. London: Macmillan.

Demarée, R. J. 1983. *The 3ḥ Ikr n Rᶜ-Stelae: On Ancestor Worship in Ancient Egypt*. Leiden: Nederlands Instituut voor het Nabije Oosten te Leiden.

DeMarrais, E., L. J. Castillo, and T. Earle 1996. Ideology, materialization, and power strategies. *Current Anthropology* 37(1): 15–32.

di Leonardo, M. and R. N. Lancaster 1997. Embodied meanings, carnal practices. In R. N. Lancaster and M. di Leonardo (eds), *The Gender/Sexuality Reader: Culture, History, Political Economy*, 1–10. New York: Routledge.

Díaz-Andreu, M. and T. Champion 1996. *Nationalism and Archaeology in Europe*. London: University College London Press.

Dolgin, J. L. 1995. Family law and the facts of family. In S. Yanagisako and C. Delaney (eds), *Naturalizing Power: Essays in Feminist Cultural Analysis*, 47–67. New York: Routledge.

du Cros, H. and L.-J. Smith (eds) 1993. *Women in Archaeology: A Feminist Critique*. Canberra: ANU Press.

Earle, T. 1997. *How Chiefs Come to Power: The Political Economy in Prehistory*. Palo Alto: Stanford University Press.

Emberling, G. 1997. Ethnicity in complex societies: archaeological perspectives. *Journal of Archaeological Research* 5(4): 295–344.

Foucault, M. 1978. *The History of Sexuality*. London: Routledge.

Foucault, M. 1980. *Herculine Barbin: Being the Recently Discovered Memoirs of a Nineteenth Century Hermaphrodite*. New York: Pantheon.

Foucault, M. 1985. *The History of Sexuality: The Use of Pleasure*. Harmondsworth: Penguin.

Foucault, M. 1986. *The History of Sexuality: The Care of the Self*. Harmondsworth: Penguin.

Friedman, F.A. 1985. On the meaning of some anthropoid busts from Deir el Medina. *Journal of Egyptian Archaeology* 71: 82–97.

Friedman, F.A. 1994. Aspects of domestic life and religion. In L.H. Lesko (ed.), *Pharaoh's Workers: The Villagers of Deir el Medina*, 95–117. New York: Cornell University Press.

Gamble, C. 1998. Palaeolithic society and the release from proximity: a network approach to intimate relations. *World Archaeology* 95(3): 426–49.

Gathercole, P.W. and D. Lowenthal (eds) 1994. *The Politics of the Past*. London: Routledge.

Gell, A. 1998. *Art and Agency: An Anthropological Theory*. Oxford: Oxford University Press.

Gero, J. 1985. Socio-politics and the woman-at-home ideology. *American Antiquity* 50(2): 342–50.

Gero, J. 1996. Archaeological practice and gendered encounters with field data. In R.P. Wright (ed.), *Gender and Archaeology*, 251–80. Philadelphia: University of Pennsylvania Press.

Gero, J.M. and M.W. Conkey (eds) 1991. *Engendering Archaeology: Women and Prehistory*. Oxford: Blackwell.

Gero, J. and D. Root 1990. Public presentation and private concerns: archaeology in the pages of National Geographic. In P. Gathercole and D. Lowenthal (eds), *The Politics of the Past*, 19–37. London: Routledge.

Gibbs, L. 1987. Identifying gender in the archaeological record: a contextual study. In I. Hodder (ed.), *The Archaeology of Contextual Meanings*, 79–89. Cambridge: Cambridge University Press.

Giddens, A. 1981. *The Class Structure of the Advanced Societies*. London: Hutchinson.

Giddens, A. 1984. *The Constitution of Society: Outline of a Theory of Structuration*. Cambridge: Polity Press.

Gilchrist, R. 1991. Women's archaeology? Political feminism, gender theory and historical revision. *Antiquity* 65: 495–501.

Gilchrist, R. 1994. *Gender and Material Culture: The Archaeology of Religious Women*. London: Routledge.

Gilchrist, R. 1997. Ambivalent bodies: gender and medieval archaeology. In

J. Moore and E. Scott (eds), *Invisible People and Processes: Writing Gender and Childhood into European Archaeology*, 42–58. London: Leicester University Press.

Gilchrist, R. L. 1999. *Gender and Archaeology: Contesting the Past*. London: Routledge.

Gilchrist, R. (ed.) 2000. *Human Lifecycles. World Archaeology* 31/3.

Hamilakis, Y. 1996. Through the looking glass: nationalism, archaeology and the politics of identity. *Antiquity* 70: 975–8.

Harvey, P. and P. Gow 1994a. Introduction. In P. Harvey and P. Gow (eds), *Sex and Violence: Issues in Representation and Experience*, 1–17. London: Routledge.

Harvey, P. and P. Gow (eds) 1994b. *Sex and Violence: Issues in Representation and Experience*. London: Routledge.

Hodder, I. 1991. Gender representation and social reality. In D. Walde and N. D. Willows (eds), *The Archaeology of Gender: Proceedings of the 22nd Annual Chacmool Conference*, 11–16. Calgary: University of Calgary Archaeological Association.

Hollimon, S. E. 1997. The third-gender in native California: two-spirit undertakers among the Chumash and their neighbors. In C. Claassen and R. Joyce (eds), *Women in Prehistory*, 173–88. Philadelphia: University of Pennsylvania Press.

Hollimon, S. E. 2000. Gender and sexuality in prehistoric Chumash society. In R. Schmidt and B. Voss (eds), *Archaeologies of Sexuality*. London: Routledge.

Hunt, L. (ed.) 1993. *The Invention of Pornography: Obscenity and the Origins of Modernity 1500–1800*. New York: Zone Books.

Jones, S. 1996. *The Archaeology of Ethnicity: Constructing Identities in the Past and Present*. London: Routledge.

Joyce, R. A. 1996. The construction of gender in Classic Maya monuments. In R. P. Wright (ed.), *Gender and Archaeology*, 167–95. Philadelphia: University of Pennsylvania Press.

Joyce, R. A. 1998. Performing the body in Prehispanic Central America. *RES: Anthropology and Aesthetics* 33(Spring): 147–66.

Joyce, R. A. 2000a. A Precolumbian gaze: male sexuality among the Ancient Maya. In R. Schmidt and B. Voss (eds), *Archaeologies of Sexuality*, 263–83. London: Routledge.

Joyce, R. A. 2000b. Heirlooms and houses: materiality and social memory. In R. A. Joyce and S. Gillespie (eds), *Beyond Kinship: Social and Material Reproduction in House Societies*, 189–202. Philadelphia: University of Pennsylvania Press.

Joyce, R. A. 2001. Performance and inscription: negotiating sex and gender in Classic Maya society. In C. Klein (ed.), *Gender in Prehispanic America*, 107–39. Washington DC: Dumbarton Oaks.

Joyce, R. A. and C. Claassen 1997. Women in the ancient Americas: archaeologists, gender and the making of prehistory. In C. Claassen and R. A. Joyce (eds), *Women in Prehistory: North America and Mesoamerica*, 1–14. Philadelphia: University of Pennsylvania.

Knapp, A. B. 1998. Who's come a long way, baby? Masculinist approaches to a gendered archaeology. *Archaeological Dialogues* 5(2): 91–106.

Knapp, A. B. and L. M. Meskell 1997. Bodies of evidence in prehistoric Cyprus. *Cambridge Archaeological Journal* 7(2): 183–204.

Kohl, P. L. and C. Fawcett (eds) 1995. *Nationalism, Politics and the Practice of Archaeology*. Cambridge: Cambridge University Press.

Kokkinidou, D. and M. Nikolaidou (eds) 1993. *Archaeology and Gender: Approaches to Aegean Prehistory*. Thessaloniki: Banias.

Koloski-Ostrow, A. O. and C. L. Lyons (eds) 1997. *Naked Truths: Women, Sexuality, and Gender in Classical Art and Archaeology*. London: Routledge.

Kristiansen, K. 1991. Chiefdoms, states, and systems of social evolution. In T. Earle (ed.), *Chiefdoms: Power, Economy, and Ideology*, 16–43. Cambridge: Cambridge University Press.

Kus, S. 1992. Toward an archaeology of body and soul. In J.-C. Gardin and C. Peebles (ed.), *Representations in Archaeology*. 168–77. Bloomington: Indiana University Press.

Laqueur, T. 1990. *Making Sex: Body and Gender from the Greeks to Freud*. Cambridge, MA: Harvard University Press.

Lesick, K. S. 1997. Re-engendering gender: some theoretical and methodological concerns on a burgeoning archaeological pursuit. In J. Moore and E. Scott (eds), *Invisible People and Processes: Writing Gender and Childhood into European Archaeology*, 31–41. London: Leicester University Press.

Lesko, B. S. 1994. Ranks, roles and rights. In L. H. Lesko (ed.), *Pharaoh's Workers: The Villagers of Deir el Medina*, 15–39. Ithaca, NY: Cornell University Press.

Lesure, R. G. 1997. Figurines and social identities in early sedentary societies of coastal Chiapas, Mexico 1550–800 b.c. In C. Claassen and R. A. Joyce (eds), *Women in Prehistory: North America and Mesoamerica*, 227–48. Philadelphia: University of Pennsylvania.

Lyons, D. 1998. Witchcraft, gender, power and intimate relations in Mura compounds in Déla northern Cameroon. *World Archaeology* 95(3): 344–62.

Marcus, J. and K. V. Flannery (eds) 1983. *The Cloud People: Divergent Evolution of the Zapotec and Mixtec Civilizations*. New York: Academic Press.

Marcus, M. I. 1993. Incorporating the Body: adornment, gender, and social identity in ancient Iran. *Cambridge Archaeological Journal* 3(2): 157–78.

McCafferty, G. G. and S. D. McCafferty 1999. The metamorphosis of Xochiquetzal. In T. Sweely (ed.), *Manifesting Power: Gender and the Interpretation of Power in Archaeology*, 103–25. London: Routledge.

McDowell, A. G. 1999. *Village Life in Ancient Egypt: Laundry Lists and Love Songs*. Oxford: Oxford University Press.

McGuire, R. H. 1982. The study of ethnicity in historical archaeology. *Journal of Anthropological Archaeology* 1: 159–78.

McKinnon, S. 1995. American kinship/American incest: asymmetries in a scientific discourse. In S. Yanagisako and C. Delaney (eds), *Naturalizing Power: Essays in Feminist Cultural Analysis*, 25–46. New York: Routledge.

Meskell, L. M. 1994. Dying young: the experience of death at Deir el Medina. *Archaeological Review from Cambridge* 13(2): 35–45.

Meskell, L. M. 1996. The somatisation of archaeology: institutions, discourses, corporeality. *Norwegian Archaeological Review* 29(1): 1–16.

Meskell, L. M. 1997. Egyptian social dynamics: the evidence of age, sex and class in domestic and mortuary contexts. Ph. D thesis, Department of Archaeology, Cambridge University.

Meskell, L. M. 1998a. An archaeology of social relations in an Egyptian village. *Journal of Archaeological Method and Theory* 5(3): 209–43.

Meskell, L. M. (ed.) 1998b. *Archaeology under Fire: Nationalism, Politics and Heritage in the Eastern Mediterranean and Middle East.* London: Routledge.

Meskell, L. M. 1998c. Intimate archaeologies: the case of Kha and Merit. *World Archaeology* 29(3): 363–79.

Meskell, L. M. 1998d. The irresistible Body and the seduction of archaeology. In D. Montserrat (ed.), *Changing Bodies, Changing Meanings: Studies on the Human Body in Antiquity*, 139–61. London: Routledge.

Meskell, L. M. 1999. *Archaeologies of Social Life: Age, Sex, Class etc. in Ancient Egypt.* Oxford: Blackwell.

Meskell, L. M. 2000. Re-embedding sex: domesticity, sexuality and ritual in New Kingdom Egypt. In R. Schmidt and B. Voss (eds), *Archaeologies of Sexuality*, 253–62. London: Routledge.

Meskell, L. M. forthcoming. *Private Life in New Kingdom Egypt.* Princeton, NJ: Princeton University Press.

Montserrat, D. 1996. *Sex and Society in Graeco-Roman Egypt.* London: Kegan Paul International.

Montserrat, D. (ed.) 1998. *Changing Bodies, Changing Meanings: Studies on the Human Body in Antiquity.* London: Routledge.

Moore, H. L. 1994. The problem of explaining violence in the social sciences. In P. Harvey and P. Gow (eds), *Sex and Violence: Issues in Representation and Experience*, 138–55. London: Routledge.

Morris, I. 1987. *Burial and Ancient Society: The Rise of the Greek City-State.* Cambridge: Cambridge University Press.

Morris, I. 1992. *Death-Ritual and Social Structure in Classical Antiquity.* Cambridge: Cambridge University Press.

Naccache, A. F. H. 1998. Beirut's memoryside: hear no evil, see no evil. In L. M. Meskell (ed.), *Archaeology under Fire: Nationalism, Politics and Heritage in the Eastern Mediterranean and Middle East*, 140–58. London: Routledge.

Nelson, M., S. M. Nelson, and A. Wylie (eds) 1994. *Equity Issues for Women in Archaeology*, Washington: Archaeological Papers of the American Anthropological Association 5.

Nelson, S. M. 1997. *Gender in Archaeology: Analyzing Power and Prestige.* Walnut Creek, CA: Altamira Press.

Nixon, L. 1994. Gender bias in archaeology. In L. J. Archer, S. Fischler, and M. Wyke (eds), *Women in Ancient Societies*, 1–23. London: Macmillan.

Nordström, H.-A. 1996. The Nubian A-Group: ranking funerary remains. *Norwegian Archaeological Review* 26(1): 17–39.

O'Shea, J.M. 1984. *Mortuary Variability: An Archaeological Investigation.* Orlando: Academic Press.

Osborne, R. 1998a. Men without clothes: heroic nakedness and Greek art. *Gender and History: Gender and Body in the Ancient Mediterranean* 9(3): 80–104.

Osborne, R. 1998b. Sculpted men of Athens: masculinity and power in the field of vision. In L. Foxhall and J. Salmon (eds), *Thinking Men: Masculinity and its Self-Representation in the Classical Tradition*, 23–42. London: Routledge.

Øvrevik, S. 1991. Engendering archaeology. Review section. *Antiquity* 65: 738–41.

Parezo, N. (ed.) 1993. *Hidden Scholars: Women Anthropologists and the Native American Southwest.* Albuquerque: University of New Mexico Press.

Parkinson, R.B. 1995. "Homosexual" desire and Middle Kingdom literature. *Journal of Egyptian Archaeology* 81: 57–76.

Paynter, R. and R.H. McGuire 1991. The archaeology of inequality: material culture, domination, and resistance. In R.H. McGuire and R. Paynter (eds), *The Archaeology of Inequality*, 1–27. Oxford: Blackwell.

Peebles, C.S. and S.M. Kus 1977. Some archaeological correlates of ranked societies. *American Antiquity* 42(3): 421–48.

Pollock, S. and C. Lutz 1994. Archaeology deployed for the Gulf War. *Critique of Anthropology* 14(3): 263–84.

Porter, D. (ed.) 1997. *Internet Culture.* New York: Routledge.

Prezzano, S. 1997. Warfare, women, and households: the development of Iroquois culture. In C. Claassen and R.A. Joyce (eds), *Women in Prehistory: North America and Mesoamerica*, 88–99. Philadelphia: University of Pennsylvania Press.

Rega, E. 1997. Age, gender and biological reality in the Early Bronze Age cemetery at Morkin. In J. Moore and E. Scott (eds), *Invisible People and Processes: Writing Gender and Childhood into European Archaeology*, 229–47. London: Leicester University Press.

Reyman, J. (ed.) 1992. *Rediscovering our Past: Essays on the History of American Archaeology.* Aldershot: Avebury.

Robb, J. 1997. Female beauty and male violence in early Italian society. In A. Olga Koloski-Ostrow and C.L. Lyons (eds), *Naked Truths: Women, Sexuality, and Gender in Classical Art and Archaeology*, 43–65. London: Routledge.

Robins, G. 1979. The relationships specified by Egyptian kinship terms of the Middle and New Kingdoms. *Chronique D'Égypte* 54(107): 197–217.

Robins, G. 1993. *Women in Ancient Egypt.* London: British Museum Press.

Robins, G. 1996. Dress, undress, and the representation of fertility and potency in New Kingdom Egyptian art. In N. Boymel Kampen (eds), *Sexuality in Ancient Art*, 27–40. Cambridge: Cambridge University Press.

Rowlands, M. 1994. The politics of identity in archaeology. In G.C. Bond and

A. Gilliam (eds), *Social Construction of the Past: Representation as Power*, 129–43. London: Routledge.

Sawicki, J. 1991. *Disciplining Foucault: Feminism, Power and the Body*. New York: Routledge.

Schmidt, R. and B. Voss (eds) 2000. *Archaeologies of Sexuality*. London: Routledge.

Schrire, C. 1995. *Digging through Darkness: Chronicles of an Archaeologist*. Charlottesville: University Press of Virginia.

Shanks, M. 1995. Art and archaeology of embodiment: some aspects of Archaic Greece. *Cambridge Archaeological Journal* 5(2): 207–44.

Shanks, M. and C. Tilley 1982. Ideology, symbolic power and ritual communication: a reinterpretation of Neolithic mortuary practices. In I. Hodder (ed.), *The Archaeology of Contextual Meanings*, 129–54. Cambridge: Cambridge University Press.

Shennan, S. (ed.) 1994. *Archaeological Approaches to Cultural Identity*. London: Routledge.

Shilling, C. and P. A. Mellor 1996. Embodiment, structuration theory and modernity: mind/body dualism and the repression of sensuality. *Body and Society* 2(4): 1–15.

Spector, J. D. 1994. *What this Awl Means: Feminist Archaeology at a Wahpeton Dakota Village*. St Paul: Minnesota Historical Society Press.

Spence, M. W. 1992. Tlailotlacan, a Zapotec enclave in Teotihuacan. In J. C. Berlo (ed.), *Art, Ideology, and the City of Teotihuacan*, 59–88. Washington: Dumbarton Oaks.

Spencer-Wood, S. M. 1991. Toward an historical archaeology of materialistic domestic reform. In R. H. McGuire and R. Paynter (eds), *The Archaeology of Inequality*, 231–86. Oxford: Blackwell.

Spriggs, M. (ed.) 1984. *Marxist Perspectives in Archaeology*. Cambridge: Cambridge University Press.

Sweely, T. 1999. Gender, space, people and power at Cerén, El Salvador. In T. Sweely (ed.), *Manifesting Power: Gender and the Interpretation of Power in Archaeology*, 155–71. London: Routledge.

Tainter, J. A. 1978. Mortuary practices and the study of prehistoric social systems. *Advances in Archaeological Method and Theory* 1: 105–41.

Tarlow, S. A. 1999. *Bereavement and Commemoration: An Archaeology of Mortality*. Oxford: Blackwell.

Thomas, J. and C. Tilley 1993. The axe and the torso: symbolic structures. In C. Tilley (ed.), *Interpretive Archaeology*, 225–324. Oxford: Berg.

Touraine, A. 1995. Sociology and the study of society. In P. Joyce (ed.), *Class*, 83–9. Oxford: Oxford University Press.

Trigger, B. G. 1989. *A History of Archaeological Thought*. Cambridge: Cambridge University Press.

Trigger, B. G. 1995. Romanticism, nationalism, and archaeology. In P. L. Kohl and C. Fawcett (eds), *Nationalism, Politics and the Practice of Archaeology*, 263–79. Cambridge: Cambridge University Press.

Turkle, S. 1996. *Life on the Screen: Identity in the Age of the Internet*. London: Weidenfeld and Nicolson.

Vance, C.S. (ed.) 1984. *Pleasure and Danger: Exploring Female Sexuality*. Boston: Routledge and Kegan Paul.

Walde, D. and N.D. Willows (eds) 1991. *The Archaeology of Gender: Proceedings of the 22nd Annual Chacmool Conference*. Calgary: University of Calgary Archaeological Association.

Wall, D. diZerega 1994. *The Archaeology of Gender: Separating the Spheres in Urban America*. New York: Plenum Press.

Wason, P.K. 1994. *The Archaeology of Rank*. Cambridge: Cambridge University Press.

Weeks, J. 1997. *Sexuality*. London: Routledge.

Weston, K. 1995. Naturalising Power. In S. Yanagisako and C. Delaney (eds), *Naturalizing Power: Essays in Feminist Cultural Analysis*, 87–110. New York: Routledge.

Wilson, D. 1997. Gender, diet, health, and social status in the Mississippian Powers Phase Turner cemetery population. In C. Claassen and R.A. Joyce (eds), *Women in Prehistory: North America and Mesoamerica*, 119–35. Philadelphia: University of Pennsylvania.

Winter, I.J. 1996. Sex, rhetoric, and the public monument: the alluring body of Naram-Sîn of Agade. In N.B. Kampen (ed.), *Sexuality in Ancient Art: Near East, Egypt, Greece and Italy*, 11–26. Cambridge: Cambridge University Press.

Woodhouse-Beyer, K. 1999. Artels and identities: gender, power, and Russian America. In T. Sweely (ed.), *Manifesting Power: Gender and the Interpretation of Power in Archaeology*, 129–54. London: Routledge.

Wright, R.A. (ed.) 1996. *Gender and Archaeology*. Philadelphia: University of Pennsylvania Press.

Wylie, A. 1991. Gender theory and the archaeological record: why is there no archaeology of gender. In J.M. Gero and M.W. Conkey (eds), *Engendering Archaeology: Women and Prehistory*, 31–54. Oxford: Blackwell.

Wylie, A. 1992. Feminist theories of social power: implications for a processual archaeology. *Norwegian Archaeological Review* 25(1): 51–68.

Yanagisako, S. and C. Delaney (eds) 1995a. *Naturalizing Power: Essays in Feminist Cultural Analysis*. New York: Routledge.

Yanagisako, S. and C. Delaney 1995b. Naturalizing power. In S. Yanagisako and C. Delaney (eds), *Naturalizing Power: Essays in Feminist Cultural Analysis*, 1–22. New York: Routledge.

Yates, T. 1993. Frameworks for an archaeology of the Body. In C. Tilley (ed.), *Interpretive Archaeology*, 31–72. Oxford: Berg.

Yates, T. and J. Nordbladh 1990. This perfect body, this virgin text: between sex and gender in archaeology. In I. Bapty and T. Yates (eds), *Archaeology after Structuralism*, 222–37. London: Routledge.

Yentsch, A.E. 1994. *A Chesapeake Family and their Slaves: A Study in Historical Archaeology*. Cambridge: Cambridge University Press.

# 9

# American Material Culture in Mind, Thought, and Deed

## Anne Yentsch and Mary C. Beaudry

This chapter takes its cue from Jacques Maquet (1993: 40): "it is essential to know what objects mean for the people who make and use them. [A] reading of objects always has to be supplemented by what people say and write about them. Objects can illuminate words; they cannot replace them." Yet large segments of history stand out where texts are non-existent or markedly silent (i.e. discussions of slavery from the slave's perspective in the American South). The concept that writing encapsulated history and provides a "natural" boundary mythologizes the span of human existence and gives primacy to a small number of centuries. Archaeology illuminates history.

Yet there is truth in the statement that the fullest range of layered meaning is obtained when one can consult an informant using her words and deeds to inform the analysis of material culture. Historical archaeology does so, and has reaped its greatest rewards thus far through its elaboration of North American history. Yet a dependence on formulaic artifact analysis and inadequate theories of material culture keep it from its full potential. We take this to be, for the colonial era in America, a study of the material residue of interaction among three cultures – red, white, and black – that elicits the cultural diversity, influence, and response of discrete, creolized ethnic communities and the subjectivity of individual actors. By the 1800s, the focus enlarges with a more numerous and diverse ethnic population and different institutional forces (i.e. industrialization, manifest destiny, divisive political beliefs, a strong national military, etc.). What archaeology offers for each era is a second, separate descriptive source that provides details, nuances of daily life, aspects of social experience, and belief systems from the perspective of

active "others" who are frequently not visible, or only partially represented, in documents. Their silence does not dishonor their influence,
emotions, creativity, and individuality in the roles each held – it stems
instead from written accounts that presuppose social separations. These
separations are bridged at archaeological sites.

Archaeologists see past life through the media of space and form
inserted within linear models of time. These are physical constraints
imposed on archaeologically derived data. The bridges begin to dissolve
when one inserts imagined peoples – members of prior cultures, or
"others." Next, archaeologists use artifacts to infer the beliefs, activities,
and the ideational organizing principles of the "other" to elicit her
culture. So, material culture is often seen only as the product of a site,
and because it is the out-growth of social action, the archaeological
"site" becomes a metonym for the past culture subsuming its communities and individual members. Yet material culture is not simply a product;
it *is* the infrastructure from which archaeological sites arise. Material
culture is *puissant* and imposes a frame upon human interaction affecting virtually every aspect of daily life.

It is and has been apparent that even as "ethnographic specimens" –
standing as metonyms for exotic "others" – objects evoke a multitude
of meanings. For example, in an 1893 pamphlet edited by Ida B. Wells,
*The Reason Why the Colored American is not in Chicago's World's
Columbian Exposition*, eminent African Americans protested the place-
ment of buildings, objects, exhibits, etc. The Exposition displaced black
citizens, ignoring their work and their contributions to national life.
Native Americans protested too. Iconic objects conveying mythic history
were on exhibit throughout. New Englanders, like Eben Horsford, found
the Italian claim that Columbus had discovered their Anglo-Saxon world
insufferable. Protesting those who accepted the link between Christopher
Columbus' voyages and New World settlement, Horsford displayed a
replica of a Viking ship to emphasize the role of northern Europeans
in voyages of discovery (Upton 1998: 84).[1] The presence and absence
of material objects was telling, illuminating the perceived hierarchy of
America as a nation.

An archaeologist excavating the Exposition would find artifacts from
two "normative" categories: (a) portable artifacts, and (b) *in situ* features that would be destroyed by excavation. The first are small things,
whereas the latter run the size gamut. Yet, no matter their size, each
speaks to culture in large ways, and their analysis is critical. Artifacts
can be analyzed for both information and knowledge (see Gosden, this
volume). They occupy two distinct cultural domains existing both as
instruments (i.e. labor-related devices) and as signs (i.e. signifiers of cul-

tural meaning) (Maquet 1993: 30). A distinction must be made in terms of the ideal versus the real and the manufacturing process versus the usage and the cycles therein. And then, to accomplish our goals, material culture has to be read for what it reveals about cultural dislocations, culture change, and the emergence of new perceptions or beliefs as to how the world works.

Artifacts hold a power that is rarely recognized by individual actors, for as "things" many reside within the taken-for-granted stratum of social action. People hold prearranged ideas about what "things" should look like or behave like that they cling to because their beliefs accord with cultural schemata. Joyner wrote, "Caught in the sensual music of conquest, the 'advanced' societies neither understand nor value the traditions" of the vanquished (1999: 167). Bluntly put, they simply don't see them. To take a modern example, computers perform in completely unexpected ways – ways that invoke grief, joy, or hours of troubleshooting. It matters little what our imperfect notions were or what a manufacturer meant to create; people must react to the reality of the object's existence and the constraints it introduces. The result is both a dislocation and a subsequent change in behavior.

## Material culture theory in historical archaeology

American and Canadian studies began linked to prehistory. Like most paradigmatic shifts, work began simultaneously as a cluster of analytical endeavors among individuals known to one another, yet not collaborating together. Thus one must look at the models of gravestones created by Deetz and Dethlefsen (1967), of folk houses developed by Henry Glassie (1975) and, following Glassie's example, of New England's material culture by Deetz (1977). In Williamsburg, Ivor Noël Hume (1963) drew on classic decorative arts models to look at small objects embedded in the stratigraphic layers of Virginia's revolutionary era sites. He used these to refine site chronologies, basing sequences on field observations and the presence/absence of artifacts with distinct date ranges (Noël Hume 1969). Stanley South (1977) drew from Noël Hume's expertise to create statistical models for ceramics that allowed him to establish chronologies and infer lifestyle.

Of all the above, the most sophisticated and circumscribing was Glassie's view of material culture, but it was not immediately apparent how to use it to look at small classes of artifacts. Glassie's perspective was synchronic; at its core was a belief in the enduring forms of material culture and expressive performance associated with "folk" working in a vernacular tradition. Glassie sought to capture the essence of folk art as it has been maintained in different cultures, accepting that within each, what was essential would shift. The focus was ordinary folk caught in the midst of social change. His elegant and insightful writing was difficult to replicate. The results often seemed intuitive and certainly not quantitative. The analysis was anthropological and discursive, not "archaeological" and succinct. His concern has been the individual artisan during periods of social transformation and the inner strength that working with traditional forms provides when the larger world (whether colonial power or global entity) imposes its will. The depth and sophisticated intellectual framework of Glassie's various works (1982, 1995, 1997, 1999) have prompted others to attempt similar research (see Upton 1996, 1998).

Glassie's scholarship is thus much like that of Clifford Geertz, whose influence on American historians and anthropologists is legend, while his effect on archaeologists is minimal. Geertz (1973) argued persuasively for a dynamic, humanistic web of culture and against any that prioritized economic, technological, or environmental factors. His model posited culture as a deep web whose interrelated components are lattice-like, connected by varied groups of relationships built from a composite of religious, social, economic, and technological values. No single thread is deterministic of the whole; individuals construct multiple meanings, invariably linked to the material world, to make sense of their lives. They both conserve traditional ways of doing things and introduce innovation. Any culture thus enfolds diverse, creative actors who leave their own imprint on communities in a variety of materials. Marshall Sahlins would add that whether or not an individual attempts to recreate a cultural pattern or set of patterns as she lives her life, culture is inevitably mutable and hence in the very attempt to precisely reuse a pattern, one will often, if not invariably, introduce change. Culture is thus reconstrued in practice and while commonalties exist, precise replicas do not. Yet, cultural continuity (essentialist in the present vernacular) also endures.

These models of culture do not do away with the patterned regularities (social process) found in all cultures, but acknowledge that the form each process assumes – its "dress" – and the context in which each is embedded can and does vary cross-culturally. Values are culturally relative; ideas about beauty and functionality are culturally relative. Similar cultural processes exist in each culture, but because of different worldviews the media of expression and the mechanisms through which each works will differ (Leach 1982). Hence the infinite variety of material phenomena we see worldwide; hence the variability in scale, in content, and symbolic attribution.

Material culture is universal; its use, style, form, substance, and symbolic meaning are culturally relative. North American preservationists, museum curators, folklorists, and art historians are among those who depend upon it. Their disciplines should produce coherent theories of material culture, but do not. It is ironic that there is not more cross-fertilization of ideas and research results; one of us has found that principles in archaeology apply equally well to all material culture domains.

This can be seen in a preliminary study of African-American quilts.[2] Older quilts used as the foundation for newer ones are akin to sealed deposits, carefully hidden beneath layers of more recent fabrics; their composition, fabric, and workmanship reveal an older time. Some possess stratigraphic sequences – simple ones to be sure – which are datable through changes in fabric hues and designs like pottery or glass. Changes in technique as simple as a shift in the size of stitches and their spacing provide one dating tool and there are others, more than can be covered here. Seriation is readily observable in the colorful designs while symbolic content is "masked" but decipherable or inferable once one learns the underlying order of the culture (accessible through oral histories). Different dimensions of cultural expression exist simultaneously within a single quilt. This information can be gleaned by careful inspection, but the analysis grows richer as one adds local knowledge, and begins to access "layered" meaning.

Secular utilitarian traits (warmth/division of space) co-mingle with attributes that encode worldview. Take, for example, a deliberate imprecision in piecing fabric or the insertion of odd lengths of cloth that are based on the Islamic precept that only God creates what is perfect and one should not depict anything that has a soul. Individual social identity is another aspect of their expressive form. Each woman knows her own quilts and distributes them as gifts to spouses, children, grandchildren, and significant others in the community, thus binding and outlining circles of reciprocity. African-American quilts also speak to gender issues through masculine and feminine motifs or men's and women's fabrics. Group dynamics appear once one understands how a woman collects her fabrics and the sociable collaboration that surrounds quilting.

Ethnicity is visible in a distinctive aesthetic underlying both pattern and color. Assimilation can be seen in the adoption and adaptation of designs drawn from popular culture and with it one can see either the intrusion of the wider world or an active merge with it – a different scene from the antebellum years when white mistresses made the rules. The complexity of quilts and their expressive values have parallels in African-American cuisine, in ethnomusicology (studies of gospel and the blues). Quilts have much to say about societal change, adaptive perception, *and* a collateral retention of age-old African traditions. African-American quilts are microcosms of social process and by working through these, people appear as vividly as they do in any artifact analysis.

Using artifacts to order stratigraphic layers or date a site is an archaeological use of material objects, and a primary objective when historical archaeology was new. The first leap away from "archaeology" came when Ivor Noël Hume convinced people that knowledge of the dates for artifacts would improve fieldwork. Noël Hume also knew the difference between ordinary objects and elegant, costly artifacts. The distinctions he drew created a milieu in which it seemed not only appropriate but necessary to discuss the lifestyles of site occupants in terms of their ceramic assemblages, their British and European pottery, their Chinese porcelain. That is to say, it became necessary to look at assemblages and determine how well they fit the criteria of wealth in western society (e.g. studies characteristic of the 1960s and 1970s – and still seen today).

## Theory in the 1970s and 1980s

### Pattern recognition

Stanley South (1977) used Noël Hume's expertise to create statistical ceramic models that gave him the information necessary to establish site chronologies and, he believed, to infer lifestyle. South believed that fixed generalizing principles ("laws") governed human behavior and under-pinned all cultural constructs. The principles were the foundations that molded site formation, spatial regularities, and artifact patterning. South imposed an immense time–space grid linked to artifact patterning recognition at sites located along the 2,000-mile Atlantic seaboard wherever British sites were found. South's model postulated that similar sites should produce artifact patterns that were similarly aligned; different sites should stand out, statistically, by their variation from the norm. Under his influence, historical archaeologists formulated research designs based on the belief that a globally uniform British system of colonization gave rise to uniform patterns of social interaction creating regularities in the material record.

South based his artifact classes on morphological and stylistic qualities: Arms, Activities, Architectural, Kitchen, Bone, Furniture, Clothing, Personal, Tobacco Pipe. These classes are still used despite incisive critiques (Deetz 1987).[3] South neither addressed their duality or multiple roles nor the cultural contexts in which each type resided. Later studies (Beaudry 1996: 477–82) have shown that a more insightful interpretation can only be made with analysis of all the varied sources of information that contain cultural data. South simply skimmed the surface.

Some historical archaeologists still focus on artifacts and eco-facts, especially faunal remains, independent of context.[4] Many strongly believe that broad comparisons reveal the essential and significant elements of history and that these are not visible in the nitty-gritty history of individual sites. They set aside the contextualized studies and knowledge bases that permit reliable comparison. This is unfortunate for South's model contains a flaw that no amount of number crunching can overcome. Much of the data suggests the British tried similar techniques and strategies in their colonizing efforts no matter the locale; certainly the Spanish followed a consistent pattern. However, native peoples in different colonies possessed dissimilar culture identities, many significantly if not startlingly unconventional by western standards. Environmental resources differed too. Granting competence to the opposing forces to use material objects in ways that their cultures dictated makes any global, culturally imposed uniformity derived from a foreign power inconceivable. Different traditions and different predicaments invariably created modified, divergent material culture assemblages.[5]

## Consumer consumption

Studies of consumer choice were closely related to pattern analysis. The approach relied upon selected categories of household refuse ranked by price and in it material culture is plainly a commodity. Ceramic analysis using George Miller's revised 1991 economic scaling model, or analysis of selected meat cuts showing diet differences dominate the venue (Landon 2000). Researchers calculate a household's monetary investment and use it to determine social rank. Concentrating on a single element – money – and a single artifact attribute – its identity as a commodity – blinds the researcher to the complexity and diversity of household makeup and how different household members interact in social and economic matters. Furthermore, there is an implicit assumption that people buy goods primarily to display or acquire a place among the upper classes; it is paralleled by the belief that poorer members of society do not deliberately acquire items to indicate their identity. Lauren Cook's 1989 essay that considered how mill workers in New England towns used tobacco pipes to express their self-identity contradicts this assumption. Cook's study shows that class as a rigid, objective social category is flawed and asset analysis by itself is inadequate to reveal working-class values.

## Marxist and Marxist-related theory

Ironically, by the 1980s, Marxist analysts were introducing people more vividly into interpretive discussions than did those who were wed to artifact patterning and consumer consumption. Initially, this work was promoted under the guise of class, becoming overtly Marxist as the decade progressed (Orser 1988). The approach captivated many because of its simplicity – two groups of individuals, one dominant, thus able to rule, and the other subordinate and destined for exploitation. An overarching assumption is the conviction that archaeology is a political activity; behind this shared principle there are, however, multiple strands of thought. The disagreements center on the operation of ideology in the past (McGuire 1992). Classical Marxists believed culture change is the outcome of two, interrelated, underlying, determinant forces: production and exchange. They single out economic factors for analytical attention, stressing inequality, class conflict, and contradictions inherent in the acquisition and distribution of wealth.

This position appealed to archaeologists working on complex societies. Theory in cultural evolution was inadequate for the elaborate systems of social ranking they had to consider (Patterson 1995: 135). Some sought a way to explore power relations, inequality, domination, and resistance (e.g. McGuire and Paynter 1991; Hall 1995; Funari et al. 1999). Some opted for a critical theory drawn from Althusser and stressed that archaeological objectives were connected to "knowing about things historically to be able to know consciously or criticize the society we live in now" (Leone and Little 1993: 162). This opened Pandora's box. Archaeologists began to argue that only descendants or "natives" should excavate the sites their ancestors created. Since this is illogical when applied to old archaeological sites (e.g. cave paintings at

Lascaux, early man sites in South America), its applicability to more recent sites is debatable. Yet, some went so far as to suggest that only "natives" should decide research issues.

In summary, the Marxist model was too closely tied to an economic framework together with its technological and environmental infrastructure to produce a holistic vision of colonial society. In reality, American culture was more varied with greater opportunity for a directed, deliberate maneuvering of objects by the white underclass and the non-white sector, whether of African or Native American origin, than a static hierarchy allowed. The influence of Marxist analysis remained confined to academic circles despite efforts to bring it to the man-in-the-street.

Marxist analysis did not touch the public in the same fashion as other research, because the public was more interested in what its members had done in the past than in the details of their exploitation. Nothing made this clearer than the furor over the excavation of the African Burying Ground in New York. Yes, the site was one where exploited slaves were laid to rest and yes, their skeletal remains did show signs of malnutrition and overwork caused by poor treatment at the hands of a dominant elite. But what the African-American community most cogently stressed were the strong, extant kinship and religious ties that remained. They spoke metaphorically: "These bones are the bones of our ancestors." Conveyed within this simple phrase are the seeds of an African theology that survived centuries. In the phrase, "some of these bones are my mother's bones going to rise; some of these bones are my father's bones; and some of these bones are mine" can be seen the rationale for a community-sponsored burial in Atlanta in 1999. Note the seamless continuity across generations, the encapsulation of time, and the application of the tenet in two cities 1,500 miles apart.[6]

## Class consciousness

Early studies of consumer consumption carry definitions of class drawn from Weber and Marx (see Meskell, this volume). Yet, class is but one of the factors shaping social interaction. It is familiar because it is part and parcel of the capitalist economic system encompassing our own lives. It is a way to explain the infrastructure of past societies converging on power, inequality, and its mediation by material culture (e.g. Paynter 1989, 1999a; McGuire and Paynter 1991). When sensitively applied, it has the benefit of making an array of people visible (e.g. Paynter 1999b). However, it both conveys and exhibits the arrogance of the dominant class through structures archaeologists do not suspect. This is particularly true for sites from the early colonial period when European nations were first in cultural contact with native peoples who had had no experience with European society and had built their cultures on different classifications of social rank. These included neither class nor the economic behavior associated with a budding capitalist society.

## Material culture theory in the 1990s

### Markets and commodification

By the 1990s, archaeologists were looking at market creation and commodification in a more sophisticated fashion, weaving threads of the Marxist focus on inequality with a consideration of minority groups as active agents. Paul Mullins (1996, 1999) also included an analysis of social interaction and belief systems. His dissertation on African Americans in Annapolis, Maryland, 1850–1930, left behind consumer consumption studies based on exchange value (price) or essentialist notions of material symbolism and cultural identity. Mullins used the "centrality of desire" – "the *belief* that an object will realize or contribute to some idealization when it is consumed" (Mullins 1999: 31, emphasis in original) – believing it to be critical in the construction and contestation of subjectivity. Subjectivity occurs when members of a subgroup forge and renegotiate a cultural identity within the bounds of specific physical conditions and power relationships that are not under their control (in Annapolis, as slaves or minority freedmen). It is a self-creating process. Subjectivity is neither essential nor imposed; it does not increase or decrease status, although it enables the development of new personas or, in the case of Mullins's subjects, the ability to express their black individuality in creative, self-sustaining ways.

Living conditions and population densities for African Americans varied across the colonies, depending on the staple crops grown. Maryland's dependence on tobacco production did not require the massive labor force that rice and sugar did. Because of the different circumstances, Mullins believed that a cultural unity or "oneness" drawn from pre-existent African models could not exist. He predicted no uniformity in African-American consumption patterns and found none. What Mullins discovered in the artifact assemblages were congruities in "consumption [that] suggest how African Americans negotiated common structural conditions and constantly transformed a shared heritage"

(1999: 187–8). The artifacts were ordinary and found at Euro-American sites too. Mullins's interest, however, was not in the artifact patterns *per se* but in the clusters of beliefs that African Americans projected onto, saw reflected in, or as flowing from, material goods. He linked nineteenth-century African-American consumption with desires for emancipation and full citizenship.

Mullins asked readers to discover, in the words of Daniel Miller (1998: 14), "why some things matter" – why some relationships between objects and peoples are significant, yet others are not. It is a dramatic departure from earlier consumer studies and it, like Delle's 1999 study of social space on coffee plantations, extends and refines Marxist theory. Yet, the analytical models continue to elicit information as opposed to knowledge. What one really wants to plumb are the layers of meaning and to be able to specify why differences exist in terms that will reveal the social dynamics involved. Because these studies situate a monolithic locus of power, they differ in dramatic ways from the interpretive strategies other historical archaeologists use.

## Household analysis and active voices

Archaeological study of the backlots of the Boott Mills boardinghouses in Lowell, Massachusetts (see, e.g., Beaudry et al. 1991; Mrozowski et al. 1996), offered a wealth of opportunities for contextual and interpretive studies of various categories of material culture at different levels. The boardinghouses represented a material record of corporate policy as well as of workers' leisure and domestic activities. The Lowell study defined the boardinghouses as corporate households, an important conceptual tool for interpreting the archaeological evidence (Beaudry 1989, 1999; Mrozowski and Beaudry 1989). The model accounted for ways in which the company-controlled structure affected the domestic lives of the residents as well as how it affected the nature of boardinghouse-keeping as a social and economic activity. It adapted Mary Douglas's concept of "active voices" for use in archaeological inquiry. It became possible to interpret patterns of consumer behavior by delineating personal versus corporate purchase and consumption patterns. Keepers bought and prepared the food and often bought both food and furnishings in bulk; the ceramic assemblage, for example, consisted primarily of plain, serviceable wares. Personal effects such as brooches and hair combs reflected the presentation of self and construction of personal identity among the female operatives; and items such as alcoholic beverage containers and clay pipes reflected activities the boardinghouse residents engaged in during leisure hours (see Beaudry et al. 1991).

A field anthropologist, Douglas framed her questions for live informants. Her method "consists in setting people's beliefs back into the social context of their lives, by careful, intensive field research" (Douglas 1982b: 9). In other words, Douglas sought both information *and* knowledge. Much artifact analysis requires an ethnographic interrogation of documents to construct "action contexts" through which an archaeologist can grasp the range of meanings artifacts take on in social interaction. The approach is akin to that used by Derrida (see Gosden, this volume); it derives from semiotics and the study of symbolism; sociological and anthropological theories of social action; and the detailed historical and cultural context of artifact use from critical readings of texts. It draws from Douglas's extensive research on goods as a system of communication (Douglas 1982a: x; Douglas and Isherwood 1979).[7] Douglas's approach to commodities, which she terms "active voice" analysis, emphasizes communication, negotiation, and manipulation (see Beaudry 1996).

Beaudry (1995: 3) observed that a crucial analytical challenge is investing the historical "chronicle" with cultural meaning and placing it within the context of cultural discourse(s). She starts with the belief that culture is concerned with meaning and representation, often symbolic, often in material form. Material culture is a way to inscribe or write on landscapes, houses, bodies, pots, animals and written texts. Historical archaeologists question varied sources on the past, considering behavior in terms of action and discourse. This enables one to expand the notion of discourse to look at action and interaction, at control and constraint, at formal and informal mechanisms, at silences as well as assertion and defiance.

In some ways this notion of "action contexts" dovetails with recent formulations of material culture as manifestations of discourse.[8] Discourse analysis selectively adopts strategies from various theories of literary criticism. It considers artifacts and the archaeological record as "texts" to be read critically, probing for forthright messages as well as ambiguous meanings that might be intended for users and producers. The approach incorporates elements of performance theory and feminist theory (particularly their calls for integration of multiple voices and differing perspectives), emphasizing the compound meanings of artifacts, especially the nuances visible through highly contextualized studies (cf. Beaudry et al. 1991; Hall 1991; Yentsch 1994; De Cunzo 1995). Such studies attend to many elements, and while some seem fixed, most are fluid or at best ambiguous. Through these elements individual subjectivities – age, sex, gender, class, race, and so on – are constructed. The approach relies upon connecting material culture, other archaeological data, and documents while acknowledging the intertextual relationship among these diverse data sets.

## Pulling culture back in

### Artifacts as texts

Despite Hodder's efforts (1990, 1991, 1999) to inspire European and American prehistorians to move toward contextual and interpretive archaeologies, it is perhaps in historical archaeology that these approaches are most fully realized. One reason is that students had begun in the 1970s to read the texts on which these approaches are based. The work of Roland Barthes, Pierre Bourdieu, Umberto Eco, Michel Foucault, Mary Douglas, Edmund Leach, Claude Lévi-Strauss, Charles Pierce, and Victor Turner was standard fare at many universities. Anthropology professors insisted that archaeology students had to know their anthropology – that it was more important, ultimately, than the tools of excavation. There were differences between the British and American schools; postmodernist theories of literary criticism, especially deconstructionism, were initially more popular at the former.

At Cambridge, Hodder (1991) used the artifact as text metaphor, insisting that "context" also meant "with-text," thus introducing an explicit analogy between contextual meanings of material objects and the meanings of written words. He argued that it was fallacious to think that "objects are only mute when they are out of their 'texts'; [when] in fact most archaeological objects are, almost by definition, situated in place and time and in relation to other archaeological objects" (Hodder 1991: 153). Through careful analysis one should be able to observe and read the network of relationships embodied within the archaeological assemblages of specific sites and to use this "content" to educe meaning (see, for example, the material expressions of Igbo relationships described by Aniakor 1996).

Henry Glassie's 1975 study of Virginia folk housing became one of the most influential American studies to examine objects as texts. Here, he constructed a Chomskian grammar for architecture that enabled a reader to pinpoint times when specific decisions are made in building and thereby to isolate stages of construction. Glassie amplified the process with a structural analysis drawn from Lévi-Strauss. Structuralism, for the most part, has been a model that archaeologists avoid in the mistaken belief that it can have no diachronic dimension. Structuralism highlights different relationships. As a culture changes, the "form" or cultural expression of a relationship shifts. Objects can mediate these relationships; individuals can invert these relationships to express a variety of views. When the norm is breached, if it is a significant norm, cultural confrontation ensues. The infringements can be deliberate violations or acts that arise innocently because one group does not understand the cultural precepts of another. A structural model – because it is based on perceptions held in mind – is particularly potent in revealing the cultural domains where alterations are occurring (Hodder 1987; Tilley 1990; Yentsch 1991b). The infinite variations in the "form" of the structural oppositions are what make culture dynamic and its imprint is left on the material world, whether man-made or natural. Consequently the configuration and path of the change creates a text.

Recently, scholars have retreated from the textual metaphor, seeking additional approaches. Some see a promise in Gottdiener's (1995) rediscovery of C.S. Peirce and have begun to look anew at artifacts as signs (i.e. semiosis). A sign is a thing that stands for something else and the two (signifier and signified) are linked by a cognitive chain. "The first link," according to Maquet, "is based on visual isomorphism" (1993: 34). The second is grounded in metonymy. When analyzing an artifact as an "instrument," the analyst focuses on the object and, perhaps, on its maker's intent. When analyzing an artifact as a "sign," the critical element is the people – the group – that gave it meaning, or signification. Archaeologically, one can speak only in terms of probabilities when it comes to such elucidation of meaning, but ethnographically it is a different world, as revealed in our examples of African-American quilts and African beads (also see Hill 1998). And it is from here that one obtains the illustrative data that enable tighter interpretation of the artifacts tied to both ethnicity and gender.

## Gender and social identity

By the late 1990s it became clear that age, gender, ethnicity, religious beliefs, and race converge in mind to create expressive forms through which individuals assert social identity (A. Praetzellis and M. Praetzellis 1992, 1998; M. Praetzellis and A. Praetzellis 1998; Scott 1994; Wall 1999; Yentsch 1991a). Some of these – posturing, walking stance, tone of voice, facial intonations, and touch – are ephemeral. When the refer-

ent base is communal (i.e. ethnicity and religious belief systems), the artifacts range widely in size and convey unity, or a harmonic integrity. Yet,
because social identity also subsumes personal identity, there are infinite
variations that revolve around similar themes (i.e. creative adaptations
that are individualistic). When the closest link is to autonomy and individuality, the artifacts can be small but, despite size, they are telling.
Sarah Williams's (1987) study in northern Kenya examined the social
meaning of beads, and how they fit within Turkana social organization
and ideology. Implicitly, Williams was also interested in women and how
their beads revealed perceptions of beauty, sociability, and wealth.[9] Beads
throughout Africa express these attributes; they also can invoke magical
powers or assert sexuality, particularly those worn around the hips.
Banned in French West Africa in the twentieth century, strands of hip
beads are now worn hidden beneath skirts where their tinkling sounds
are considered unique to each woman (because body movement and
clothing differ as do beads) and potent couriers of sexual communication. This article, together with other bead studies (Yentsch 1995; Stine
et al. 1996), remind us that small things need not be forgotten and that
the power invested in them is not proportional to their size. Now
archaeologists are mining the rich data contained in a site's "small finds"
and pulling them out of descriptive appendices for closer inspection.

Beaudry is now taking the artifacts of needlework and sewing beyond
dating and identification (i.e. further than the information stage), and
past "engendered" artifacts by using multiple classes of evidence in an
interpretation based on the "active voice" (Beaudry n.d.). As with
Beaudry's prior Lowell study, the approach involves various stages and
diverse scales of analysis that permit construction of multidimensional
historical and cultural contexts. These, in turn, elicit the social frame in
which the objects were used. The first step is weaving together various
lines of evidence – or recontextualization – to learn how items functioned
in social settings. Next comes an inquiry into the classificatory logic
underpinning the "gendered" nature of sewing. Finally, a close reading
of cases in which the "usual" symbolic import of sewing implements is
subverted through symbolic inversion or in which anomalies appear is
required. Finally, Beaudry will be able to interpret how needlework
implements were deployed in constructions of feminine identity.

Feminist art historian Rozsika Parker (1984: 5) concludes that "the
development of an ideology of femininity coincided historically with the
emergence of a clearly defined separation of art and craft." By the seventeenth century, embroidery was used to inculcate femininity in young
girls, so much so that people perceived a woman's ability to embroider
as an innate trait. An ideology of femininity as natural to women evolved

in the eighteenth century, and, subsequently, embroidery came to signify femininity and a leisured, aristocratic lifestyle – proof of gentility through its association with nobility. The art was critical in maintaining the status of a household and spoke to the value of a man's wife as well as to his economic assets, signifying feminine traits such as obedience, docility, and love of home. "Finally, in the nineteenth century, embroidery and femininity were entire[ly] fused, and the connection was deemed to be natural. Women embroidered because they were naturally feminine and were feminine because they naturally embroidered" (Parker 1984: 11). Women responded by using these ideologies even as they continued to be expressive elements within the dogma. Embroidery provided support and satisfaction for women for more than three centuries. It gave them a covert method of negotiating the constraints of femininity. They could create personal, womanly meanings yet, on the surface, appear to live up to the archetype of the passive, silent, vain and frivolous, even seductive, needlewoman.

Parker's observations form the framework for Beaudry's examination of both the material culture of fancy needlework and the artifacts of ordinary sewing. Here the contextual, interpretive approach – which draws on deeper levels of knowledge – makes one alert to the different meanings and potential ideological import of small objects.

Thimbles, for instance, are common small finds on historical sites and are often seen merely as practical objects. But because they were such common and necessary accessories for the needleworker, thimbles took on special significance. Monogrammed thimbles leave no doubt as to the close identification of some women with their needlework tools. Indeed, thimbles became emblematic of the values embedded in the ideology of femininity, including class membership. Seventeenth-century court records contain many instances of women who were accused of violating sumptuary laws (or worse) by possessing silver thimbles, bodkins, or other needlework tools. In one instance a young housemaid who specialized in fancy embroidery either treated herself to a silver thimble because of pride in her work, a desire to enhance her identity as a needlewoman, or was given it as a particularly meaningful gift. Her possession of a silver thimble caused a court case full of hostility and bitter accusations of theft, following discovery of the offending silver thimble in a place where it should not have been (i.e. among a housemaid's belongings). Reconstructing the symbolic import of something seemingly as humble as a thimble in the construction and negotiation of personal identity and class, and its ability to foster or break down social cohesion reinforces our awareness of how objects become highly charged with hidden import. They send coded messages that the archaeologist must decipher if she wants her material culture analysis to progress from information retrieval into the realm of layered cultural knowledge.

Just as small finds detail the lives of ordinary people and suggest parameters of existence not immediately apparent in the common artifacts used to date a site or indicate socioeconomic standing, the interpretation of landscape also indicates how texts persist across the generations.

## Culture writ large

### The built environment

The richness of landscape archaeology done by historical archaeologists is unparalleled (Leone 1984; A. Praetzellis and M. Praetzellis 1989; Kelso and Most 1990; Paynter 1990; Yamin and Metheny 1996; Miller and Gleason 1994; Hall 1991; see also Thomas, this volume). Landscape archaeology also forces the researcher to escape a site's confines and to fly over its topographic boundaries. It reveals ways in which the transitory nature of human life is deliberately overcome through the passage of mnemonic devices preserved on the land from one generation to the next (Yentsch 1988) in explicit ruins, topographic contours, and the arrogation of natural resources.

Take ruins. Some ruins are icons for prestigious ancestors (King 1996); the tabby remains of slave quarters evoke the *slave-owning* elite of Georgia's sea islands (Vlach 1993). These icons are so significant that people put up with their decayed walls in twentieth-century towns like Beaufort, South Carolina. In rural areas, fragmentary memorials exist as neglected, crumbling frame houses whose doors were shut when black folk died or moved away. Additional icons in the highlands speak to Native Americans forced from the land, but do so in muted tones because the centuries have erased the ephemeral elements that once told most about the "others" who lived there.

This is the case with one home in northwest Georgia preserved for its stunning architecture and not because it was built by Cherokee chief James Vann. Today, the mansion and a single, dramatically smaller service building stand as representations of Euro-American lifestyles.[10] In 1804, Chief James Vann used the aesthetic principles of "grand" architecture and landscape design to invert the social order. Vann built a mansion, overtly European with Cherokee ornamentation, whose vista included two Appalachian mountain ranges to the east and west, a tributary of the Conasougo River, the mission and school at Spring

Place below his hilltop home, and several hundred acres of surrounding fields where 200 slaves labored. Exterior outbuildings were built in a vernacular Native American style – storehouses, barns, sweathouses, and so on.

More is taking place here than when elites built homes for display. Rather, we have a liminal man of mixed race who negotiated a powerful presence/position for himself and his family. Vann blended the traditions of two cultures to facilitate success in both while exploiting the labor of a third to accrue wealth and become one of the richest men in North America. Here we see the power of material culture to form and express social identity in a complex, intermingled tangle of cultural ties. Neither Marxist models, models of consumer consumption, nor formulaic pattern analysis can do justice to the assemblage present at this site. It is no accident that the State of Georgia let the site fall into disrepair as it passed from one white man's hands to another's after the forced migration of Cherokees along the Trail of Tears. This site, like that of Vergelegen in South Africa (Markell et al. 1995), possessed too much symbolic potency for survival in a state of grace until Americans, as a nation, passed to a point where we could validate the accomplishments of indigenous peoples. In truth it is not yet successfully done at Chief Vann's home. Nor, because of his mixed heritage and dubious reputation, has it assumed the role of sacred space that some sites possess. Yet if one imagines the missing buildings and peoples the estate with red and black folk in a variety of dress, it becomes a dramatically different place. It expresses Cherokee values and absorbs the natural landscape, some of which probably was sacred land when the mansion was built.

## Natural space as sacred space

Landscape studies also renewed interest in the environment *per se*. Some symbolic alterations to the natural world possess both a focus and a visibility that make their symbolism undeniable (e.g. Serpent Mound in Ohio [built ca. AD 1050] or stone effigies at Easter Island). Archaeologists might argue over the symbolism and the intent of the makers, but few would deny that cultural meaning was deeply imbued into the feature. It is more troublesome to ascribe a symbolic dimension to landscapes that exhibit minimal differentiation from natural phenomena.

In Georgia, the Creeks and Cherokees continued to view water and special riverine locales as their predecessors did. In some cases, mounds both mark the location and give visibility to the feature (e.g. Mississippian Mounds outside Macon, Georgia, at the confluence of the

Ocmulgee and Oconee rivers). In other cases, oral history still records the association (e.g. Hurricane Shoals on the North Oconee River; a Coweta chief's home near shoals in the Chattahoochee). These areas are presumed to be sacred space even as the woods surrounding African-American communities in the southeastern United States were and, in some cases, still are. Oral informants provide vivid descriptions of their sojourns in these places, as shown in this passage by African-American artist, Jonathan Green.

> The woods were also sacred space used in religious quests. . . . We were sent alone into the forest to pray for seven days and seven nights. So, the forest and the land became our closest friend. It was a place where we dreamed and recited to elders the dreams we had had. It was a time when the land and what lived within it kept us company and provided comfort.
>
> I can remember being out in the forest for days praying – for exactly what I really didn't know. But I'd been told to go there, to go out, pray and seek God. I remember the times when I was so incredibly hungry and I'd look up and miraculously a pear tree or some other fruit tree would appear. I learned to thank the land for providing me with food. (Yentsch 1999)

Highly personal encounters thus highlight how the natural world functioned as sacred space within culturally prescribed situations. These suggest the richness of cultural attributions to the things created by humans and used by humans. While similar detail can't be infused into many past landscapes, one can use analogy to infer a symbolic content.

Richard Stoffle (1997; see also Stoffle et al. 1997) does this for the Colorado River region of the western United States where he worked among the southern Paiute. It took years, he writes, before he realized *the depth* of the river's meaning. Many times Stoffle attended family gatherings where a ritual bucket of water was presented. The group prayed over it in Paiute "like talking to a person; thanking them for providing life to the family members. After the prayer, each family member drank from a common ladle filled with the water." It reminded Stoffle of Christian ceremonies such as communion and he realized "that water was never taken casually" (Stoffle 1997: 2).

As elders shared knowledge of the meaning – the life in fact – embedded in the natural world, Stoffle's understanding grew. He learned that even small rocks could be alive and that, like mountains, rivers, and minerals, each had distinct personalities. With time, he realized what it meant for something to be near a river:

A medicine plant has the power to cure, but this power is greater if it is growing near the Colorado River. A red paint is sacred, but it is somehow more sacred because it comes from next to the Colorado River. A curing rock is strong and unique, but one that lives in the middle of the Colorado River is perhaps the strongest known. . . . What does it mean, then, for something to be near the Colorado River? It means everything – even life itself. (Stoffle 1997: 2)

In both the southern Paiute beliefs and the African-American religious quests we see parallel cultural universes in action. They coexist quietly side by side with mainstream American culture. They are accessible to sensitive observers, but can be easily overlooked especially when issues of power or economics are at play. They are not always obtainable in archaeological analysis, but their very presence – the life and vitality they possess in today's world – suggests their presence in the past.

## Conclusion

Julian Thomas (1998: 107–8) notes that while some reject taking textual metaphors too literally, there have been so many successful efforts at treating artifacts as text-like, or artifact use as if it were a staged performance, that it is counterproductive to reject the textual metaphor altogether. Any metaphor that proves informative and can throw light on human relationships with the material world deserves consideration, and there is no reason that one is a better metaphor than the other, as long as we avoid reifying the metaphor or retreating into essentialism or mind/matter dualities, or both. What is genuinely needed, Thomas stressed, is a recognition of "the unresolved character of the relationship between discourse, symbolism, and materiality" (1998: 108).

There is a spirit that lives within people that empowers them to take small, simple things and large complex entities and use these as they will. It is human volition and its imagery and power that draws us, in part, to archaeology – to a world filled with things, cultural things, with visible and invisible meanings. Large, sculptural monuments can express a nation's intent and character and may even serve as a mythic charter for behavior. Yet, small incised marks on pots or paintings hidden in caves, while speaking to a smaller audience, are equally evocative reminders that material culture is as rich and complex as human society itself – and has as long a history as humankind.

Why not take the whole modern world and use it as an *atelier* to observe how different groups interact and express identity, to pinpoint what they do in times of environmental stress, of culture contact, and of unstoppable change to the material world that surrounds them? Cultures differ because of predicament, temperament, environment, and ideational factors, yet humanity remains the same. We should use ethnographic approaches that let us tap into the layered meanings material objects have had in the recent past and we may be able to use the techniques so developed to project meaning onto far older artifacts.

## NOTES

1  In a parallel situation, Native Americans in the Northwest have protested the identification of Kennewick Man as Caucasian. Kennewick Man lived some 9,000 years ago along the coast of Oregon and, if the forensic attribution of his skeletal remains as Caucasoid are correct, then there is limited evidence that American Indians were not the only occupants of the northern hemisphere prior to Columbus' voyage in 1492. This contradiction in what is seen as "real history" has potential implications of great magnitude. As one might imagine, the debate over the Kennewick remains has already entered the legal system and political ramifications are already visible. Another similar situation involves the mummies in China who are clearly Caucasian and whose remains were hidden in a Chinese museum for that very reason. The Chinese initially did not want to admit that their culture could have had western penetration and perhaps exhibited western influences over 2,000 years ago. National purity demands otherwise.

2  Yentsch's study of African-American women in Georgia (in progress).

3  Colono-ware cooking pots, for example, are not in the kitchen grouping, but are listed as signifying other "activities" such as trade with Native Americans or ceramic production by African Americans. Tobacco pipes are a set unto themselves and while they are certainly useful in establishing site chronologies, they are clearly of as personal a nature as other items listed in the personal category.

4  Sites are characterized on the percentage of recovered fragments using sherd counts rather than vessel counts. There is often little consideration given to the repercussions of breakage rates grounded in ware attributes or site use; sherd sizes and weights are nominally examined. Site structure, site formation processes, or contextual relationships among artifacts and soil strata receive scant attention. This restricts the information available.

5  The English produced different shell-edged ceramics for different markets (Deetz, personal communication); Chinese porcelain vessels that appear in many South African assemblages differ from those seen on North American sites in quantity, quality, and vessel form.

6  What had happened over a period of time was the objectification of human skeletal remains within the discipline of archaeology; they were seen as objects of material culture. What interviews with Native Americans and African Americans clearly reveal is that human skeletal remains are *not* objects, but the residue of people with whom they still feel a close connection. Other interviews by the authors indicate that what people want from the past is new information and empowerment, data that they can take and make an active, positive entity in their lives (i.e. Ethics 2000 classes at Armstrong Atlantic State University). There is a suspicion that those who keep bringing up the ways in which a minority group was exploited are doing so because they feel an identity with the dominant group and thus derive satisfaction or pleasure from pointing out how "others" were treated. It is as though the discussion of exploitation of past peoples also serves to validate differential treatment in the present (through a psychological process known as "mirroring"). Unless one is very careful to point out ways in which these practices from the past can be subverted in present life, the result is anger on the part of students. Similar anger and grief is well documented in videos on both the African Burial Ground and Native American burial sites (*Contested Bones*).

7  This approach is familiar to historians through the work of Rhys Isaac (1980), who, like many anthropologically trained historical archaeologists, was strongly influenced by Douglas's work. In her work Beaudry shows how an "active voice" approach provides a compelling alternative to recent studies that stress dominant ideologies or domination and resistance and leave people as cultural actors out of the picture. See Tilley (1990) for explication of structuralist and poststructuralist approaches.

8  It is important to note here that this is not, however, congruent with *discourse theory* as presented in the work of theorists such as Ricoeur, Bourdieu, Giddens, or Foucault, who lodge discourse with social structures and systems rather than with the individual (for a recent critique of discourse theory, see Meskell 1999: 18–32).

9  It is noteworthy that, in the 1980s, this study was not cast as one that empowered women, yet it preceded the first international meeting of archaeologists where gender was the main theme – the 1989 Chacmool Conference (Walde and Willows 1991) and the path-breaking *Engendering Archaeology: Women and Prehistory* (Gero and Conkey 1991).

10  Vann, the son of a Scottish trader, is often described in disparaging terms. Henry Malone wrote of him as "far-famed, little beloved and greatly feared" while another biographer, Lela Latch Lloyd, said he was "a domineering demon." Nonetheless, he was literate, a diplomat who persuaded the new federal government to run a federal highway past the location where he planned to build, and far-sighted enough to invite Moravian missionaries into the region if they would educate his son.

REFERENCES

Aniakor, C. 1996. Household objects and the philosophy of Igbo social space. In M. J. Arnoldi, C. M. Geary, and K. L. Hardin (eds), *African Material Culture*, 214–42. Bloomington: Indiana University Press.

Beaudry, M. C. 1989. Household structure and the archaeological record: examples from New World historical sites. In S. MacEachern, D. J. W. Archer, and R. D. Garvin (eds), *Households and Communities: Proceedings of the 21st Annual Chacmool Conference*, 84–92. Alberta: Department of Archaeology, University of Calgary.

Beaudry, M. C. 1995. Introduction: ethnography in retrospect. In M. E. D'Agostino, M. Winer, E. Prine, and E. Casella (eds), *The Written and the Wrought: Complementary Sources in Historical Anthropology*, 1–15. Kroeber Anthropological Society Papers 79. Berkeley: Department of Anthropology, University of California.

Beaudry, M. C. 1996. Reinventing historical archaeology. In L. A. De Cunzo and B. Herman (eds), *Historical Archaeology and the Study of American Life*, 473–97. Winterthur: Wintherthur Museum.

Beaudry, M. C. 1999. House and household: the archaeology of domestic life in early America. In G. Egan and R. L. Michael (eds), *Old and New Worlds*, 117–26. Oxford: Oxbow Books.

Beaudry, M. C., n.d. Culture, material culture, and gender identity: interpreting the artifacts of needlework and sewing. MS in preparation.

Beaudry, M. C., L. J. Cook, and S. A. Mrozowski 1991. Artifacts and active voices: material culture as social discourse. In R. H. McGuire and R. Paynter (eds), *The Archaeology of Inequality*, 150–91. Oxford: Blackwell.

Cook, L. J. 1989. Tobacco-related material and the construction of working-class culture. In M. C. Beaudry and S. A. Mrozowski (eds), *Interdisciplinary Investigations of the Boott Mills, Lowell, Massachusetts. Volume III: The Boarding House System as a Way of Life*, 209–29. Cultural Resources Management Study no. 21. Boston: National Park Service, North Atlantic Region.

De Cunzo, L. A. 1995. Reform, respite, ritual: an archaeology of institutions; the Magdalen Society of Philadelphia, 1800–1850. *Historical Archaeology* 29(3): iii–168.

Deetz, J. 1977. *In Small Things Forgotten: An Archaeology of Early American Life*. Revised edn, 1996. New York: Doubleday.

Deetz, J. 1987. Harrington histograms versus Bindford mean dates as a technique for establishing the occupational sequence of sites at Flowerdew Hundred, Virginia. *American Archeology* 6(1): 62–7.

Deetz, J. F. and E. Dethlefsen 1967. Death's head, cherub, urn and willow. *Natural History* 76(3): 28–37.

Delle, J. A. 1999. *An Archaeology of Social Space: Analyzing Coffee Plantations in Jamaica's Blue Mountains*. New York: Plenum Press.

Douglas, M. 1982a. Preface. In M. Douglas (ed.), *In the Active Voice*. London: Routledge and Kegan Paul.

Douglas, M. 1982b. Passive voice theories in religious sociology. In M. Douglas (ed.), *In the Active Voice*, 1–10. London: Routledge and Kegan Paul.

Douglas, M. and B. Isherwood 1979. *The World of Goods: Toward an Anthropology of Consumption*. New York: W. W. Norton.

Funari, P. P. A., M. Hall, and S. Jones (eds) 1999. *Historical Archaeology: Back from the Edge*. London: Routledge.

Geertz, C. 1973. *The Interpretation of Cultures*. New York: Basic Books.

Gero, J. and M. Conkey (eds) 1991. *Engendering Archaeology: Women and Prehistory*. Oxford: Blackwell.

Glassie, H. 1975. *Folk Housing in Middle Virginia: A Structural Analysis of Historic Artifacts*. Knoxville: University of Tennessee Press.

Glassie, H. 1982. *Passing the Time in Ballymenone: Culture and History of an Ulster Community*. Philadelphia: University of Pennsylvania Press.

Glassie, H. 1991. Studying material culture today. In G. L. Pocius (ed.), *Living in a Material World: Canadian and American Approaches to Material Culture*, 253–66. St. Johns: Institute of Social and Economic Research, Memorial University of Newfoundland.

Glassie, H. 1995. *The Spirit of Folk Art: The Girard Collection at the Museum of International Art*. New York: Abrams.

Glassie, H. 1997. *Art and Life in Bangladesh*. Bloomington: Indiana University Press.

Glassie, H. 1999. *Material Culture*. Bloomington: Indiana University Press.

Gottdiener, M. 1995. *Postmodern Semiotics: Material Culture and the Forms of Post-modern Life*. Oxford: Blackwell.

Hall, M. 1991. High and low in the townscapes of Dutch South America and South Africa: the dialectics of material culture. *Social Dynamics* 17(2): 41–75.

Hall, M. 1995. The architecture of patriarchy: houses, women and slaves in the eighteenth century South African countryside. In M. E. D'Agostino, M. Winer, E. Prine, and E. Casella (eds), *The Written and the Wrought: Complementary Sources in Historical Anthropology*, 61–73. Kroeber Anthropological Society Papers 79. Berkeley: Department of Anthropology, University of California.

Hill, S. H. 1998. *Weaving New Worlds: Southeastern Cherokee Women and their Basketry*. Chapel Hill: University of North Carolina Press.

Hodder, I. 1987. The meaning of discard: ash and domestic space in Baringo. In S. Kent (ed.), *Method and Theory for Activity Area Research: An Ethnoarchaeological Approach*, 424–48. New York: Columbia University Press.

Hodder, I. 1990. *The Domestication of Europe*. Oxford: Blackwell.

Hodder, I. 1991. *Reading the Past: Current Approaches to Interpretation in Archaeology*. 2nd edn. Cambridge: Cambridge University Press.

Hodder, I. 1999. *The Archaeological Process: An Introduction*. Oxford: Blackwell.

Isaac, R. 1980. Ethnographic method in history: an action approach. *Historical Methods* 13(1): 43–61.

Joyner, C. 1999. *Shared Traditions: Southern History and Folk Culture*. Urbana: University of Illinois Press.

Kelso, W. and R. Most (eds) 1990. *Earth Patterns: Essays in Landscape Archaeology*. Charlottesville: University Press of Virginia.

King, J. 1996. "The transient nature of all things sublunary": romanticism, history and ruins in nineteenth-century southern Maryland. In R. Yamin and K. B. Metheny (eds), *Landscape Archaeology: Reading and Interpreting the American Historical Landscape*, 249–72. Knoxville: University of Tennessee Press.

Landon, D. 2000. Zooarchaeology in historical archaeology. In T. Majewski and C. E. Orser, Jr. (eds), *Handbook of Historical Archaeology*. New York: Kluwer Academic/Plenum.

Leach, E. R. 1982. *Social Anthropology*. Oxford: Oxford University Press.

Leone, M. P. 1984. Interpreting ideology in historical archaeology: the William Paca Garden in Annapolis, Maryland. In D. Miller and C. Tilley (eds), *Ideology, Power, and Prehistory*, 25–35. London: Cambridge University Press.

Leone, M. P. and B. Little 1993. Artifacts as expressions of society and culture: subversive geneaology and the value of history. In S. Lubar and W. D. Kingery (eds), *History from Things: Essays on Material Culture*, 160–81. Washington: Smithsonian Institution Press.

McGuire, R. 1992. *A Marxist Archaeology*. New York: Plenum.

McGuire, R. and R. Paynter (eds) 1991. *The Archaeology of Inequality*. Oxford: Blackwell.

Maquet, J. 1993. Objects as instruments, objects as signs. In S. Lubar and W. D. Kingery (eds), *History from Things: Essays on Material Culture*, 30–40. Washington: Smithsonian Institution Press.

Markell, A., M. Hall, and C. Schrire 1995. The historical archaeology of Vergelegen, an early farmstead at the Cape of Good Hope. *Historical Archaeology* 29(1): 10–34.

Meskell, L. 1999. *Archaeologies of Social Life: Age, Sex, Class, et cetera in Ancient Egypt*. Oxford: Blackwell.

Miller, D. 1998. Why some things matter. In D. Miller (ed.), *Material Cultures: Why Some Things Matter*, 3–21. Chicago: University of Chicago Press.

Miller, G. L. 1991. A revised set of CC index values for classification and economic scaling of English ceramics from 1787 to 1860. *Historical Archaeology* 25(1): 1–25.

Miller, N. F. and K. L. Gleason (eds) 1994. *The Archaeology of Garden and Field*. Philadelphia: University of Pennsylvania Press.

Mrozowski, S. A. and M. C. Beaudry 1989. Archaeology and the landscape of corporate ideology. In W. M. Kelso and R. Most (eds), *Earth Patterns: Essays in Landscape Archaeology*, 189–208. Charlottesville: University Press of Virginia.

Mrozowski, S. A., G. H. Ziesing, and M. C. Beaudry 1996. *Living on the Boott: Historical Archaeology at the Boott Mills Boardinghouses, Lowell, Massachusetts*. Amherst: University of Massachusetts Press.

Mullins, P. R. 1996. Negotiating industrial capitalism: mechanisms of change among agrarian potters. In L. A. De Cunzo and B. L. Herman (eds), *Historical Archaeology and the Study of American Culture*, 151–91. Winterthur, DE: Winterthur Museum.

Mullins, P. R. 1999. *Race and Affluence: An Archaeology of African America and Consumer Culture*. New York: Kluwer Academic/Plenum.

Noël Hume, I. 1963. *Here Lies Virginia*. New York: Knopf.

Noël Hume, I. 1969. *A Guide to Artifacts of Colonial America*. New York: Knopf.

Orser, C. E. 1988. The archaeological analysis of plantation society: replacing status and caste with economics and power. *American Antiquity* 53(4): 735–51.

Parker, R. 1984. *The Subversive Stitch: Embroidery and the Making of the Feminine*. The Women's Press: London.

Patterson, T. 1995. *Towards a Social History of Archaeology in the United States*. Fort Worth, TX: Harcourt Brace.

Paynter, R. 1989. The archaeology of equality and inequality. *Annual Review of Anthropology* 18: 369–99.

Paynter, R. 1990. Afro-Americans in the Massachusetts historical landscape. In P. Gathercole and D. Lowenthal (eds), *The Politics of the Past*, 49–62. London: Unwin Hyman.

Paynter, R. 1999a. Epilogue: class analysis and historical archaeology. *Historical Archaeology* 33(1): 184–95.

Paynter, R. 1999b. Negotiating the color line in Western Massachusetts. Paper presented at the 4th World Archaeological Congress, Cape Town, January.

Praetzellis, A. and M. Praetzellis 1989. "Utility and beauty should be one": the landscape of Jack London's ranch of good intentions. *Historical Archaeology* 23(1): 33–44.

Praetzellis, A. and M. Praetzellis 1992. Faces and façades: Victorian ideology in early Sacramento. In A. E. Yentsch and M. C. Beaudry (eds), *The Art and Mystery of Historical Archaeology: Essays in Honor of James Deetz*, 75–99. Boca Raton, FL: CRC Press.

Praetzellis, A. and M. Praetzellis 1998. A Connecticut merchant in Chinadom: a play in one act. *Historical Archaeology* 32(1): 86–93.

Praetzellis, M. and A. Praetzellis 1998. Further tales of the Vasco. *Historical Archaeology* 32(1): 55–65.

Scott, E. M. (ed.) 1994. *Those of Little Note: Gender, Race, and Class in Historical Archaeology*. Tucson: University of Arizona Press.

South, S. 1977. *Method and Theory in Historical Archaeology*. New York: Academic Press.

Stine, L. F., M. A. Cabak, and M. D. Groove 1996. Blue beads as African-American cultural symbols. *Historical Archaeology* 30(3): 49–74.

Stoffle, R. 1997. Paper on file at the University of Arizona.

Stoffle, R., D. B. Halmo, and D. E. Austin 1997. Cultural landscapes and traditional cultural properties: a southern Paiute view of the Grand Canyon and Colorado River. *American Indian Quarterly* 21(2): 229–49.

Thomas, J. 1998. The socio-semiotics of material culture. *Journal of Material Culture* 3(1): 97–108.

Tilley, C. (ed.) 1990. *Reading Material Culture: Structuralism, Hermeneutics and Post-structuralism*. Oxford: Blackwell.

Upton, D. 1996. Ethnicity, authenticity and invented tradition. *Historical Archaeology* 30(2): 1–7.

Upton, D. 1998. *Architecture in the United States*. New York: Oxford University Press.

Vlach, J. 1993. *Back of the Big House: The Architecture of Plantation Slavery*. Chapel Hill: University of North Carolina Press.

Walde, D. and N. Willows (eds) 1991. *The Archaeology of Gender: Proceedings of the 22nd Annual Chacmool Conference*. Calgary: Archaeological Association of the University of Calgary.

Wall, D. 1999. Examining gender, class, and ethnicity in nineteenth-century New York City. *Historical Archaeology* 33(1): 102–17.

Wells, I. B. (ed.) 1893. *The Reason Why the Colored American is not in the World's Columbian Exposition*. Chicago: privately printed by Ida B. Wells.

Williams, S. 1987. An "archaeology" of Turkana beads. In I. Hodder (ed.), *The Archaeology of Contextual Meanings*, 31–8. Cambridge: Cambridge University Press.

Yamin, R. and K. B. Metheny (eds) 1996. *Landscape Archaeology: Reading and Interpreting the American Historical Landscape*. Knoxville: University of Tennessee Press.

Yentsch, A. 1988. Legends, houses, families, and myths: relationships between material culture and American ideology. In M. C. Beaudry (ed.), *Documentary Archaeology in the New World*, 5–19. Cambridge: Cambridge University Press.

Yentsch, A. 1991a. Engendering visible and invisible ceramic artifacts, especially dairy vessels. *Historical Archaeology* 25(4): 132–55.

Yentsch, A. 1991b. The symbolic divisions of pottery: sex-related attributes of English and Anglo-American household pots. In Randall McGuire and Robert Paynter (eds), *The Archaeology of Inequality*, 192–230. Oxford: Blackwell.

Yentsch, A. 1994. *A Chesapeake Family and their Slaves: A Study in Historical Archaeology*. Cambridge: Cambridge University Press.

Yentsch, A. 1995. Beads as silent witnesses of an African-American past: social identity and the artifacts of slavery in Annapolis, Maryland. In M. E. D'Agostino, M. Winer, E. Prine, and E. Casella (eds), *The Written and the Wrought: Complementary Sources in Historical Anthropology*, 45–60. Kroeber Anthropological Society Papers 79. Berkeley: Department of Anthropology, University of California.

Yentsch, A. 1999. The marshlands: expressing memories of land and family in art. MS on file at Jonathan Green Studios, Naples, Florida.

# 10

# Postcolonial Archaeology
## Issues of Culture, Identity, and Knowledge

## *Chris Gosden*

All archaeology today is postcolonial. This is true in a chronological sense, in that most former colonies have become independent and we live in a world coping with the consequences of colonialism. But it is only partially true in an intellectual or political sense, as much archaeology is still pursued with little feel for the colonial origins of the discipline, the impact of postcolonial theory, or the new political circumstances giving more control over archaeological activities to indigenous people in places like the United States or Australia.

There is a lot of potential ground to cover under the rubric of post-colonial archaeology and I shall not look at archaeology's colonial roots, as I have covered this elsewhere (Gosden 1999; see also Rowlands 1998), but I shall consider in detail the potential impact of postcolonial theory on archaeology and at the new intellectual and legal context of archaeology in many parts of the world. Postcolonial theory, as far as it can be discussed as a single entity, is a series of discussions about the sorts of cultural forms and identities created through colonial encounters. Theorists such as Homi Bhabha (of whom more below) developed the idea that colonialism is not about the meeting of different cultural forms, colonizer and colonized, who maintain their own separate identities, but about the creation of hybrid and creole cultures resulting from sustained colonial contact. These arguments, which I find compelling, although hard to disentangle from the prose of many postcolonial writers, are in direct contradiction to the growing body of law surrounding the repatriation of human remains and cultural artifacts, which states that the legal basis for claims is some form of cultural integrity and continuity with the prehistoric cultures which produced the remains. In order to claim ancestral bones and objects, indigenous peoples around the world have to prove that they are not creolized or hybrid cultures, but have maintained some essential identity through time and into the present. Postcolonial theory, which is in tune with broader trends of western academic thought moving away from any essentialized notion of culture, runs in direct contradiction to ideas of culture which need to be developed by indigenous people as the basis for their political strategies in the present. In this chapter I would like to explore some of the contradictions between academic thought on the postcolonial situation and the political and legal strategies pursued by indigenous peoples in gaining some control over archaeological work on their histories, which are often embedded in broader struggles for legal and cultural renewal.

## Postcolonial theory and archaeology

Colonial structures were constructed over five centuries and saw the movement from plantation, to colony, to empire. Many of the formal structures of colonialism have been dismantled over the last five decades, although it might be argued that this sudden demise is more apparent than real, with the colonialism of nation-states being replaced by that of transnational companies. Be that as it may, taking apart the old structures of colonialism has led to a questioning of the forms of thought that went with them and this includes subjects like archaeology and anthropology, both of which were intellectual outgrowths of colonialism. Many have argued that the present state of the world, where colonies are few but the colonial legacy is omnipresent, requires new forms of thought and discussion. These new forms go jointly under the name of postcolonial theory, although as we shall see a single title is misleading for such a complex phenomenon. Complexity is partly due to the variety of theoretical influences, but also to the shape-shifting nature of colonialisms and their subsequent histories.

At the core of postcolonial theory is an attack on any view of essentialism in culture. This derives initially from problems of agency. The clichéd view of colonialism is that it was something imposed on the "natives" by the colonizers, with all the power to shape colonial regimes and cultures deriving from the latter. This implies a static and monolithic view of culture and of colonial encounters as the meeting of two discrete cultures, with the stronger colonists overwhelming those colonized. A view of this kind does not stand up when matched against reality:

Colonial cultures are complex mixtures of their original parts, where these parts do not remain separate from each other but blend into something new. The hybrid nature of a colonial culture means that all participants in that culture, colonizers and colonized, have vital inputs into the structures of power, domination, and resistance that result. Foucault said that power is inherent in all human relationships and this view lies at the heart of the notion of hybridity: all participants in a colonial culture bring something of their own to the culture; all have agency and the power to shape their world, although this is nuanced and constrained in different ways. Another core element of postcolonial views is an emphasis on culture. Older views, critical of colonialism, tended to focus on economic and political aspects of colonial histories and the basic facts of economic exploitation and dispossession (Frank 1966; Wallerstein 1974, 1980 – see also Frank 1993 for how forms of capital accumulation may have operated in prehistoric times). Postcolonial theory's emphasis is on culture: the architecture, tropes of speech and writing, habits of dress and forms of ritual associated with domination and resistance in the colonial world. Culture is approached through some of the tools of literary theory and cultural forms are often seen as texts to be deconstructed. This has given the cultures of colonialism a very immaterial look, where the materiality of cultural forms has not been at the center of the analysis, although this has changed as anthropologists have started to focus on colonial cultures. A further feature of postcolonial thought worth emphasizing is the attempt to identify and weed out colonial habits of thought within the western intellectual tradition. This is not simply a matter of criticizing progressivist histories which privilege the west, but of understanding the sets of metaphors and views of the cultural process which throw an advantageous light on western thought and culture, with everything else seeming to lie in its shadow. Postcolonial theory may suggest new directions for archaeological analysis, but it cannot be used uncritically or unchanged. As well as the lack of concern for material culture, which must be central to any archaeological analysis, postcolonial approaches contain no real theory of history or change, tending to consist of vignettes or snapshots of one time and place. Another charge that postcolonial theorists vehemently deny is a lack of real political involvement in the struggles of the present, and some such as Edward Said are obviously fully involved with present problems. Perhaps a more realistic accusation is that the forms of struggle, such as those to do with land and culture I will talk about below, have had little impact at the level of theory, where the colonial text and its deconstructions appear to be what moves theoretical debate.

The first theorist to be considered is Edward Said, who was the earliest and best-known writer, partly due to his active involvement with the Palestinian cause. Said can be seen as the most influential of the postcolonial theorists. His book, *Orientalism* (Said 1978), has a basic premise that the West has created and maintained a simplified, clichéd, and essentialized view of the East through much of its history. Continuing structures of representation produce the East as inferior, being variously voiceless, sensual, female, despotic, irrational, and backward, as against the West's view of itself as masculine, democratic, rational, moral, dynamic, and progressive. These characterizations come through even in the writing of people who are sympathetic to the East. Said uses Foucault to show how the academic and cultural apparatus of the West produced this "truth" about the East, so that cultural works joined seamlessly to political action and the writings of Kipling might subtly reinforce claims to intervene in, or further westernize, conquered territories. Like Foucault, Said is pessimistic about the possibility of resistance, by either subject peoples or those within the West who reject the dominant stereotype, and he sees Orientalism as dating back to the Greeks, at least, so that this cliché has become a natural part of the West's perception of the non-western world.

It does not take much thought to pick out any number of archaeological writers who have been unconscious purveyors of orientalism: Gordon Childe's contrast between the deadening theocratic structures of Egypt and Mesopotamia on the one hand and the lively individualistic spirit of barbarian Europe on the other is a prime example which could be multiplied many times (Childe 1930). An interesting antidote to these views of history is contained within the controversial writings of Bernal (1987, 1991) on the origins of classical civilization.

Said's work has had a major influence on people in the West writing on eastern history and culture. *Orientalism* has also come in for much criticism: it is said to be bad history, creating a stereotype out of much more varied views of the East by the West; it leaves out the dimension of gender and it only analyzes western discourse and argues with western academics who ignore the voice of the colonized and their discourse (Clifford 1988; Young 1990). Said (1993) has gone on to look at the general effect that imperialism has had on western culture and the lack of acknowledgment of this influence. He also now sees the existence of a common culture throughout the world rooted in the experience of colonialism, linking colonized and colonizer alike. Working through this common history can lead to a common dialog of liberation.

Derrida had a major influence in shaping the thought of the second of the postcolonial theorists I will consider, Gayatri Spivak. Derrida con-

centrates almost exclusively on the manner in which meaning is constructed and the means by which dominant meanings might be disrupted.
The notion of text is crucial to his view and by this he means not just
written texts, but all structures of signification through which meanings
are created. Derrida starts from the margins of texts, eschewing more
conventional forms of criticism which concentrate on the overall structure of the plot and the intentions of the author. Derrida focuses on what
authors did not intend, those revealing slips of the tongue or loose ends
in construction which at first sight seem irrelevant but on further consideration provide a vital clue to the whole. Derrida seizes on a loose
end to deconstruct the text, to unravel its basic assumptions and logic,
but also to highlight the things which the text passes over in silence. His
deconstructive method is perfectly suited to analysis of the influence of
colonialism in European thought and the postcolonial theorists have
seized on deconstruction as a means of showing the vital presence of
colonialism at the margins of the core texts of western culture. Colonial
forms of life provide background shadow to highlight the development
of the notion of the rational, controlled, individualized white male which
lies at the heart of western liberal humanism. Such a figure could only
be developed through implicit contrasts with the mass of black people,
swayed by their emotions and imperfectly individuated, to be found, it
was thought, in all areas outside Europe. The deconstructive method,
highlighting the contrasts necessary to create western humanism, poses
considerable challenges for both archaeology and anthropology as both
are outgrowths of liberal philosophy, and are engaged in the conscious
study of the Other which has played such a major role in the unconscious creation of western thought.

For Spivak deconstruction is not the exposure of error, but is rather
about how truths are produced. This investigation into the creation of
truth is to ensure that other, more liberating truths are produced. Deconstructing classic colonial texts and revealing their logics will prevent
radical politics unwittingly reproducing the habits of thought they seek
to undermine. Following Derridean deconstruction Spivak employs a
number of strategies, such as the seeking out of minor characters like St
John Rivers, the missionary to India, found in *Jane Eyre*. A further technique is catachresis, which involves ripping ideas and images out of their
normal contexts and deploying them randomly and unexpectedly. This
is the antithesis of the creation of essentialized figures, such as the Indian
or the Asian, who appear constantly in colonial literature. Essentialism
of this type is impossible, because of the unstable nature of all subjects.
Following Lacan, who sees all individuals as emerging through a symbolic order inscribed in language, Spivak feels that all human subjects

are multiple, made up of the conflictual meanings of the codes which help construct them. In colonial situations, where colonizer and colonized alike are continually constructing different codes in opposition to each other, character is by no means straightforward, but continually reordered through changing sets of relationships.

Spivak, by contrast, has created no all-embracing scheme for colonial discourse, such as is found in *Orientalism*, nor is she confident of the millennial outcome to which Said now looks forward. Rather she concentrates on the variety of colonial experiences and histories, and a major element seen to structure this variety is gender, so that women's experiences loom large. She also gives more place to local voices, with much less of a concentration on colonial conversations. There is considerable acknowledgment of change over time in colonial regimes, so that the diasporas created through slavery are seen as very different from the diasporas resulting from economic migrations in the postwar period. Furthermore, Spivak makes a point of exploring her position as a western-based critic of colonialism in a "workplace engaged in the ideological production of neo-colonialism" (Spivak 1987: 210). Such a varied range of emphases in her work derives in part from the disparate nature of the theoretical positions Spivak draws on, mixing feminism, deconstructionism, and a political economic strand of Marxism. Her links with the Subaltern Studies Group (Guha 1988) have also led to influence from Gramsci (who coined the term "subaltern"), but also to a critique of their revisionist histories (Spivak 1987).

Spivak's emphasis on the symbolic construction of individuals and reality as a whole comes into conflict with her more Marxist analysis of the political and economic realities underlying colonial relations. It is very difficult to hold simultaneously that there are certain objective conditions of exploitation and repression, but that also the whole is constructed through symbolic schemes creating particular reality effects. To her credit, Spivak acknowledges, and even revels in, such contradictions which might help illuminate some of the contradictory aspects of the colonial process (Moore-Gilbert 1997: 99). A further complication is how far Spivak is guilty of "nativism," that is, claiming privileged insight into the Indian point of view through being Indian herself, albeit based in the United States and far removed from the oppressed women of that subcontinent. At different times within her writings she appears as a representative of Third World women and as a distanced academic, although this is a problem all cultural analysts share, as the position of analyst almost always distances the writer from those being analyzed.

Further ambiguities are to be found in the work of Homi Bhabha. Bhabha, like Spivak, is concerned to expose the creation of simplified and clichéd views of the colonial world. Complexity existed at the level of identity and also in the domain of knowledge, where contradiction was common. The native could be "both savage (cannibal) and yet the most obedient and dignified of servants (the bearer of food); he is the embodiment of rampant sexuality and yet innocent as a child; he is mystical, primitive, simple-minded and yet the most worldly and accomplished liar and manipulator of social forces" (Bhabha 1994: 82). For Bhabha, too great a concentration on the division between colonizer and colonized is pernicious. Both patrol officer and native were involved in complex sets of negotiations and mutualities and each operated through "forms of multiple and contradictory beliefs" about the other (Bhabha 1994: 95). However, as a measure of control the colonizers attempted to both fix the identity of the colonized in their own minds, and to alter it, with the Anglicized Indian being a case in point. However, although some Indians were encouraged to develop features of English culture this does not mean that English culture was a static entity and it too was a colonial product. Colonial contacts helped create Englishness and it was not just the Indians that were Anglicized, but also the English themselves. This is the point that Jones (1997) made about the Roman Empire, that the Romans came into being as Romans through their empire. Perhaps this is a truth about all forms of imperialism: Rather than being simply the imposition of the colonial culture on the natives, native and colonizer are created through the relations of colonialism. The colonial experience was much more contradictory and complex than that contained in simple histories emphasizing either domination or resistance.

Not only were everday aspects of cultural life created through colonialism, but also trends of thought. It has only recently started to be realized how much subtle influence colonial relations have had on political, economic, and social philosophies. It is also ironical that postmodernism, which has set itself up as a general critique of current ways of life, often sees western values as the norm. Only the West has taken part in the creation of modernity and equally only the western world has created the conditions of postmodernity, leaving out any non-western agency in the creation of global culture and relations. If in fact, as Bhabha holds, all cultures have hybrid origins and are creole forms, then all cultures in the world today are created through modernity and have played a part in creating the modern world. Lacan, Derrida, and Foucault all can be criticized for assuming western culture as a norm in their work. For instance, it could be said of Lacan that he does not recognize that different modes of forming individual identities exist throughout the globe and that he does not recognize the specificity of varying forms of gender, race, and class and the multitude of historical and social contexts in which these are created. It is odd that Said, Spivak, and Bhabha do not subject their French influences to the same criticism as they do other works.

The ideas of these three theorists have much to offer archaeologists. Said's critique of Orientalism could be extended to the views of the past developed by many prehistorians. A history of subtle denigration has been written through the use of crude categories like band, tribe, chiefdom, and state organized within a progressive view of world history, with the implication that only states are fully dynamic in world-historical terms and even then some are more dynamic than others. China, India, Mesopotamia, Egypt, Great Zimbabwe, or the Aztecs are just some of those who were felt not to maintain themselves at the cutting edge of world history (see Abu-Lughod [1989] for a critique of Euro-centric ideas used in analyzing the rise of capitalism). The values attached to these historical achievements can be reversed through a focus on the brute aspects of colonialism, with European states being seen to have most blood on their hands and the other states in the list being less destructive of other forms of life. Spivak's deconstructionist enterprise has much to offer archaeology, where even though we have moved away from some of the grander narratives of the past, most of us still operate with a set of concepts with Eureocentricism at the core. Archaeology's colonial origins also need further probing: the sets of analogies from Native American stone tool using groups which allowed people to start to think through European prehistory are only the tip of the iceberg in terms of the intellectual and social influences colonialism had on archaeology from the sixteenth century onwards. Such deconstruction could result in a radically different form of archaeology. In many ways Homi Bhabha's thought is becoming most directly influential and the notion of hybrid and creole cultures is being used to disrupt older more unitary notions of culture, as recently exemplified by Rowlands (1994a, 1994b) on European cultural origins. For a brilliant use of similar ideas, without explicit discussion of postcolonial theory, see Woolf (1998) on the creation of Roman imperial culture in Gaul. Some use of postcolonial theory of the type developed by Bhabha is to be found also in historical archaeology, although Foucault's thoughts on the origins of the modern world and the technologies of state and personhood are more directly influential (see the survey by Delle et al. 1999).

It is not just a case of what postcolonial theory can do for archaeology, but we also need to think about the transformations that archaeology can bring about in postcolonial theory. Colonialism was profoundly material: the whole driving force of colonial expansion was the extraction of wealth of varying kinds and the whole culture of colonialism was marked by differences of clothing, buildings, and bodies which need to be taken seriously as material things and not simply as texts (Tarlo 1996; Thomas 1991, 1994). Archaeology, due to the nature of its evidence, has to take material things seriously and any use of postcolonial theory will require us to think how a consideration of objects will alter the theory. Lastly, archaeologists are aware that modern colonialism is not the only one and that over the last 5,000 years there have been a plethora of social expansions which might be labeled "colonial," raising the question as to whether the Incas or the Chinese state can be understood in the same terms as colonial forms of the last few centuries. Archaeologists are also aware that some of the panoply of power used by the Romans, for instance, has been recycled in more modern times to give legitimation to recent regimes.

A further area where postcolonial theory is lacking is in any real engagement with the present political struggles of indigenous peoples for land and renewal of cultures. This is an area of postcolonial engagement which has transformed archaeology in many parts of the world and will eventually have effects on archaeologists everywhere.

## Postcolonial archaeology and indigenous rights

Archaeology has become much more politically engaged in the last two decades and this is most manifest in relationships with indigenous people. Such changes could be broadly seen as deriving from settler nations' attempts to come to terms with the indigenous peoples they dispossessed and a major part of this attempt at accommodation is through rethinking culture and history. Where archaeologists have seen themselves as disinterested scientists producing a past of interest for people everywhere, indigenous people have viewed archaeology as the final act of usurpation in which white society, having cut away the basis for people's control over their present, has now removed any control over the construction of the past. Being able to construct their own past is a vital precondition for the resurrection of culture in the present. Indigenous control over the past does not necessarily mean that local people will not work with archaeologists (although some clearly are deeply suspicious of the discipline – see Deloria 1970, but also Biolsi and Zimmerman 1997); but it does make for new sets of relationships, research goals, and forms of publication. New relationships are partly a matter of changing attitudes and partly of changes to the law in various parts of the world that necessitate greater consultation and links between indigenous peoples and archaeologists. Organizations such as the World Archaeological Congress are vital in creating channels of communication (Ucko 1987, 1995). Obviously these issues have been most pressing in places with internal colonies, such as the various nations of Native Americans, Aboriginal groups in Australia, and Maori tribes in New Zealand. This is an area that is changing fast and is very regionally diverse, even within one country, and all I can do here is highlight some of the current issues.

In many ways these changes have been most pronounced in the United States with the passing of the Native American Graves and Protection and Repatriation Act (Public Law 101–601, known generally as NAGPRA) in 1990. As the title of the Act indicates, the crucial points at issue are what, to whites, might seem an overly specific issue, the right to dispose of human bones and bodies (Hubert 1989 has shown that the European attitude to dead bodies is emotionally charged and not at all straightforward). Discussions about human remains have become the fulcrum on which all the issues concerning cultural property and the rights of so-called scientific archaeology as against different worldviews have shifted. The major arguments can be summarized quite neatly, but require far more thought and discussion than any brief summary might imply. The hard kernel of the archaeological argument is that freedom of research and action is necessary to allow disinterested western researchers to survey, excavate, and analyze sites in a manner only influenced by the dictates of science. Human physical and cultural remains tell us of a general human story and scientific institutions are creating the story of long-term human evolution and shorter-term local history in a manner that will be of interest and accessible to all humankind. Giving back human remains, or not excavating a site because it is sacred, is to lose access to potentially vital information about the past and to impoverish our knowledge of ourselves. The indigenous argument is more local than global and states that there is a moral and cosmological need to treat human remains and other cultural items in a manner according to local forms of respect. Failure to do so may result in danger from the spiritual forces of the universe and mean that local people are not discharging their custodianship of land and ancestral spirits in a responsible manner. There is also obviously the issue of control. After centuries of dispossession and an inability to speak out, indigenous people want the right to create their own past in a manner that makes sense to them and accords with local cultural logics and this may well mean saying no to archaeologists, or at least those not willing to work in accord with local sentiments.

The NAGPRA legislation has shifted the debate by giving native Americans control of their heritage under certain defined standards. It is worth looking in some detail at a particular case in which the issues are brought out in a concrete manner. On October 6, 1991 some 756 lots of skeletal material, representing perhaps 1,000 individuals, were interred in the Alutiiq village of Larsen Bay, Kodiak Island, Alaska, just a short distance from where they had been dug up some fifty years previously by Aleš Hrdlička, a physical anthropologist at the Smithsonian Institution. The reburial of the human remains followed some eight years of negotiations between the Smithsonian and the Larsen Bay community and these negotiations brought to light many of the crucial issues surrounding such cases and helped settle precedents for the future (Bray and Killion 1994). Hrdlička, a Czech immigrant to the United States, was a crucial figure in physical anthropology between the wars. Late in his life, in the 1920s and 1930s, he became interested in the peopling of the Americas and the routes that the first colonists might have taken between Siberia and North America. This led him to research in Alaska, both doing anthropometric measurements of the existing inhabitants and looking for sites to excavate for prehistoric human remains. Much of Alaska disappointed him, as it was so heavily eroded that few older deposits remained. However, Kodiak Island in the Gulf of Alaska had comparatively good conditions of deposition and he was led to the Uyak site in Larsen Bay through information from a local cannery manager and his wife. The Uyak site (known to Hrdlička as "Our Site") comprised a settlement and a cemetery, which we now know spanned from ca. 3000 BP to AD 1500. To say that Hrdlička excavated is to imply a sophistication that was lacking from his field approach. However, he carried out four summer seasons of crude digging at Uyak between 1932 and 1936, recovering some 1,000 individuals and numerous artifacts from three roughly defined stratigraphic units. He left little adequate documentation for his excavation or provenance for his finds. He also had extremely poor relations with the local Indian population, who obviously had considerable reservations about Hrdlička's mass exhumation of bodies they considered related to themselves. Hrdlička was a single-minded scientist, for whom the questions and answers of his own research were paramount. McGuire (1994: 180) mentions the case of Hrdlička removing the bodies of Yacqui people, killed by the Mexican army three weeks before, from the massacre site and sending them off to the American Museum of Natural History in New York. Memories of Hrdlička's disregard of local people's feelings in Larsen Bay were crucial in promoting the case for repatriation in the late 1980s, highlighting the fact that it is the nature of the relationship between western investigators and indigenous people that is important and how things are done is as influential in subsequent events as what was done.

Once returned to the Smithsonian, the Uyak site skeletons represented 5 percent of the total physical anthropology collections and were seen by the institution as of major scientific importance, despite all the deficiencies in their manner of excavation. People at the Smithsonian were aghast when the Larsen Bay community first made moves to repatriate the skeletons. This followed a resolution of the Larsen Bay Tribal Council in May 1987 to try and gain return of the skeletal material, which was itself part of more general attempts by the community to revitalize the culture of the region (Pullar 1994: 17). Righting the wrongs of the past was basic to the health of the community in the present. The Bray and Killion volume (1994) contains a fascinating account of the negotiations between the Smithsonian and the community, with many of the main viewpoints found in all such cases well expressed: the physical anthropologist distressed at the lack of opportunity to do more work on skeletons of interest; the museum director and director of the Arctic Studies Center who shifted their positions considerably and honorably and who felt they had learned a lot by the experience; the emotional relief experienced by the community once the skeletons were reinterred; and the evolving legal and moral positions of all involved. Although the repatriation of skeletal remains is not only, or even primarily, a legal issue, it is worth thinking about the law for a moment, as (oddly) this highlights many of the intellectual issues at stake.

The Larsen Bay negotiations straddled the NAGPRA legislation, starting prior to its formulation and concluding just after its enactment in law. The case had some influence on the legislation and brings out the issues of culture and history that lie at the heart of the legislation. Since NAGPRA the legal basis for a repatriation claim of skeletal remains or certain classes of artifacts is cultural affiliation. This is defined in the act as "a relationship of shared group identity that can be reasonably traced historically or prehistorically between a present day Indian tribe or Native Hawaiian organization, and an identifiable earlier group." There are problems here of what constitutes groups in the present and the nature of their claims. Three groups are currently recognized as having claims: lineal descendants; tribal members; other individuals or groups who claim some degree of Native American heritage. Lineal descendants have a straightforward claim in law, showing the importance of genetic inheritance in these issues. People making claims on the basis of a general Native American cultural affiliation can have their claims dismissed – a case brought by American Indians Against Desecration (AIAD) against a developer, who planned to disturb human remains, was dismissed as they could not show "ancestral ties to persons whose remains were excavated at the site" (quoted in Bray and Grant 1994: 155). It is those in the middle, tribal members, who may have varying degrees of legal claim. This is partly due to conflicting forms of evidence. NAGPRA allows that admissable evidence for cultural affiliation can be geographic, genealogical, biological, archaeological, anthropological, linguistic, folkloric, and historic information. In the Larsen Bay case there was something of a contradiction between local oral history, which claimed that the modern village residents were descendants of the Koniag people who had always lived on the Kodiak Island, and the evidence from archaeological analysis of the mortuary assemblages, which suggested a break in the history of the site. The biological evidence was more equivocal than either of these, suggesting a mixing of Native American groups and an admixture of Russian and Euro-American characteristics. The Smithsonian agreed to repatriate the remains before the case came to law, but it was felt that the Larsen Bay villagers may not have been able to mount a claim to all the remains that would have been upheld by the law as it then stood (Bray and Grant 1994: 157). The Smithsonian were obviously motivated by political considerations surrounding the case, rather than its strict legality. Nevertheless, many legal arguments over cultural affiliation rest on intellectual premises that would be questioned by many anthropologists and archaeologists and at times by Native peoples themselves.

Essentialized notions of culture constitute the best basis for any claim in law, which makes it hard to allow for the complex colonial and precolonial histories of many groups or the fact that some groups may not have boundaries and identities which were fixed and defined in western views. It does not need skilled deconstruction to show that the law is rooted in notions of timeless and primitive tribal groups, implicitly contrasted to fast-changing and unstable western cultures.

This is a situation also found in other parts of the world. In Australia, the current state of land law is that in order for Aboriginal people to reclaim land they must show a continuing attachment to it and this attachment is not only physical but cultural and ritual. If people can show that they have been hunting and gathering on the land, but also caring for it through the use of proper ceremony, then their claim is a strong one, as long as the land is not already covered by western legal title (a major limitation). Part of the demonstration of ritual care is through continued use of sites with rock art and aspects of the Dreamtime, a period during which ancestral figures created the features of the landscape through journeys across it. People maintain links to the land by the use in ceremony of sacred objects and through creating dance, song, and painting. The deepest of these links in both a historical and semantic sense is to the ancestral landscape, providing continuity such that the Dreamtime still exists to structure contemporary action. Land is also genealogy, a set of links to known ancestors. A hunting or gathering expedition is never a purely pragmatic business, but a means by which young people get to know their past and older people maintain their links with the dead. The landscape has a group aspect, creating the history of the group as a whole, but it is also individual, as each person has their own unique set of links to the land, due to genealogy and the pattern of their life. The end of funeral rites often involves the burning of the country associated with a person, to make it safe for the living to enter.

Human remains and their reburial have caused considerable debate in Australia between Aboriginal people and archaeologists and amongst the general public. Most contentious of these have been fossils of Pleistocene age, such as the forty individuals dating from between 9000 and 15,000 BP from Kow Swamp in Victoria. These represented the world's largest collection of skeletal remains from a single late Pleistocene/early Holocene site and caused an outcry when the Victorian government returned these remains to the Echuca Aboriginal community for reburial. Les Hiatt, a past president of the Australian Institute of Aboriginal Studies, wrote to a national newspaper, *The Australian* (August 2, 1990) to say that he applauded the return of recent Aboriginal human remains, but that fossil material was "surely the heritage of all humankind. It would be ludicrous to suggest that remains of Homo sapiens neanderthalensis should be returned to the people of Düsseldorf for ritual burial or destruction. If such a proposal was made, we would quickly dismiss it as the product of misplaced sentimentalism, philistinism or political opportunism" (quoted in Fforde 1997: 77). The World Archaeological Congress, by contrast, had in 1989 passed the Vermillion Accord in Vermillion, South Dakota, which recognized the legitimacy of concerns indigenous people had for all their ancestors regardless of age. This also appears to be the Australian legal position, as the federal Aboriginal and Torres Strait Islander Heritage Protection Act (1984) allows for the "satisfactory disposal of remains held contrary to expressed Aboriginal wishes" by empowering the Minister for Aboriginal Affairs to order the delivery of remains to himself or Aboriginal people "entitled to them, and willing to accept responsibility for them, in accordance with Aboriginal tradition" (*A Guide to How the Act Works*, 1984, p. 13). The Australian Archaeological Association (AAA) has also developed a Code of Ethics, adopted in 1991, which acknowledges Aboriginal control over the skeletal remains and enjoins regular communication between archaeologists and Aboriginal communities to resolve what should happen to remains and the way forward for further study. The AAA also set up a consultancy, held by Steven Webb (a physical anthropologist), to liaise with Aboriginal communities concerning the scientific values of such studies and to explore the benefits for Aboriginal communities of the study of human remains.

Although in the early stages discussions surrounding human remains generated more heat than light, the result has been to set up connections between Aboriginal communities and archaeologists which are evolving into new relationships. Once the idea has been established that it is impossible to carry out archaeology, of the prehistoric period at least, without some form of consultation with indigenous communities, then this brings about fundamental changes in the way in which archaeology is done. The notion has grown up of "covenantal archaeology" which takes place through a worked set of agreements between archaeologists and local people as to aims, methods, forms of analysis, and the eventual disposition of artifacts deriving from excavations (Zimmerman 1997). This has led archaeologists away from a generalized liberal view of knowledge, which sees information about the past as being of potential interest to people everywhere, to more locally based views, deriving from culturally specific notions of history and what is appropriate subject matter for debate. A number of issues come to the fore, such as culturally different notions of the construction of the past. Sahlins (1985) has written that all history is culturally ordered and that all culture is historically ordered. Archaeologists and anthropologists are now trying to probe the complexities involved in such a succinct statement. In many parts of the world collaborative work is being carried out into the nature of history (Dening 1992, 1996; Douglas 1992; Wiessner and Tumu 1998). This will add a new dimension to what Hodder (1986) has called contextual archaeology, where finds should not only be understood in the contexts of sites and assemblages from which they come, but also, partially at least, from the viewpoints of people in the local area. A view like this raises again new issues of how far it is possible to generalize about the prehistories of varying regions. A useful distinction might be that between information and knowledge. Knowledge is tied to a particular cultural context and relative to especial sets of concerns and forms of history. Knowledge of the past for many indigenous people is not of purely intellectual interest, but is tied to issues of custodianship for the land and past human generations. Knowledge comes from a real personal and group engagement with the issues at hand and may derive from different sources, with oral history and genealogy being as important as archaeological material (Anyon et al. 1996). Information, on the other hand, is rather more generalized, deriving from some universal premises informing archaeology and of interest to people beyond a local group. Many archaeologists would be interested in the manner in which material culture is meaningful and might use specific situations to explore this general premise. Cases can be compared and contrasted in discussions as to whether, for instance, the notion of biography is a useful one in understanding the changing meaning of material culture. For local people, the main concern is to look at the history of particular sets of meanings attached to objects and their historical and spiritual significances. One set of objects can potentially be discussed in different manners, as both knowledge and information, with each discussion being aware of, and sensitive to, the rules by which the other discussion works. It would not be a good idea to reify the distinction between knowledge and information too much, but such distinctions may be helpful in understanding the links between the global and local concerns about history in the age of the World Wide Web and the global consideration of local issues (Hodder 1999).

We should also bear in mind that in long-colonized parts of the world the relationship between archaeologists and local people will not just be a bipartite one. There will be a multiplicity of groups and claims on the past, not all of which are in harmony with others. For instance, the situation in South Africa is extremely complicated, as many different groups have territory within the borders of the nation state and the colonial history of the country has brought groups from many parts of the world to the southern end of the African continent (Schrire 1995; Boonzaier et al. 1996). The collapse of apartheid has meant that many hidden histories can now be probed for the first time, but most involve complex and painful stories involving links between archaeologists, historians, and a variety of different groups (Hall and Markell 1993). A situation of serial dispossession, where one group after another attempts to dispossess its predecessors, can be found in many parts of the world (Honeychurch 1997) and makes telling any such history a fraught and contested process.

One set of indigenous communities never consulted are local communities in Britain and Europe. In Britain and elsewhere in Europe there is no legal requirement to ask permission to excavate from local communities. Once the landowner has agreed and any national body, such as English Heritage or the National Trust, which might have some form of legal control over the site, has given permission, then the consultation process normally ends. This ignores the fact that local people have strong cultural and emotional attachments to sites and may wish to have some say in what is done to them. A stress on local values also raises questions of cultural affiliation strongly: does local residence alone qualify one for a say over what happens at sites? Should the length of a family's history in the area be taken into account and might a village of people commuting to London, who have moved there in the last few decades, have less influence on what is done to the area's archaeological sites than people who trace their local roots back to the Anglo-Saxon period? These are issues which have not yet been tackled in any adequate manner in Europe, showing that the lessons of consultation learned elsewhere in the world have not been taken to heart in areas in which issues of identity and control appear unproblematical, but may not be so. It may be that postcolonial concerns need to infuse the heartlands of colonialism.

## Final thoughts

Intellectual and political changes deriving from the context of postcolonialism have formed a new context for archaeology and archaeologists are only just starting to come to terms with this. Trigger (1985: 3) noted, in relation to Canada's history and prehistory, that until recently many white North Americans assumed that native peoples would be assimilated by white society, or simply die out (a view common in other parts of the world: McGregor 1997). The question was not one of consultation, but rather of documentation, to preserve records of vanishing ways of life before they disappeared for ever. Native American society was used as a series of examples of global social typologies. They were seen as bands, tribes, and chiefdoms, informing Europeans about aspects of a progressive history, which had the settler societies at the pinnacle of progress. Postcolonial theory and practice has now made all aspects of these views untenable. Native societies do not represent pristine examples of social formations unfortunately destroyed by white settlers. Rather they should be seen as hybrid or creole social forms arising from the complexities of colonialism and combining indigenous responses and resistance, as well as outside impact (Peers 1999). Despite the effects of disease, dispossession, and massacre, native societies persist into the present, demonstrating the resilience and strength of their cultural forms. Postcolonial archaeology needs to uncover the hybrid nature of colonialized societies that have come to be in the last few centuries and the longer-term precolonial histories of these groups. The agency of native peoples in the past in creating colonial forms has a strong echo in the present, where demands for archaeologists to create more locally sensitive views of history are now backed by legislation. This means that present research must be a collaborative project between archaeologists and local people and that this can only come about once the injustices of the past have been redressed, which will often mean the return of skeletal or cultural material considered to have been inappropriately obtained, stored, or displayed. Archaeology and the broader colonial societies will be ultimately much healthier for these changes.

However, the picture is by no means all rosy and there is still a large residue of anger and resentment on both sides. There are also deep issues of culture, identity, and knowledge to be confronted. Postcolonial theory can be seen partly as an assault on the notion of essentialized cultural forms, cultures which have some central and unchanging essence to them. Archaeologists and native peoples alike have worked with such views of culture in the past and legislation, plus political imperatives, may encourage simplified notions to persist. A group claiming rights to land or cultural property would be ill-advised to stress in a court of law that theirs is a hybrid and complex history, which makes a simple notion of cultural integrity difficult to sustain. A stress on cultural integrity can also lead to contests between native groups, where a parcel of land may have had a complex history of ownership in the past, and an oversimplified view of the group and of ownership may lead one group to press a claim where many have equal rights. Archaeologists have to engage in these debates not just in particular cases, but also to try and shift the general context of lawmaking to embrace a more realistic view of the entangled history of groups through taking account of colonial and pre-colonial histories. Such discussions might also be useful in a place like the British Isles, where notions of history and cultural integrity are heavily contested. Lastly, archaeologists need more subtle ways of dealing with the intellectual results of their work. Aboriginal Australians are used to working with concepts of secret and public stories about their art and ritual, so that a painting or a dance can be interpreted in quite different manners depending on the level of knowledge of the viewer or participant (Morphy 1992). Archaeologists might also have to embrace the notion of layered knowledge, with some discussions so tied to the local context that they cannot be easily revealed to outsiders, and with other forms of knowledge which are locally based but not restricted, and then with types of information which can fit into larger discussions of colonialism, history, and material culture. The output of archaeology would then be a process of negotiation as to both the intellectual premises on which the endeavor rested and the suitability of the results for broad publication. Such negotiated outcomes recognize the plurality of interests in the past and the political needs of the present, but involve thought about culture, knowledge, and identity which will further transform archaeological studies of the past.

NOTE

I am very grateful to Gwyneira Isaac for advice, discussion and key references.

REFERENCES

Abu-Lughod, J. L. 1989. *Before European Hegemony: The World System A.D. 1250–1350*. Oxford: Oxford University Press.
Anyon, R., T. J. Ferguson, L. Jackson, and L. Lane 1996. Native American oral traditions and archaeology. *Society for American Archaeology Bulletin* 14: 14–16.
Bernal, M. 1987. *Black Athena I: The Fabrication of Ancient Greece 1785–1985*. New Brunswick: Rutgers University Press.
Bernal, M. 1991. *Black Athena II: The Archaeological and Documentary Evidence*. New Brunswick: Rutgers University Press.
Bhabha, H. 1994. *The Location of Culture*. London: Routledge.
Biolsi, T. and L. J. Zimmerman (eds) 1997. *Indians and Anthropologists: Vine Deloria Jr. and the Critique of Anthropology*. Tucson: University of Arizona Press.
Boonzaier, E., C. Malherbe, A. Smith, and P. Berens 1996. *The Cape Herders: A History of the Khoikhoi of Southern Africa*. Cape Town: David Philip.
Bray, T. L. and L. G. Grant 1994. The concept of cultural affiliation and its legal significance in the Larsen Bay repatriation. In T. L. Bray and T. W. Killion (eds), *Reckoning with the Dead: The Larsen Bay Repatriation and the Smithsonian Institution*, 153–7. Washington: Smithsonian Institution Press.
Bray, T. L. and T. W. Killion (eds) 1994. *Reckoning with the Dead: The Larsen Bay Repatriation and the Smithsonian Institution*. Washington: Smithsonian Institution Press.
Childe, V. G. 1930. *The Bronze Age*. Cambridge: Cambridge University Press.
Clifford, J. 1988. *The Predicament of Culture: Twentieth Century Ethnography, Literature and Art*. Cambridge, MA: Harvard University Press.
Delle, J., M. P. Leone, and P. R. Mullins 1999. Archaeology of the modern state: European colonialism. In G. Barker (ed.), *Companion Encyclopedia of Archaeology*, 1107–59. London: Routledge.
Deloria, V. 1970. *Custer Died for your Sins: An Indian Manifesto*. New York: Avon.
Dening, G. 1992. *Mr. Bligh's Bad Language: Passion, Power and Theatre on the Bounty*. Cambridge: Cambridge University Press.
Dening, G. 1996. *Performances*. Chicago: Chicago University Press.

Douglas, B. 1992. Doing ethnographic history, the case of fighting in New Caledonia. In J. Carrier (ed.), *History and Tradition in Melanesian Anthropology*, 86–115. Berkeley: University of California Press.

Fforde, C. 1997. Controlling the dead, an analysis of the collecting and repatriation of Aboriginal human remains. Ph.D. thesis, Department of Archaeology, University of Southampton.

Frank, A.G. 1966. The development of underdevelopment. *Monthly Review* 18: 17–31.

Frank, A.G. 1993. Bronze Age world system cycles. *Current Anthropology* 34: 383–429.

Gosden, C. 1999. *Anthropology and Archaeology: A Changing Relationship*. London: Routledge.

Guha, R. (ed.) 1988. *Selected Subaltern Studies*. Oxford: Oxford University Press.

Hall, M. and A. Markell (eds) 1993. *Historical Archaeology in the Western Cape*. South African Archaeological Society Goodwin Series 7. Cape Town: University of Cape Town Press.

Hodder, I. 1986. *Reading the Past*. Cambridge: Cambridge University Press.

Hodder, I. 1999. *The Archaeological Process*. Oxford: Blackwell.

Honeychurch, L. 1997. Crossroads in the Caribbean: a site of encounter and exchange in Dominica. *World Archaeology* 28: 291–304.

Hubert, J. 1989. A proper place for the dead: a critical review of the "reburial" issue. In R. Layton (ed.), *Conflict in the Archaeology of Living Traditions*, 131–66. London: Routledge.

Jones, S. 1997. *The Archaeology of Ethnicity: Constructing Identities in the Past and Present*. London: Routledge.

McGregor, R. 1997. *Imagined Destinies: Aboriginal Australians and the Doomed Race Theory, 1880–1939*. Melbourne: Melbourne University Press.

McGuire, R. 1994. Do the right thing. In T.L. Bray and T.W. Killion (eds), *Reckoning with the Dead: The Larsen Bay Repatriation and the Smithsonian Institution*, 180–3. Washington: Smithsonian Institution Press.

Moore-Gilbert, B. 1997. *Postcolonial Theory: Contexts, Practices, Politics*. London: Verso.

Morphy, H. 1992. *Ancestral Connections*. Chicago: Chicago University Press.

Peers, L. 1999. "Many tender ties": the shifting contexts and meanings of the S Black bag. *World Archaeology* 31: 288–302.

Pullar, G.L. 1994. The Qikertarmiut and the scientist: fifty years of clashing world views. In T.L. Bray and T.W. Killion (eds), *Reckoning with the Dead: The Larsen Bay Repatriation and the Smithsonian Institution*, 15–25. Washington: Smithsonian Institution Press.

Rowlands, M. 1994a. Childe and the archaeology of freedom. In D.R. Harris (ed.), *The Archaeology of V. Gordon Childe*, 35–54. London: UCL Press.

Rowlands, M. 1994b. The politics of identity in archaeology. In G.C. Bond and A. Gilliam (eds), *Social Construction of the Past: Representation as Power*, 129–43. London: Routledge.

Rowlands, M. 1998. The archaeology of colonialism. In K. Kristiansen and

M. Rowlands *Social Transformations in Archaeology: Global and Local Perspectives*, 327–33. London: Routledge.

Sahlins, M.D. 1985. *Islands of History*. Chicago: University of Chicago Press.

Said, E.W. 1978. *Orientalism*. New York: Vintage.

Said, E.W. 1993. *Culture and Imperialism*. New York: Knopf.

Schrire, C. 1995. *Digging through Darkness*. Johannesburg: Witwatersrand University Press.

Spivak, G. 1987. *In Other Worlds: Essays in Cultural Politics*. London: Routledge.

Tarlo, E. 1996. *Clothing Matters: Dress and Identity in India*. London: Hurst.

Thomas, N. 1991. *Entangled Objects: Exchange, Material Culture and Colonialism in the Pacific*. Cambridge, MA: Harvard University Press.

Thomas, N. 1994. *Colonialism's Culture: Anthropology, Travel and Government*. Cambridge: Polity Press.

Trigger, B.G. 1985. *Natives and Newcomers: Canada's "Heroic Age" Reconsidered*. Kingston: McGill-Queen's University Press.

Ucko, P. 1987. *Academic Freedom and Apartheid: The Story of the World Archaeological Congress*. London: Duckworth.

Ucko, P. (ed.) 1995. *Theory in Archaeology: A World Perspective*. London: Routledge.

Wallerstein, I. 1974. *The Modern World System, I*. New York: Academic Press.

Wallerstein, I. 1980. *The Modern World System, II*. New York: Academic Press.

Wiessner, P. and A. Tumu 1998. *Historical Vines: Enga Networks of Exchange, Ritual and Warfare in Papua New Guinea*. Bathurst, NSW: Crawford House.

Woolf, G. 1998. *Becoming Roman: The Origins of Provincial Civilization in Gaul*. Cambridge: Cambridge University Press.

Young, R. 1990. *White Mythologies: Writing History and the West*. London: Routledge.

Zimmerman, L. 1997. Remythologising the relationship between Indians and archaeologists. In N. Swidler, K.E. Dongoske, R. Anyon, and A.S. Downer (eds), *Native Americans and Archaeologists: Stepping Stones to Common Ground*, 44–56. Walnut Creek: Altamira Press.

# 11

# Archaeological Representation

## The Visual Conventions for Constructing Knowledge about the Past

*Stephanie Moser*

## Introduction

The field of archaeological representation addresses the ways in which knowledge about the past is constructed through the different modes of presenting our disciplinary findings. On one hand there are academic modes of representation such as the various types of archaeological writing, conference presentations, and archaeological illustration. On the other hand there are "non-academic" modes of representation that communicate to a far wider audience, such as museum displays, popular books, the print media, fiction writing, and film and television. While some work has been done on the academic modes of representation, very little has been done on non-academic discourses about the past. The premise of research on archaeological representation is that both of these modes of communication – academic and non-academic – are responsible for the construction of archaeological theories about the past. Indeed, the theory of archaeological representation asserts that non-academic forms of presentation are not merely by-products of academic research, but rather that they have their own distinctive ways of participating in the process of making meaning.

Late in the 1980s and early in the 1990s postprocessual archaeologists highlighted the need to reflect on the nature of archaeological representation, claiming that the ways in which we write the past play a significant role in determining its meaning. "Archaeological poetics" was defined as a subject of inquiry, where the aim was to identify the forms of how archaeological knowledge is communicated, or the style with which archaeology designs and produces its pasts (Shanks 1992; Tilley 1993). Despite this wide-ranging objective, the focus of discussion centered on archaeological writing and the textuality of archaeological discourse. In calling for an awareness of the manner in which archaeologists represented the past through text, postprocessual theorists demonstrated how language shaped meaning. While this was an important connection to make, the emphasis was clearly on academic discourse as representation; the popular dimensions of archaeological representation were neglected. Scholars who published on the textual dimensions of representation, such as Michael Shanks, Chris Tilley, and Ian Hodder, argued that the more popular areas of archaeological representation also required attention, but since then little systematic work has been done on the subject. It would seem that there was an inherent assumption that academic modes of representation were more important in shaping archaeological knowledge than non-academic ones. But is this true?

## The neglect of archaeological representation

The archaeological community has been slow in recognizing the role of popular representations of the construction of archaeological knowledge. Part of the explanation is that questions concerning the presentation of the past in non-academic discourses have traditionally been relegated to the field of public archaeology. This area lacks status as an "important" field in the methodological and theoretical literature of mainstream archaeology. Furthermore, we academics, living in our ivory towers, tend to assume that popular representations of the past have a primary role in shaping the public's perception of archaeology, but that they do not have a significant impact on the production of knowledge about the past. Thus, we see ourselves as somehow being immune from the popular realm and consider the subject of archaeological representation as being outside the domain of our professional responsibility. This notion needs challenging as it is based on a false distinction between science and culture. Understanding the way our disciplinary findings are represented is our responsibility because the forms and media used to communicate our work have a significant impact on the ideas we have about the past and about archaeology.

When giving conference presentations and public talks, archaeologists often use popular images of the past but they tend to engage with them as a source of amusement, or when some great injustice has been done in the portrayal of a particular ancestor or site. This reflects the assumption that representations are unproblematic and that they do not require any interpretation. But representations demand serious attention because they so greatly influence the wider public's perception of archaeology and the past. More important still, representations need to be understood because they affect *us* – the archaeologists who are seeking to produce reliable accounts of the past. We too are part of the so-called wider public. While it is true that our interpretations are represented by other professionals, such as museum designers, illustrators, filmmakers, artists, and popular science writers for example, it is also the case that these people make their own contributions to the process of making meaning. On one hand, they select particular aspects of archaeological interpretations and emphasize them, but on the other hand, popular representations can make their own statements and actually create ideas about the past. Furthermore, archaeological representations not only feed back into the way we formulate our research questions; they shape ideas we have about ourselves as professionals (see Moser 1999). Indeed, in many cases it would be fair to say that popular representations of the discipline inspire us to study archaeology and ultimately become archaeologists. This point has been made in relation to palaeontology, where Mitchell (1998: 282) has argued that while the cultural status of the dinosaur is driven and influenced by its scientific status, scientists are influenced – maybe even driven – by the myths, metaphors, and images that surround the objects they study.

The notion that representations are not simply by-products of academic research is a view that other cultural historians have developed in relation to the investigation of how science and culture interact. In his analysis of the representation of prehistoric animals in film, Mitman (1993) accounts for the scientific community's neglect of popular culture in terms of a diffusionist model of knowledge creation. According to this model, knowledge is created by scientists and then reused or diffused into popular culture – thus it is seen as a one-way process. Another author who challenges the separation of popular culture and science is Mitchell, who has examined the proliferation of dinosaur imagery in the twentieth century. He states that "the dinosaur image is not, then, *simply* a popularisation of scientific understanding, a mere vehicle for reporting and representing scientific knowledge. The visual image is also a key element in the process of scientific thinking and discovery as such, not just as a descriptive afterthought or afterimage, but as constitutive element, a speculative, theoretical construction" (Mitchell 1998: 55). A similar argument was made in relation to the production of reconstruction drawings of our hominid ancestors in their inferred habitats, where it was demonstrated how the images constituted theories about human evolution (Moser 1992).

## Archaeological representation as a new field of inquiry

In the 1980s questions concerning archaeological representation started to be addressed in the context of examining the socio-political dimensions of archaeological practice. North American archaeologists in particular highlighted how politics and social values shaped representations of the past in both the academic and popular realms. People such as Mark Leone, Tom Patterson, and Joan Gero explored different aspects of how the discipline was represented to wider audiences. While Leone (1981) addressed the aspects of representation in museum displays, Patterson (1986) looked at the way class shaped accounts of the past, and Gero (1985) discussed the gendered dimensions of presenting the discipline. With socio-politically orientated studies it became clear that the ways in which knowledge was constructed were contingent on numerous social factors. With this established, it became possible to consider the role of popular representations in the production of knowledge.

The fact that the topic of representation is slowly gaining recognition in archaeology is evidenced by a growing body of literature on the many different genres of communicating the past. At this stage the majority of work examines the role of illustration (see below); however there is a growing literature on museum display and site presentation that is sensitive to representation issues in archaeology (e.g. Arnold et al. 1998; McManus 1996; Stone and Molyneaux 1994; Walsh 1992). In addition to this, work has also been done on film (Piccini 1996; Serceau 1982; Solomon 1998; Wyke 1997), popular magazines (Gero and Root 1990), literature (Evans 1983; Girdwood 1984; Landau 1991), souvenirs (Beard 1992), re-enactment (Sansom 1996), and children's books (Burtt 1987). Most recently, the topic of computer and multimedia representation has been delineated. Besides examining the issues associated with GIS and interpretation, researchers are beginning to consider the implications of virtual reality and the three-dimensional reconstructions of sites (Forte and Siliotti 1996; Higgins et al. 1996; Dingwall et al. 1999).

When it comes to the development of a general theory of archaeological representation, it is the work on the visual images of the past that has most clearly demonstrated the way representations influence scientific thought. During the last decade a number of authors have documented how images function in relation to the research process (e.g. Gifford Gonzalez 1993; James 1997; Moser 1992, 1993, 1996, 1998; Moser and Gamble 1997). While progress has been made in outlining the major areas of visual production in archaeology and their general significance (e.g. Molyneaux 1997), we still need to know exactly how representations make their own statements and create knowledge about the past. In *Ancestral Images* the crucial role of reconstruction drawings in shaping ideas about human origins was demonstrated (Moser 1998). Here it was shown that from classical times a visual vocabulary for explaining our origins was created. This vocabulary quickly became a powerful iconographic tradition that has had an everlasting impact on our consciousness. When seeking to account for human evolution, scientists of the twentieth century found it difficult, if not, impossible to avoid being influenced by the visual concepts set up by those working in pre-scientific traditions. The reason why images have been so successful in accounting for human evolution is that the artists and illustrators working in classical, medieval, Renaissance, and antiquarian traditions singled out a set of potent symbols or icons that communicated the essence of our primal existence. Archaeologists have not discarded these visions but continue to slot their ideas into the established pictorial frameworks.

## Visual culture and the concept of representation

A general characteristic of contemporary society is our fascination, indeed obsession, with the visual. Our attempts to make sense of the world and communicate with each other are increasingly made through the growing range of visual technologies. When it comes to learning about the past, we have always relied heavily on pictorial representation to help us imagine the lives of our distant ancestors. The visual portrayal of ideas about the past has played a key role in the quest to understand the past, and illustrations have had tremendous power in disseminating ideas throughout society and fixing them in popular culture. Thus, representation in archaeology can be defined as the production of meaning through a visual language of communicating the past. Meaning is not constructed through words and then visually portrayed; rather it is created through a set of pictorial conventions that are laden with symbolic content.

What has changed, as a result of the growing dominance of visual culture, is that the visualization of the past in media other than two-dimensional illustrations has become very prolific. Multimedia educational resources, computer games, interactive virtual reality displays, movies and reproduction merchandise have also begun to contribute to the way we understand the past. In order to make sense of these developments it is important to understand the broader impact of such visual technologies on society. Much is currently being written about visual culture, and all of it shows how central the visual world is in producing meanings. Investigating the trend in postmodern culture to increasingly communicate through the visual, scholars such as Mirzoeff (1998: 5) state that "Western culture has consistently privileged the spoken word as the highest form of intellectual practice and seen visual representations as second-rate illustrations of ideas. Now, however, the emergence of visual culture as a subject has contested this hegemony." The significance of images is relatively straightforward – as Rogoff (1998: 15) asserts, "images convey information, afford pleasure and displeasure, influence style, determine consumption and mediate power relations." The visual mode of communication thus becomes key in the production of meanings about our past, present, and future.

Before addressing the question of how representations construct meaning in archaeology, it is important to look at how archaeological representation is related to research in other disciplines. Work on the concept of representation has been undertaken in both the social studies of science and cultural studies. In the former, scholars have looked at how scientific knowledge is shaped by different forms of representation such as lab reports and illustrations (e.g. Lynch and Woolgar 1990; Baigrie 1996; Jones and Galison 1998). In cultural studies, scholars have highlighted representation as a key concept in the study of culture, defining it as being about the communication of ideas using language, signs, and images (e.g. Hall 1997). In both areas representation is seen as being a process that involves the production of meaning via the act of describing and symbolizing.

Social studies of science have yielded an excellent array of studies on palaeontological imagery, which is one of the major areas of popular presentation. Rudwick (1992), Rupke (1993), and Mitman (1993) have all redressed the neglect of pictures as agents of meaning, showing how dinosaur iconography has had a deeply formative influence in constructing knowledge of prehistoric times. They dismantle the notion that popular culture is divorced from science by tracing the history of illustrative traditions and outlining their close connection to research assumptions and biases. Most recently, as noted above, Mitchell has looked at the proliferation of dinosaur images in all areas of popular culture, including shopping malls, theme parks, advertisements, sitcoms, and cartoons. He explains the cultural significance of the dinosaur in contemporary society by examining the underlying meaning of all the images that surround us. His justification for this quest is well explained:

> the most difficult problem with the cultural meaning of the dinosaur is resisting the temptation to settle for quick and easy answers. People assume, quite rightly, that it takes a great deal of special knowledge and training to interpret the fossil remains of a dinosaur. But they assume, quite wrongly, that the traces of popular fascination with dinosaurs can be explained with a bit of common sense. (Mitchell 1998: 10)

After examining the ways in which the dinosaur is consumed in popular culture, he asserts that it is a central cultural icon of the twentieth century that has emerged as the global symbol of modern humanity's relation to nature (1998: 77).

Cultural and art historians have contributed to the delineation of the theory of representation by outlining the symbolic power of representations. As Hall (1997: 5) states, representations signify – "they are the vehicles or media which carry meaning because they operate *as symbols*, which stand for or represent (i.e. symbolise) the meanings we wish to communicate." I would add that they also communicate meanings that we may not be aware of or wish to convey. These ideas have much relevance for archaeological representation, where distinct languages making use of symbols and a variety of other conventions are used to define the past and the archaeological profession.

## The conventions of archaeological representation

In this chapter I identify the conventions of archaeological representation, as it is by understanding these that we can understand how representations construct knowledge. For example, visual images do not only have a common-sense meaning (i.e. this picture shows a hairy man with a spear), they carry a message and thus require interpretation.

Archaeological representations "make meaning" because they employ devices that are not used in written and verbal communication. These devices can be described as conventions that appeal to our sense of reasoning in ways that text does not. The issue is not so much what representations are (e.g. pictures, films, displays) but how these genres actually communicate. For instance, in looking at a museum display, it is not the subject of the display that requires understanding, but how the arrangement of material culture produces particular meanings about that subject. Similarly, in looking at a picture of life in the Neolithic for example, it is not the theme of the picture that demands our interrogation as much as it is the methods by which the picture convinces us of the inevitability of that theme. Representation is not a straightforward practice in the sense that it constitutes its own language; representations utilize a range of conventions that make up this language. By assembling a range of conventions in a representation a whole system of making meaning has been developed by illustrators. I suggest that the key conventions characterizing archaeological representation are iconography, autonomy, longevity, authenticity, singularity, dramatism, and persuasiveness. These findings are based on my analysis of pictorial reconstructions; however, they can be revised in relation to other types of representation, such as films.

## *Iconography*

In 1548 a beautiful woodcut featuring the theme of prehistoric life was published in a German translation of Vitruvius' book *De architectura* (figure 11.1). This vivid picture, which is full of activity and excitement, reveals how fire had already taken on an important iconographic role in the depiction of the past. The wild flames of the fire are placed right in the centre of the picture as they carry so much meaning in the explanation of our evolution. In 27 BC Vitruvius had written about the brutish existence of the first humans before they learnt to work together. He identified the discovery of fire as being critical to this transformation, suggesting that the taming of fire by humans facilitated the invention of speech. When Vitruvius' ideas were brought to life by illustrators of the sixteenth century, they singled out the visual motif of fire and it quickly became a key icon in the visual language of the past. The frequent repetition of this motif in the many different illustrated editions of Vitruvius' book indicates that the illustrators of the time found it a useful device for communicating a particular point or meaning. By highlighting the flaming fire in scenes of humanity's primitive beginnings, illustrators were constructing their own vision of the past. Through their efforts fire became an icon that signified the turning point in the history of human culture. Reuse of this icon in other images ensured that fire

**Figure 11.1**   The discovery of fire (from Vitruvius 1548)

came to convey an essence of what it meant to be civilized. Subsequent artists appropriated the motif and 500 years later the visual icon of fire still conveys this idea.

So what do we mean when we refer to the creation of icons as a convention of archaeological representation? Essentially, illustrators through time have actively created visual motifs in relation to ideas expressed about the past. These motifs have taken on a distinctive meaning, becoming icons that communicate an essence. Such icons are successful in conveying meaning because they are frequently repeated and also because they function like stereotypes. Because representations are distinguished by their aim to compress as much information as possible into a single picture, they reduce information to its barest essentials. In effect they act as a summary that is instantly recognizable. Icons are thus very useful as a means of communicating something immediately and effectively. Iconographic images of the past are particularly useful at evoking a familiar concept that has already been established in other images. In this sense only limited visual details are required in order to get the message across. Indeed, only a vague resemblance to the subject in question is required in order to communicate the meaning desired. While the iconographic aspect of representations helps to make ideas more comprehensive because they require no explanation, it also leads to the constraint of concepts and ideas, pushing understandings of the past in particular directions.

## *Autonomy*

The stunning painting of an ancient Pict that was produced by Jacques Le Moyne de Morgues around 1585 is a prime example of the autonomous nature of representations (figure 11.2). Representations don't simply replicate ideas expressed in academic discourse, they construct their own meanings and have a life of their own. This image was thought to convey the ideas of the classical authors on the appearance of the early Britons; it was also thought to be influenced by images of New World Indians. While these elements can easily be identified in the picture, it is clear that the artist does far more than just sum up current views of historic ancestors. For instance, the decision to decorate the figure from head to foot in flowers is based on the assertion that ancient Picts tattooed their bodies. Rather than portraying this idea with a few simple lines and patterns, Le Moyne de Morgues has paraded his artistic skill in depicting flowers by featuring lavish specimens in great detail. Thus, while certain elements of the picture can ostensibly be seen as being historically inspired, their impact derives more from their artistic success.

In addition to historical and ethnographic sources, the artist drew on a wide variety of other materials for inspiration, including costume drawings, botanical illustration, and not least his own imagination. The result was a unique vision, which was a very important attempt to reconstruct prehistoric life and had a great impact on subsequent conceptions of the ancient Britons. Le Moyne de Morgues created a visual idea, which has

**Figure 11.2**   *A Young Daughter of the Picts* (ca. 1585), painting by Jacques Le Moyne de Morgues (Yale Centre for British Art, Paul Mellon Collection)

become an entrenched tradition in the history of visual representation. Images of naked, decorated "Celts" draw on this original vision, which clearly had a life of its own apart from academic discourse and scholarly inquiry. What we can see from this example is how artistic conventions, and the desire to produce a visually successful composition, can contribute to the creation of knowledge about the past.

## Longevity

In a striking engraving of the ancient Germans published by Philip Cluverius in 1616, we can see how the general image of a primitive naked warrior was beginning to persist as a visual idea (figure 11.3). One of the key features of representations is their longevity, which refers to the way in which images replicate or recycle aspects of earlier images. Thus, while this picture introduced a seventeenth-century audience to the lives of ancient Germans, it was showing them something they were already familiar with. The nakedness, primitive fur garments, and spears were all established pictorial conventions that had been used in other iconographic traditions. For example, classical iconography had utilized the motifs of nakedness and fur garments as signifiers of outsider status. Longevity refers to the way in which the meanings of these motifs were transported into "new" images seeking to present knowledge about different topics. Cluverius' work was very significant in the history of antiquarianism because he was the first scholar to produce a comprehensive set of engravings describing life in ancient Germany. Despite the detailed rendering of different tribes wearing distinctive regional dress and holding different weapons, the images retain elements of earlier images.

The longevity of representations relates to the fact that iconic images are extremely difficult to replace; they persist and live on despite being disproved, updated, or replaced. Also connected to longevity are the problems associated with recycling. Once created, representations are recycled and reproduced in many other contexts. This may be explained by the visual "success" of a particular picture, i.e. because it is dramatic and eye catching, but also because it is much easier to use something that already exists rather than create something entirely new. This is especially the case for visions of the past, where a basic repertoire of pictorial motifs that communicated primitiveness, wildness, and lack of civilization was effectively created very early on.

## Authenticity

An unusual illustration of ancient Britons published by Joseph Strutt in 1779 was specifically aimed at correcting previously inaccurate pictures

**Figure 11.3**   Ancient Germans (from Cluverius 1616)

of the past (figure 11.4). This picture marked an important step in the development of reconstructions as explanatory devices as it placed a premium on authenticity. A concern with authenticity has since become one of the key features of the success of archaeological representations.

**Figure 11.4**   Figures of ancient Britons (from Strutt 1779)

This refers to the way in which representations incorporate as much detailed evidence as possible. Items of dress and personal adornment, armor, and hairstyles all become important in reinforcing the authenticity and thus believability of a picture. While the concern with authenticity already existed before Strutt (1779) produced his images of ancient life, what changed was the introduction of a particular artistic convention to better convey the "reality" of the past. Strutt was an engraver and historian who expressed great frustration at the quality of pictures of historical ancestors that were becoming popular in history books in the late eighteenth century. He noted the tendency to portray one generic vision of an ancestor and so invented the "composite reconstruction," in which a range of ancestors are pictured together in one scene. This device, together with meticulous detail on costumes and armor, was thought to enhance the reliability of his interpretation, but a paradox exists in the sense that temporal and regional difference has been falsely compressed into a single image.

The attribute of authenticity thus refers to the way in which "accuracy" is emphasized in archaeological representations, yet illusion is used to achieve this. Representations are usually defended as being authentic, but by combining information from different sources, they create a pastiche that is completely artificial. Furthermore, the authentic tone of representations is reinforced by the artistic convention of realism. The pictures we see of our ancestors are often so detailed in their execution that they are accepted as if they were photographs. The result of this is that even though we have not experienced the past we are so convinced by the image that we feel as if we have actually seen it.

## Singularity

The violent scene depicted in Henri Cleuziou's book of 1887 captures a moment of the past that we have seen in numerous images (figure 11.5). One of the most captivating aspects of representations is the way in which a precise moment in time is depicted in order to convey some essence of what life was like in the past. The singularity of representations refers to the way one view or one vision is selected, often leaving us with a very limited way of looking at the past. In this picture we can see why the moment of combat between an ancient hunter and wild animal is so popular as a vision of antiquity. However, this moment is very singular and leaves out so much else that could be told about our early existence. Clearly, the theme of "man versus beast" is chosen to capture the essence of life as it was in distant times because it is so engaging and active. The struggle for occupation of the cave is also symbolic of our forebears' quest to conquer the animal kingdom and dominate the evolutionary process.

The nature of representations is such that they typically present one view of the past. Single images are used to sum up key perspectives on a topic, but they suggest one interpretation rather than showing alternative ideas about what may have happened. Associated with the convention of singularity is the construction of a standard sequence of images, which together portray a story. In this practice images function as a snapshot that is part of a greater narrative.

## Dramatism

The painting entitled *Un rapt* by Paul Jamin of 1888 uses a highly dramatic scene to tell the story of prehistoric France (figure 11.6). Dramatism is a characteristic of many representations, ensuring they have a long-lasting impact on the viewer. The nature of representations as highly visual documents ensures that they are constructed to shock and entertain their viewers. Pictures have strong emotional associations, and they can speak to us directly by capturing aspects of human experience which

**Figure 11.5** "Man the conqueror of the cave bear" (from du Cleuziou 1887)

are not as effectively communicated via words. The image of a young woman being abducted by a brutish man, who is in turn being attacked by another man, has a high emotive content. The fact that the picture illustrates prehistoric life is almost of secondary importance, as the scene would attract attention whatever period was being portrayed.

Representations, such as this scene of struggle, have a sense of immediacy and impact that renders them extremely powerful forms of

**Figure 11.6**  *Un rapt* (1888), painting by Paul Jamin (© photo du Musée des Beaux-Arts de la Ville de Reims)

**Figure 11.7**   *Cro-Magnon Artists* (1924), mural by Charles Knight (courtesy American Museum of Natural History Library)

argument. For instance, we are so beguiled by the activity taking place in the scene that we absorb the details that make up the picture in a gratuitous manner. Garments, personal items, and artifacts are reduced to being props in an ostensibly artistic vision. But props such as these are critical in presenting the past and defining how people once lived. We accept such details as if they were unproblematic, not realizing how the accumulation of details in representations lends to their authenticity.

## Persuasiveness

The mural of ancient artists produced by Charles Knight for the American Museum of Natural History in 1924 is a highly persuasive representation because it is full of familiar ideas about art and gender (figure 11.7). One of the most important qualities of representations is their inherent plausibility and thus persuasiveness. Because representations embody some of our most basic assumptions about the past they immediately appeal to our sense of reason. For instance, because scenes of men in their studios had dominated pictures of artistic production for so long it was difficult to conceive of the past in any other way. Knight's vision of the specific contexts in which prehistoric art was produced was informed by current views on art and craft production more than by any evidence found at archaeological sites. The ascribing of gender roles was also based on society's views of the sexual division of labor.

The persuasiveness of representations lies in their ability to be so immediate. Images of distant times do not require labored efforts in order to be understood because they rely so heavily on accepted interpretive frameworks. Such frameworks are typically drawn from our own experience and thus they seem plausible. By slotting archaeological evidence into these familiar pictorial compositions, illustrations contributed to the construction of particular theories about past lifeways.

## Conclusion

Different representational practices characterize different disciplines. In the case of archaeology, illustrative traditions are central. From the initial point of unearthing archaeological deposits, the archaeologist makes sense of the past by visually representing it. At the other end of this spectrum there are communicators and consumers of archaeological knowledge, seeking to explain the past through visual summaries of information. Their summaries, often climaxing in a three-dimensional recreation of ancient life, are so easy to absorb that they immediately become ingrained in our consciousness. Representations are successful in achieving this because they blend scientific knowledge with accepted or assumed frames of reference. Thus, popular presentations go beyond simply fulfilling our desire to "see" the past to playing a role in our "academic" construction of the past. For instance, the assumed frames of reference embodied within representations (which are often ideas about gender relations, the nature of evolution, or domestic lifestyles) are subconsciously transferred into theories, explanations, and accounts of humanity's past.

The significance of the theory of archaeological representation is that it draws attention to a key problem in the construction of disciplinary knowledge. This problem concerns the way in which visualizations of the past have become intimately linked with knowing or understanding the past. The process or mechanisms by which this blurring of boundaries occurs (i.e. representations = knowledge) need to be unraveled so that we can clearly distinguish seeing and knowing. The conventions identified here inform us of some of the ways in which representations make meaning. More specifically, they reveal how visual images are an extremely powerful means of explaining the past because they allow us to experience it.

The field of archaeological representation is based on the premise that archaeological knowledge is not simply established by archaeologists and then filtered down into the popular realm, as if these were two separate activities where one is a result of the other. The idea that the knowledge we create "filters down to the masses" and ends up in a Hollywood movie or museum display suggests that we are the only ones who create meaning about the past. This is a false and indeed dangerous assumption; representations are not inconsequential to the development of intellectual arguments, they are an integral part of the research process.

## REFERENCES

Arnold, J., K. Davies, and S. Ditchfield (eds) 1998. *History and Heritage: Consuming the Past in Contemporary Culture*. Shaftesbury: Donhead.

Baigrie, B. (ed.) 1996. *Picturing Knowledge: Historical and Philosophical Problems concerning the Use of Art in Science*. Toronto: University of Toronto Press.

Beard, M. 1992. Souvenirs of culture: deciphering (in) the museum. *Art History* 15(4): 505–32.

Burtt, F. 1987. "Man the hunter": bias in children's archaeology books. *Archaeological Review from Cambridge* 6(2): 157–74.

Cleuziou, H. du 1887. *La Création de l'homme et les premiers âges de l'humanité*. Paris: C. Marpon and E. Flammarion.

Cluverius, P. 1616. *Germaniae antiquae*. Lugduni Batavorum (Leiden): Apud Ludovicum Elzevirium.

Dingwall, L., S. Exon, V. Gaffney, S. Lafin, and M. Leusen (eds) 1999. *Archaeology in the Age of the Internet*. London: BAR International Series 750.

Evans, C. 1983. Wildmen, pulp and fire – archaeology as popular fiction. *Archaeological Review from Cambridge* 2: 68–70.

Forte, M. and A. Siliotti (eds) 1996. *Virtual Archaeology: Great Discoveries Brought to Life through Virtual Reality*. London: Thames and Hudson.

Gero, J. 1985. Socio-politics and the woman-at-home ideology. *American Antiquity* 50: 342–50.

Gero, J. and D. Root 1990. Public presentations and private concerns: archaeology in the pages of *National Geographic*. In P. Gathercole and D. Lowenthal (eds), *The Politics of the Past*, 19–48. London: Routledge.

Gifford Gonzalez, D. 1993. You can hide, but you can't run: representations of women's work in illustrations of Palaeolithic life. *Visual Anthropology Review* 9(1): 23–41.

Girdwood, A. 1984. The imaginative response to archaeology in late nineteenth-

and early twentieth-century literature. *Archaeological Review from Cambridge* 3: 29–37.

Hall, S. 1997. *Representation: Cultural Representations and Signifying Practices*. London: Sage.

Higgins, T., P. Main, and J. Lang 1996. *Imaging the Past: Electronic Imaging and Computer Graphics in Museums and Archaeology*. London: British Museum Press.

James, S. 1997. Drawing inferences: visual reconstructions in theory and practice. In B. Molyneaux (ed.), *The Cultural Life of Images*, 23–48. London: Routledge.

Jones, C. A. and P. Galison 1998. *Picturing Science, Producing Art*. London and New York: Routledge.

Landau, M. 1991. *Human Evolution as Narrative*. New Haven: Yale University Press.

Leone, M. 1981. The relationship between artefacts and the public in outdoor history museums. *Annals of the New York Academy of Sciences* 376: 301–14.

Lynch, M. and S. Woolgar (eds) 1990. *Representation in Scientific Practice*. Cambridge, MA: MIT Press.

McManus, P. M. (ed.) 1996. *Archaeological Displays and the Public*. London: Institute of Archaeology, UCL.

Mirzoeff, N. 1998. What is visual culture? In N. Mirzoeff (ed.), *The Visual Culture Reader*, 3–13. London: Routledge.

Mitchell, W. J. T. 1998. *The Last Dinosaur Book*. Chicago: University of Chicago Press.

Mitman, G. 1993. Cinematic nature: Hollywood technology, popular culture, and the American Museum of Natural History. *Isis* 84: 637–61.

Molyneaux, B. (ed.) 1997. *The Cultural Life of Images*. London: Routledge.

Moser, S. 1992. The visual language of archaeology: a case study of the Neanderthals. *Antiquity* 66: 831–44.

Moser, S. 1993. Gender stereotyping in pictorial reconstructions of human origins. In H. du Cros and L. Smith (eds), *Women in Archaeology: A Feminist Critique*, 75–92. Canberra: Department of Prehistory, Research School of Pacific Studies.

Moser, S. 1996. Visual representation in archaeology: depicting the missing-link in human origins. In B. Baigrie (ed.), *Picturing Knowledge: Historical and Philosophical Problems concerning the Use of Art in Science*, 184–214. Toronto: University of Toronto Press.

Moser, S. 1998. *Ancestral Images: The Iconography of Human Origins*. Sutton: Stroud (Ithaca: Cornell University Press).

Moser, S. 1999. The cultural dimensions of archaeological practice: the role of fieldwork and its gendered associations. In A. Wylie and M. Conkey (eds), *Doing Feminist Archaeology*. Santa Fe: School of American Research.

Moser, S. and C. Gamble 1997. Revolutionary images: the iconic vocabulary for representing human antiquity. In B. Molyneaux (ed.), *The Cultural Life of Images*, 184–212. London: Routledge.

Patterson, T.C. 1986. The last sixty years: towards a social history of Americanist archaeology in the United States. *American Anthropologist* 88: 1–26.

Piccini, A. 1996. Filming through the mists of time. *Current Anthropology* 37: 87–111.

Rogoff, I. 1998. Studying visual culture. In N. Mirzoeff (ed.), *The Visual Culture Reader*, 14–26. London: Routledge.

Rudwick, M.J.S. 1992. *Scenes from Deep Time: Early Pictorial Representations of the Prehistoric World*. Chicago: University of Chicago Press.

Rupke, N.A. 1993. Metonymies of empire: visual representations of prehistoric times, 1830–90. In R.G. Mazzolini (ed.), *Non-verbal Communication in Science prior to 1900*, 513–28. Florence: Leo S. Olschki.

Sansom, E. 1996. Peopling the past: current practices in archaeological site interpretation. In P.M. McManus (ed.), *Archaeological Displays and the Public*, 118–37. London: Institute of Archaeology, UCL.

Serceau, D. 1982. Prehistory in film. *Revue du Cinema* 377: 110–13.

Shanks, M. 1992. *Experiencing Archaeology*. London: Routledge.

Solomon, J. 1998. A treasure hard to attain: images of archaeology in popular film with a filmography. *Archaeology* 51(2): 90–1.

Stone, P.G. and B. Molyneaux (eds) 1994. *The Presented Past: Heritage, Museums and Education*. London: Unwin and Hyman.

Strutt, J. 1779. *The Chronicle of England, or a complete history, civil, military and ecclesiastical, of the ancient Britons and Saxons, from the landing of Julius Caesar in Britain, to the Norman Conquest*. London: T. Evans and R. Faulder.

Tilley, C. 1993. *Interpretative Archaeology*. Oxford: Berg.

Vitruvius, P.M. 1548. *Vitruvius Teusch. Alles mit schoenen kunstlichen figuren and antiquiteten, und sonderlichen commentarien zu mehrerem bericht*. Nuremberg.

Walsh, K. 1992. *The Representation of the Past: Museums and Heritage in the Post-modern World*. London: Routledge.

Wyke, M. 1997. *Projecting the Past: Ancient Rome, Cinema and History*. London and New York: Routledge.

# 12

# Culture/Archaeology
## The Dispersion of a Discipline and its Objects

## Michael Shanks

### Archaeology – two cultural locales

The museum and landscape – these are two of archaeology's cultural locales. Most of us will have made a visit to one of the great international museums. Somewhere like the Louvre in Paris. Its galleries display artifacts, mostly old, and many from archaeological sites. They are on display because, by some at least, they are considered worthy of attention. They have exhibition value. Why? It is difficult to dissociate the museum from art, from artifacts held to represent aesthetic and cultural achievement (Shanks and Tilley 1992: ch. 4). The finest examples of their kind. Paradigms. For people everywhere to admire, wonder at. And here in an old royal palace in Paris, Walter Benjamin's capital of the nineteenth century (Benjamin 1983).

The Venus de Milo stands ritually encircled by visitors, solitary, punctuating the pattern in the marble floor of the gallery. It was acquired after a scramble on the part of several aristocrats to grab it after it first turned up on a beach of a Greek island. It was an adventure story rivaling those of Indiana Jones (Shanks 1996: 150). Winckelmann, aesthete and art historian, loved sculpture like this, though he didn't know the piece, and was more interested in Roman copies of Greek sculpture. But he epitomizes that romantic shift to a new way of looking and appreciating art and the Greeks (Shanks 1996: 56–8). In a fundamental reevaluation of art history and the cultural significance of art works, he reenergized the classical tradition. In a lyrical prose he celebrated the aesthetic wonders of fragments left in the Vatican collection. His archaeology was simultaneously historical and transcendent. With Winckelmann we look back to the Greeks and their works, or what is left of them, to experience those human cultural values which escape time itself. We still live with the remains of this cultural ideology of Hellenism (Morris 1994).

And the tension between historical provenance and universal value is there also in works from times other than ancient Greece. Islamic and Chinese ceramics may fill galleries too, on the basis of their attestation to the same transcendent cultural values.

Places then of cultural pilgrimage, these museums in the capital cities of the modern nation state (Horne 1984). Cultural treasure houses built upon the desire to acquire and own a transnational heritage, the right to which modern imperial states considered theirs by virtue of global reach and power. So often this heritage has been seen as Graeco-Roman. The nineteenth-century European states competed to acquire the best; their museums are less able to do so now, but the art market remains a determining force in the field of cultural value, dominated by corporate and institutional capital, such as the immense resources of the Getty Foundation.

The art object is at one interface of archaeology and culture. But another romantic, Herder, and again at the end of the eighteenth century, complained of this association of cultivation with universal human value or progress and western culture, writing instead of *cultures* in the plural, in an appreciation of the works and values of other societies. This anticipates an anthropological sense of culture as way of life. It was probably Tylor's book *Primitive Culture* of 1870 which formalized this use, though tying it to evolutionary models of human development, from primitive to civilized.

Ethnic or national identity is also found on display in the museum, signified by archaeological artifacts. The Venus de Milo is simultaneously for all humankind, *and* (ancient) Greek. We find galleries in the Louvre of Roman, Egyptian, Celtic, Assyrian works (of art), alongside French, Italian, British painting and sculpture. Behind the classification and ordering is the equation of cultural work and some essential quality of identity.

Not in the Louvre, but in many other museums, we may be able to look upon the works of peoples categorized according to a more specialized and archaeological meaning of culture. Gordon Childe is associated with this sense of culture as recurring sets of associated artifacts or traits held to represent a people or society (discussed by Renfrew and Bahn 1996: 443–5). It emphasizes the expressive or stylistic components of identity over issues of value. In prehistoric archaeology and in the absence of written sources, these cultures may be named after "type"

sites, regions, or artifacts – the Mousterian culture of the Middle Palaeolithic period (after le Moustier); the Bronze Age Beaker folk (after a
type of ceramic vessel); the TRB (Trichterbecker) culture group (another
class of ceramic); the Wessex culture (a region of southern England). That
such "culture-historical" interpretation is now academically discredited
has not been fully accepted. Many archaeologists still orient their work
around this concept of culture. Culture-historical classification of archaeological remains, particularly prehistoric ones, is still the norm.

For archaeologists it is not enough that their collections of artifacts
make cultural sense, whether it is in terms of artistic value or marker of
identity; they must also be linked to a place, a setting. The key term here
is landscape and the pivotal concept mediating archaeology and culture
is identity.

The equation between people, their culture, and the land they inhabit
is central to the time-space systematics of the discipline of archaeology,
as just outlined. It is an equation crucial to the coherence of the new
nation states of modern Europe. It is encapsulated in the cultural attachment to land so characteristic of romantic nationalism.

Johannes Fabian (1983) has convincingly clarified the dependence of
anthropological knowledge upon travel and encounters with other cultures in other lands. This confrontation between western Enlightenment
reason and a cultural (and colonial) other was transposed upon time and
history – those cultures that help us understand who we are live over
there and back then, while we are here and now.

But landscape is a complex articulation of inhabitation, place, and
value. It is a term as complex and ideologically charged as culture
(Williams 1976: 76–82). It should not be forgotten that the roots of the
term still lie in the notion of an aesthetic cultivation of the view or aspect.
Landscape painting and architecture improves upon nature according to
particular aesthetic or cultural values. This submission of place to reason
and imagination imbricates time and history. The landscape genre in the
hands of Claude Lorrain and Poussin, the myriad of landscape painters
from the seventeenth and eighteenth centuries, landscape architects like
Repton, Uvedale Price, and Capability Brown, was always explicitly or
implicitly a relationship to history and sensibility to be found in land
itself (Smiles 1994). History – ancient monuments and ruins, classical,
medieval, prehistoric. Sensibility - attitudes to the land which refer back
to ideologies of the Roman campagna and classical pastoral. History and
sensibility – a celebration of the rural, often over the urban and industrial, those scarring features of modernity.

Stephen Daniels (1993) has shown how the aesthetic of landscape has
been central to the construction of national identity in Britain and the

United States. Powerfully affective, it provides a deep cultural milieu, mapping out values and attachments. Landscape provided a basis for locating new communities of nationhood in a kind of collective cultural memory of belonging. Memory has come to need the earth; for there are places where memories are stored, places which carry the mark of time. These are monuments and landforms which give history and shape to human communities, nations included. Consider, for example, the legacy of this concept of landscape in Britain. The English countryside is one of interwoven traces and layers of previous inhabitation, punctuated by monuments and the relics of times gone by; a particular cultural ecology of narratives, plants and creatures, geology, language, music, customs, architectures, traces, archaeological sites, and finds. It is where the English belong and find their roots, though others may appreciate its beauties.

Those tensions noted in the concept of culture, between universal human values, the qualities of particular cultures, and the aspiration to cultivated intellectual or artistic activity, are here present also in landscape. Images of land the world over, photographs and paintings, are generated from the same aesthetic models. A place may qualify for the status of world heritage site on the basis of universal criteria or values applied without reference to geography or time. Yet narratives of identity may be considered to lie in the land itself, in an attachment of land, language, culture, and people. In spite of social mobility and diaspora, land may still provide a basis for belonging, and the notion of aboriginal folk culture, deeply rooted in place, remains potent (see the complementary arguments in Chris Gosden's chapter).

## The concept of culture – a contested field

It was only in the eighteenth century that the concept of culture began to acquire its present-day meanings (Williams 1976: 77–8). It first referred to cultivation, to being cultivated, possessing civilized traits and values. As indicated, it was only later that culture came to have a plural sense of a way of life, a sense which led to its anthropological use, formalized in the discipline in the twentieth century (Kroeber and Kluckhohn 1952).

Association with value has been retained in a recruitment of the term in ideological positioning associated with the class organization of the modern industrial state. Many intellectuals and academics from Thomas Arnold onward have set up an opposition between the high cultural values of a canon of works, often entrusted to an educated elite, and the cultural artifacts of and produced for the industrial working classes, considered transient. It is certainly the case that more and more resources have been dedicated to the production of popular cultural artifacts. Adorno and Horkheimer (1979) coined the term "culture industry" to refer to this articulation of economic and cultural interest. Dominated by the production of Americanist cultural goods by transnational mega-corporations like Sony and Disney, the culture industry spans the globe and popular consciousness. Mass or popular culture has often been derided or considered as an ideological expression of the false consciousness of the industrial masses (*contra* Swingewood 1977). It is the issue, for example, of the difference and respective values or qualities of a play by Shakespeare and an episode of the American TV series *Baywatch*, reputedly the most watched TV program in the world. The prehistorian Grahame Clark explicitly invoked the distinction when he proposed (1979, 1983) a direct correlation in human history between great cultural work and elite social groups, the corollary being that egalitarian societies invest in the lowest common cultural denominator and fail to produce cultural works of lasting value.

This highlights the role of the cultural critic (Adorno 1981). Some intellectuals and academics have seen their role as cultural policemen or guardians, upholding values, judging and condemning work not considered worthwhile. This implies a position for the critic outside of society. Other cultural critics have reacted against the polarization of art and popular culture. It has also been a significant issue in modernist fine and applied arts, focusing upon the nature of the art object. It is encapsulated in the disputes over the value of some gallery pieces that make no reference to traditional artistic media, skills, and qualities. In 1917, as one of the founding acts of modernism, Marcel Duchamp placed a urinal in a gallery exhibition. This could be considered a work of art, in that it was an artist that placed the artifact in an art gallery. But, of course, this "readymade art" provoked a hostile reaction from those who believed art was their high culture. The general point is that when culture is understood as a discourse of excellence, preserving timeless and universal human treasures, it actually translates class and other forms of social inequality into *cultural capital*. This is a form of value monopolized by certain elite groups, such as those who patronize art and its galleries. Hence criticism of cultural value has raised awareness of ethnocentrism and the involvement of social power in the construction of knowledge and understanding. So in the museum it is often western culture that is valued and on display and other cultures are seen through western eyes.

Cultural Studies grew as an interdisciplinary field from the 1950s, bracketing value under an anthropological suspension of judgment, instead of polarizing high and low culture. This opens up the study of all kinds of cultural artifacts other than those claimed as works of art. So Richard Hoggart (1957) pioneered with his study of popular working-class culture in Britain. No longer were only great works worthy of study and interpretation (Turner 1996). This has led to a broad interdisciplinary interest in culture operating under a definition such as the following. Culture: the social production and reproduction of meaning, the social sphere of making sense which unites production and social relations; a field of signification through which a social order is communicated, reproduced, experienced, and explored. The interest in systems of meaning and signification is part of the "linguistic turn" in the humanities and social sciences to issues of culture and communication (for anthropology, see Leach 1976).

## Archaeology and the concept of culture

Archaeology may make references to art and humanity. It has an interest in classical *civilized* culture, *primitive* other or older cultures. The discipline has developed its own culture concept uniting material relics with peoples of the past. Archaeology has thus been an important part of the interplay and evolution of the references and meanings of the culture concept.

More generally, it is clear that archaeology and anthropology were central to the cultural development of the advanced capitalist nation states of the nineteenth century. Political revolution (Britain in the seventeenth century, France and the United States at the end of the eighteenth) and the threat of it accompanied the forging of a new form of political unity through the industrial nation state (Hobsbawm 1990). From the beginning nation states have been founded upon a fundamental tension. On the one hand, they have invoked, as unifying force and legitimation, Enlightenment ideas of popular will and sovereignty, and universal human rights. And the form of the nation state itself has been exported globally from its origins in early modern Europe. On the other hand, they are all locally circumscribed, each independent of similar polities on the basis of regional, ethnic, linguistic, and/or national identity and history (Turner 1990). Archaeology and anthropology, disciplines formalized at the beginning of the nineteenth century, offered powerful ways of working on these new *cultural* issues.

A crucial factor in ideas of national identity was the imperialist and colonial experience of travel and other cultures (Pratt 1992). Both archaeology and anthropology have been powerful media in these cultural geographies of the imagination. Ethnography confronted the industrial west with its alternative and provided a foil or difference, against which western nations might understand themselves. Archaeology provided material evidence of folk roots of the new state polities, while also attaching the imperial states to the cultural peaks of history measured by artistic values and encapsulated in objects acquired, often from abroad, for the museums. This has been one of the main cultural successes of archaeology – to provide the new nation states of the eighteenth and nineteenth centuries with histories and origin stories rooted in the *material* remains of the past (Díaz-Andreu and Champion 1996). Myths of ancestry were articulated in new national narratives, stories of belonging and common (civilized) community (the latter particularly identified with Graeco-Roman culture). Both archaeology and anthropology provided specific symbols and evidences used to create exclusive and homogeneous conceptions of identity rooted in national traditions, conceptions of race, ethnicity, and language. Moreover, archaeology provided an extraordinary immediacy apparently accessible without academic training – finds which could be displayed to speak for themselves in the new museums, the cultural treasure houses of imperial power, repositories of ancestral remains. Many archaeologies around the world continue to perform this role of providing material correlates for stories and myths of identity and belonging (Trigger 1984; Kohl and Fawcett 1995; Olivier and Coudart 1995; Meskell 1998).

## Culture contested

Conceptions of modern identity are still dependent upon the idea of the nation state and upon the formation of nation states in the nineteenth century. But recent history shows clearly their instability. They often have no obvious cultural justification in geography, history, race, or ethnicity. Nation states are social constructions (Anderson 1991; Bhabha 1990). Growing out of the demise of old empires, nation states have frequently been connected with Enlightenment notions of human rights and rational government (democracy and representation), relying on these to unify people around a common story of their national identity. Such unified history and culture has always failed to cope with diversity. The distinction between nation and nation state has frequently collapsed into contention, with ideas of self-determination and freedom, identity and unity colliding with the suppression of diversity, domination, and exclusion that overrides a genuine egalitarian pluralism (Chatterjee 1993).

The tension between universal political and cultural forms and values, and local cultural textures, has shifted emphasis in recent decades. Nation states now have less power and agency, which is in stark contrast to the ever-increasing influence of structures and movements of corporate and transnational capital. In a period of rapid decolonization after the Second World War this *globalization* is about the transformation of imperial power into supranational operations of capital, communications, and culture. This *postcolonial* world is one of societies, including new nation states, that have escaped the control of the empires and ideological blocs of western and eastern Europe. An ideological unity is engineered through the culture industry, the mass media, and mass consumption – a predominantly American culture. And the integrated resources of the global economy lie behind this (Curti and Chambers 1996; Featherstone et al. 1995; Featherstone 1990; Spybey 1996).

But with international capital, global telecommunications, and world military order, the nation state continues to be a major structural feature of this postmodern scene. It remains a major focus of regional cultural identity. The postcolonial state is heavily and ironically dependent upon notions of the state and nation developed in Europe, and so too it is dependent upon the same sorts of ideological constructions of national identity developed through history, archaeology, and anthropology (Hobsbawm and Ranger 1983). Hence a key tension or contradiction in globalization involves the fluid free market between nations, epitomized in multinational and corporate capital and based upon ideologies of the free individual operating beyond boundaries of any one polity, and ideologies of difference, ideologies of local identity. Here the nation, nation state, and nationalism remain potent.

And here archaeology remains a vital cultural factor, in the context too of ideas of heritage. For the crucial cultural issue is the ways local communities engage with these processes of globalization. And the ways they do compare with the ways colonized communities dealt with imperial colonial powers; the interpenetration of local and global cultural forces is a feature of modernity since at least the nineteenth century. It is not simply a one-way process of influence, control, dissemination, and hegemony, with an American western homogenized culture taking over and supplanting local identity. It is not just top-down dominance, but a complex interplay of hegemony, domination, and empowerment. The key question or issue is the way external and internal forces interact to produce, reproduce, and disseminate global culture within local communities. To be asked is to what extent the global is being transformed by peripheral communities; to what extent, by appropriating strategies of representation, organization, and social change through access to global systems, are local communities and interest groups empowering themselves and influencing global systems.

Here then is a broad context for the interface of archaeology and culture. There is the part archaeology plays in the construction of national and cultural identities (Rowlands 1994). A key is an encounter with materiality and regional focus, the ruins of a local past, setting the homogenization of processes like nationalism, colonization, and imperialism against the peculiarities of history and geography. This is about the relation between local pasts and those global methods, frameworks, and master narratives which may suppress under a disciplinary and cultural uniformity the rich pluralism and multicultural tapestry of peoples and histories. So what is now termed "world archaeology" (in relation to the mission of the World Archaeological Congress) implies questions of whether genuine local pasts (Shanks 1992: 109), implicit in local and distinct identities, are possible. Archaeology's focus on obdurate remains suggests the possibility of a material resistance to the ideologies of a homogeneous world uniform in its accommodation with the commodity form and principles of the global market.

Theories of culture connect with this postcolonial and postmodern scenario. Conspicuously it has not been possible to locate culture in essential or universal values or identities, yet any concept of culture remains inseparable from value and identity. Culture is therefore best treated as something which is constructed, emergent from social practice, and changing; it is not a unified body of symbols and values. Historian E. P. Thompson preferred to think of culture less as a whole way of life, more of a "whole way of struggle." Being about values and identities, often in crisis in a modern world of change and dislocation, invoked in ideologies of the state and the maneuvers of class hegemony, culture is always political and contested.

Definitions and uses of the concept vary quite considerably, as I have tried to show. This is part of its contested character. Less something that is easily defined, culture is a field of debate, a field of discourse. Accordingly cultural criticism and interpretation may be treated as historically specific and interventionist, raising consciousness, forging new cultural meanings, provoking dispute, rather than standing back detached behind eternal verities.

This discursive component is prominent in poststructuralist cultural critique. The unity of the human subject has been challenged, the individual, subjectivity, and agency decentered and dispersed, through language, text, and discourse. Primary foundational narratives and ideologies have been subject to withering critique. Two targets relevant to discussion here have been essential and proprietorial notions of culture and identity. Our identities are not something inherited or acquired, as essential qualities of our character or life, but are perpetually reconstructed in relations with others and with cultural artifacts. Postcolonial theory, closely allied to poststructuralist thought, has, as Gosden shows in chapter 10, similarly attacked these same notions of culture. This has occurred through its focus on culture contact in colonial settings, the insistence that contact and border zones do not display the sort of frictions and relations we are led to expect from theories of fixed, stable, and coherent cultural identities.

Anthropological and archaeological theories of culture lend strong support to this thesis of hybridity and articulation. Woolf has raised profound questions of the stability and coherence of cultural identity in the Roman Empire (Woolf 1998). Anthropologist James Clifford (1988, 1997) has elegantly explored syncretic culture in his studies of art, travel, tourism, and identity. And the traditional Childean concept of culture has been displaced by appreciations of the subtleties of style, function, and artifact design (after Shennan 1978; Conkey and Hastorf 1990; Carr and Neitzel 1995).

To return to that other cultural locale of archaeology, consider how landscape is a syncretic field. The space of landscape is at once cultural and natural, connecting values, modes of perception and representation, experiences, artifacts, histories, natural histories, dreams, identities, narratives, memories in networks of cultural ecology. Everything that goes with living in a place. Though historically layered and composed of tracks and traces, landscape is beyond simple conceptions of depth and surface, beyond the linearity of chronology, narrative, and physical cartography. Lived meaningful inhabitation, of varying time depth and subject to varying degrees of fragmentation and loss through time, landscape is a multitemporal and complicated, folded *cultural topology*. Any practice of "deep mapping," which might aim to capture this complexity, must itself be hybrid, syncretic, diverse (Pearson and Shanks 1996, 2000).

## Archaeology – a mode of cultural production

Let me now pull together some implications of this discussion of culture and landscape for archaeologists and their discipline. The orthodox line is to separate archaeology from culture, while recognizing the importance of (cultural) *context* for what archaeologists do. This is to take that distanced standpoint of the academic or intellectual following the methods and practices of their discipline. I wish to oppose this standpoint and separation of discipline and culture. While it maintains a disciplinary or discursive unity, it leaves unaccountable the work and works of archaeologists, other than as epistemology and method (cf. also Shanks 2000 on cultural politics).

Instead I propose that we accept that archaeology deals in cultural artifacts, and its works have cultural effect. Archaeology is a mode of cultural production in which work is done upon the remains of the past (McGuire and Shanks 1996). This makes it impossible to separate archaeology as a method and epistemology from a cultural context. On the contrary, the unity and boundaries of the discipline are challenged, according to those same arguments against essentialism that have been employed for culture. Archaeology is no more, or no less, than the work of its practitioners. While the discipline may define and police its community, values, and principles, its "culture," and establish an orthodoxy or integrity, there is nothing *essential* about this unity or coherence.

To accept archaeology as cultural work thus requires the *dispersion* of its disciplinary subject and object. This is implicit in those interdisciplinary fields such as cultural studies, material culture studies, cultural geography, comparative literature, theory itself. They construct linkages and translations across diverse disciplinary spaces, turning liminal issues into primary foci.

Two studies I have undertaken over the last fifteen years can be used as illustration here. The first was a year of research with Chris Tilley into the design of beer cans and bottles (Shanks and Tilley 1992: ch. 7). It was planned as a comparative study of material culture, to try out some ideas we had developed for understanding the style and design of artifacts. A key interpretive tactic was to place beer cans into the context of alcohol consumption in two modern states of northern Europe – Britain and Sweden. The results of our study (accounting for the look of beer packaging) turned out to be less important than what we found out about ways of understanding cultural artifacts. First, it proved impossible to demarcate a coherent object of study. It just was not the case that the design of beer cans could be set in appropriate contexts in order to reach some understanding. We traced relevant connections with the cans through the brewing industry (back to the eighteenth century), marketing and advertising, the history of packaging, sites of mass consumption, the culture of drink, class differences, health-related issues, state licensing/legislation, state interest in alcohol production and consumption, even yeasts and pasteurization. There was no object and context, simply networks of connection. Second, it was clear that there could be no understanding of beer cans which posited a line of creative determination or agency that had society, culture, and its individuals expressing themselves (in whatever way) through material artifacts. I couldn't actually answer who designed the cans, even though we met with the people employed by breweries who decided what words and imagery should go on them. It seemed to be more about norms, expectations, aspirations, an indeterminate state interest in control (albeit finding very concrete expression in taxation and legality), and the congeniality of the bar or pub. These cultural subjects have agency. Who makes culture? It's not just people – the beer cans themselves are involved!

I later focused upon a class of "art" objects, perfume jars from an ancient Greek city. I was ready this time to tackle what Stuart Hall and others have called the *circuit of culture* – from production, consumption, regulation of social life, to representation and identity (DuGay et al. 1997). Rather than methodology I began with a single artifact (one of the perfume jars) and a principle – to follow whatever connections I could find engendered by its design and what I term *its lifecycle* (Shanks 1998, 1999) – the circuit of culture. Interpretation exploded into pottery manufacture, techniques of painting, reflections upon pictures of animals, soldiers and flowers, perfume and its consumption in temples and graves, experiences of war, mobility and travel (as the pots were widely exported), homoeroticism and the warrior band. The issue I faced throughout was containment: where and on what grounds should I stop exploring? For it was only to create a particular disciplinary intervention (write a book on classical archaeology) that I contained the dispersion according to chronology and subject matter (the early city state in the Mediterranean in the first millennium BC). The task of historiography became just this narrative containment as I set up the sources to outline the options facing the pot painter, as well as the shape of archaic bodies, ideologies of certain kinds of cultural association – men armed, actually or metaphorically, for war.

The containment was in no way inherent or essential to the perfume jars that were my initial object of interest. I could have ignored chronology entirely, or gone beyond the cultural space of the early Greek state, while still being rigorously empirical. It could have been quite a different story. Of course.

I particularly confirmed for myself that the category material culture is something of a tautology. I was dealing with traces of an ancient social fabric. Division into matters of mind and materiality, or objects and cultural signification or value, were specious and distracting. The soldiers' bodies were real, were felt, suffered, trained, enjoyed, and some have ended as archaeological sources. At the same time these are all cultural dispositions and performances, literally embodying the ideological conflicts and values, or so I argued, of the early state. The soldiery and their life as citizens of the new state necessarily involved the accoutrement of weapons, the artifacts of lifestyle. They were nothing without these, just as the ideologies of citizenry and war were nothing without bodies to uphold them. I was dealing with cyborgs. And just as the people of these cities, from potters to sea captains to slaves, were its historical agents, so too were cultural factors like a particular experience of travel, whose elements I tracked through a series of source materials.

So rather than demarcating archaeological methods, objects, and interests, I traced connections. Cognate terms which can be applied to this include translation and social linkage, and articulation (Shanks 1999: ch. 1). The historiographical task facing me as archaeologist and ancient historian was how to write about hybrid forms.

## The archaeological

If archaeology is part of the cultural sphere itself, how then are we to distinguish archaeology? What makes archaeology distinctive? Do we look to its communities and subcultures? Is archaeology simply its practitioners and their ways of life? Is archaeology the way archaeologists do what they do?

Under a dispersion of the discipline's subject and object, I propose that we think less of archaeology, and instead of *the archaeological*. This concerns social fabric itself, the materiality of all of society's components. The archaeological is particularly about remnants, morbidity, entropy, traces, decay, the grubby underside of things, stuff lost or overlooked in the gaps.

The archaeological has affinities with many of modernity's foundational experiences. It may even be described as one of (post)modernity's root metaphors (on the importance of metaphor, see Lakoff and Johnson 1980). I have already outlined some of these: experiences of immediate encounter with history in the earth; artifacts collected and owned as signifiers of identity; delving deep to find authenticity and identity; metaphors of roots, stratigraphy, subsurface structures finding expression at the surface; the archaeological component of cultural tourism. Freud's archaeological interests are now well documented (Lowenthal

1985: 252–5), so it would seem appropriate that the archaeological should provide such a stimulating metaphor for his understanding of the human psyche. His medical and symptomatic logic of therapy and interpretation of a layered mind has been connected with a broad cultural field of speculative modelling (Ginzburg 1989; Eco and Sebeok 1983). This is concerned with traces, tracks, and details and includes forensic detection, some branches of art history (concerned with attribution of works to artists through stylistic details), as well as archaeology. The great classical archaeologist and art historian Sir John Beazley had much in common with Sherlock Holmes (Shanks 1996: 37–41). A great appeal of the archaeological is its affinities with the work of the detective (for the subtlety of this cultural field see Merivale and Sweeney 1999).

The archaeological refers to the social fabric. As I have tried to indicate through my examples in the last section, the distinction between social or cultural and material, "the social" and its "fabric," is not easy to uphold. The archaeological is quintessentially hybrid. The social is a world of hybrids (Law 1991). This point is given much significance by the recent work of anthropologists of science and sociologists of technology who have radically challenged the orthodox separation of science, its objects, and the natural world from social relations and cultural values (for example Mackenzie and Wajcman 1985; Pickering 1992; Bijker and Law 1992; Fuller 1997; Latour 1987). In this interdisciplinary development we hear no longer of science applied to society, or of the social context of technology. Instead science becomes a cultural achievement, technology *has* politics, and Edison, rather than inventing the light bulb, is shown to have engineered a heterogeneous or hybrid network of artifacts, scientific equations, dreams, capital, political good will, people, and a laboratory in Menlo Park (Hughes 1983). Bruno Latour (1993) has even defined modernity in terms of its hybridity, attributing its scientific and material success to a particular and paradoxical hybrid politics of representation in both the citizen body and natural world. His work on science and material culture has led him to develop an explicit (and evolutionary) archaeology of people, technics, and knowledge (Latour 1999: ch. 6).

## A cultural agenda for archaeology

I end with a checklist of cultural issues which I consider as archaeological. Examples given are meant to make further open connections within this *culture/archaeology*.

## Challenging the canon of great works

The values of the art market permeate the world of archaeological objects. A task is to scrutinize them.

Note should be taken here of strategies in the art world which question the transcendence and status of the art object, or locate it in transient or immaterial forms. This is one of the guiding principles of modernism. Consider, for example, performance-based art (Goldberg 1998), arte povera (Christov-Bakargiev 1999), installation and conceptual art (Art and Design Editorial 1994; DeOliveira et al. 1994).

## Difference instead of identity

As has been already well indicated in this volume, postcolonial theory takes us beyond a plurality of self-contained cultures, by challenging proprietorial and essentialist notions of cultural identity. The issue concerns constructions of community in the absence of a secure notion of identity.

## Exploring hybridity

The social fabric is one of hybrid forms. Cyborgs are not just a creation of science fiction. People-object articulations, they are the norm.

Look to borders and mixtures. Consider the implications of genetic modification and artificial intelligence (Haraway 1991, 1997). Guillermo Gomez-Peña and Roberto Sifuentes have created the ethno-cyborg in their performance-based border art which is about chicano identity and its ritual/material accoutrements and stereotypes (Gomez-Peña and Sifuentes 1996; http://riceinfo.rice.edu/projects/cybervato).

## Poetics of assemblage

Exploring hybridity may require a poetics of assemblage (Shanks 1992: 43–7; 1999: ch. 1). This is based upon articulation as a process of bringing to expression and connecting what otherwise might remain unconnected or unrealized. It emphasizes how the compositions of things and cultural identities alike are neither immutable, nor unified.

We should think of fields rather than objects. Consider a classic of interpretation in cultural studies – the account of the Sony Walkman by DuGay et al. (1997). Consider the museum exhibitions curated by filmmaker Peter Greenaway (1991, 1993, 1997) – extraordinary collections of artifacts grouped through bricolage or montage that present non-linear histories and dispersed anthropologies (of the body, classification, flight . . .).

Assemblage relates to collection, and though this is constantly denied, archaeology is a branch of collecting (Schnapp 1996: 11). Susan Pearce (1992, 1997) has provided an introduction to the diverse energies of collection in relationship to personal and cultural identity.

The singular object or artifact, unclassified or unclassifiable according to conventional understanding, may break through history and the ordinary and engender wonder or fascination – this is, for me, the attraction of the Museum of Jurassic Technology in Los Angeles – an out-of-time wunderkammer from the pages of Borges (Weschler 1995).

## Embodiment and the performative

The social fabric is felt and suffered as well as thought and valued. Attention is drawn to the embodiment and corporeality of society and culture.

This is now a well-developed field of thought and writing. Consider, for example, the relevance of the concept of performance. Identity has been argued to be a performative accomplishment. Social practice as performance is not about the expression or representation of a quality such as identity. Performance enacts and produces that to which it refers. So gender, for example, is both a doing and a thing done (Butler 1993). Performance thus complements arguments against essentialism: it presupposes that the acting self must enunciate itself rather than represent a given identity.

Concerning the performance of cultural identity, consider how heritage interpretation is founded upon performative and theatrical metaphors – the past is staged for the visitor (Kirschenblatt-Gimblett 1998). Paul Connerton (1989) has linked social memory with the enactment of cultural rituals.

## Non-linear histories and deep maps – realizing new temporal spaces

Rather than reconstruct or resurrect the past, reflections here upon culture/archaeology suggest a different strategy of creating new articulations through an indeterminate chronology. Surface and depth are subsumed beneath connectivity. Challenges to depth metaphors of historical roots and appreciations of the folded cultural topology that is place and landscape introduce possibilities of flat chronologies, non-linear histories, and deep maps – new conceptions of space and place, temporality and history.

In academic fields this is the further refinement of critical historiography, cultural geography, and ethnography.

Take, for example, the cultural mappings of modernity made by Alan Pred (1995). Deleuze and Guattari (1988) and Manuel De Landa (1997) have written explicit non-linear histories. Paul Carter has explored the colonization of space in historical Australia through the cultural accretion of mapping, naming, narratives, and textualities in his book *The Road to Botany Bay* (1987). Wilson Harris, Guyanese novelist and critic, makes fascinating use of metaphors of palimpsest and fossil beds in his understanding of history, race, and culture in the Carribean (Harris 1996).

## The lure of the local

How are we to travel and be guided round these new temporal spaces between global homogeneity and the unique locale?

Lucy Lippard (1997, 1999) has connected these questions with new art practices and experiences of travel and tourism in two suggestive compendia.

## Against mimesis

Theories of performativity and hybridity mean that we may not be able to easily represent culture and experience according to orthodox models of mimesis (by which is meant a naturalistic reproduction of what is represented).

How are we to write about things and people? Should archaeologists aim to use all the power of computer-generated virtual realities to rebuild and repeople antiquity? This grand mimetic dream lies behind many projects in academic archaeology and heritage interpretation.

Peggy Phelan (1993, 1997) and Elin Diamond (1997) have confronted the topic of mimesis from within performance theory in fascinating reflections upon the representation of performances in academic writing.

## The return of the real

In spite of the postmodern impulse to surface, simulation and signification, and empty pastiche supposedly in the place of authentic roots and history (Poster 1988), many artists are exploring realms and textures of corporeality and materiality.

Many are profoundly archaeological in their interest in decay, morbidity, historical accretion, patina, ruin, and remnant. Look for examples in Grunenberg's (1997) definition of a new gothic sensibility. Damien Hirst (1997) notoriously explores these issues in many of his works – the archaeological formation process of rot, the conservator's practice of pickling.

In the sphere of popular fascination with forensics read Gordon Burn (1998) on serial killer Fred West – a real-life horror story of bodies buried in basements and walls tied together in a suburban history of home extensions and sexual perversity. It is a gruesome story of mortuary practices and architectural history revealed in the real excavation of the scene of a crime.

## New modes of engagement and patterns of association

The archaeological community is its own connected culture of people/things. Models of IT-based hypertext have been proposed as a critical medium for connecting people, mixed media, sources, and commentaries (for example, Landow 1994, 1997). The internet may provide spaces where may be constructed experiences and meanings which engage us intimately, which creatively address the issues of culture/ archaeology in a postmodern and postcolonial idiom. Ultimately the sphere of culture/archaeology is about the construction of communities, of whatever kind – how we make ourselves.

### REFERENCES

Adorno, T. 1981. Cultural criticism and society. In *Prisms*, 17–34. Cambridge, MA: MIT Press.

Adorno, T. and M. Horkheimer 1979. *Dialectic of Enlightenment*. London: Verso.

Anderson, B. 1991. *Imagined Communities: Reflections on the Origin and Spread of Nationalism*, 2nd edn. London: Verso.

Art and Design Editorial 1994. *Performance Art into the 1990s*. London: Academy Group.

Benjamin, W. 1983. *Das Passagen-Werk*. Frankfurt: Suhrkamp.

Bhabha, H. (ed.) 1990. *Nation and Narration*. London: Routledge.

Bijker, W. and J. Law (eds) 1992. *Shaping Technology/Building Society*. Cambridge, MA: MIT Press.

Burn, G. 1998. *Happy like Murderers*. London: Faber and Faber.

Butler, J. 1993. *Bodies that Matter: On the Discursive Limits of Sex*. London: Routledge.

Carr, C. and J.E. Neitzel (eds) 1995. *Style, Society and Person: Archaeological and Ethnological Perspectives*. New York: Plenum.

Carter, P. 1987. *The Road to Botany Bay*. London: Faber and Faber.

Chatterjee, P. 1993. *The Nation and its Fragments: Colonial and Postcolonial Histories*. Princeton: Princeton University Press.

Christov-Bakargiev, C. 1999. *Arte Povera*. New York: Phaidon.

Clark, G. 1979. Archaeology and human diversity. *Annual Review of Anthropology* 8: 1–20.

Clark, G. 1983. *The Identity of Man*. London: Methuen.

Clifford, J. 1988. *The Predicament of Culture: Twentieth Century Ethnography, Literature and Art*. Cambridge, MA: Harvard University Press.

Clifford, J. 1997. *Routes: Travel and Translation in the Late Twentieth Century*. Cambridge: Harvard University Press.

Conkey, M. and C. Hastorf (eds) 1990. *The Uses of Style in Archaeology*. Cambridge: Cambridge University Press.

Connerton, P. 1989. *How Societies Remember*. Cambridge: Cambridge University Press.

Curti, L. and I. Chambers (eds) 1996. *The Post-Colonial Question: Common Skies, Divided Horizons*. London: Routledge.

Daniels, S. 1993. *Fields of Vision: Landscape Imagery and National Identity in England and the United States*. Cambridge: Polity.

De Landa, M. 1997. *A Thousand Years of Nonlinear History*. New York: Swerve/Zone.

Deleuze, G. and F. Guattari 1988. *A Thousand Plateaus: Capitalism and Schizophrenia*. London: Athlone Press.

DeOliveira, N., N. Oxley, and M. Petry 1994. *Installation Art*. London: Thames and Hudson.

Diamond, E. 1997. *Unmasking Mimesis: Essays on Feminism and Theater*. London: Routledge.

Díaz-Andreu, M. and T. Champion (eds) 1996. *Nationalism and Archaeology in Europe*. London: University College London Press.

DuGay, P., S. Hall, L. Janes, H. Mackay, and K. Negus 1997. *Doing Cultural Studies: The Story of the Sony Walkman*. London: Sage/Open University.

Eco, U. and T. Sebeok (eds) 1983. *The Sign of Three: Dupin, Holmes, Peirce*. Bloomington: Indiana University Press.

Fabian, J. 1983. *Time and the Other: How Anthropology Makes its Object*. New York: Columbia University Press.

Featherstone, M. (ed.) 1990. *Global Culture: Nationalism, Globalisation and Modernity*. London: Sage.

Featherstone, M., S. Lash, and R. Robertson (eds) 1995. *Global Modernities*. London: Sage.

Fuller, S. 1997. *Science*. Buckingham: Open University Press.

Ginzburg, C. 1989. *Clues, Myths and the Historical Method*. Baltimore: Johns Hopkins University Press.

Goldberg, R. 1998. *Performance: Live Art since 1960*. New York: Harry Abrams.

Gomez-Peña, G. and R. Sifuentes 1996. *Temple of Confessions: Mexican Beasts and Living Santos*. New York: Powerhouse.

Greenaway, P. 1991. *The Physical Self*. Rotterdam: Boymans–van Beuningen Museum.

Greenaway, P. 1993. *Some Organising Principles/Rhai Egwyddorion Trefn*. Swansea: Glyn Vivian Art Gallery.

Greenaway, P. 1997. *Flying over Water/Volar Damunt l'Aigua*. London: Merrell Holberton.

Grunenberg, C. (ed.) 1997. *Gothic: The Transmutations of Horror in Late Twentieth Century Art*. Cambridge, MA: MIT Press.

Haraway, D. 1991. *Simians, Cyborgs and Women: The Reinvention of Nature*. London: Free Association.

Haraway, D. 1997. *Modest_Witness@Second_Millennium: FemaleMan©_Meets_OncoMouse™*. London: Routledge.

Harris, W. 1996. *Jonestown*. London: Faber and Faber.

Hirst, D. 1997. *I Want to Spend the Rest of My Life Everywhere, with Everyone, One to One, Always, Forever, Now*. London: Booth-Clibborn.

Hobsbawm, E. 1990. *Nations and Nationalism since 1780*. Cambridge: Cambridge University Press.

Hobsbawm, E. and T. Ranger (eds) 1983. *The Invention of Tradition*. Cambridge: Cambridge University Press.

Hoggart, R. 1957. *The Uses of Literacy: Aspects of Working Class Life*. London: Chatto and Windus.

Horne, D. 1984. *The Great Museum: the Re-presentation of History*. London: Pluto Press.

Hughes, T.P. 1983. *Networks of Power: Electrification in Western Society 1880–1930*. Baltimore: Johns Hopkins University Press.

Kirschenblatt-Gimblett, B. 1998. *Destination Culture: Tourism, Museums, and Heritage*. Berkeley: University of California Press.

Kohl, P.L. and C. Fawcett (eds) 1995. *Nationalism, Politics and the Practice of Archaeology*. Cambridge: Cambridge University Press.

Kroeber, A.L. and C. Kluckhohn 1952. *Culture: A Critical Review of Concepts and Definitions*. Cambridge, MA: Peabody Museum.

Lakoff, G. and M. Johnson 1980. *Metaphors We Live By*. Chicago: Chicago University Press.

Landow, George P. (ed.) 1994. *Hypertext Theory*. Baltimore: Johns Hopkins.

Landow, George P. (ed.) 1997. *Hypertext 2.0*. Baltimore: Johns Hopkins.

Latour, B. 1987. *Science in Action: How to Follow Scientists and Engineers through Society*. Milton Keynes: Open University Press.

Latour, B. 1993. *We Have Never Been Modern*. London: Harvester Wheatsheaf.

Latour, B. 1999. *Pandora's Hope: Essays on the Reality of Science Studies*. Cambridge, MA: Harvard University Press.

Law, J. (ed.) 1991. *A Sociology of Monsters: Essays on Power, Technology and Domination*. London: Routledge.

Leach, E. 1976. *Culture and Communication*. Cambridge: Cambridge University Press.

Lippard, L. 1997. *The Lure of the Local: Senses of Place in a Multicentered Society*. New York: New Press.

Lippard, L. 1999. *On the Beaten Track: Tourism, Art and Place*. New York: New Press.

Lowenthal, D. 1985. *The Past is a Foreign Country*. Cambridge: Cambridge University Press.

Mackenzie, D. and J. Wajcman (eds) 1985. *The Social Shaping of Technology: How the Refridgerator Got its Hum*. Milton Keynes: Open University Press.

McGuire, R. and M. Shanks 1996. The craft of archaeology. *American Antiquity* 61: 75–88.

Merivale, P. and S.E. Sweeney (eds) 1999. *Detecting Texts: The Metaphysical Detective Story from Poe to Postmodernism*. Philadelphia: University of Pennsylvania Press.

Meskell, L. (ed.) 1998. *Archaeology under Fire: Nationalism, Politics and Heritage in the Eastern Mediterranean and Middle East*. London: Routledge.

Morris, I. 1994. Archaeologies of Greece. In I. Morris (ed.), *Classical Greece: Ancient History and Modern Archaeologies*, 8–48. Cambridge: Cambridge University Press.

Olivier, L. and A. Coudart 1995. French tradition and the central place of history in the human sciences: preamble to a dialogue between Robinson Crusoe and his Man Friday. In P. Ucko (ed.), *Theory in Archaeology: A World Perspective*, 363–81. London: Routledge.

Pearce, S. 1992. *Museum Objects and Collections: A Cultural Study*. Leicester: Leicester University Press.

Pearce, S. 1997. *Collecting in Contemporary Practice*. London: Alta Mira Sage.

Pearson, M. and M. Shanks 1996. Performing a visit: archaeologies of the contemporary past. *Performance Research* 2: 42–60.

Pearson, M. and M. Shanks 2000. *Theatre/Archaeology: Reflections upon a Hybrid Genre*. London: Routledge.

Phelan, P. 1993. *Unmarked: The Politics of Performance*. London: Routledge.

Phelan, P. 1997. *Mourning Sex: Performing Public Memories*. London: Routledge.

Pickering, A. (ed.) 1992. *Science as Practice and Culture*. Chicago: University of Chicago Press.

Poster, M. (ed.) 1988. *Jean Baudrillard: Selected Writings*. Cambridge: Polity.

Pratt, M.-L. 1992. *Imperial Eyes: Travel Writing and Transculturation*. London: Routledge.

Pred, A. 1995. *Recognizing European Modernities: A Montage of the Present*. London: Routledge.

Renfrew, C. and P. Bahn 1996. *Archaeology: Theories, Methods, and Practice*, 2nd edn. London: Thames and Hudson.

Rowlands, M. 1994. The politics of identity in archaeology. In G. Bond and A. Gilliam (eds), *Social Construction of the Past: Representation as Power*, 129–43. London: Routledge.

Schnapp, A. 1996. *The Discovery of the Past: The Origins of Archaeology*. London: British Museum Press.

Shanks, M. 1992. *Experiencing the Past: On the Character of Archaeology*. London: Routledge.

Shanks, M. 1996. *Classical Archaeology: Experiences of the Discipline*. London: Routledge.

Shanks, M. 1998. The life of an artefact. *Fennoscandia Archaeologica* 15: 15–42.

Shanks, M. 1999. *Art and the Early Greek State: An Interpretive Archaeology*. Cambridge: Cambridge University Press.

Shanks, M. 2000. Archaeology/politics. In *Blackwell Companion to Archaeology*, ed. J. Bintliff. Oxford: Blackwell.

Shanks, M. and C. Tilley 1992. *Re-constructing Archaeology: Theory and Practice*, 2nd edn. New Studies in Archaeology. London: Routledge.

Shennan, S. 1978. Archaeological cultures: an empirical investigation. In I. Hodder (ed.), *The Spatial Organisation of Culture*, 56–68. London: Duckworth.

Smiles, S. 1994. *The Image of Antiquity: Ancient Britain and the Romantic Imagination*. New Haven: Yale University Press.

Spybey, T. 1996. *Globalization and World Society*. Cambridge: Polity.

Swingewood, A. 1977. *The Myth of Mass Culture*. London: Macmillan.

Trigger, B. 1984. Alternative archaeologies: nationalist, colonialist, imperialist. *Man* 19: 355–70.

Turner, B. (ed.) 1990. *Theories of Modernity and Postmodernity*. London: Sage.

Turner, G. 1996. *British Cultural Studies: An Introduction*, 2nd edn. London: Routledge.

Tylor, E. 1870. *Primitive Culture: Researches into the Development of Mythology, Philosophy, Religion, Language, Art, and Custom*. New York: Holt.

Weschler, L. 1995. *Mr. Wilson's Cabinet of Wonder: Pronged Ants, Horned Humans, Mice on Toast, and Other Marvels of Jurassic Technology*. New York: Vintage.

Williams, R. 1976. *Keywords: A Vocabulary of Culture and Society*. London: Fontana.

Woolf, G. 1993. *Becoming Roman: The Origins of Provincial Civilization in Gaul*. Cambridge: Cambridge University Press.

# Index